Global Secularisms in a Post-Secular Age

Religion and Its Others

Studies in Religion, Nonreligion, and Secularity

Edited by
Stacey Gutkowski, Lois Lee, and Johannes Quack

Volume 2

Global Secularisms in a Post-Secular Age

Edited by
Michael Rectenwald, Rochelle Almeida,
and George Levine

DE GRUYTER

The hardcover edition of this book was published in 2015.

ISBN 978-1-5015-1564-4
e-ISBN (PDF) 978-1-61451-675-0
e-ISBN (EPUB) 978-1-61451-931-7
ISSN 2330-6262

Library of Congress Cataloging-in-Publication Data
A CIP catalog record for this book has been applied for at the Library of Congress.

Bibliographic information published by the Deutsche Nationalbibliothek
The Deutsche Nationalbibliothek lists this publication in the Deutsche Nationalbibliografie;
detailed bibliographic data are available on the Internet at http://dnb.dnb.de.

© 2017 Walter de Gruyter Inc., Boston/Berlin
Printing and binding: CPI books GmbH, Leck
♾ Printed on acid-free paper
Printed in Germany

www.degruyter.com

Preface and Acknowledgements

On November 15 and 16, 2013, in New York City, the Global Liberal Studies program of New York University held an international conference entitled "Global Secularisms." In the call for papers, the conference committee, headed by Michael Rectenwald, appealed to scholars and creative authors from the major divisions of the academy, including the humanities, social sciences, and sciences, as well as to independent scholars, writers and activists from outside the academy. The conference welcomed engagement with questions involving secularism and the arts, culture, economics, feminism, history, international relations, philosophy, politics, religion, and science.

The conference attracted participants from Belgium, Germany, India, Italy, the Netherlands, Norway, Spain, the UK, the US, and Turkey, representing numerous universities including the University of Antwerp, Brown University, the University of Chicago, Columbia University, European University Institute, George Washington University, Harvard University, the University of London, Northwestern University, the University of Oslo, the University of Pittsburgh, Princeton University, Rutgers University, SUNY Binghamton, UC-Davis, and Yale University, as well as New York University. Also represented were the Centre for the study of Developing Societies in India, UNESCO, and One Law for All in Great Britain. The conference included panels on politics, the public sphere, theory, education, history, the nation, narrative, "sacred" and "secular" spaces, science, and post-secularism in context, among other topics. Given that our objective was exploration and not advocacy, the conversations were both generative and rife with controversy. Discussions included defenses of (and attacks on) the wearing of the burqa and the niqab in western public spaces and state ceremonies, the (re)emerging importance of religion in the politics of Turkey and India, secular and/or religious education in various nation states, the importance of secularism to science, strenuous defenses of secularism against the new "post-secular" dispensation, and many other topics.

Following the conference, we asked several presenters to rethink and revise their presentations on the basis of the case studies and theoretical and historical reflections presented by other speakers. With one exception, the present collection is a result of the conference and the subsequent reflection and revision by the volume's editors and authors on the issues involved. With a few chapters, particularly those by George Levine, Philip Kitcher, and Bruce Robbins, we have aimed at retaining the sense of a delivered talk. In one case, we solicited a chapter by authors who were unable to attend. Those conference participants whose essays are not included here either were unable to contribute, or their papers simply did not fit well within the structure of the book as we envisioned it. Their absence is in no way reflective of a lack of quality or importance to the conversation.

As the current volume would not be possible without the conference that preceded and generated it, we owe a significant debt of gratitude to the Liberal Studies Program of New York University, and especially to its Dean, Fred Schwarzbach. Given the presentation of a somewhat costly conference that brought in ten plenary speakers and thirty-four other participants, we are grateful that Dean Schwarzbach recognized the importance of the topic and its relevance and timeliness for a relatively new program in Global Liberal Studies. Dean Schwarzbach had the vision to see the value of such an event, and furthermore, found a way to make it happen, financially and institutionally. As he noted at the opening of the conference, the event was a signal moment for Global Liberal Studies and its institutional home, the Liberal Studies Program of New York University.

Speaking of institutional support, we are also indebted to the financial wizardry and logistical expertise of the program's Director of Administration, Billy Helton, and to Angelo Cruz, conference budget administrator, for their hard work and acute problem solving. We thank Shirley Smith-Smalls, our program faculty administrative assistant, who arranged hotel and travel for all plenary speakers and booked conference rooms. We would like to thank our NYU faculty colleagues who served on the conference committee, including Emily Bauman, Sean Eve, Brendan Hogan, Mitra Rastegar, Martin Reichert, Anthony Reynolds, Tilottama Tharoor, Elayne Tobin, and Kyle Wanberg. They helped to revise the call for papers, select papers, and arrange panels. Special thanks go to Emily Bauman, whose innovative ideas for panels was a great help; Elayne Tobin, whose advice and help with food and other matters was invaluable; and Anthony Reynolds, who artfully designed the poster. NYU's Liberal Studies Program includes wonderful students, some who served as conference volunteers. This cast includes Elena Ferraro, Katalina Park, Annelise Bell, Andrea Maehara, Amrita Ramanathan, Harim Kim, Rebecca Brown, and Helen Wang.

We are grateful for the assistance we received from De Gruyter Acquisitions Editor Alissa Jones Nelson, whose vision for this work and help in preparing it for publication guided us throughout preparation of this manuscript.

Michael Rectenwald would like to thank Rochelle Almeida for her tireless work and endless patience with the taxing demands of this volume. Rochelle became closely involved with this volume at the point when the presented papers evolved into chapters to be collated and edited for publication. Her editorial insights and acumen, as well as her endurance and ebullient spirit have been indispensable to this project's completion. Rochelle's contributions of paragraphs on Asia in the Introduction prove essential. Michael would also like to thank his partner, Sarah Skaggs, for her support throughout this and other projects on which he has recently worked. Michael is deeply grateful to George Levine, without whose help and contacts, he would not have been able to assemble such an impressive cast of conference plenary speakers, or to include several of them as contributors to the present volume. The current project owes much to Michael having overheard George (at the Dickens Universe) mention a conference he had tried to arrange at NYU Tisch on secularism.

Rochelle is indebted to Michael Rectenwald, her co-editor and colleague at New York University, with whom it has been an honor to work on a very important volume upon a topic of increasing global significance. Rochelle also wishes to thank her husband, Llewellyn Almeida, for his support and assistance during the time she devoted to editing these chapters and preparing them for publication.

The editors also thank Ross Wolfe and Lori R. Price for reading versions of the Introduction and Lori R. Price for her proofreading and bibliographical work on a few chapters.

And finally, the editors wish to thank the contributors to this volume, who worked hard to frame their essays as chapters within the volume's parameters and whose scholarly interest and expertise on the complex issue of secularism enables the conversation to continue on a global scale. Without their research and commitment to scholarship, this volume could never have been possible.

Table of Contents

Part II: Case Studies: Global Secularisms

A The Political Sphere

Part II: Case Studies: Global Secularisms

B The Public Sphere

Michael Rectenwald and Rochelle Almeida

Introduction: Global Secularisms in a Post-Secular Age

By now, it is nearly a commonplace observation to note that secularism – until quite recently simply assumed to be the basis of modern nation states and the public sphere – is a contested and even "beleaguered" cultural, social, and political formation.[1] Once regarded as the *sine qua non* of public democratic life and the requisite integument of international relations, the secular was taken to be unmarked ideologically, as the mere absence or negation of obsolescing "religion." Linked to this regard for secularism as an unmarked, neutral category was the standard secularization thesis, according to which modernity itself was characterized by, if not understood as predicated upon, the progressive decline of religion – its relegation to the private sphere, its diminishing hold on individual belief, and its loss of authority in separate and increasingly differentiated spheres of discourse and activity.

However, within the past two or three decades, both the status of secularism as a relatively unproblematic feature of modernity and the secularization thesis as a standing explanation for its regnant status have been deeply shaken. A crisis of secularism is widely recognized. Secularism is currently a vexed topic fraught with complex and difficult global implications and consequences. While scholarship on secularism has seen a dramatic upsurge, questions related to secularism have become increasingly urgent and involve enormous real-world implications. These include the battles over "Sharī'ah law" in Europe and the Middle East, and the renewed importance of religion in the politics of India and Turkey. They also include the challenges posed for and by laicism in France. One might also point to the emergence of the "new atheism" and its political meanings in the West, and the battles over the authority of science in the United States. At stake also is secularism's supposed role for arbitrating armed religious conflict, and its place in political and legal struggles over the shape of the public sphere in multiple contexts. The questions involving secularism prove essential and significant.

In recent years, secularism has been taken to task not only for its differential treatment of various religions within the state but also, and more fundamentally, for its putative imposition of cultural norms and values, political prerogatives,

---

1 Rajeev Bhargava, "Political Secularism," in *The Oxford Handbook of Political Theory*, eds. John S. Dryzek, Bonnie Honig, and Anne Phillips (Oxford: Oxford University Press, 2006), 636–55.

and hegemonic impulses within and across political landscapes and the public sphere. As the chapters in this volume make clear, secularism has been far from a neutral arbiter of religious practices and expression in its various contexts. Including other charges, secularism has been seen as deeply implicated in colonial and imperialist projects. Meanwhile, the standard secularization thesis, once a staple of social science theory, has been called into question, if not outright reversed, even by some of its more prominent, erstwhile proponents. Some scholars question the assumption that the modern social order is undergoing, or indeed has ever undergone, the process of secularization.[2] In the late 1990s, pointing to the continued popularity of churchgoing in the United States, the emergence of New Age spirituality in Western Europe, the growth of fundamentalist movements and religious political parties in the Muslim world (even before the terrorist attacks of September 11, 2001), the evangelical revival sweeping through Latin America, and the upsurge of ethno-religious conflict in international affairs, sociologist Peter Berger recanted his earlier faith in secularization and descried a new "religious resurgence" or desecularization.[3] Similarly, Jürgen Habermas, a major social theorist and signal advocate of secularism in the public sphere, has attended to the persistence of religion and called for a new role for it in politics and public life, as well as adoption of the term "post-secularism" to describe the relations between the secular and the religious in the current era.[4] Indeed, while important thinkers have reasserted versions of the secularization thesis, and others have attempted to retain it with significant revisions,[5]

---

2 See for example the title of a conference held at The New School for Social Research: "We Have Never Been Secular," http://blogs.ssrc.org/tif/2010/02/01/we-have-never-been-secular-re-thinking-the-sacred/. Accessed August 31, 2014.

3 In particular, Peter L. Berger, once an important secularization theorist, reversed his long-standing position on secularization in *The Desecularization of the World: Resurgent Religion and World Politics* (Washington, D.C.: Ethics and Public Policy Center, 1999), esp. at 1–18.

4 Jürgen Habermas, "Notes on Post-Secular Society," *NPQ: New Perspectives Quarterly* 25.4 (2007): 17–29. In March of 2007, Habermas delivered his now famous lecture on "post-secularism" at the Nexus Institute of the University of Tilberg, Netherlands. Habermas pointed to three factors that characterize modern social orders as post-secular: 1) the broad perception that many global conflicts hinge on religious strife and the changes in public consciousness and weakening of confidence in the dominance of a secular outlook that such acknowledgement accedes; 2) the increased importance of religion in various public spheres; and 3) the growing presence in Europe and elsewhere of immigrant or "guest workers" and refugees with traditional cultural backgrounds.

5 For the persistence of the secularization thesis, see Steve Bruce, *God Is Dead: Secularization in the West* (Malden, MA: Blackwell Pub, 2002). For a significant revision, see Pippa Norris and Ronald Inglehart, *Sacred and Secular: Religion and Politics Worldwide* (West Nyack, NY, USA: Cambridge University Press, 2004). Norris and Inglehart advance the "existential security hy-

there is little doubt that it has been significantly weakened. Secularism and secularization, that is, are no longer regarded unquestionably as the vaunted pillars of modern democratic society, or modernity itself.

On the other hand, some thinkers insist that secularism, despite post-secular claims to the contrary, represents the only means of negotiating sectarian strife and establishing and maintaining a democratic state. Secular humanists continue to insist that secularism is the best way to achieve real human flourishing. Yet the very meanings of the words "secularism" and "religion" have been questioned, and the secular/religious binary has been significantly troubled.[6] For some, the crisis of secularism represents a significant potential loss. The questions at stake include whether secularism, promoted by the West as a universal doctrine and since debunked from its perch and understood as provincial and particularistic, can be recuperated and its incomplete universalism universalized, its secularism (re)secularized.[7]

Given the dynamic and shifting roles and meanings of secularism in contemporary societies, a brief review of its history may be in order. Etymologically, the notion of the "secular" was originally contrasted not to religion, but to eternity. Derived from the Latin, *saeculum*, the word secular is related to time, and the French word for century, *siècle*. The secular thus stood for occurrences in worldly time as opposed to otherworldly eternity, to temporal as opposed to spiritual power. From late thirteenth-century Latin Christendom, the secular came to refer to clergy who lived outside of monastic seclusion, serving parishioners as they sought to live Christian lives under secular conditions. The cloistered monks on the other hand were referred to as "religious." Thus, the word secular signified the worldly or mundane, and also became closely associated with the profane in contrast to the sacred. From the designation of a lesser state of religiosity within the western Christian imaginary, the secular eventually came to refer to that which stood outside of the Church altogether, as an antipode to the religious. Secularization, meanwhile, first referred to the expropriation of

---

pothesis" as the explanation for secularization or the lack thereof. According to this thesis, as populations become relatively secure economically and otherwise, religiosity tends to decline. The denizens of post-industrial societies are demonstrably less religious than those living in agricultural or industrial economies. Meanwhile, although secularization is increasing as regions become post-industrial, religious populations are growing relative to secular ones, owing to the fact that in traditional societies the birthrate is much higher than in secular societies.

6 Janet R. Jakobsen and Ann Pellegrini, "Introduction: Times Like These," in *Secularisms*, eds. Janet R. Jakobsen and Ann Pellegrini (Durham: Duke University Press, 2008), esp. 9–17.
7 See especially, Étienne Balibar, *Saeculum: Culture, Religion, Idéologie* (Paris: Éd. Galilée, 2012).

church property during the Protestant Reformation, and later was extended to designate any transference of religious authority to persons or institutions with non-religious functions. In contemporary parlance, secularism has connoted the separation of church and state, a supposedly neutral space for arbitrating religious and other claims, or a successor to disappearing religion(s). Secularization has signified the (progressive) decline in importance and influence of religion in the political sphere, public life and private commitment, and has become nearly synonymous with modernity itself.

Secularism received renewed scholarly attention with the publication of Charles Taylor's monumental *A Secular Age* in 2007.[8] In this arguably paradigm-shifting study of secularism and secularization, Taylor undertook a complete revision of the accounts of secularization, taking the secularization thesis to task for its reliance on what he called "subtraction stories," or narratives of the progressive loss and compartmentalization of religious belief attendant upon the rise of science, industrialization, urbanization, and so forth. Drawing on Max Weber's notion of pre-modern enchantment and modern disenchantment, Taylor argues that, as a consequence of disenchantment resulting from religious reformism that began before the Protestant Reformation, faith was ultimately undermined as a default position, requiring that "belief" become a matter of positive declaration. Against the subtraction stories of the standard secularization thesis, Taylor advances his notion of "secularity 3," which describes a *condition* comprising both belief and unbelief, and everything in between. Unbelief ultimately became a distinct possibility for a growing number, including non-elites, for the first time. According to Taylor, the secular age is marked not by the progressive rise of unbelief or decline of religion or religiosity, but rather by a condition under which choices are opened up for belief, unbelief, a suspension between the two, as well as other creedal commitments. Secularity in Taylor's third sense is a new "naïve framework" for all those living within modernity, indeed representing a space opened up for unbelief but also amounting to an overarching *optative* state that comprehends unbelief and belief and the irresolution and continuing challenge that they pose to one another. But secularity also embodies a "fully exclusive humanism," which greatly pressures religious belief and conditions its fragility.

This conception of secularity significantly challenges the standard secularization thesis and redefines secular modernity in terms of a new "social imaginary" or background condition of lived experience. Quite apart from sociological

---

8 Charles Taylor, *A Secular Age* (Cambridge, MA: Belknap Press/Harvard University Press, 2007).

accounts of church attendance and other indices of secular ascendance or putative religious decline, Taylor's study obviates or skirts such quantitative evidence in favor of a historical narrative that arrives at an existential-phenomenological predicament characterizing modernity. Against the positing of a new desecularization or post-secular dispensation, Taylor's conception of secularity theoretically accounts for the fragility and vacillations of religious belief and unbelief, perhaps even making sense of the putative "religious resurgence" observed by Peter Berger and others.[9] Certainly, causal factors would need to be located for such resurgences, but secularity comprehends such fluctuations as possibilities in advance. Furthermore, the notion of secularity as developed by Taylor may help us to comprehend the nature or quality of religious commitment under modernity. For Taylor, not only is belief "fragilized" by unbelief but also its very structure is changed, since believers, along with unbelievers, all operate under the "immanent frame" of secularity. The question becomes whether or not belief – in transcendence in particular – is any longer what it once was. The answer to this question may prove important for how we regard the various forms of religiosity across the globe today.

Taylor's work prompted several significant responses, including *Varieties of Secularism in a Secular Age*, *Rethinking Secularism*, and *The Joys of Secularism*, among others.[10] Given its exclusive focus on the West, *A Secular Age* has been faulted not only for its apparent provinciality or ethnocentrism, but also, and more importantly, for its intra-Christian understanding of the development of western secularism. Although Taylor provided an explanation for this exclusivity – the task at hand already threatened to exceed the compass of a single work; other studies might address the historical development of secularism in various regions – Taylor's internalist perspective, it has been argued, misses the role played by non-Christian societies. Like Taylor, Talal Asad also figures the secular as a social formation that developed initially within Latin Christendom in particular.[11] However, unlike Taylor, Asad sees western secularism's development as

---

9 Michael Warner, Jonathan VanAntwerpen, and Craig J. Calhoun, *Varieties of Secularism in a Secular Age* (Cambridge, MA: Harvard University Press, 2010), 22: "[B]ecause [Taylor's] third sense of the secular comprehends precisely those forms of religiosity that are now most widely mobilized, resurgence of religion is not evidence of a new post-secular dispensation."

10 Warner, et al., *Varieties of Secularism in a Secular Age*; Craig J. Calhoun, Mark Juergensmeyer, and Jonathan VanAntwerpen, *Rethinking Secularism* (Oxford/N.Y.: Oxford University Press, 2011); George L. Levine, *The Joy of Secularism: 11 Essays for How We Live Now* (Princeton, N.J: Princeton University Press, 2011).

11 Talal Asad, *Formations of the Secular: Christianity, Islam, Modernity* (Stanford, Calif.: Stanford University Press, 2003).

contingent upon the West's interactions and exploits in the Middle East and elsewhere. According to Asad, in its management of colonies, the West encountered diverse belief systems and cultural practices that it came to understand in terms of "religion." Its understanding of these beliefs and practices was conditioned upon Protestant Christianity as the context for the development of western secularism. For Asad, secularism is far from a neutral or innocent formation; rather, it is fully implicated in colonial and imperialist projects. Yet Asad does not figure secularism as simply a colonialist imposition. Rather, secularism developed differently as it interacted with different religious and regional contexts. Secularism is not the mere unfolding of an Enlightenment universal within particular local situations. The secular and the religious are co-constituting formations and secularism is always contingent upon its relationship with the particularity of its religious other. Thus, while Asad, and Saba Mahmood, whose work follows in his paradigmatic footsteps, treat secularism as a western construct that is not easily transported and transposed onto other contexts, those contexts nevertheless condition the development of secularism. Likewise, secularism should always be understood as plural and variable.

Along similar although not identical lines, the political theorist Rajeev Bhargava has argued for the existence of a distinctive (although not "unique" or conceptually novel) Indian secularism that developed outside of the reach of European colonialism and which he argues currently provides much needed lessons for western democracies.[12] Bhargava serves to underscore the multiplicity and substantive content of secularism, but also its contingent and variable character. Secularism is not an empty container or timeless wall between the state and the public sphere on the one hand, and religious belief and practice on the other. Rather, it is purposive and content-full, with "positive" values of its own, which change depending on the context. If anything, Bhargava sees secularism as a flexible and necessary concept of modernity, and one that we should work to refurbish and support.

Following the work of Bhargava, as well as Janet R. Jakobsen and Ann Pellegrini,[13] in this volume, the editors take as a point of departure the fact that secularism is plural, that various secularisms have developed in various contexts and from various traditions around the world, and that secularism takes on different social and cultural meanings and political valences wherever it is expressed. Further, in accord with the first volume in this series, we hold that

12 See especially Rajeev Bhargava, "The Distinctiveness of Indian Secularism," in *The Future of Secularism*, ed. T.N. Srinivasan (Delhi: Oxford University Press, 2006), 20–53.
13 Jakobsen and Pellegrini, *Secularisms*.

"[u]niversalist theories of secularization are singularly ill-suited for exploring secularities beyond the West."[14] At the same time, however, we acknowledge the hegemonic *desiderata* of secularism's universalizing claims. That is, we see the importance of recognizing secularism as an Enlightenment legacy that exhibits universalizing ambitions. Thus, it is necessary to keep in mind both the doctrinal claims of secularism – its supposed difference from religion(s), its association with "progress" and modernity, its assertions of rationality and neutrality, its claims of exclusivity in connection with public life – as well as how this doctrinal logic unfolds in various contexts. Given this conception of secularism as both universalizing doctrine and particular instantiation, the chapters in this volume provide numerous points of contact between theoretical/historical reflection and empirical case studies on secularisms in context. With this anthology, we aim to fill a chasm between sweeping theoretical analyses of secularism on the one hand and accounts relating to the lived experiences of the formations as they have evolved in different parts of the world on the other. We believe it is unlike any another work in the field for its delivery of both theoretical scope and empirical granularity on a global scale.

Recognizing that secular traditions have developed differently around the world and that this multiplicity must necessarily inform and complicate the conceptual theorization of secularism as a universal doctrine delivered wholesale from the Enlightenment, we have sought to gain clearer and more nuanced appreciations of the complexities of the concept of secularism from empirical case studies. Analyses of different regions, we believe, enrich our understanding of the meanings of secularism, providing comparative range to our notions of secularity, while adding dimension to our understanding of regional conditions and conflicts themselves. We maintain that theoretical and historical reflections over the meanings of secularism benefit from such empirical studies, serving to illustrate theories while also challenging traditional understandings that otherwise may remain unchallenged from within the more or less purely theoretical debates. At the same time, theoretical/historical treatments of secularism, we believe, help to inform our understanding of secularisms in context, enabling us to discern the principles at stake in the various regional expressions of secularity and/or religiosity globally. Theoretical and historical accounts help us to refine, contextualize, and revise our understandings of contemporary empirical findings.

---

14 Marian Burchardt, Monika Wohlrab-Sahr, and Matthias Middell, *Multiple Secularities Beyond the West: Religion and Modernity in a Global Age* (Boston: De Gruyter, 2015), 3.

We also take for granted that secularism is currently a contested category – not only in terms of its definition and its political and social meanings but also in terms of its clear and unproblematic opposition to religion(s). This is not at all to suggest that secularism is simply another religion; it is, in fact, a distinct social formation with its own characteristics and histories. But the secular has always defined itself as against religion(s), and, in the process, has defined religion(s) as such. Our point is that this definitional process is variable and context contingent and that while secularism is always content-full, its content is not fixed or stable; the secular is an adaptable category that takes its shape, content and meaning in connection with and in distinction from the religions with which it interacts and against which it defines itself. In fact, several chapters in this volume complicate and challenge the stability, meaning and universality of the secular/religious binary. The question becomes whether or not secularism can be more or other than an opportunistic formation serving particularized ends in different contexts.

While it certainly has served and may continue to serve democratizing functions, while also posing as a solution for non-particularistic education, secularism, *per se*, can no longer be understood as a fixed idea and simply posited as "progressive" as against religion(s) understood as "conservative." Likewise, while inclusive of defenses and elaborations of secularism, this collection has also aimed to register recognition – in the title and in many of the chapters as well – of the post-secular understanding. A polyvalent and contested term, *post-secularism* may signify a skepticism and/or antagonism toward secularism in recognition of the persistence or "resurgence" of religion. Connected with post-colonialism, post-secularism may regard secularism as a legacy of colonialist enterprises and a disguise for the domination of a particular (Christian/western) order. While recognizing these significations, by post-secularism, we refer especially to "an attempt to overcome the antinomy of secularism/religion."[15] Post-secularism accords to religion an enduring value – a place at the table in politics, a voice in the public sphere, and an abiding role in private life. Post-secularism recognizes the persistence of religion and marks an acknowledgement of religious and secular pluralisms. It recognizes the ethical resources and community-building efficacy that religious systems and practices can offer and acknowledges the function of religion in constructing and defending cultural identities. Further, post-secularism may amount to a refutation of the standard secularization thesis. According to post-secularism, the secularization thesis

---

15 Vincent Geoghegan, "Religious Narrative, Post-secularism and Utopia," *Critical Review of International Social and Political Philosophy* 3.2–3 (2000): 205–24, at 206.

has been empirically disproven. Rather than a descriptive characterization of modernities, the secularization thesis, post-secularism suggests, is a normative imperative and a (failed) self-fulfilling prophecy of secular advocates. Yet, rather than taking sides with either secularists or post-secularists, this anthology focuses on the debates themselves – in relation to the new, global understanding that the volume facilitates – aiming at a more or less inclusive representation of the controversies surrounding secularisms globally.

The "global" designation in this volume's title not only registers the inclusion of a broad representation of secularisms from around the world but also the fact that virtually every region's version of secularism has been affected by global Others, or "globalization." While the majority of the chapters in the volume recognize and account for the "global" in this latter sense, we should note that a few do so hardly at all. This is largely due to the fact that in such chapters, the authors either treat a particular historical moment of secularism when its global content was less apparent or merely incipient, or they examine secularism in the abstract. But, as most of the volume's chapter make clear, the developments of actually-existing, contemporary secularisms and religions have "benefitted" from globalization and the circulation of global capital, as well as from the political impacts of nation states or other regional actors promoting or responding to global capital or military aggression. In the context of globalization and secularity, it is important to note that fundamentalism, far from being the reestablishment of traditional religiosity, is a modern formation dependent for its very existence on secularisms and their challenges to traditional religion. Likewise, globalization has impacted secularisms and religiosities and their viability or lack thereof in various contexts. In terms of political secularism, in the dichotomy between secularism as the absence of religion from the political and public spheres on the one hand, and the more pluralistic notion of secularism as multi-religious co-existence on the other, the world's rapid globalization, particularly since the last quarter of the twentieth century, has played a key role. The political and economic pressures of globalization have impacted national ideologies in struggles over just what kind of secularism, if any, would emerge victorious in particular nation states, often as individual nations have vied for international acceptance as "modern," where modern almost invariably had been recognized as secularist – until quite recently, that is.

Turkey's positioning for inclusion in the European Union is a classic case in point of the role that global context can have on matters of secularity and religiosity. Kemal Attaturk's modernization project was aimed at drawing Turkey into the international fold, within which westernized ideas of enlightenment, progressivism and rationality were placed in tandem with the religious observance of its predominantly Islamic population. But events surrounding September

11, 2001, and perceptions of Islamic orthodoxy in its aftermath, led to western suspicion of overt signs of Islamization in public space, so that the wearing of the hijab, for example, came to be associated with fanaticism. As Turkey struggled to declare its modernity in the rush for inclusion in the EU (largely for strategic economic advantage), its notions of secularism were redefined and rearticulated for the post-9/11 era. Turkey represents a clear case study of the way that nationalist ideology with regards to secularism has been impacted by a globalization that made international bilateral cooperation paramount in the zeitgeist following glasnost and perestroika in the former Soviet Union, and the fall of the Berlin Wall. The erasure of European geographical boundaries and the creation of Schengen Area plurality led, willy-nilly, to new conditions for the admission or, conversely, the exclusion of nation-states. At a time when growing Islamic influence in government was perceived as having a negative impact on the country's democratic secularist image, Turkey hastily proffered to the international community its supposed commitment to religious pluralism. Thus, its inclusion in the EU depended upon an emphasis on a pluralistic secularity, as against the recent (re)assertion of Islamic heritage.

China, too, in its bid to gain international approval as it surges ahead toward global financial dominance, is at pains to underscore perceptions of religious tolerance. This preoccupation fuels a pan-western cultural revolution that is clearly visible in modern Shanghai, where just impatience with poverty and deprivation is interacting with the products of global capital to create what we may call a "brand secularism," which is quite obviously globalized. Thus, as McDonald's, KFC, the Gap, and Louis Vuitton represent the commodification of a traditionally frugal Chinese culture, rendering it rapidly consumerist, regard for religious practice is also undergoing a metamorphosis. Paradoxically, a thriving state-directed capitalist economy in China is developing a seeming hand-in-glove relationship with a robust new religiosity. In the face of the actually existing communism that was China, Buddhist temples, for instance, had been relegated to the status of mere tourist attractions. But, the revival of religious services in Anglican churches in the urban metropolis and the large audiences they attract point to a renewed interest in organized religion as ironically synonymous with progress and modernization. While strict state economic regulation keeps the country on a disciplined march, the regime is determined to vitiate perceptions of its control in the daily lives of its burgeoning populace. And although the Communist Party still dominates political life, globalization and a new kind of secularism are tempering the party's totalitarian rigidity.

India is yet another paradoxical example of an altered national secularism – with the rejuvenation of Hindu enthusiasm within a climate of rapid technological and economic globalization. However, while in the case of Turkey, eagerness to conform with western notions of secularism have determinedly kept Islamic influence at bay, in India, as in China, globalization has succeeded in reviving religious fervor. Represented as a secular nation for decades by the dominant Congress governments that shaped India's Nehruvian vision, ironically, the country's inclusion as an emergent giant in the BRIC nations has been concurrent with the adoption of an aggressively Hindu nationalism. Indeed, in the India of recently-elected Prime Minister Narendra Modi, a younger generation, seemingly anxious to abandon Nehru's socialism together with his secularist vision, yearns for a quasi-capitalist business environment in which the immediate financial rewards for individual ambition, enterprise, and risk-taking are seen as far more urgent imperatives than the maintenance of a climate within which religious and social minorities might co-exist without fear of Hindu hegemony. The elite intelligentsia that championed secularism in India has become stridently polarized in recent decades and has developed a profoundly left/right binary that is routinely contested by a powerfully emergent lower middleclass that seemingly has little regard for minority sentiment. It insists that altered definitions of secularism commensurate with the assertion of Hindu nationalism will in no way threaten India's diverse minority communities. It is much too early to know the extent to which the political power of the rightwing Hindu-dominated parties will affect democratic secularism in India in the long run. The prevailing notion, however, is that just as long as India's economy delivers, those hungry for the erasure of Nehru-Gandhian austerity in a New India will willingly sacrifice "academic" notions of pluralist equality and inter-communal fraternity. Indeed, since he achieved a landslide victory on promises of bringing prosperity to the greatest number of Indians, it would seem that, in Modi's India, middleclass pecuniary interests will likely triumph over "elitist" and "western" notions of secularism. Turkey, China and India, while undergoing major transformations in terms of secularism, are just a few of the major areas where secularism is being challenged and/or redefined.

1 Mapping Global Secularisms: The Structure of the Book

This anthology brings together theoretical and historical interventions, as well as empirical case studies from anthropology, cultural and literary studies, history, international relations, political science, religious studies, sociology and other fields, in order to illustrate the "on-the-ground" working out of secularisms as they interact with various religious, political, social, and economic contexts.

The central questions this anthology asks are the following: What is the state of secularism globally, and what are its prospects? This collection offers a synoptic introduction to the situation of secularisms in what has been called a post-secularist era (Part I), and detailed case studies of secularisms globally (Part II). Thus, it works to represent the state of the debate regarding global secularisms today, and to consider the prospects for secularisms under various conditions. Part I lays the historical, theoretical and philosophical groundwork for the rise and development of secularisms and post-secularism, including chapters that deal with the state of secularism and the kinds of secularisms that may be possible. This section provides a framework for the extensive discussions of the various expressions of secularism and post-secularism globally, which follow in the next section.

Part I begins with a broader time frame for secularism's emergence than is generally accorded it, as Stijn Latré explores the evolution of religion and politics in the "axial age," when ancients such as Confucius and Lao Tse in China, the Upanishad texts and the Buddha in India, Zarathustra in Persia, the Jewish prophets in Palestine and the Greek philosophers presented concepts of secularism with which modern scholars continue to grapple. Latre compares the views of Marcel Gauchet and Robert Bellah on the axial dynamics of secularization and religious evolution before moving on to the German debate between Karl Lowith and Hans Blumenberg and touching briefly on Karl Jaspers's interpretation of the axial. Modern discourse led, he says, to the loss of the concept of "transcendence," which has always been linked to immanence. Gauchet, who dwells on transcendence in the axial period, states that it plays a key role on the path to a disenchanted world. Latre examines well-known passages from Shakespeare's plays to determine the manner in which the concept of Providence was understood as playing a role in guiding human action. He ends his chapter with the conclusion that secular aspirations saw the light of day in the religious and philosophical reforms of the axial age. Interestingly, a resurgence in transcendence has recently emerged, and with it, a universal meaning – the spirit of free thinking that, as Jaspers believed, co-exists with the fruits of science and technology in the twentieth-first century.

The section continues with an exploration of the history of Secularism proper, a movement founded by George Jacob Holyoake in Britain in 1851–52. Michael Rectenwald characterizes Holyoake's Secularism, which marks the first ever use of the term, and contrasts it with that of his rival for the control of the Secularist movement, Charles Bradlaugh. This historical exploration is motivated by concerns over the fate of secularism and the contemporary claims of post-secularism. Rectenwald asserts that Holyoake's brand of Secularism represented "the co-existence of secular and religious elements subsisting under a common umbrella," not the negation of religion. Thus, Holyoake's Secularism, he argues, anticipated Taylor's notion of "secularity 3" by over 150 years, and obviates the need for a new post-secular dispensation. Rectenwald champions the kind of "positive," pluralistic Secularism advocated by Holyoake, over the negative, "evacuative" Secularism of Bradlaugh.

In his chapter, the prominent secularist philosopher Philip Kitcher brings the discussion of secularism as a "positive" program into the contemporary theoretical moment, drawing on his earlier proposals for an "enlightened secularism,"[16] arguing here that a purely "negative" secularism is "at least intellectually incomplete." In the vein of Holyoake, Kitcher argues that to be successful, secularism must provide "secular surrogates for religious institutions." One of the most important secular surrogates is that for the grounding of value – or a secular ethics. Rather than adopting one of the several ethical systems that historically have been proposed as surrogates – Benthamite utilitarianism, a theory of moral sentiments, etc. – Kitcher proposes that we look to anthropology and primatology to see just how ethics have developed in human and human-like societies. When we do, we find that ethics are not transcendental value systems imposed from without, but rather historical developments of "agreed-on rules for joint living" derived from "human attempts to construct life together." Kitcher extends his analysis on the development of ethics to the question of meaning, which secularism has often been deemed incapable of supplying. Again, meaning need not be leveraged on a transcendental object, but may be grounded in projects contributing to a more lasting and larger social body, projects that are nevertheless temporal. Such a notion of meaning should be an adequate substitute for religious systems based in the transcendental and the eternal.

Shifting the discussion to the sociopolitical, Özlem Uluç Kucukcan undertakes an analysis of the emergence and development of a post-secular from a "pre-post-secular" public sphere. Kucukcan argues for the inadequacy of the earlier, secular public sphere for the representation of the rights of religious minorities in modern nation states, and details the conditions and requirements of the new post-secular public sphere as articulated by Jürgen Habermas. Kucukan argues that while Habermas's post-secular public sphere is not a comprehensive answer for secular states as they face the challenges of a post-secular age, it nevertheless represents a significant improvement over its predecessor. More work is

---

16 See Philip Kitcher, "Science, Religion, and Democracy," *Episteme: A Journal of Social Epistemology* 5 (2008): 5–18; "Militant Modern Atheism," *Journal of Applied Philosophy* 28 (2011): 1–13; and *Science in a Democratic Society* (New York: Prometheus Books, 2011).

needed to understand why religious formations and adherents find secular counterparts inimical to their very existence, and vice versa.

In his study, centered on a theoretical framework inaugurated by Jürgen Habermas, Patrick Loobuyck examines the role of religious education in a post-secular world, with special reference to multicultural environments. Loobuyck grapples with the role of religious education from a Habermasian, post-secular perspective. Habermas's work, he states, provides an important opportunity to enter the religious education debate from the perspective of political philosophy. Loobuyck considers the possible ramifications of a religious education program and its long-term impacts, while also explaining the paradigm shifts that brought important policy changes to western schools with multicultural demographics. He concludes that in post-secular societies, the aims of religious education are broad and include learning about different religions, contributing to students' personal development, creating intercultural skills, attaining religious literacy, and preparing students for participation as citizens in a pluralistic world.

As one of the leading lights in the debates over the role and significance of secularism in a (post)modern, "post-secular" world, in his chapter, Rajeev Bhargava subjects the meanings and implications of secularism and post-secularism to close scrutiny. Given the characterization of the term "post-secular" as putatively distinct from the "secular," Bhargava argues that, while Europe and the North Atlantic might very well be transitioning from a secular to a post-secular condition, for other parts of the world, the historical narrative is inapt. Adapting (and inverting) Bruno Latour's memorable, and for some, contemptuous title, Bhargava concludes that, according to the sense of the terms "secular" and "post-secular" that this narrative implies, in India at least, "we have always been post-secular."[17] Thus, the chapter questions not only the validity and relevance of a historical narrative more suited to Europe and North America but also the relevance of the term "post-secular" in connection with other contexts. Going further, we might add here that the notion of the post-secular can be understood as always already predicated upon the standard secularization thesis. That is, the post-secular designation only becomes necessary, or possible, given an at least implicit, prior acceptance of progressive secularization, which is subsequently subject to rejection or revision. If we have never been secularized in this sense, then we have never been secular (or post-secular) in the sense resulting from it.

---

17 Bruno Latour, *We Have Never Been Modern* (Cambridge, MA: Harvard University Press, 1993).

While Bhargava argues that (in India) we have always been post-secular, the prominent literary critic and broadly engaged intellectual George Levine suggests that in the United States in particular, we have hardly been secular and ought never to *become* post-secular. Levine asserts that for secularists like him, secularism is a deeply felt commitment, "a way of being in the world," rather than, we may suppose, a mere doctrine or intellectual conviction. Levine claims for secularism what William Connolly calls the "visceral register;" lost in Taylor's historicism and the challenges of post-secularism is the facticity of secularity as "a condition rather like breathing." After arguing for this existential-phenomenological sense of secularism, Levine suggests that the secular is a historical achievement that coincides with evidence-based, scientific reasoning. In its concern for cultural sensitivity and pursuit of religious accommodation, Levine warns that post-secularism is "in danger of giving away the store." Thinking particularly of the US context, he implies that post-secular concessions to religious sensibilities may be dangerous, pointing to the crisis of global warming and the religious obstructionism that may preclude effective responses to it. More pressing than our attention to "the religion/secular binary," he argues, must be our commitment to a fair and just world achieved through ethical and legal practices that ultimately depend on secular principles – even as we simultaneously acknowledge that the latter "have developed out of religious traditions."

Literary historian and theorist Bruce Robbins ends this section with an argument against the oft-repeated saw: "there are no atheists in foxholes." Acknowledging the difference between secularism and atheism, Robbins nevertheless implies that the atheist life has something to teach us about the importance and role of secularism. The claim that there are no atheists in foxholes is an argument not against atheism, Robbins cleverly asserts, but against foxholes. Foxholes are something that we can prevent, by preventing war. If we had more atheists, we would have fewer foxholes, and if we had fewer foxholes, we would have more atheists. Secularism, he argues, is perhaps our best means for preventing war. Robbins suggests that by acting in historical, linear time, human agents may exert control over some things, although not everything. Assuming the control humans may have depends on recognizing our own agency and forgoing, without replacement, transcendent aid and goals. Robbins argues for the very "subtraction" of value and meaning that Taylor rejects as an inadequate understanding of the development of secularism, in a sense obviating Kitcher's call for secular substitutes for religious meaning. But only in a sense – for Robbins suggests that although transcendent goals and comforts must be "subtracted" with nothing necessarily posited to replace them, he implies that ethics and meaning are provided by our contingent circumstances and depend upon the immediate care of ourselves and others.

Part II draws on the expressions of secularism and post-secularism from around the globe, tracing in detail the interactions between religious and secular values, norms and practices in cultural production, education, politics, public ceremony, public policy, international relations, and more. Chapters represent the diversity and particularity of secularisms as they exist today on nearly every continent. This section is divided into two subsections: the political and the public sphere.

Initiating the treatment of the political sphere, Rochelle Almeida's chapter on the projected annulment of public or gazetted religious holidays in India points to the escalating fears of minority communities, particularly in light of the recent accession to power of a blatantly right-wing Hindu nationality party. She argues that minorities in India – whether religious-, caste- or gender-related – had already, since the country's independence from Great Britain in 1947, suffered violations of their human rights by a gradual curtailment of their civil benefits (even while under successive so-called secularist Congress governments). Almeida thus expresses concern for what she sees as doubly vulnerable communities, such as Muslims and Christians, that privileges bestowed upon them might be swiftly revoked in the era of Prime Minister Narendra Modi. At risk, Almeida argues, is a conception and variety of secularism that might protect such minorities.

Arolda Elbasani and Murat Somer examine the evolution of secularism in Turkey and Albania. They argue that, having developed under European secular models, both nation states have regulated and disciplined Islam, while at times (especially in Turkey) harnessing it to state-directed ends. The authors examine the institutional devices through which state has controlled the visibility, function, and impact of Islam, while Islam itself has been "reformed" and "rationalized" in the process. Elbasani and Somer conclude that in contemporary Albania, secularism has been represented in terms of a relative interreligious equality, while in Turkey a dominant Islam has been endorsed for a cohesive national identity and social uniformity. Thus, in Turkey, the secular is in some sense "Islamic," while in Albania the secular is more multi-religious. Under such differing national conditions, religious elements have had to negotiate, adapt, and compete for space and recognition within particularized secular forms. The chapter thus makes clear how secularism and religion have differentially shape-shifted in relation to one another in various contexts. The discussion should eliminate any notion that may remain in the secular imaginary of the possibility for the simple extension of a universalized secularism, at least under existing conditions.

Ayşe Seda Müftügil examines the legislative introduction in 1982 of compulsory "religion education" in Turkey. Although the addition to the curricula of a mandatory course in religion has been attributed solely to the discretion of the military junta, Müftügil argues that academics and civilian groups played a significant role both in shaping the content of religion education and pursuing its adoption and particular implementation by the state. Müftügil suggests that scholars of Turkish history have overlooked this partially determinative role. To remediate this lack, Müftügil interviewed Beyza Bilgin, the first professor of religion education and the academic most responsible for making it a compulsory subject. Drawing from the interview and previously unexamined textbooks, legal documents, and transcripts from scholarly debates, Müftügil explains how and why religion education was consolidated and became mandatory, despite the Turkish constitutional provision of secularism. She also examines how this mandatory course considered, or did not consider, the particular needs and interests of religious minorities. Thus, the chapter illustrates how particular religious objectives may be instituted and justified, even while drawing on secular state doctrines.

Jonathan Beloff's chapter represents an indictment of the role of the Catholic Church in Rwanda in connection with the notorious genocide of 1994 that killed 1.2 million Tutsis and Hutus in one hundred days. If anything positive has emerged from so dark a phase in recent African history, it may be the secularization of government and social institutions. As Rwanda attempts to recover from multiple horrors in its brief post-colonial history, its emphasis on secularism may ultimately enable it to create a place for itself within the vast post-secularist canvas of African diversity.

Turning our attention to South America, Jonathan Scott addresses what he suggests should be considered a new Latin American secularism. In Latin America, Scott argues, geo-political unity and the rejection of neoliberalism are fostering an economic revolution of sorts, which is either ignored or utterly misrepresented in the North American media. A broad contingent of Latin American countries have successfully resisted North American financial hegemony, within a space where oil reserves allow formerly colonized nations to assert their global significance. As they attempt to shed the legacy of imperial dominance and the influence of Wall Street, Scott argues, a new form of secularism is emerging – based not so much on opposition to Christianity as upon the objective of addressing the needs of the poor and propertyless, who stand to gain by more equitable distribution of the region's rich natural resources. Scott's chapter should remind us that secularism, at least as initially founded by Holyoake, was first and foremost a movement for the amelioration of the material and cultural conditions of the laboring classes.

Despite the religious symbolism of its domestic politics and the religious rhetoric of its international affairs, US foreign policy expertise has been essentially secular in orientation. That is, notwithstanding public pronouncements, foreign policy experts have regarded other political actors, especially other nation-states, as behaving according to their putative secular interests. However, as Gregorio Bettiza shows, that too has changed. Bettiza surveys multi-disciplinary developments among foreign policy experts in academia and think tanks since 9/11. Bettiza asserts that talking about religion is no longer considered taboo within the arenas of policy elites in the United States. In fact, religious considerations have not only been integrated into discussions of US foreign policy – they have been emphasized. While secularism is integral to the US Constitution and the political sphere, in international affairs, a sea change has been wrought through (at least a perceived) "desecularization" of the global political landscape. The result is that US foreign policy has been re-conceptualized in post-secular terms.

Turning to the public sphere, in a cross-cultural study, Roberta Newman compares the mortuary memorials in Nanjing, China, and Gettysburg, Pennsylvania – the Memorial Hall to the Victims of the Nanjing Massacre, and the Gettysburg National Military Park, respectively. Newman notes that such monuments were developed as sites for the articulation of a national spirit that encompasses what she terms "spiritual magnetism." Such memorials speak to the anguish of loss and healing power of remembrance, regardless of global location. Thus, Newman argues, although such sites of pilgrimage may have been intended to have strictly secular-national significance, given the solemnity of their occasions and their recollection of ancestors, it is perhaps inevitable that they have acquired a sacred status. Newman's chapter thus represents a troubling of the secular/religious binary.

In her chapter on the intersections of politics, religion and economics, Chika Watanabe notes similar tensions in contemporary Japan between religion on the one hand and development on the other. She focuses on a Japanese NGO, the organizational product of a Shinto-based new religious group called Ananaikyo. Its founder, Yonosuke Nakano, spoke of the "Great Spirit of the Universe" and "Great Nature" as the source of all life and beings – supposedly as an alternative to traditional religion. Yet, as Japan has struggled with diminished global status in the post-World War II era, Watanabe explains, organizations such as Ananaikyo have altered their mission statements so as to obscure their religious legacies. Although it is eligible to receive government subsidies, in recent years, Ananaikyo has become suspect, its legacy considered "fishy" and "cultish." A blurring of the religious/secular binary has characterized the politics of development and environmental science. As environmentalism continues to take priority in Japan, Watanabe states that such projects are both hopeful and hazardous, for while promising a sustainable future, the renewal of Shinto politics is reminiscent of the nationalist and imperialist aspirations of the early twentieth century. Watanabe thus reminds us not only of the blurring of the secular and the religious but also the possibilities for the religious to be mobilized for secular ends.

Elayne Oliphant examines an unconventional art exhibition space, the College des Bernardins in Central Paris, and its implications for the secular/religious binary. As a traditionally sacred space owned and operated by the Catholic Archdiocese, visitors have been dismayed that such an iconoclastic modern artist as Claudio Parmiggiani was permitted to display his work as the first exhibitor. The response to modern art in the College exemplifies a French public reluctant to relinquish the sacred associations of both Catholic religious spaces like the Cathedral of Notre Dame and museum spaces for traditional art such as Palais de Versailles or the Centre Pompidou. Indeed, they are reluctant to see their churches reduced to museums, especially when the exhibitions housed within them contest notions of what is meant by "art" and "French" culture. Yet, Oliphant argues, the Catholic Church is paradoxically able to produce secular spaces precisely by mobilizing the tension between its religious history in France and the contemporary secularity that has emerged from that history. At stake is a contradiction within secular France such that only Catholicism can be rendered "secular" and "French," while Islam, in particular, remains hopelessly "religious" and other-than-French. Thus, Oliphant's study represents a sophisticated analysis of the differential construction of the "religious" by the "secular," and vice versa.

In the United States, the attainment of secular political power has necessarily required the display of religious, particularly Christian, belief. In his chapter, Charles Louis Richter shows how irreligion came to be regarded as anathema to national interests, and thus, by implication, how religion came to be regarded as essential to the same. Richter provides a cogent genealogy of the production of equivalence between North American nativism and an animus toward irreligion. Richter shows how a nineteenth-century public sphere relatively free of religious intolerance was transformed such that a conspicuous religiosity became a shibboleth of national loyalty. In 1898, an epitaph could unreservedly and proudly declare Lewis Knapp "thoroughly infidel to all ancient and modern humbug myths." Within a few years, however, irreligion would be synonymous with atheism, anarchy, and eventually, communism. Two events inaugurated this sudden shift in public judgment: the death of the "Great Agnostic" Robert Ingersoll, and anarchist/atheist Leon Czolgosz's assassination of President William McKinley. Not far behind, the specters of fascism, socialism, and communism lurked – "foreign" ideologies perceived as un-American and anti-America. In the aftermath of the terrorist attacks of September 11, a near century-long association of irreligion with foreign, existential threats was extended to Islam. Richter's chapter thus demonstrates the sense in which the US brand of political secularism is compatible with a requirement that Christian belief, at least on the part of national political figures, be declared in the public sphere, and that nationalist ideology be draped in quasi-religious symbolics. It is this apparent contradiction between political secularism and religious expression in the public sphere that causes so much confusion where the secularism of the United States is concerned.

In the final chapter and one connected primarily with secularism in the US, James McBride draws on Marx's notion of the commodity fetish to argue that while largely displaced and disarticulated from traditional cult objects, religious consciousness has found a new locus in the commodity. McBride traces the role of advertising in the activation and promotion of commodity fetishism. The implication is that contemporary capitalist society – in the US and throughout the global capitalist marketplace proliferating from it – remains religious in character. Thus, for McBride, secularization, at least as described in the standard secularization thesis, never happened; rather, modernity is marked by re-enchantment through the products of capitalist production and consumption.

2 Secularism: Diagnosis and Prognosis

As stated above, this volume takes as its central purpose the investigation of two questions: What is the state of secularism globally, and what are its prospects? Given the collection's theoretical and historical treatments of secularism and its explorations of secularisms globally, we hope to arrive at least a diagnosis, if not a prognosis, for global secularisms. A diagnosis necessitates the kind of open and sometimes conflicting reports that Part II of this volume represents. A prognosis depends upon predicting the unfolding of circumstances in secularism's several contexts and assessing its viability within and as part of those circumstances. Thus, a prognosis depends on both sections of this volume. However, while diagnosis may be within our grasp at present, prognosis will be necessarily more difficult. As Jacques Berlinerblau suggests in his Introduction to *Secularism on the Edge*, "[t]he academic discipline of secularism needs to experience a 'discovery' period. Simply put, more data is necessary before conclusions can be drawn."[18] Nevertheless, having presented and examined additional

---

18 Jacques Berlinerblau, "Introduction: Secularism and Its Confusions," in *Secularism on the Edge: Church-state Relations in the United States, France, and Israel*, eds. Jacques Berlinerblau, Sarah Fainberg, and Aurora Nou (New York, NY: Palgrave Macmillan, 2014), 1–16, at 9.

data, we *can* confirm with a degree of confidence that secularism is indeed "beleaguered" – both theoretically and politically. We point to the chapters in Part II for evidence of this embattlement.

With an even greater confidence, however, we can assert that secularism's prospects are *not entirely* beyond its control. That is, the fortunes of global secularisms hinge not solely on the cultural, political, regional, and religious environments in which they are embedded. Rather, successes will depend largely upon the efficacious articulation of secularism's value, both as idea, and as political apparatus. This badly needed articulation, however, appears to be encumbered by conceptual and terminological difficulties owing not only to secularism's provincial provenance but also to its mobilization by foes and friends alike. Likewise, the theoretical/historical explorations that we have included here are not mere speculative jaunts. As a philosophical idea and a political tool, secularism depends upon well-articulated definitions and demarcations. And the implications of such definitions and demarcations need to be explored. This volume represents, we hope, a contribution to such definitions, demarcations, and explorations.

Furthermore, the contexts of secularism will need to be understood in order to address the situation of secularism(s) in particular cases. Such contexts include not only the role(s) that secularism has played historically within various nation states and across regions but also the composition and character of secularism's historical religious partners and opponents. The sometimes historically biased, divisive, and even oppressive character of secularism in various settings must be acknowledged and attended to. In order to assert a role within and across states, secularism's fraught relationships –including its tacit endorsement of particular religions (as against others) in various settings – will need to be taken seriously and redressed.

Generally, some form of what Habermas calls "post-secularism" will be necessary for the successful articulation and promotion of secularisms. In stating this, we are not recommending the supersession of secularism as such. Nor do we mean to take a normative stance with reference to particular forms of secularism. Rather, we make this observation based upon the broad conditions for secularism in multiple contexts, and based on what we see as the best chances for secularisms globally. Thus, our use of the "post-secular" designation echoes Habermas's insistence that even for secular ends, recognition and sensitivity is best yielded to religious expression in the public and political spheres. Further, we suggest that the translation of religious language into a secular (or perhaps post-secular) discourse will be a vital component of secularisms in the future.

Additionally, we suggest that some types of doctrinal secularism will likely be non-adaptive in many post-secular contexts. Perhaps unsurprisingly, we refer here to the "hard naturalism"[19] that Habermas describes as scientistic secularism, a secularism that attempts to justify itself and its polemical stance with regards to religion strictly on scientific grounds, despite the fact that the claims of the hard naturalist "cannot be scientifically justified"[20] as such. Scientistic secularism[21] anticipates the extirpation of religions and religiosity from public life. And, drawing on reason and the presentation of scientific evidence, it also actively works to accomplish this end. It asserts that the co-existence of the secular and the religious is virtually impossible, or at least highly undesirable.

However, as a dialectical other of religion under secularity, scientistic secularism appears to consolidate that which it aims to eliminate. At the same time, it derives its own identity and solidity from the religion that it reifies and subsequently opposes. We consider it an unfortunate circumstance that some western organizations for the promotion of secularism apparently commend forms of hard naturalism or "hard secularism."[22] Basically, we see such "eliminationist"[23] secularisms not only as inefficacious for the promotion of secular ends in many contexts, but also as positively obstructive of the same.

Other forms of hard naturalism are not institutionalized so much as proliferated culturally. For example, the "new atheism" is a scientistic, hard secularism that adheres to the standard secularization thesis and that "suffers no [religious] fools."[24] Accusations of Islamophobia, racism, and the cheerleading of western imperialism in the Middle East render the new atheism extremely unlikely to travel far beyond its rather narrow scope in North America, Great Brit-

---

19 Jürgen Habermas, "Notes on Post-Secular Society," 27.

20 Jürgen Habermas, "Notes on Post-Secular Society," 27.

21 Massimo Pigliucci, "New Atheism and the Scientistic Turn in the Atheism Movement," *Midwest Studies in Philosophy* 37.1 (2013): 142–53, at 144: "Scientism here is defined as a totalizing attitude that regards science as the ultimate standard and arbiter of all interesting questions; or alternatively that seeks to expand the very definition and scope of science to encompass all aspects of human knowledge and understanding."

22 See, for example, "One Law for All," at http://www.onelawforall.org.uk/. Accessed September 19, 2014. For the notions of "hard" and "soft" secularism and "hard" and "soft" secularity, see Barry A. Kosmin, "Introduction: Contemporary Secularity and Secularism," in Barry A. Kosmin, and Ariela Keysar, eds. *Secularism & Secularity: Contemporary International Perspectives* (Hartford, CT: Institute for the Study of Secularism in Society and Culture, 2007), 1–13.

23 Colin Campell, *Toward a Sociology of Irreligion* (London: Macmillan, 1971), 54.

24 Razib Khan, "The Selfish Genius, Mind Your Manners Dr. Dawkins!" *Discover Magazine* (August 24, 2009). http://blogs.discovermagazine.com/gnxp/2009/08/the-selfish-genius-mind-your-manners-dr-dawkins/. Accessed September 19, 2014.

ain, and presumably, parts of continental Europe.[25] But even within its native environs, the new atheism has been sharply criticized by secular, atheist theorists.[26] Actually existing global secularisms thus would do well to reject such forms of secularism as the new atheism and other variants of hard naturalism.

Finally, the tendency of global secularisms may be toward softer institutional secularisms within broad post-secular frameworks. For example, Islam has posed a challenge to France's stringent laicism. Short of secular retrenchment in such settings, we should expect continued religious challenges and eventual accommodations of religious expression and practice. Of course, much will depend on the perception of Europe's religious others, especially the figuration of Islam by the West more broadly. By and large, however, global secularisms may be becoming more labile, expansive, and pluralistic – resembling, that is, Taylor's notion of secularity 3 – as they adapt to increasingly broadened and differentiated spheres of religious activity and expression. Perhaps what looks like a crisis of secularism is actually its evolution and diversification.

Works Cited

Asad, Talal. *Formations of the Secular: Christianity, Islam, Modernity.* Stanford, CA.: Stanford University Press, 2003.

Balibar, Étienne. *Saeculum: Culture, Religion, Idéologie.* Paris: Éd. Galilée, 2012.

Berger, Peter L. *The Desecularization of the World: Resurgent Religion and World Politics.* Washington, D.C.: Ethics and Public Policy Center, 1999.

Berlinerblau, Jacques. "Introduction: Secularism and Its Confusions." In *Secularism on the Edge: Church-state Relations in the United States, France, and Israel,* edited by Jacques Berlinerblau, Sarah Fainberg, and Aurora Nou, 1–16. New York, NY: Palgrave Macmillan, 2014.

Bhargava, Rajeev. "Political Secularism." In *The Oxford Handbook of Political Theory,* edited by John S. Dryzek, Bonnie Honig, and Anne Phillips, 636–55. Oxford: Oxford University Press, 2006.

Bhargava, Rajeev. "The Distinctiveness of Indian Secularism." In *The Future of Secularism,* edited by T.N. Srinivasan, 20–53. Delhi: Oxford University Press, 2006.

Bruce, Steve. *God Is Dead: Secularization in the West.* Malden, MA: Blackwell Pub, 2002.

Burchardt, Marian, Monika Wohlrab-Sahr and Matthias Middell. *Multiple Secularities Beyond the West: Religion and Modernity in a Global Age.* Boston: De Gruyter, 2015.

---

25 Be Scofield, "Reason and Racism in the New Atheism Movement," *Tikkun Daily* (January 26, 2012), http://www.tikkun.org/tikkundaily/2012/01/26/reason-and-racism-in-the-new-atheist-movement/. Accessed September 19, 2014.

26 Pigliucci, "New Atheism and the Scientistic Turn in the Atheism Movement."

Calhoun, Craig J., Mark Juergensmeyer and Jonathan VanAntwerpen. *Rethinking Secularism.* Oxford/N.Y.: Oxford University Press, 2011.

Campbell, Colin. *Toward a Sociology of Irreligion.* London: Macmillan, 1971.

Geoghegan, Vincent. "Religious Narrative, Post-secularism and Utopia." *Critical Review of International Social and Political Philosophy* 3.2–3 (2000) 205–24.

Habermas, Jürgen. "Notes on Post-Secular Society." *NPQ: New Perspectives Quarterly* 25.4 (2007): 17–29.

Jakobsen, Janet R. and Ann Pellegrini. "Introduction: Times Like These." In *Secularisms,* edited by Janet R. Jakobsen and Ann Pellegrini, 9–17. Durham: Duke University Press, 2008.

Khan, Razib. "The Selfish Genius, Mind Your Manners Dr. Dawkins!" *Discover Magazine,* August 24, 2009. Accessed September 19, 2014. http://blogs.discovermagazine.com/gnxp/2009/08/the-selfish-genius-mind-your-manners-dr-dawkins/.

Kitcher, Philip. "Science, Religion, and Democracy." *Episteme: A Journal of Social Epistemology* 5 (2008): 5–18.

Kitcher, Philip. "Militant Modern Atheism." *Journal of Applied Philosophy* 28 (2011): 1–13.

Kitcher, Philip. *Science in a Democratic Society.* New York: Prometheus Books, 2011.

Kosmin, Barry A. "Introduction: Contemporary Secularity and Secularism." In *Secularism & Secularity: Contemporary International Perspectives,* edited by Barry A. Kosmin and Ariela Keysar, 1–13. Hartford, CT: Institute for the Study of Secularism in Society and Culture, 2007.

Latour, Bruno. *We Have Never Been Modern.* Cambridge, MA: Harvard University Press, 1993.

Levine, George L. *The Joy of Secularism: 11 Essays for How We Live Now.* Princeton, N.J: Princeton University Press, 2011.

Norris, Pippa and Ronald Inglehart. *Sacred and Secular: Religion and Politics Worldwide.* West Nyack, NY: Cambridge University Press, 2004.

"One Law for All," at http://www.onelawforall.org.uk/. Accessed September 19, 2014.

Pigliucci, Massimo. "New Atheism and the Scientistic Turn in the Atheism Movement." *Midwest Studies in Philosophy* 37.1 (2013): 142–53.

Scofield, Be. "Reason and Racism in the New Atheist Movement." *Tikkun Daily.* January 26, 2012. http://www.tikkun.org/tikkundaily/2012/01/26/reason-and-racism-in-the-new-atheist-movement/. Accessed September 19, 2014.

Taylor, Charles. *A Secular Age.* Cambridge, MA: Belknap Press/Harvard University Press, 2007.

Warner, Michael, Jonathan VanAntwerpen, and Craig J. Calhoun. *Varieties of Secularism in a Secular Age.* Cambridge, MA: Harvard University Press, 2010.

"We Have Never Been Secular." Conference held at The New School for Social Research, The New School, New York, NY. Accessed August 31, 2014. http://blogs.ssrc.org/tif/2010/02/01/we-have-never-been-secular-re-thinking-the-sacred/.

Part I: **Histories & Theories of the (Post)Secular**

Stijn Latré

The Fall of the Sparrow: On Axial Religion and Secularization as the Goal of History

Why is it that belief in God has become one option among others in our days, whereas the same belief was evident around 1500? This is the way Charles Taylor frames the question about the *genealogy* of secularization in the West.[1] I will not provide yet another in depth assessment of Taylor's monumental *A Secular Age*. Instead, I will focus on what I believe to be a common aspect of recent, more or less philosophical theories of secularization and religious evolution, i.e. the focus on the importance of the "axial age." Before comparing Marcel Gauchet and Robert Bellah's views on the axial dynamics of secularization, I briefly present the precursor of recent genealogical theories of secularization, the German debate between Karl Löwith and Hans Blumenberg. Since most authors who today write on axial religion refer to Karl Jaspers' use of the term, I will also briefly dwell on Jaspers' presentation of the axial in *Vom Ursprung und Ziel der Geschichte*.[2] The body of my paper will then consist in comparing Bellah and Gauchet on the role they ascribe to the dynamics of axial religion.[3]

1 "Smaller" genealogies of secularization: Löwith and Blumenberg

The Jewish philosopher Karl Löwith has questioned modernity and its self-acclaimed originality. In *Meaning in History*,[4] Löwith coined a new (philosophical) secularization paradigm, that of *modernity as an illegitimate transfer* of previously religious elements to a worldly level. The transfer is illegitimate, because one

---

1 Charles Taylor, *A Secular Age* (Cambridge, MA: Belknap Press/Harvard University Press, 2007), 25.
2 Karl Jaspers, *The Origin and Goal of History*, trans. Michael Bullock (New Haven and London: Yale U.P., 1953).
3 Since Taylor and Bellah are rather congenial thinkers, I will focus on Bellah in a comparison to Gauchet. For a comparison between Taylor and Gauchet, see Cloots, Latré and Vanheeswijck, "The Future of the Christian Past: Marcel Gauchet and Charles Taylor on the Essence of Religion and its Evolution" in *The Heythrop Journal*. Forthcoming, first published online November 2013.
4 Karl Löwith, *Meaning in History The Theological Implications of the Philosophy of History* (Chicago, Illinois: University of Chicago Press, 1949).

cannot untie secular concepts or practices from their religious framework, without perverting the original purpose of the religious concepts and practices. For example, the Christian concept of hope was deeply intertwined with a transcendent, eschatological perspective on life after death. It was by no means directed towards an inner-worldly total solution for suffering. Redemption was solely possible in the afterlife. It was only with the Franciscan movement inaugurated by Joachim of Fiore that the priority of transcendent eschatology over inner-worldly affairs was questioned. Löwith considers modernity as the heir of this Franciscan movement. When modernity transforms Christian hope into the modern idea of progress, totalitarian ideologies see their chance to promote inner-worldly goals leading to ultimate salvation *in this life*. To underline their undeniable kinship with religious schemes, Marcel Gauchet has called these totalitarian views – Marxism, fascism – "secular religions."[5]

Hans Blumenberg objected to Löwith's paradigm of secularization as an illegitimate transfer of religious concepts to modern, secular concepts. He defended modernity's original claims in his classic book *The Legitimacy of the Modern Age.*[6] Secularization did not come about by an illegitimate transition from Christian hope to the modern idea of progress. Medieval eschatology was not primarily based on the hope for salvation, but on the fear of condemnation. This fear was theologically deepened by the nominalist account of a voluntarist and almighty God, who could at any time alter the ratio of his own creation arbitrarily and totally whimsically. Hence man could no longer be considered as the image of a God whose almighty will and thinking infinitely transcend the human condition, nor could nature be seen as the reflection of a divine plan of creation. As a result, man was left on his own, squeezed between an almighty but capricious *Deus absconditus* on the one hand, and a whimsical and irrational nature on the other. According to Blumenberg, this predicament gave rise to the modern idea of self-assertion (*Selbstbehauptung*): man had to enhance his unenviable position by becoming master and commander of nature by his own rationality, and not by understanding God's rationality. Modern science developed in this context as a perfectly legitimate endeavor.

The debate between Löwith and Blumenberg revolved around the relationship between Christianity and modernity in very specific historical figures: that of the Franciscan Joachites in the case of Löwith, and that of nominalism in Blumenberg's account. While these two perspectives on secularization remain

---

5 Marcel Gauchet, *L'Avènement de la démocratie, t. III. À l'épreuve des totalitarismes, 1914–1974* (Paris: Gallimard, 2010).
6 Hans Blumenberg, *The Legitimacy of the Modern Age* (Cambridge, MA: MIT Press, 1983).

true for their part, Taylor, Gauchet and Bellah esteem that they only tell a relatively small part of the story.

2 Karl Jaspers on Axial Religion

Ground for this suspicion lies in Karl Jaspers' *Vom Ursprung und Ziel der Geschichte*, where Jaspers questioned Christianity's centrality in the rise of modernity by pointing to the importance of what he coined as the era of "axial religion," roughly situated between 800 and 200 B.C. In this period "man, as we know him today, came into being. For short we may style this the "Axial period."[7] In this period of constitutive importance for human history, new philosophies and religions were formed around central figures and writings, such as Confucius and Lao Tse in China, the Upanishad texts and Buddha in India, Zarathustra in Persia, Jewish prophets in Palestine, and Greek philosophers.

What do these figures and their religions have in common? According to Jaspers, they all break with a mythical understanding of the cosmos. Rationality and *logos* start to fight mythical traditions. These new understandings of the cosmos substitute the transcendence of the one God for the polytheism of multiple demons, untrue figures of the divine (Jaspers 1949, 21). If myths persist, it is because they are transformed and serve now in more rational narratives. Along with the articulation of transcendence comes the articulation of divine moral perfection: *"Die Gottheit wurde gesteigert durch Ethisierung."* ("Religion was rendered ethical, and the majesty of the deity thereby increased.")[8] Humanity as a whole undergoes a rationalization, a *Vergeistigung* ("spiritualization") in Jaspers' terms.[9] The human being gets disentangled from its tacit understanding of the mysteries of being. Humanity is now open to new possibilities. For the first time in history, human beings can ask *questions*. The first philosophers are born. These passages from Jaspers are almost literally taken over by Gauchet, as we will shortly indicate. However various the ways may be in which the new experiences of being are experienced, what stands out is that human beings transcend themselves (*über sich hinausgreifen*), in that they become aware of

---

7 Jaspers, *The Origin and Goal of History*, 1.
8 Karl Jaspers, Vom Ursprung und Ziel der Geschichte, (München: Piper Verlag, 1949), 21. English trans. *The Origin and Goal of History*, 3. Note that the English translation is somewhat inadequate: instead of using "majesty," I would prefer "transcendence," because that word is mentioned only two lines before this quotation, and thus provides the context for the "increase of the deity."
9 Jaspers, *Vom Ursprung*, 21. Eng. *The Origin and Goal of History*, 3.

their own being within the totality of being, and that they from now on have to go some ways *on their own.* The axial period revealed capacities that were later called "reason" (*Vernunft*) and "personality."[10]

3 Gauchet versus Bellah: Anthropological Presuppositions[11]

Gauchet and Bellah diverge from Jaspers in that they no longer presuppose an abstract origin and goal of history. Their interests lie elsewhere: they purport to offer a historical-sociological analysis of religion, with the focus on the interplay between religion and politics. This interplay even constitutes the thread of Gauchet's argument in *The Disenchantment of the World*,[12] as is obvious from the subtitle, "A Political History of Religion." However, Gauchet's analysis of the connection between religion and politics leans heavily on a number of anthropological presuppositions. Elsewhere, Gauchet has depicted his philosophical and sociological views as *antroposociologie transcendentale.*[13] I shall now dwell on the connections Gauchet establishes between anthropology, sociology and transcendental theory.

Gauchet's anthropology bears the signature of Sartre. According to Sartre, the human being is always squeezed between the mere givenness of reality (*en-soi*) and human freedom, the capacity to transcend the merely given (*pour-soi*). When the human being chooses to hand over its freedom to some other authority, it objectifies itself and becomes *en-soi.* This is what Sartre called the state of *mauvaise foi.*[14] The human betrays her identity as *pour-soi* when giving up her freedom in order to surrender to the security and comfort of a given identity. According to Gauchet, this is exactly what happens collectively at the dawn of mankind. Without having a clear conscience of the event, humanity so to speak col-

---

10 Jaspers, *Vom Ursprung,* 22. Eng. *The Origin and Goal of History,* 4.
11 Sections 3 and 4 of this chapter are an adaptation of Stijn Latré, "The Axial Age and the Dynamics of Transcendence" in Stijn Latré, Guido Vanheeswijck, Walter Van Herck (eds.), *Radical Secularization? An inquiry into the religious roots of secular culture* (New York: Bloomsbury, 2015).
12 Marcel Gauchet, *Le désenchantement du monde. Une histoire politique de la religion* (Paris : Gallimard, 1985). Trans. Oscar Burge, *The Disenchantment of the World: A Political History of Religion* (Princeton, NJ: Princeton Univ. Press, 1997).
13 Marcel Gauchet, *La condition historique* (Paris: Gallimard, 2003), 10.
14 Jean-Paul Sartre, *L'être et le néant. Essai d'ontologie phénoménologique* (Paris: Gallimard, 1943), 81–106.

lectively "chose" in favor of *dépossession*, dispossession, the misappropriation of what is most intimate to human existence: freedom as autonomy. Hence humanity has "chosen"[15] to hand over its freedom to the gods. So-called primitive religion is born. Gauchet thus applies the Sartrian fundamental anthropology to the way people organize their living together in groups. The first groups of hunter-gatherers surrender their freedom collectively to the gods. For Gauchet, religious evolution will consist of the gradual recovery of this "freely" sustained dispossession.

This form of anthropo-sociology is transcendental, because the basic scheme of human subjectivity sketched above will set the preconditions from which human history unfolds. Once the original dispossession is questioned, human political history will continue to oscillate between the choice for a founding alterity and heteronomy on the one hand, and freedom and autonomy on the other. It is striking how close Gauchet comes to Jaspers in this respect, though he rejects the latter's presupposition of an "origin" and "telos" of history.[16] For Gauchet and Jaspers alike, it is as if the discovery of human freedom – and thus "transcendence," see below – unleashes the true but until now hidden nature of humanity.[17]

As soon as this transcendental scheme is applied to the history of politics and religion, it may cause the impression that Gauchet is trying to explain, in a Hegelian fashion, every phase of history as the consequence of logical antecedents. Gauchet's transcendental analysis of history does indeed intend to demonstrate how, in view of a given historical relation between religion and politics, only a limited number of possibilities lie open for realization in the future. However, it is entirely open to historical contingency which possibilities will eventually prevail. In addition, Gauchet's transcendental analysis is not *a priori*, but *a*

---

15 Gauchet uses the word "choix," but deliberately puts it between quotation marks. These marks indicate that Gauchet does not want to refer to a deliberate and fully conscious choice, nor to a necessary event. Rather, Gauchet wants to refer to a contingent event: humanity could have started otherwise, as it were with full exercise of capacities of freedom and autonomy. It was by no means necessary for humanity to take that path, but as a matter of fact, humanity did start off with dispossession (Gauchet 1985, 20–21).

16 Marcel Gauchet, *L'Avènement de la démocratie, t. I. La révolution moderne* (Paris: Gallimard, 2007), 14.

17 Jaspers, *Vom Ursprung*, 22: "Es ist der eigentliche Mensch, der im Leibe gebunden und verschleiert, durch Triebe gefesselt ,seiner selbst nur dunkel bewußt, nach Befreiung und Erlösung sich sehnt, und sie in der Welt schon erreichen kann." *The Origin and Goal of History*, 3–4: "It is the specifically human in man which, bound to and concealed within the body, fettered by instincts and only dimly aware of himself, longs for liberation and redemption and is able to attain to them already in this world."

posteriori: logical structures of history can, in most cases, only be revealed a long time after events took place, because causes and consequences are then easier to track, albeit never without difficulties and methodological restraints. I emphasize the status of Gauchet's transcendental method because the reader may eventually be surprised about the various convergences between the "transcendental" Gauchet and the "empirical" Bellah I will lay bare below.

Bellah's anthropological views do not depart from the tension between givenness and freedom, but are rooted in scientific knowledge about the development of human capacities. In a few quick notes, Bellah situates the evolution of humanity within a much larger framework of the evolution of life on earth. He adheres to an "emergentist" view, which he contrasts with a "determinist" view and for which he mentions Monod and Weinberg as main proponents. The emergentist view holds that apparently chaotic phenomena contain the capacity for self-organization[18] under circumstances which are not entirely reducible to mere coincidence. Bellah names the supposedly accidental transition from the unicellular bacteria prokaryotes to the multicellular organism eukaryotes as an instance of such an "emergence". The emergentist view[19] equally holds that newly composed forms of life show a complexity and creativity that cannot be explained by mere reference to their composing parts. The determinist view, by contrast, asserts that all organisms can be reduced to their constituting parts, and that nothing genuinely new can emerge.[20]

Bellah's account of the development of human capacities like play and ritual enactment seamlessly fits the emergentist view. Whereas small organisms showcase a baffling capacity for adaptation, to the degree that new developments cannot be explained away by mere reference to accidental material conditions, cultural products such as play, ritual and religion display a similar capacity for adaptation and creativity. Although every transition builds on preceding developments, religious transformations testify to that remarkable capacity for adaptation, a capacity overlooked by Gauchet in his account of so-called "primitive" religion.

Despite the wide variety of human cultures, Bellah seems to discern a common denominator. He considers the dialectics between what he calls "the world of ordinary life" and "some other world" in which concerns of everyday existence can be temporarily set aside, as crucial to the human species. Bellah refers

---

18 Robert N. Bellah, *Religion in Human Evolution: From the Paleolithic to the Axial Age* (Cambridge (Mass.)/London: The Belknap Press of Harvard UP, 2011), 57.
19 Bellah, *Religion in Human Evolution*, 57–58.
20 Bellah, *Religion in Human Evolution*, 97–104.

to Alfred Schutz's contrast between *ordinary* reality and *non-ordinary* reality.[21] Sports, play and religion pertain to the "other world." Bellah sustains this hypothesis with findings from psychology. Maslow speaks about "Deficiency cognition," related to the world of everyday needs, whereas "Being cognition" refers to an experience of the fullness of being, to a world where daily needs are fulfilled and in which there is time and space for other activities that are at first glance non-instrumental to surviving. Religion and symbolic representation take place at the level of "Being cognition." It goes without saying that the two levels are not entirely independent. What happens in times of "leisure" may also have useful effects in "real" life. Children imitate adults while playing. Medieval tournaments are for sport, but are equally training sessions for real war situations. Boundaries are permeable from the other side as well. In the middle of D-cognition activities, such as harvesting the crops, a sudden experience of B-cognition may emerge, when the farmer looks at the crops he is harvesting as a symbol of his intimate connection to nature, or of his fragile dependence on natural phenomena. Like Charles Taylor in *A Secular Age*,[22] Bellah refers to the tree described by Vaclav Havel during his imprisonment in Hermanice. The tree becomes a symbol of a higher fullness of being, breaking the daily routine of life in prison[23].

Although Bellah does not depart from a transcendental axiom, but from an, at first glance, merely empirical description of the evolution of human capacities, his point of view eventually comes close to Gauchet's: human beings are capable of transcending the surroundings in which they are initially fully embedded. This happens in activities of the B-cognition type. Within this eventually isomorphic anthropological framework, Bellah and Gauchet disagree about the role of religion. According to Bellah, religion is of the B-cognition type, practiced in times of leisure and abundance, though rituals may strengthen group cohesion and thus contribute to the efficient organization of activities centered on D-cognition. Gauchet, by contrast, does not define religion as pertaining to the realm of "time off" or "free play," but as dispossession, that is, as the *refusal* of freedom. At least, he does so while writing about so-called "primitive" religion. Gauchet allows freedom within the heart of religion as soon as the state has emerged in human history. That brings us to the next part, about the issue of the periodization of human history with regard to the relation between religion and politics.

---

21 Bellah, *Religion in Human Evolution*, xv and 147.
22 Taylor, *A Secular Age*, 728–29.
23 Bellah, *Religion in Human Evolution*, 5–8.

4 The evolution of religion and politics in the Axial Age

Dividing history into distinct phases is always tricky, and both Gauchet and Bellah are well aware of the pitfalls on this route. Despite these difficulties, they both end up with similar results, which is surprising in light of the very few references both thinkers make to each other's work.[24] Nonetheless, the scope of the books by Bellah and Gauchet here discussed differs: Gauchet covers in *Disenchantment* the entire history of the relation between religion and politics, whereas Bellah confines himself in *Religion in Human Evolution* to the period extending from the Paleolithicum to the axial age.[25] For the purpose of this chapter, I will mainly focus on their accounts of the axial age.

Gauchet and Bellah look at human history from different angles. Gauchet studies the rise of western democracy. In his narrative, he needs the "logic of the religious" to account for political changes, and vice versa. Bellah's focus lies on religion itself, though he cannot neglect the interplay between religion and politics. Up to the axial religion, religious history has unfolded in three stages, according to both scholars. The first phase is called "tribal religion" by Bellah and *religion primitive* by Gauchet. Bellah names the second stage "archaic religion," where Gauchet speaks of "the emergence of the State" or "hierarchic society," which Karl Jaspers named *Hochkultur* ("high culture").[26] Both Gauchet and Bellah refer to axial culture as the third stage in human history, on which I will now dwell.[27]

According to Bellah, the period of axial religion constitutes the most fundamental rupture in cultural history. He quotes Erik Voegelin, who depicted the

---

24 In *Religion in Human Evolution*, Bellah refers only once to Gauchet. Gauchet is generally sparse with references, but refers once to Bellah (Gauchet, *Le désenchantement du monde*, 28), to the latter's book Beyond Belief.
25 Bellah assembled scholars of different fields to discuss what comes after the axial age in Robert N. Bellah, Hans Joas (eds.), *The Axial Age and Its Consequences*.
26 Jaspers, *Vom Ursprung*, 25 and passim.
27 It should be noted that Gauchet does not explicitly divide his narrative into the stages I have just mentioned, but that this division imposes itself on the reader as his story unfolds. The fourth stage is Christianity as the "religion for the departure from religion," as Gauchet famously put it, in continuity with the Jewish tradition. The fifth stage corresponds to our present days, in which the role of religion as the structuring principle of society has come to its end, and has given way to democratic societies based on autonomy.

axial age as a "leap in being,"[28] words that were probably copied by Gauchet as *fracture dans l'être*,[29] albeit in the context of the emergence of the state. A similar vocabulary can be found in Jaspers.[30] The "leap in being" is essentially the rift between the world of gods and the world of men, the breaking of the unity that Gauchet already saw at work in the previous stage, and that leads to a gradually increasing separation of religion and politics. Bellah's account of the axial period can be summarized in four features, whereby the first three explain why this fundamental shift in culture came about. The fourth one is rather a formulation of this cultural breach than an explanation.

The first characteristic of axial religion is the immediate relation of God to his People or to religiously moved individuals, as we can find them in the Jewish tradition, and more specifically among the Jewish prophets.[31] The king is no longer divine, and the access to the divine is no longer necessarily mediated by the king or the priest. Moses never becomes king, but remains a prophet of God. The distance between politics and religion is growing.[32] Whereas Egyptian pharaohs typically had built large pyramids, no one knows where Moses is buried. Worldly and religious affairs are increasingly separated.[33]

A similar process occurs in the Eastern traditions. Bellah quotes a famous proverb from Taoism, which utters a dire social critique on imperial authority and its confucianist legitimation: "Follow the Dao and not the ruler, follow justice and not the father."[34]

Bellah explores the Jewish tradition, Ancient Greece in its Golden Age of the fifth century BC, India and China as examples of the axial spirit. Gauchet likewise refers to the Jewish prophets, and to Greek thinking.[35] He also highlights the immediate relation to the divine as a social innovation. One can bring to mind the classic example of Sophocles' Antigone, telling the story about the dilemma between loyalty to divine laws and loyalty to political authority. In Euro-

---

28 Bellah, *Religion in Human Evolution*, 271: "After mentioning Max Weber as a precursor, I need to mention two other scholars who developed Jaspers's idea further after he had put "the axial age" on the map. One of these is Eric Voegelin in his massive five-volume Order and History, where he speaks of "multiple and parallel leaps in being" in the first millennium BCE."

29 Gauchet, *Le désenchantement du monde*, 47.

30 Jaspers, *Vom Ursprung*, 21: "Aus dem unbefragten Innesein des Lebens geschieht die Lockerung."

31 Bellah, *Religion in Human Evolution*, 303 en passim.

32 Bellah, *Religion in Human Evolution*, 309.

33 Bellah, *Religion in Human Evolution*, 311.

34 Bellah, *Religion in Human Evolution*, 471.

35 Gauchet, *Le désenchantement du monde*, 141–155.

pean culture, Lutheran Protestantism is another example of an immediate relation to God that provokes social critiques.

"Second-order thinking" is, according to Bellah, the second feature of the axial period. It denotes logic, thinking about thinking, and more generally philosophy as such: all texts containing general reflections on the human being, the cosmos, the gods and their relations. Ancient Greece is the prime example of this second feature of the axial spirit. A subcategory of second-order thinking is the ability to imagine alternative social realities, to reflect on different possible political constellations.[36] Modes of human self-assessment also increase. The Greek tragedies explore the depths of the human soul.[37] The ability to think on a metalevel also takes form in the ontological dualism between the realm of mere appearance and the realm of being, which has become classic since the debates between Parmenides and Heraclites.[38]

The third feature of the axial period has also been articulated emphatically by Charles Taylor in *A Secular Age* and *Dilemmas and Connections*,[39] and centers around the moral revolution of the axial period. The gods lose their ambivalent moral status and become morally pure and perfect. The true God can only be morally good. The morally good is henceforth connected to activities which transcend the level of ordinary life (in the idiom that Bellah borrows from Schutz), or human flourishing (Taylor). One can easily draw from the Jewish or (postaxial) Christian tradition in this respect, but Bellah also refers to eastern traditions. There, sociological concepts undergo shifts of meaning as a consequence of the quest for moral perfection. The word *shi* from Chinese tradition originally denotes "lower nobility." In the period of the Warring States (5th-3rd century BC), its meaning shifts to "lower class of bureaucrats," and gradually slides to "educated people" in general in later times.[40] In order to gain access to the Chinese bureaucratic apparatus, candidates have to pass state exams, based on intellectual knowledge of Chinese language and Confucianist classics. Hence political office is in principle freely accessible and no longer tied to hereditary succession. Chinese culture is the first one, worldwide, to incorporate these democratic principles in its political apparatus, before Christianity and without needing the latter as "the religion to depart from religion", as Gauchet has it. Thus China has al-

---

36 Bellah, *Religion in Human Evolution*, 352.
37 Bellah, *Religion in Human Evolution*, 356.
38 Bellah, *Religion in Human Evolution*, 375.
39 See also my book review essay, Stijn Latré, "From the Field to the Forest. A Book Review Essay on Charles Taylor's Dilemmas and Connections" in *Bijdragen, International Journal in Philosophy and Theology* 72.4, 2011, 456–65.
40 Bellah, *Religion in Human Evolution*, 408.

ready developed at this early stage the bureaucratic tools Gauchet deems necessary for democracy.[41]

The fourth and final feature that Bellah attributes to the axial period is the growing awareness of transcendence. At first sight, this term does not seem to add something significant to the phrasing of the "leap in being". Transcendence is always linked to immanence. Schutzian ordinary life and Maslow's D-cognition belong to the realm of immanence, our sensory, daily life. Next to, above or outside this reality, a second reality exists, non-ordinary life (Schutz) or B-cognition (Maslow), a structure of categorical dualism which Bellah already sees operating within tribal religion.

This implicit duality of tribal religion is deepened in the axial period. Now the question arises on which levels this happens, considering transcendence against the yardstick of the three axial features mentioned above. The answer is straightforward: all three features have recourse to transcendence. In her relation to God/ a god, the individual is obviously connected to what she regards as transcendent reality. The metaphysical opposition between appearance and reality appeals to a transcendent realm beyond the senses. And it goes without saying that the moral articulation of the universally good *beyond human flourishing* also leans on a notion of transcendence. When Bellah makes use of the concept of transcendence, it is not always clear whether he denotes the religious, logic, ontological or moral meaning of the concept. He only distinguishes multiple dimensions of transcendence on one single occasion, when he discusses the idea of "two worlds" in ancient China. In this context, Bellah mentions both a formal transcendence, i.e. the capacity of our thinking to transcend immediately given reality, and a substantial form of transcendence, i.e. the religious belief in "heaven" (*Tian*). In addition, this religious form of transcendence entails a moral dynamics of belief in salvation.[42]

Gauchet dwells much longer on the deepening of transcendence in the axial period than Bellah. According to him, the "dynamics of transcendence" plays the key role on the path to a disenchanted world. When the divine is situated in a separate world, the distance to our sensory, immanent world may grow. Gauchet primarily refers to "western" examples. In Thomistic thinking, God is the transcendent Creator, whose *ratio* is diffused in nature. If one wishes to understand the godly super-nature rationally, one is to study nature scientifically as the "book of God". Less intellectual souls can have recourse to the Revelation. For nominalist thinking, however, God's will and intellect are ineffable. While engag-

---

41 Bellah, *Religion in Human Evolution*, 479. Gauchet, *Le désenchantement du monde*, 260–67.
42 Bellah, *Religion in Human Evolution*, 475–77.

ing in this world, we never know if we are dealing with the sacred, because we cannot know whether the order in nature is the result of absolute divine decree. God may will this order differently at any time. Since nature cannot simply be taken as the reflection of divine will, it is open to free scientific inquiry. If nature may not be the "book of the Creator", and if we cannot defend ourselves against the capricious will of an almighty God, at least we can buffer ourselves against the whims of nature, like pestilence and other natural calamities. In Thomism and nominalism alike, the deepening of transcendence leads to growing independence of the immanent world, to a widening gap with the transcendent, and a new impetus for science.[43]

Gauchet situates the deepening of transcendence within a western setting. In his view, the eastern traditions try to bridge the gap and restore the unity of being. They would want to return to the "reign of the One".[44] Here Gauchet seems to follow the interpretation of Max Weber, whose analysis is questioned by Bellah. In *Konfuzianismus und Taoismus*, Weber argues that China in general and Confucianism in particular do not know any field of tension between an immanent and a transcendent realm.[45] As indicated above, Bellah does plea for a transcendent dimension in Chinese tradition: on the formal-operative level of logical thinking, and on the ontological and religious[46] level by reference to the importance of "Tian" (heaven). In the context of his criticism of Weber, Bellah also adds[47] the presence of moral transcendence in the idea of salvation[48]. In

---

43 Within the scope of this chapter, I am unable to delve deeper into Gauchet's interesting thoughts on the dynamics of transcendence. See Gauchet, *Le désenchantement du monde*, 47–80 for more details. The general line of Gauchet's thoughts is that the deepening of transcendence progressed, so that western culture eventually lost sight of the religious as the structuring principle of society. For a more detailed account of Gauchet's views on the dynamics of transcendence, see also Cloots, Latré and Vanheeswijck, "The Future of the Christian Past: Marcel Gauchet and Charles Taylor on the Essence of Religion and its Evolution" in *The Heythrop Journal*. Forthcoming, first published online November 2013.

44 Gauchet presumably denies transcendence in the eastern traditions in terms of an ontological meaning, but may recognize in these traditions a moral, logical or even non-substantial religious transcendence. In *Le désenchantement du monde* (xviii), he notes that the West deepens the dualism, while the East tries to deny a substantial "second world" by developing the notion of "empty being": " Elle [the development of axial religion, sl] a emprunté deux voies clairement divergentes: la voie du compromis entre le maintien de la structure religieuse originelle et l'intégration des contenus nouveaux – la voie des religions orientales et de la pensée de l'être comme vide; et la voie extrémiste, à l'opposé, de la subjectivation du divin et de la division structurale du matériel et du spirituel, [...] – le monothéisme juif."

45 Bellah, *Religion in Human Evolution*, 476.

46 "Religious" here denotes an impersonal concept of "Heaven," not a personal God.

47 Bellah, *Religion in Human Evolution*, 476.

addition, the Confucian notion of *ren* does not simply refer to the inner worldly virtues of a gentleman or *junzi*. *Ren* also contains a notion of the universal good beyond ordinary life. Reason enough for Bellah to think that the Confucian *Analects* is not the merely secular text many interpreters presuppose it to be.[49] Likewise, Indian texts also exhibit moral transcendence. The meaning of *dharma* shifts from ritual observance to the moral prescript to respect the existing metaphysical order. Ascetic renouncers even withdraw from ordinary life so as to do justice to certain dimensions of *dharma*.[50]

No matter how, the deepening of transcendence in all mentioned areas – logical, religious, ontological and moral – caused religion to still "be" in the world, but no longer *of* the world. Politics could neither sustain its grip on religion, nor vice versa.

5 The Axial Shakespeare

I want to conclude with some reflections on the relation between axial dynamics and modern culture. For this purpose, I first quote three passages from two of William Shakespeare's most notorious and brilliant plays:

As flies to wanton boys are we to the gods,
They kill us for their sport.
(*King Lear* 4.1.38 – 39)[51]

There's a special Providence in the fall of a sparrow.
(*Hamlet* 5.2.215 – 16) [52]

Doubt thou the stars are fire,
Doubt that the sun doth move,
Doubt truth to be a liar,
But never doubt I love.
(*Hamlet* 2.2.115 – 118)

---

48 About the notion of salvation, Bellah (2011, 477) writes: "If Confucianism had depended entirely on a political form of salvation, it might have met the same fate; surely its powerful personal Faith in transcendent morality at whatever cost is what allowed it to survive political failure time and time again."

49 Bellah, *Religion in Human Evolution*, 412.

50 Bellah, *Religion in Human Evolution*, 508.

51 William Shakespeare, *King Lear*, edited by R.A. Foakes, *The Arden Shakespeare Series* (Walton-on-Thames, Surrey: Thomas Nelson and Sons, 1997).

52 William Shakespeare, *Hamlet*, edited by Harold Jenkins, *The Arden Shakespeare Series* (London and New York: Routledge, 1982).

In the context of this chapter, the first quotation refers to the stage of pre-axial religion, where the boundaries between gods, human beings and nature are porous, and where Homeric gods may kill Greek and Trojan warriors "for their sport". As we have seen, the axial period articulated the *transcendence* of the gods, or of the one single God. We have also seen how this articulation of transcendence went along with an *ethical purification* of the divine. The "axial mind" can no longer bear the thought that the gods arbitrarily toy with nature and human lives. The ambivalence of good and evil inherent in the pre-axial conception of divinity gives way to a morally univocal conception of the divine.

Hence, the idea of Providence could arise. The problem of evil may persist in the calamities of nature and deeds of men. But, in the end, these events are steered by a benevolent and omnipotent God. Shakespeare's Hamlet has recourse to this divine Providence to justify his own actions. Since even the fall of a sparrow happens according to divine providence, why then would the actions of a prince of Denmark be exempt from divine plotting?

One can indeed observe an intimate relation between the idea of divine Providence and human actions. One could argue that the idea of Providence runs counter to the idea of human freedom. Whatever human beings endeavor, the meaning of their actions was already foreseen by a divine intellect. This may seem continuous with the realm of the Greek gods, with their arbitrary and fatal decisions affecting mankind. But in a paradoxical way, this is not the case. Instead of submitting ourselves to quietism in the light of divine Providence, this very idea of Providence may also trigger an unremitting engagement with this world, the *secular* world.

How so? If God has become unambiguously benevolent, and my actions in the world lead to success, then I prove to myself, and more importantly, to my fellow human beings, that the course of my life is blessed by divine Providence, that I will be saved at the end of times. This line of argument was, of course, developed by Max Weber in his famous essay on the Protestant ethic and the spirit of capitalism.[53] Weber connects the spirit of capitalism – seeking evermore success and money, a spirit of reinvesting the fruits of labor in a capitalist enterprise in order to make even more money – to Protestant or more specifically, to Calvinist ethics. The doctrine of Predestination indeed urges people to strive for innerworldly success *ad maiorem gloriam Dei*, but also as a means to prove to oneself and the community that one belongs to the pre-elected people. Excessively enjoying the fruits of labor, as the traditionalist ethics of the *Ancien Régime* aristoc-

---

53 Max Weber, *The Protestant Ethic and the Spirit of Capitalism*, trans. Talcott Parsons (New York: Scribner's Sons and London: Allen and Unwin Ltd, 1930).

racy upheld, has now become a sin, for it is exactly in the calling (*Beruf*) of one's profession that one can best serve God. If we try to connect Weber's "small" genealogy of secularization – in the way I have called Löwith's and Blumenberg's accounts small genealogies – to the "larger" axial theories I described above, it is fascinating to see that Weber also connects the austerity of Calvinist ethics and the proof of pre-election to the deepening of transcendence: "The combination of faith in absolutely valid norms with absolute determinism and the complete transcendentality of God was in its way a product of great genius."[54]

As we see in Weber, and, of course, also in Blumenberg and Gauchet, the deepening of transcendence may lead again to the affirmation of the absolute power of divine will. But what then is the difference with the pre-axial gods of the Greeks? As the previous paragraphs already suggest, it is exactly this deepening of transcendence. Once the transcendence of God is articulated, it can either be considered as rational and benevolent to human beings (Thomist theology), or as employing an absolute but possibly capricious and even deceitful will (nominalist theology).

The last quotation from Shakespeare echoes this nominalist theology. Divine creation could not be subjected to any rational order after all. What if the stars are not fire, or truths turn out to be lies? If God has an absolute will, human beings are left alone with their own capacities –including, as we have seen, the capacity of self-affirmation ("Never doubt *I* love") and science. In post-Copernican times, human rationality is capable of judging for itself whether the sun does move or not.

To sum up: the "secular" aspirations of humanity saw light in the religious and philosophical reforms of the axial age. Jaspers believed that the axial revolution had a *universal* meaning: the spirit of free thinking that went along with it has gradually conquered the planet, as have its fruits of science and technology.[55]

Today, this globalization of the secular is questioned from many angles which are represented by other papers in this book. A global secularity as the "end of history" has given way to various global secularisms and non-secularisms, where relations between religion and politics may differ. But what might at least stand out in the variety of secularisms, is that they were in some respect made possible by a deepening of transcendence, in the multi-layered meaning I

---

54 Max Weber, *The Protestant Ethic*, 126.
55 Jaspers, *Vom Ursprung und Ziel der Geschichte*, 26: "Die Achsenzeit beginnt zwar zunächst räumlich begrenzt, aber sie wird geschichtlich allumfassend." See also p. 27: "Die Achsenzeit assimiliert alles übrige. Von ihr aus erhält die Weltgeschichte die einzige Struktur und Einheit, die durchhält oder doch bis heute durchgehalten hat."

indicated above, even if this very transcendence was lost sight of in the course of history. We might still need some understanding of transcendence, if only to understand our secular or post-secular age.

Works Cited

Bellah, Robert N. *Beyond Belief. Essays on Religion in a Post-Traditional World*. New York: Harper & Row, 1970.
Bellah, Robert N. *Religion in Human Evolution: From the Paleolithic to the Axial Age* Cambridge (Mass.)/London: The Belknap Press of Harvard UP, 2011.
Bellah, Robert N., and Joas, Hans, eds. *The Axial Age and Its Consequences*. Cambridge (Mass.)/London: The Belknap Press of Harvard UP, 2012.
Blumenberg, Hans. *The Legitimacy of the Modern Age*. Cambridge, MA: MIT Press, 1983.
Gauchet, Marcel. *Le désenchantement du monde. Une histoire politique de la religion*. Paris: Gallimard, 1985.
Gauchet, Marcel. *The Disenchantment of the World: A Political History of Religion*, trans. Oscar Burge. Princeton, NJ: Princeton UP, 1997.
Gauchet, Marcel. *La condition historique*. Paris: Gallimard, 2003.
Gauchet, Marcel. *L'Avènement de la démocratie, t. I. La révolution moderne*. Paris: Gallimard, 2007.
Gauchet, Marcel. *L'Avènement de la démocratie, t. III. À l'épreuve des totalitarismes, 1914–1974*. Paris: Gallimard, 2010.
Jaspers, Karl. *Vom Ursprung und Ziel der Geschichte*. München: Piper Verlag, 1949.
Jaspers, Karl. *The Origin and Goal of History*, trans. Michael Bullock. New Haven and London: Yale U.P., 1953.
Löwith, Karl. *Meaning in History The Theological Implications of the Philosophy of History*. Chicago, Illinois: University of Chicago Press, 1949.
Sartre, Jean-Paul. *L'être et le néant. Essai d'ontologie phénoménologique*. Paris: Gallimard, 1943.
Shakespeare, William. *Hamlet*, edited by Harold Jenkins, *The Arden Shakespeare Series*. London and New York: Routledge, 1982.
Shakespeare, William. *King Lear*, edited by R.A. Foakes, *The Arden Shakespeare Series*. Walton-on-Thames, Surrey: Thomas Nelson and Sons, 1997.
Taylor, Charles. *A Secular Age*. Cambridge, MA: Belknap Press/Harvard University Press, 2007.
Weber, Max. *The Protestant Ethic and the Spirit of Capitalism*, trans. Talcott Parsons. New York: Scribner's Sons and London: Allen and Unwin Ltd, 1930.

Michael Rectenwald

Mid-Nineteenth-Century British Secularism and its Contemporary Post-Secular Implications

In the late 1840s, a new philosophical, social, and political movement evolved from the freethought tradition of Thomas Paine, Richard Carlile, Robert Owen, and the radical periodical press. The movement was called "Secularism."[1] Its founder was George Jacob Holyoake (1817–1906).[2] Holyoake was a former apprentice whitesmith turned Owenite social missionary, "moral force" Chartist, and leading radical editor and publisher. Given his early exposure to Owenism and Chartism, Holyoake had become a freethinker. With his involvement in freethought publishing, he became a moral convert to atheism. But his experiences with virulent proponents of atheism or infidelity and the hostile reactions to infidelity on the part of the state, church, and press induced him to develop in 1851–52 the new creed and movement he called Secularism.

In retrospect, Holyoake claimed that the words "Secular," "Secularist," and "Secularism" were used for the first time in his periodical the *Reasoner* (founded in 1846), from 1851 through 1852, "as a general test of principles of conduct apart from spiritual considerations," to describe "a new way of thinking," and to define "a movement" based on that thinking, respectively.[3] In using these new derivatives, he redefined in positive terms what had been an epithet for the meaner concerns of worldly life or the designation of a lesser state of religiosity within the western Christian imaginary. His bold claims for the original mobilization of the terms are corroborated by the OED.[4] Never before Holyoake's mobilization

---

1 The foundational texts of Secularism include George Jacob Holyoake, *Secularism, The Practical Philosophy of the People* (London: Holyoake & Co., 1854) and George J. Holyoake, *The Principles of Secularism Illustrated* (London: Austin & Co, 1870).

2 Lee Grugel, *George Jacob Holyoake: A Study in the Evolution of a Victorian Radical* (Philadelphia: Porcupine Press, 1976), 2–3. In addition to Grugel's biography, for biographical sketches of Holyoake, see Edward Royle, *Victorian Infidels: The Origins of the British Secularist Movement, 1791–1866* (Manchester: University of Manchester Press, 1974), esp. at 3–6, 72–74, and 312; and Joseph McCabe, *Life and Letters of George Jacob Holyoake*, 2 vols. (London: Watts & Co., 1908).

3 George Jacob Holyoake, *English Secularism: A Confession of Belief* (Chicago: Open Court Pub. Co., 1896), 45–9.

4 *The Oxford English Dictionary*, http://ezproxy.library.nyu.edu:2181/view/Entry/174621?re directedFrom=Secularism#eid. Accessed September 4, 2014.

had "secular" been used as an adjective to describe a set of principles or "secularism" as a noun to positively delineate principles of morality and epistemology. The Secular principle was in effect an ontological demarcation stratagem, dividing the metaphysical, spiritual or eternal from "this life" – the material, the worldly or the temporal: "Secularity draws the line of demarcation between the things of time and the things of eternity."[5] Like Thomas H. Huxley's later agnosticism, Secularism deemed that whatever could not be "tested by the experience of this life" should simply be of no concern to the science practitioner, progressive thinker, moralist or politician. The "Secularist" was one who restricted efforts to "that province of human duty which belongs to this life."[6] But, as in Huxley's agnosticism, atheism was not a prerequisite for Secularism. Secularism represented "unknowingness without denial."[7] Holyoake did warn against the affirmation of deity and a future life, given that reliance on them might "betray us from the use of this world" to the detriment of "progress" and amelioration, but belief was not a disqualification for the pursuit of scientific knowledge or progress, only a possible obstacle. One's beliefs in the supernatural were a matter of speculation or opinion to which one was entitled, unless such beliefs precluded positive knowledge or action.

It is important to distinguish Holyoake's brand of Secularism from that of his eventual rival for the leadership of the Secularist movement, Charles Bradlaugh. Unlike Bradlaugh, for Holyoake the goal of freethought under Secularism was no longer first and foremost the elimination of religious ideology from the public sphere. Holyoake imagined Secularism as superseding and superintending both theism *and* atheism – from the standpoint of a new scientific, educative, and moral system. Holyoake insisted that a new, secular moral and epistemological system could be constructed alongside, or above, the old religious one. On the other hand, against Holyoake's assertions, Bradlaugh maintained that the primary task of Secularism was to destroy theism; otherwise the latter would impede the progress of the new secular order.[8]

Mid-century Secularism thus represents an important stage of nineteenth-century freethought – an intervention between the earlier infidelity of Carlile

---

5 *Reasoner* 12 (1852): 127, footnote. Holyoake thus advanced a demarcation argument over a century before Karl Popper in *The Logic of Scientific Discovery* (New York: Basic Books, 1959).
6 *Reasoner* 12 (1852): 34.
7 Holyoake, *English Secularism*, 36–37.
8 In *Toward a Sociology of Irreligion* (London: Macmillan, 1971), 54, Colin Campbell referred to these two approaches as the "substitutionist" (Holyoake) and "eliminationist" (Bradlaugh) camps.

and "Bradlaugh's rather crude anti-clericism and love of Bible-bashing."[9] While this new movement inherited much from the earlier infidelity of Carlile and Owen, Holyoake offered an epistemology and morality independent of Christianity, yet supposedly no longer at war with it. Had Holyoake's Secularism amounted to nothing more than this, it would nevertheless represent a significant historical development. Yet, mid-century Secularism is also significant in terms of the development of modern secularity, as it is now understood.

By the term "secular," Holyoake did not mean the mere absence or negation of religion, but rather a substantive category in its own right. Holyoake imagined and fostered the co-existence of secular and religious elements subsisting under a common umbrella. The secular and religious were figured as complementary and co-constituting aspects of what we might now call an overarching secularity, but which Holyoake called Secularism. Holyoake's Secularism thus maps very well onto Charles Taylor's notion of secularity as a condition that comprehends unbelief and belief, the secular and the religious, and the irresolution and continuing challenge that they pose to one another.[10] This understanding of Secularism is at odds with the standard secularization thesis according to which religion is progressively eliminated from the public (and perhaps even the private) sphere. Holyoake understood and advanced a notion of what we now understand as "secularity" over a century and a half before Taylor's account of it in *A Secular Age.*

In this chapter, I examine the development of Secularism as a movement and creed but also connect it to modern notions of the secular and secularity. I begin by sketching Holyoake's periodical and pamphleteering career in the 1840s, distinguishing it from that of another prominent freethinker, Charles Southwell, and showing how Holyoake eventually developed Secularism as a moral program – to escape the stigma of infidelity, but more importantly to move freethought toward a positive declaration of materialist principles as opposed to the mere negation of theology. I treat Holyoake's Secularism in terms of class conciliation between artisan-based freethinkers and middle-class skeptics, literary radicals, and liberal theists, and as a branch of Secularism distinct from that led by Bradlaugh. I conclude with further remarks regarding the significance of mid-century Secularism as a historic moment within modern secularity.

---

9 Bernard Lightman, "Ideology, Evolution and Late-Victorian Agnostic Popularizers," in ed. James Moore, *History, Humanity and Evolution: Essays for John C. Greene* (Cambridge: Cambridge University Press, 1989), 287–88.

10 Charles Taylor, *A Secular Age* (Cambridge, MA: Belknap Press/Harvard University Press, 2007).

1 From Infidelity to Moral Philosophy

In 1841, the former Owenite Social Missionary, Charles Southwell – with Maltus Questell Ryall, "an accomplished iconoclast, fiery, original, and, what rarely accompanies those qualities, gentlemanly," and William Chilton, a radical publisher and "absolute atheist" – founded in Bristol a periodical that its editors claimed was "the only exclusively ATHEISTICAL print that has appeared in any age or country," entitled *The Oracle of Reason, or Philosophy Vindicated.*[11]

Charles Southwell might, with important exceptions, be thought of as the Ludwig Feuerbach of British infidelity in the early 1840s, at least as Karl Marx characterizes the latter in *The German Ideology* (1845).[12] In this work, contemporaneous with the founding of *The Reasoner* (1846), Marx argued that the Young Hegelian Feuerbach was merely substituting one kind of *consciousness* for another, "to produce a correct consciousness about an existing fact; whereas for the real communist it is a question of overthrowing the existing state of things."[13] Marx argued that as warriors against religious concepts for the purposes of human liberation,

> "[t]he Young Hegelians consider conceptions, thoughts, ideas, in fact all the products of consciousness, to which they attribute an independent existence, as the real chains of men [...] it is evident that the Young Hegelians have to fight only against these illusions of consciousness. Since, according to their fantasy, the relationships of men, all their doings, their chains and their limitations are products of their consciousness, the Young Hegelians logically put to men the moral postulate of exchanging their present consciousness for human, critical or egoistic consciousness, and thus of removing their limitations."[14]

An atheist martyr, the criticism cannot be applied to Charles Southwell without qualifications. His writing constituted a political act with material and polit-

---

11 *Oracle* 1 (1842): ii. In George Jacob Holyoake, *Sixty Years of an Agitator's Life*, 2 vols. (London: T. F. Unwin, 1892), Vol. 1, 142, Holyoake described Chilton as "a cogent, solid writer, ready for any risk, and the only absolute atheist I have ever known."
12 The differences were many, such as the fact that Southwell was an artisan-class radical, not a university-educated philosopher trained in German philosophy. But J. M. Robertson, *A History of Freethought in the Nineteenth Century* (New York: G P Putnam's Sons, 1930) Vol. 1, 75, compares the atheism in the *Oracle* to positions developed by Feuerbach. For biographical sketches of Southwell, see Royle, *Victorian Infidels*, 69–73; and Robertson, *A History of Freethought in the Nineteenth Century*, Vol. 1, 73.
13 Karl Marx, *The German Ideology: Including Thesis on Feuerbach*, (Amherst N.Y.: Prometheus Books, 1998), 29–105, esp. at 65.
14 Marx, *The German Ideology*, 36.

ical consequences. While writing of "practical rights" with "practical powers," as opposed to "abstract rights," which were "mere chimeras," Southwell wanted to prove his rights in actual practice. However, the end he hoped to effect was in fact a revolution in ideas, which would, he thought, eventuate a change in material circumstances – precisely what Marx critiqued in Feuerbach.[15]

My aim is not to engage in an extended comparison of English infidelity and post-Hegelian German philosophy, but rather to underscore the irony of Southwell's abstraction of atheistic materialism from its socio-historical context in order to contrast it with the direction freethought was soon to take under Holyoake. Generally, Southwell warred on the level that Marx referred to as ideological, seeing religious ideas as the "chains of men." Southwell gave the sense of atheism as a purely intellectual affair, as the proclamation of a truth that had arisen at different times in places, including ancient Greece, but that had been continually thwarted by priests of all ages.[16]

Soon growing impatient with the lack of response to his philosophical disquisitions,[17] however, Southwell opened the fourth number of the *Oracle* with a caustic and belligerent article entitled "The Jew Book." Now, he took aim at the sacred text, which proved more dangerous and thus more effective for his purposes.

> That revolting odious Jew production, called BIBLE, has been for ages the idol of all sorts of blockheads, the glory of knaves, and the disgust of wise men. It is a history of lust, sodomies, wholesale slaughtering, and horrible depravity, that the vilest parts of all other histories, collected into one monstrous book, could scarcely parallel! Priests tell us that this concentration of abominations was written by a god; all the world believe priests, or they would rather have thought it the outpouring of some devil![18]

As James Secord notes, Southwell's polemic may be regarded as an "ugly attempt to exploit popular anti-Semitism to mock the Bible."[19] Southwell later admitted in his autobiography, *Confessions of a Freethinker*, the he had purposively written

---

15 Charles Southwell, *Oracle* 1 (1841): 1.
16 Southwell, *Oracle* 1 (1841): 28.
17 See *Oracle* 1 (1842): 2–4, 19–21, 27–9, 35–7. As William Carpenter and Charles Southwell noted in *The Trial of Charles Southwell: (editor of "the Oracle of Reason") for Blasphemy, Before Sir Charles Wetherall [i.e. Wetherell] Recorder of the City of Bristol, January the 14th, 1842 (London: Hetherington, 1842)*, 2–7, several of these articles ("Is There A God?") were also cited in the indictment as counts of blasphemy.
18 Southwell, *Oracle* 1 (1841): 25.
19 James A. Secord, *Victorian Sensation: The Extraordinary Publication, Reception, and Secret Authorship of Vestiges of the Natural History of Creation* (Chicago: University of Chicago Press, 2000), 307.

to provoke the authorities.[20] On the date of its publication, Southwell was arrested for blasphemy and taken to Bristol Jail.[21] His trial became a *cause celebre* in the liberal press.[22] His self-defense was unsuccessful, however, and on January 15, 1842, he was fined 100 pounds and sentenced to a year's imprisonment.[23]

With Southwell incarcerated and unable to manage the publication, George Jacob Holyoake became the editor of the *Oracle*. Under Holyoake's editorship, a change in rhetoric was immediately evident. Holyoake would not change the *Oracle*'s purpose – to "deal out Atheism as freely as ever Christianity was dealt out to the people"[24] – but he refrained from such odiously provocative and offensive denunciations as Southwell's "The Jew Book," moving the mission of the *Oracle* toward a positive declaration of atheistic and materialist principles, and away from a mere negation of theism.[25] Cleric baiting and Bible roasting were replaced by more eloquently impassioned pleas, exemplifying a principle of free speech without an ethic of vitriolic attack. Eschewing incendiary rhetoric, Holyoake sought sympathy for atheism on the basis of the conditions of poor workers and the failure of the Christian state to remedy them. Like Thomas Cooper, the Chartist poet and leader in Leicester, Holyoake saw Christianity as irrelevant to the suffering of the poor, and although not as depressive, like John Barton in Elizabeth Gaskell's Hungry Forties novel, *Mary Barton* (1848), he was "sadly put about to make great riches and great poverty square with Christ's Gospel."[26] His loss of faith had been occasioned by moral repugnance over the apparent indifference of the Christian state to the conditions of the suffering majority. Holyoake's was, first and foremost, a moral conversion.[27] As he stated in a lecture in Sheffield on "The Spirit of Bonner in the Disciples of Jesus," "the persecution of my friend [Southwell] ... has been, within these few weeks, the cradle of my doubts and the grave of my religion. My cherished confidence is gone, and my FAITH IS NO MORE."[28] During his childhood, Holyoake's sister had died

---

20 Charles Southwell, *Confessions of a Freethinker* (London, circa 1850), 66.

21 He remained there for seventeen days until an offer of bail was finally accepted.

22 See in particular, article by "Publicola" in the *Weekly Dispatch*, 19 December, 23 January, and 30 January 1842.

23 Southwell and Carpenter, *The Trial of Charles Southwell*, 102.

24 Southwell, *Oracle* 1 (1842): 1.

25 Maltus Questell Ryall, *Oracle* 1 (1842): 67.

26 Elizabeth C. Gaskell, *Mary Barton: A Tale of Manchester Life* ... : *in Two Volumes* (London: Chapman and Hall, 193, Piccadilly, (Late 186, Strand), 1850), Vol. 2, 297.

27 Royle, *Victorian Infidels*, 76–7.

28 George J. Holyoake, *The Spirit of Bonner in the Disciples of Jesus, Or, the Cruelty and Intolerance of Christianity Displayed in the Prosecution, for Blasphemy, of Charles Southwell, Editor of the Oracle of Reason: A Lecture* (London: Hetherington and Cleave, 1842), 4.

while his mother was away from home paying the Church rates and Easter dues. Conditioned by this personal loss from material want and its connection to religious observation, Holyoake had been predisposed to lose his faith in divine providence. His continual exposure to worldly want and suffering eventually spelled the end of whatever faith he may have had.[29]

As Holyoake saw it, want and knowledge were collaborators vying against superstition for control of the mid-century mind. "With the progress of knowledge, spirit and spiritual things have evaporated like ether poured out in the sunbeams."[30] Spirituality was a mirage that might have been utterly eradicated by knowledge, but because knowledge was, like Prometheus, still "changed to the rocks of superstition, and plucked at by the vultures of theology [...] suffering teaches lessons where reason could not impart truth."[31] What reason could not do in the bidding against religious superstition, the social conditions were accomplishing by deprivation.[32]

Holyoake acknowledged that the diffusion of knowledge and the spread of powerful ideas were not always sufficient to win converts to materialism. However, without the spread of knowledge, unbelief might arise only after it was too late to do any good. The diffusion of knowledge was likewise necessary to promote unbelief in order that material conditions might be improved.

While the *Oracle* still retained remnants of the old infidelity, Holyoake and company squarely shifted the focus to "the Condition of England question."[33] By the early 1840s, the freethought radicals had integrated what has been termed "the new analysis" into their loosely assembled "program" of reform. The "old analysis," an extended attack on "Kingcraft and Priestcraft," on taxes and sinecures, which also encompassed Republicanism, or alternatively the rhetoric of universal (male) suffrage, gave way under the new context of advancing industrialism. While retaining something of the old analysis, the new analysis was largely economic and drew on the work of Thomas Hodgskin, Charles Hall,

---

29 Also, Holyoake's daughter died while he served a sentence for blasphemy in Cheltenham Jail in 1841–42.

30 Holyoake, *Oracle* 1 (1842): 81.

31 Holyoake, *Oracle* 1 (1842): 81–2.

32 Holyoake, *Oracle* 1 (1842): 81. The rise of atheism during the Hungry Forties seems to contradict "the existential securality hypothesis" proffered by Pippa Norris and Ronald Inglehart in *Sacred and Secular: Religion and Politics Worldwide* (West Nyack, NY, USA: Cambridge University Press, 2004).

33 Thomas Carlyle coined the phrase in chapter one of *Chartism* (1839). Friedrich Engels contributed to the discourse in 1844 with *The Condition of the Working Class in England*. See Michael Levin, *The Condition of England Question: Carlyle, Mill, Engels* (New York: St. Martin's Press, 1998).

and Robert Owen to include a criticism of the competitive system of economic exploitation and of political economists, especially Thomas Malthus, as its primary apologists.[34] The Hungry Forties had done for materialism what a war of ideas never could, and as if validating Owenite doctrine, the force of circumstances made for the birth of a new emphasis.

When Southwell declined to resume editorship of the *Oracle* upon his release from Bristol Jail, Holyoake and company decided to fold the publication; yet they were committed to keeping freethought publishing alive. *The Movement And Anti-Persecution Gazette* was founded on December 16, 1843, allegedly to continue the mission of the *Oracle* and to report the activities of the Anti-Persecution Union.[35] Assisted by Ryall, Holyoake would be the primary editor and contributor. Central to the *Movement* was its departure for freethinking journalism. Not only did the editors maintain the tonal and rhetorical moderation characteristic of the *Oracle* after the removal of Southwell but also the *Movement* launched the "third stage" of freethought. As Holyoake saw it, the first two stages, free inquiry and open criticism of theology, were essential, but not constructive. The third stage, however, involved the development of morality: "to ascertain what rules human reason may supply for the independent conduct of life [...]"[36] The difference in emphasis marked what Holyoake later referred to as the "positive" side of freethought, which would not simply destroy theism, but replace its moral system with another. With this, Holyoake echoed Auguste Comte, who held that "nothing is destroyed until it has been replaced."[37]

The *Movement* was perhaps the first freethought periodical in Britain to emphasize a predominantly constructive approach, considering its duty to be to work toward the improvement of the conditions of the working classes, adopting to the circumstances of the Hungry Forties the Benthamite motto – carried as the epigraph following the title of every number – "to maximize morals, minimize

---

34 Patricia Hollis, *The Pauper Press: A Study in Working-Class Radicalism of the 1830s* (Oxford: Oxford U.P., 1970), 203 – 58, esp. at 204.

35 The Anti-Persecution Union was formed primarily in response to the imprisonment for blasphemous libel of Charles Southwell and grew out of the "Committee for the Protection of Mr. Southwell." Subscriptions for the Union and its establishment were announced in *Oracle* 1 (1842): 72. Maltus Q. Ryall was its first secretary; Holyoake became its secretary by 1843; see *Movement* 1 (1843): 5 – 7.

36 Holyoake, *English Secularism*, 34.

37 Quoted in Holyoake, *English Secularism*, 34. See also George J. Holyoake and Charles Bradlaugh, *Secularism, Scepticism, and Atheism: Verbatim Report of the Proceedings of a Two Nights' Public Debate between Messrs. G. J. Holyoake & C. Bradlaugh: Held at the New Hall of Science ... London, on the Evenings of March 10 and 11, 1870* (London: Austin, 1870), iv.

religion."[38] Inaugurating the development of a liberalized moral system independent of theology and relying on a rational application of methods derived from the observation of society, the *Movement* began an undertaking parallel to the positivism of Auguste Comte in France, while anticipating the social and political philosophy of John Stuart Mill's *On Liberty* (1859).[39]

2 The Upward Mobility of Freethought

The Reasoner was founded by Holyoake with the fifty pounds he won for his five entries into the Manchester Unity of Oddfellows contest for the best new lectures, to be read to graduates into the Oddfellowship.[40] The publication became the central propagandist instrument for freethought. By the time he began the new weekly Holyoake was a leading freethinker. His earlier position as an Owenite Social Missionary, his well-publicized trial for blasphemy, his secretariat of the Anti-Persecution Union, and his editorship of the leading freethought journals, had secured his reputation.[41] The *Reasoner* became the longest-standing freethought publication of its time, publishing from 1846 to 1861. The first series ended in 1861, soon after the introduction of Charles Bradlaugh's *National Reformer* in 1860. The cessation of the first series marked the effective end of Holyoake's singular prominence in the Secular movement, as Bradlaugh, the "Iconoclast," founded the National Secular Society in 1866, and became its first and long-standing President, until 1890, a year before his death. Of the publications with which Holyoake had been involved to date, he often suggested that the *Reasoner* most nearly characterized his own ideas, style and rhetoric, although these changed over time.[42]

In the *Reasoner*, Holyoake was not only interested in distancing himself from the old infidel rhetoric but also he had another kind of freethought movement in mind. While maintaining his right to the profession of atheism, he came to advocate the accommodation of other than atheistic views within a broader movement. Unbelievers, deists, monists, Utilitarians, and liberal theists might all cooperate, provided that together they promoted a morality, politics, economics,

---

38 The motto was carried as the epigraph following the title of each number.

39 John S. Mill, *On Liberty* (London: John W. Parker and Son, West Strand), 1859.

40 Holyoake, *Sixty Years of an Agitator's Life*, Vol. 1, 204–08.

41 For accounts of Holyoake's trial, see George Holyoake, *The History of the Last Trial by Jury for Atheism in England: A fragment of Autobiography* (London: Watson, 1850), and "The Trial," in Holyoake, *Sixty Years of an Agitator's Life*, Vol. 1, 157–63.

42 George Holyoake, "Letter to Paul Rodgers," *Reasoner* 3 (1847): 485–92, at 488.

and science of worldly improvement. While a seemingly contradictory position that alienated and angered some, it represented the differentiation of a religious public sphere, within which belief and unbelief coexisted by means of an over-arching secularity. Secularism thus marked a new stage in secularity itself, evincing a recognition that religious belief was unlikely to disappear.

In July of 1849, Holyoake initiated his foray into radical middle-class literary circles with a review of the George Henry Lewes's *The Life of Maximilien Robespierre* in the *Reasoner*.[43] He sent a copy of the review along with other numbers of the periodical to the biography's author at Bedford Place. Although unsure how long the papers had "been lying there" before taking notice, by August, Lewes had read the review and was impressed with its "tone & talent," although "dissent[ing] from most of its conclusions." In the company of Thornton Hunt, the son of radical poet Leigh Hunt, Lewes fired off a missive to the *Reasoner* offices and invited Holyoake for a cigar the following Monday, a night that Hunt was also available.[44] Thus began lasting friendships that signaled Holyoake's most significant literary success and began the bridge building to respectable society that would gain him admittance into the salons of numerous literary, political and scientific luminaries of the day. The connections initiated the cross-pollination of working- and middle-class freethought that resulted in the development of Secularism proper. Doubtless, Holyoake's notoriety as a leading artisan radical and journalist, who was still safe to associate with – at this point presumably the last to serve jail time for atheism[45] – had facilitated this welcome into this middle-class radical society, where he met and discussed politics and philosophy with the legatees of philosophical radicalism, including Francis Place, Robert Owen, W.H. Ashurst, Francis Newman, Thornton Hunt, George Henry Lewes, Harriet Martineau, Herbert Spencer, Louis Blanc, and others.[46] A few of these heterodox thinkers would even contribute articles to the *Reasoner*.

As a liberal activist, rising journalist and son of the heterodox poet Leigh Hunt, Thornton Hunt was a gentlemanly counterpart of Holyoake. The two became fast friends despite Holyoake's humbler background and Hunt's open af-

---

43 *Reasoner* 7 (1849): 33 – 7; 49 – 53.
44 George Henry Lewes to George Holyoake, 8 August 1849, The National Co-operative Archive, Manchester (subsequently NCA).
45 Holyoake, *The History of the Last Trial by Jury for Atheism*.
46 McCabe, *Life and Letters of George Jacob Holyoake*, Vol. 1, 145; Royle, *Victorian Infidels*, 154 – 55; Barbara J. Blaszak, *George Jacob Holyoake (1817 – 1906) and the Development of the British Cooperative Movement* (Lewiston, NY: The Edwin Mellen Press, 1988), 17; Rosemary Ashton, *142 Strand: A Radical Address in Victorian London* (London: Vintage, 2008), 8 – 9.

fair with Lewes's wife, Agnes.[47] Such libertinism if undertaken by a working-class radical like Holyoake would have been a greater scandal. By the end of 1849, Hunt already considered Holyoake an intimate to be included in his various activist schemes. His organizational plans for a "Confidential Combination" of freethinkers and a "Political Exchange" may have proven significant for Secularism. Edward Royle considers the Political Exchange foundational.[48] But the draft proposals that Hunt sent to Holyoake suggest that the Confidential Combination, with which the former has been confused, was envisioned as a means to enlist wary middle-class freethinkers into an anonymous group where they might voice advanced opinions on "politics, sociology, or religion" without fear of reprisal.[49] The Political Exchange, on the other hand, never came to fruition, and Hunt's proposal makes clear that it was intended as a public group for the comingling of persons of various political persuasions, not as an organization for the advancement of radical thought.[50] Considering Hunt's confessions to Holyoake in correspondence regarding his position on marital relations and his lack of respect for "the existing moral code in this country,"[51] one may surmise that the "sociology" to be discussed at the Confidential Combination had at least something to do with marital policy and a scientific system of morality, and "religion" with secular ideas, both of which might involve "opinions considerably in advance of those which they [publicly] avow."[52] The club's purpose was to circumvent "[t]he tyranny which keeps down the expression of opinion in our time, [which] though less dangerous than it has been in times past, is more domesticated, more searching, and constraining."[53] This anonymous club no doubt included Holyoake, Lewes, Hunt, Herbert Spencer, W. Savage Landor, W.J. Linton, W.E. Forster, T. Ballantine, and George Hooper, all of whom became contributors to the *Leader*, the liberal paper founded in 1850 by Hunt and Lewes, with Holyoake as its business manager.[54] Francis W. Newman, whose book *The Soul, its Sorrows and Aspirations* (1849) greatly impressed Holyoake, was among those, including Hunt and the pantheist William Maccall, who encouraged the forma-

---

47 As is well known, Lewes was meanwhile having an affair with Marian Evans (formerly Mary Ann Evans and soon to adopt the penname of George Eliot).
48 Royle, *Victorian Infidels*, 154.
49 Thornton Hunt to George Holyoake, 18 December 1849, NCA.
50 Thornton Hunt to Henry Travis, 21 October 1850, Holyoake Papers, Bishopsgate Institute Library, London.
51 Thornton Hunt to George Holyoake, 13 September 1852, NCA.
52 Thornton Hunt to George Holyoake, 18 December 1849, NCA.
53 Thornton Hunt to George Holyoake, 18 December 1849, NCA.
54 Royle, *Victorian Infidels*, 154.

tion of a club.[55] The members met at the Whittington Club at the old "Crown and Anchor" on the Strand. There Holyoake regularly conversed with Herbert Spencer, whom Holyoake described as having "a half-rustic look" and "gave the impression of being a young country gentleman of the sporting farmer type."[56] Spencer and Holyoake remained life-long friends, with regular correspondence continuing to 1894.[57]

Another overlapping milieu included the Muswell Hill circle, based in the Ashurst family home, which was also a center for radicalism and republicanism – notably in support of Giuseppe Mazzini. W. H. Ashurst, "[Robert] Owen's lawyer and advisor to a generation of radical leaders," encouraged Holyoake in the development of the new Secularist movement and with one hundred pounds bankrolled the reissue of the *Reasoner* in 1849.[58] It was to Ashurst, writing to the *Reasoner* under the pseudonym "Edward Search," that Holyoake owed the use of the words "Secular" and "Secularist" to describe the new branch of freethought then under formation. Holyoake added the word "Secularism" to describe "the work we have always had in hand."[59] The anonymous club was undoubtedly a breeding ground of middle-class support for the budding Secularist movement and served to germinate the program of Secularism eventually expounded by Holyoake.[60]

Many from this same circle of London writers also met at 142 Strand, the home and publishing house of John Chapman, the publisher of the *Westminster Review*, the organ of philosophical radicalism.[61] Contributors to the periodical included Lewes, Marian Evans (formerly Mary Ann Evans and soon to adopt the penname of George Eliot), Herbert Spencer, Harriet Martineau, Charles Bray, George Combe, and, by 1853, Thomas Huxley. Many of the *Westminster* writers showed an interest in the writings of Auguste Comte "and in his platform for social improvement through a progressive elaboration of the sciences."[62] Marian

---

55 Royle, *Victorian Infidels*, 158.

56 McCabe, *Life and Letters of George Jacob Holyoake*, Vol. 1, 162–63.

57 Herbert Spencer to George Holyoake, 17 September 1894, NCA.

58 Royle, *Victorian Infidels*, 154–55.

59 *Reasoner* 11 (London, 1851): 88.

60 See Margot Finn, *After Chartism: Class and Nation in English Radical Politics, 1848–1874* (Cambridge: Cambridge University Press, 1993), esp. 142–87.

61 Ashton, *142 Strand*; for Holyoake, see esp. 8–9. Another, overlapping circle centered on W. J. Fox and the Unitarian South Place Chapel. See Barbara Taylor, *Eve and the New Jerusalem: Socialism and Feminism in the Nineteenth Century* (Cambridge, MA: Harvard Univ. Press, 1993), 60–74.

62 Paul White, *Thomas Huxley: Making the "Man of Science"* (Cambridge: Cambridge University Press, 2003), 70.

Evans reviewed for the *Westminster* Robert William MacKay's *The Progress of the Intellect* (1850), a work of Comtean orientation.[63] Holyoake came to know Comte's ideas through his association with Lewes and Evans, as well through Harriet Martineau, who was then preparing her translation of his *Positive Philosophy*. Holyoake's contact with Comtean ideas was essential for the step that he was contemplating – to take freethought in a new direction.[64] In the *Reasoner* in the 1850s, Holyoake regularly cited Comte's famous phrase, "Nothing is destroyed until it is replaced," which he appropriated for Secularism.[65] Like Comte, Holyoake believed that religion had to be replaced with a "positive" creed rather than being simply negated by atheism. Martineau approvingly noticed the new direction that Holyoake was taking freethought:

> The adoption of the term Secularism is justified by its including a large number of persons who are not Atheists, and uniting them for action which has Secularism for its object, and not Atheism... [I]f by the adoption of a new term, a vast amount of impediment from prejudice is got rid of, the use of the term Secularism is found advantageous.[66]

The *Westminster Review* ran an article on Secularism in 1853, stressing that with Secularism, freethought had "abandoned the disproof of deity, contenting itself with the assertion that nothing could be known on the subject."[67] In 1862, the *Westminster* claimed, rather wishfully, that Secularism had become the belief system of the silent majority of the working classes, whatever the number of those who subscribed to its periodicals or associated with its official organizational structures.[68] Here, the author echoed the earlier remarks about Secularism by Horace Mann in his Introduction in 1854 to the 1851 census on religious worship.[69]

---

63 George Eliot, "Mackay's Progress of the Intellect," *Westminster Review* 54.2 (October 1850): 353–68.

64 Royle, *Victorian Infidels*, 156.

65 Later, Holyoake claimed that Comte suggested that he had adopted the phrase from Louis Napoleon. See Holyoake and Bradlaugh, *Secularism, Scepticism, and Atheism*, iv and 54.

66 Harriet Martineau, *Boston Liberator* (November 1853), quoted in the *Reasoner* 16.1 (1854): 5. The quote circulated widely and was found as far afield as the *Scripture Reader's Journal* for April 1856, 363–64.

67 Ebenezer Syme, "Contemporary Literature of England," *Westminster Review* (1853): 246–88.

68 William Binn, "The Religious Heresies of the Working Classes," *Westminster Review* 77 (1862): 32–52.

69 Horace Mann, *Census of Great Britain, 1851: Religious Worship in England and Wales* (London: G. Routledge, 1854), 93.

In short, Holyoake's role in the middle-class London literary and intellectual *avant garde* meant that he had moved from the radical artisan fringes to become a central figure; his "'Secularism' was their watchword," and the *Reasoner* the leading propagandist organ.[70] By the early 1850s, the cross-pollination between the middle- and working-class freethought movements was well underway. Holyoake's reviews and notices of the works of Francis Newman, Lewes, Martineau and others in the *Reasoner*, together with his work at the *Leader* and the notices of his Secularism in the *Westminster*, completed a two-way circuit of exchange. Holyoake's alliance of artisan and middle-class advocates preceded by over thirty years the more successful attempt by the son of the famous Secularist Charles Watts, Charles Albert Watts, who appropriated the idea of agnosticism for his *Agnostic Annual* in 1884, "to move towards an alliance with eminent middle-class unbelievers and away from secularism's radical working-class roots."[71] Secularism, while never disavowing its class roots, had by mid-century already forged alliances with eminent middle-class unbelievers and liberal theists, who were attracted to the new movement's program of greater inclusion.

Holyoake was admittedly flattered by his reception among middle-class intellectual circles, and boasted of it in his writing. He paid tribute to Eliot and Lewes in his book *Bygones Worth Remembering* (1905), stating that until he had been accepted into such company his had been "an outcast name, both in law and literature." His inclusion in the *Leader* was "the first recognition of the kind I have received."[72] But this conciliation with non-atheists and middle-brow radicals was seen by many of Holyoake's older working-class acquaintances as the gentrification of working-class infidelity as it merged with the gradualist, middle-class scientific meliorism ascribed to George Eliot by Charles Bray and others:

> She held as a solemn conviction ... that in proportion as the thoughts of men and women are removed from the earth ... are diverted from their own mutual relations and responsibilities, of which they alone know anything, to an invisible world, which alone can be apprehended by belief, they are led to neglect their duty to each other, to squander their strength in vain speculations ... which diminish their capacity for strenuous and worthy ac-

---

70 Adrian Desmond, *Huxley: From Devil's Disciple to Evolution's High Priest* (Reading, MA: Addison-Wesley, 1997), 160.
71 Bernard Lightman, "Huxley and Scientific Agnosticism: the Strange History of a Failed Rhetorical Strategy," *British Journal for the History of Science* 35.3 (2002): 271–89, at 284.
72 George Holyoake, *Bygones Worth Remembering* (London: T.F. Unwin, 1905), 64.

tion, during a span of life, brief indeed, but whose consequences will extend to remote posterity.[73]

This view was representative of Secularism, which evolved philosophically in connection with such middle-class influences and was developed by Holyoake expressly in order to accommodate them.

3 Atheism and Secularism

A fundamental division, as Royle points out, not only took hold between the major two camps of Secularism, but also within them.[74] The primary split dated to the early 1850s and went to the definition of Secularism itself. From the beginning of the movement and creed, Holyoake had differentiated Secularism from the older freethought movement, shifting its emphasis from a "negative" to a "positive" orientation. Philosophically, this entailed what he and others sometimes called a "suspensive" skepticism, which included not only denying atheism as a requisite commitment but also definitively disavowing any declarative assertion on the question of deity. As Holyoake argued (rather misleadingly) in the celebrated debate with the Reverend Brewin Grant in 1853, "[w]e have always held that the existence of Deity is 'past finding out,' and we have held that the time employed upon the investigation might be more profitably devoted to the study of humanity."[75] In terms of strategy, as we have seen, this position meant cooperation between unbelievers and believers; the invitation to join the Secularists extended not only to Christian Socialists such as Charles Kingsley and his ilk but also to liberal theists with reformist politics, such as Francis M. Newman and James Anthony Froude. In terms of principle, it meant that Holyoake's Secularism, as opposed to Bradlaugh's, was specifically not atheist.

Many leading freethinkers rejected the construction that Holyoake had put on freethought with his Secularism, however. These included, as we have seen, Charles Southwell; but it also included Holyoake's brother Austin, Robert Cooper, and most importantly, Charles Bradlaugh. With Bradlaugh's meteoric rise

---

73 George Eliot quoted in Edith Simcox, "George Eliot," *The Nineteenth Century* 9 (May 1881): 787; Edith Simcox quoted in Jane Hume Clapperton, *Scientific Meliorism and the Evolution of Happiness* (London: K. Paul, Trench & Co, 1885), vii-viii.

74 Edward Royle, *Radicals, Secularists and Republicans: Popular Freethought in Britain, 1866–1915* (Manchester: University of Manchester Press, 1980), 120.

75 Brewin Grant and George Holyoake, *Christianity and Secularism: Report of a Public Discussion between Brewin Grant and George Jacob Holyoake, Esq.* (London: Ward, 1853), 8.

to prominence in the Secular field in the 1860s, the divide between the Secularist camps became more pronounced. In 1850, Holyoake had chaired a freethought meeting and invited the young Bradlaugh, at the mere age of seventeen, to speak on "The Past, Present, and Future of Theology."[76] By the late 1850s, Bradlaugh had found a vehicle for his trenchant atheism in the *Investigator*, a periodical edited by Robert Cooper. By 1860, he had become the co-editor of the *National Reformer*, founded in the same year. He had also usurped Holyoake's position as the President of the London Central Secularist Society. Yet in an attempt to close the ranks of the Secularist body, in November 1861, Bradlaugh invited Holyoake to join the *National Reformer* as a special contributor. Holyoake accepted, and even signed a letter entitled, "One Paper and One Party," published in the periodical. Beginning in January 1862, Holyoake was responsible for curating three pages – either of his own writing, or from his associates. But in February a correspondent to the paper complained of the paper's diversity of opinion and asked what the *Reformer* definitively advocated regarding religion. Bradlaugh's answer effectively marked the end of Holyoake's involvement: "Editorially, the *National Reformer*, as to religious questions, is, and always has been, as far as we are concerned, the advocate of Atheism." The consequence was a fall-out between Bradlaugh and Holyoake that included a financial dispute, with Holyoake apparently demanding a year's salary, after having only served three months in his capacity as "chief contributor."[77]

By 1870, the lines were even more severely drawn. In a debate between Holyoake and Bradlaugh (chaired by Holyoake's brother, Austin, by then a follower of Bradlaugh), the topic was the place of atheism within Secularism. By then the President of the National Secularist Society (NSS), Bradlaugh asserted that "[...] Atheism is the logical result to all who are able to think the matter out" – and that Holyoake's reasoning was simply flawed.[78] Holyoake, for his part, remained as firm as ever that Secularism did not "include" atheism, but concomitantly, that it did not "exclude" atheists,[79] a point which Bradlaugh considered illogical.[80] Holyoake further suggested that making atheism a condition of Secularism was to delay the work of Secular improvement indefinitely, while atheism

---

76 Janet E. H. Courtney, *Freethinkers of the Nineteenth Century* (New York: E.P. Dutton, 1920), 105.

77 Hypatia B. Bonner and J. M. Robertson, *Charles Bradlaugh: A Record of His Life and Work* (London: TF Unwin, 1895), 128–30.

78 Holyoake and Bradlaugh, *Secularism, Scepticism, and Atheism*, vii.

79 Holyoake and Bradlaugh, *Secularism, Scepticism, and Atheism*, 19–20.

80 Holyoake and Bradlaugh, *Secularism, Scepticism, and Atheism*, 11.

made its "immense sweep" of theological notions.[81] Instead, Holyoake contended that Secularism should be established independently of theology as a creed that had positive principles of its own. He quoted a contributor to the *National Reformer* (again, his brother, Austin), who had asserted that it was "impossible to advocate Secular principles apart from Atheism [...] There is no man or woman who is willing to listen to Secular views, knowing they are intended to set up a system entirely apart and devoid of all religion."[82] George Holyoake did not spare his brother criticism:

> You set up Secular principles *for their own value.* Many persons are Secularists who can see religion even in this. *The provision is not to set up a thing "devoid of all religion," but to set up a thing distinct in itself,* and you have no more right to say it is set up apart from the religion, than the clergyman has a right to say, when you set up Secular knowledge apart from his creed, that you intend thereby to set it up *devoid* of religion or public piety.[83]

We see here that by Secularism Holyoake meant a substantive doctrine, not the mere absence or negation of religion or religious belief. For this reason, it could (logically or otherwise) stand parallel to (or above) religious systems. Moreover, he was even willing to allow Secularism to be construed as a religion in its own right. This was a more acceptable option for him than including atheism as a necessary element of Secularism. The gulf separating his views and those of Bradlaugh was thus seemingly impassable, and no further attempts at rapprochement took place.

4 Conclusion: Secularism as Post-Secularism

As introduced and developed by Holyoake, mid-century Secularism appeared to solve many of the problems posed by and for freethought radicalism itself, such as the *desideratum* to conduct free and open inquiry and expression without abdication to religious authority and unhampered by the legal and customary threats encountered in a theocracy. Holyoake modified freethought by pruning its atheistic rhetoric, allowing free thinkers to deny the supernatural and to disavow its clergy in matters relating to knowledge and morals, without the expected bombast and negation. By excluding questions of belief from morality and positive knowledge, Secularism opened up a space where working-class and gen-

---

81 Holyoake and Bradlaugh, *Secularism, Scepticism, and Atheism*, 19.
82 Holyoake and Bradlaugh, *Secularism, Scepticism, and Atheism*, 8–9.
83 Holyoake and Bradlaugh, *Secularism, Scepticism, and Atheism*, 8–9, emphasis added.

teel radicals, atheists, theists, and "agnostics" could potentially cooperate for the material improvement of humanity, especially the working classes. Many freethinkers, both those of his own generation, and those to follow, differed with Holyoake's conception of Secularism, and either rejected it outright, or modified it for their own purposes. As I have suggested, the major division between the Holyoake and Bradlaugh camps was based primarily on the question of atheism.

Remarkably, the two different types of Secularism that I have discussed survive to this day in the forms and understandings of general modern secularism. (And, so does confusion between them.) Under Bradlaugh's model, arguably the received contemporary understanding, the mission of secularism is evacuative, the category of the secular is negative and hegemonic, and secularization is understood as progressive and teleological. That is, Bradlaugh's Secularism amounted to a *belief* in what we now understand as the standard secularization thesis.[84] On the other hand, under Holyoake's model, Secularism is constructive, the category of the secular is positive and substantive, and secularization is understood as an increasingly developing, complex plurality of belief, unbelief, and suspension between the two, along with other creedal commitments. With his Secularism, Holyoake tacitly acknowledged the unlikelihood that Enlightenment rationality, extended into the nineteenth century, would utterly eradicate religious belief. That is, Holyoake grasped a sense of secularity as involving recognition and cooperation between religion and its others, a vision of the public and political spheres not unlike that which Jürgen Habermas has recently described as "post-secular."[85] Rather than (or even while) expecting its disappearance according to a model of secularization (or Secularism), that is, Holyoake argued that the secularist had best accommodate religious discourse within a public sphere notable for its uneven and forever incomplete secularization. In fact, secularization and Secularism represented just this incompletion and permanent unevenness.

Once freethought entered this "positive" phase – one of positing a substantive moral and epistemological value system, as opposed to merely antagonizing religious believers and negating theism – it could develop into a new, more in-

---

84 David Nash suggests that such a belief is in fact common among contemporary sociologists and others who maintain the standard secularization thesis, regardless of empirical evidence and theoretical disputation to the contrary. See "Reconnecting Religion with Social and Cultural History: Secularization's Failure as a Master Narrative," *Cultural and Social History* 1 (2004): 302–25.

85 Jürgen Habermas, "Notes on Post-Secular Society," *NPQ: New Perspectives Quarterly* 25.4 (2007): 17–29.

clusive, sophisticated creed and movement. Edward Royle and others have suggested that this development should be understood in terms of a kind of limited ecumenism, as the transformation of a religious sect into a denomination.[86] However, such an interpretation fails to grasp the secular as a category distinct from and yet necessarily related to and dependent upon the religious. With Holyoake's Secularism, freethought was not, or no longer, an entirely religious movement *per se*. Instead, freethought no longer contended for metaphysical sovereignty precisely on the grounds of theology itself. Or to put it another way, with mid-century Secularism, some freethinkers began to understand secularity differently. Rather than positing the category of the secular as mere the negation or absence of religion and belief, thus keeping it securely within the religious ambit, secularity had come to be understood in terms like those deployed by Charles Taylor in *A Secular Age*. Secularity (called Secularism by Holyoake and company) was understood and described as a distinct development, a new stage resulting in an overarching *condition* that embraced unbelief and belief, the secular and the religious.

The implications of historical Secularism are several. First, because it was not a form of atheism, we should not understand Secularism primarily as an anti-religious formation. Secularism, as first conceived, was not established to "overcome religion."[87] In fact, it was explicitly intended to supersede atheistic freethought in order to unite believers and unbelievers, religion and irreligion. Second, that is, Secularism was first and foremost a form of religious and non-religious *pluralism*. It acceded to the persistence of religion and a plurality of beliefs. Thus, as I have hinted above, Secularism was always already "post-secular" from its inception. Like Taylor's notion of secularity, only 150 years earlier, Holyoake's Secularism effectively pre-empted most versions of post-secularism.[88]

Finally, as I think the historical record of Secularism makes clear, Holyoake's Secularism is closer to a model for our contemporary moment than the kind promoted by Charles Bradlaugh. Whether we recognize a "religious resurgence," or merely acknowledge that the academy and other institutions are only now recognizing the persistence of religion, we are living in a post-secular age. At such a

---

86 Royle, *Victorian Infidels*, 160–62.

87 Graeme Smith suggests that organized Secularism was meant to "overcome religion;" see *A Short History of Secularism* (London: I. B. Tauris, 2008), 174–75.

88 Michael Warner, Jonathan VanAntwerpen, and Craig J. Calhoun, *Varieties of Secularism in a Secular Age* (Cambridge, MA: Harvard University Press, 2010), 22: "[B]ecause [Taylor's] third sense of the secular comprehends precisely those forms of religiosity that are now most widely mobilized, resurgence of religion is not evidence of a new post-secular dispensation."

time as ours, a broad tent, pluralistic secularism is needed. Secularism as negation is simply untenable. With the philosopher Ian James Kidd, we may understand the abiding presence of religion in terms of a (William) Jamesean psychologism such that religious "temperaments" are liable to persist.[89] Or, with the sociologist Peter Berger, we may see a religious resurgence and broad "desecularization" underway.[90] Or finally, with Charles Taylor, we may explain both possibilities in terms of an overarching or background condition called "secularity." In any case, it should be eminently clear that, if secularism is to survive at all, it must negotiate and cooperate with religion and religious believers – for the foreseeable future.

Works Cited

Archive Collections

London, Bishopsgate Library, George Jacob Holyoake Archive
Manchester, Co-operative Union Archive, Holyoake Correspondence

Periodicals

Boston Liberator
The Oracle of Reason, or Philosophy Vindicated
The Leader
The Movement And Anti-Persecution Gazette
The Nineteenth Century
The Reasoner And Herald of Progress (Various subtitles hereafter)
Scripture Reader's Journal
The Westminster Review

Primary and Secondary Sources

Ashton, Rosemary. *142 Strand: A Radical Address in Victorian London*. London: Vintage,
    2008.

---

89 Ian James Kidd, "A Phenomenological Challenge to 'Enlightened Secularism,'" *Religious Studies* 49.3 (September 2013): 377–98.
90 Peter L. Berger, *The Desecularization of the World: Resurgent Religion and World Politics* (Washington, D.C.: Ethics and Public Policy Center, 1999), esp. at 1–18.

Berger, Peter L. *The Desecularization of the World: Resurgent Religion and World Politics.* Washington, D.C.: Ethics and Public Policy Center, 1999.

Blaszak, Barbara J. *George Jacob Holyoake (1817–1906) and the Development of the British Cooperative Movement.* Lewiston, NY: The Edwin Mellen Press, 1988.

Bonner, Hypatia B. and J. M. Robertson. *Charles Bradlaugh: A Record of His Life and Work.* London: TF Unwin, 1895.

Campbell, Colin. *Toward a Sociology of Irreligion.* London: Macmillan, 1971.

Clapperton, Jane Hume. *Scientific Meliorism and the Evolution of Happiness.* London: K. Paul, Trench & Co, 1885.

Courtney, Janet E. H. *Freethinkers of the Nineteenth Century.* New York: E.P. Dutton, 1920.

Desmond, Adrian. *Huxley: From Devil's Disciple to Evolution's High Priest.* Reading, MA: Addison-Wesley, 1997.

Finn, Margot. *After Chartism: Class and Nation in English Radical Politics, 1848–1874.* Cambridge: Cambridge University Press, 1993.

Gaskell, Elizabeth C. *Mary Barton: A Tale of Manchester Life … : in Two Volumes.* London: Chapman and Hall, 193, Piccadilly, (Late 186, Strand), 1850. Vol 2.

Grant, Brewin and George Holyoake. *Christianity and Secularism: Report of a Public Discussion between Brewin Grant and George Jacob Holyoake, Esq.* London: Ward, 1853.

Grugel, Lee. *George Jacob Holyoake: A Study in the Evolution of a Victorian Radical.* Philadelphia: Porcupine Press, 1976.

Habermas, Jürgen. "Notes on Post-Secular Society." *NPQ: New Perspectives Quarterly* 25.4 (2007): 17–29.

Hollis, Patricia. *The Pauper Press: A Study in Working-Class Radicalism of the 1830s.* Oxford: Oxford U.P., 1970.

Holyoake, George Jacob. *The Spirit of Bonner in the Disciples of Jesus, Or, the Cruelty and Intolerance of Christianity Displayed in the Prosecution, for Blasphemy, of Charles Southwell, Editor of the Oracle of Reason: A Lecture.* London: Hetherington and Cleave, 1842.

Holyoake, George Jacob. *The History of the Last Trial by Jury for Atheism in England: A fragment of Autobiography.* London: Watson, 1850.

Holyoake, George Jacob. *Secularism, The Practical Philosophy of the People.* London: Holyoake & Co., 1854.

Holyoake, George Jacob. *The Principles of Secularism Illustrated.* London: Austin & Co, 1870.

Holyoake, George Jacob. *Sixty Years of an Agitator's Life,* 2 vols. London: T. F. Unwin, 1892.

Holyoake, George Jacob. *English Secularism: A Confession of Belief.* Chicago: Open Court Pub. Co., 1896.

Holyoake, George Jacob. *Bygones Worth Remembering.* London: T.F. Unwin. 1905.

Holyoake, George Jacob and Charles Bradlaugh. *Secularism, Scepticism, and Atheism: Verbatim Report of the Proceedings of a Two Nights' Public Debate between Messrs. G J. Holyoake & C. Bradlaugh: Held at the New Hall of Science … London, on the Evenings of March 10 and 11, 1870.* London: Austin, 1870.

Kidd, Ian James. "A Phenomenological Challenge to 'Enlightened Secularism.'" *Religious Studies* 49.3 (September 2013): 377–98.

Levin, Michael. *The Condition of England Question: Carlyle, Mill, Engels.* New York: St. Martin's Press, 1998.

Lightman, Bernard. "Huxley and Scientific Agnosticism: the Strange History of a Failed Rhetorical Strategy." *British Journal for the History of Science* 35.3 (2002): 271–89.

Lightman, Bernard. "Ideology, Evolution and Late-Victorian Agnostic Popularizers." In *History, Humanity and Evolution: Essays for John C. Greene*, edited by James Moore, 287–88. Cambridge: Cambridge University Press, 1989.

Mann, Horace. *Census of Great Britain, 1851: Religious Worship in England and Wales.* London: G. Routledge, 1854.

Marx, Karl. *The German Ideology: Including Thesis on Feuerbach.* Amherst N.Y.: Prometheus Books, 1998.

McCabe, Joseph. *Life and Letters of George Jacob Holyoake*, 2 vols. London: Watts & Co., 1908.

Mill, John S. *On Liberty.* London: John W. Parker and Son, West Strand. 1859.

Nash, David. "Reconnecting Religion with Social and Cultural History: Secularization's Failure as a Master Narrative." *Cultural and Social History* 1 (2004): 302–25.

Norris, Pippa and Ronald Inglehart. *Sacred and Secular: Religion and Politics Worldwide.* West Nyack, NY, USA: Cambridge University Press, 2004.

Popper, Karl. *The Logic of Scientific Discovery.* New York: Basic Books, 1959.

Robertson, J. M. *A History of Freethought in the Nineteenth Century.* New York: G P Putnam's Sons, 1930.

Royle, Edward. *Victorian Infidels: The Origins of the British Secularist Movement, 1791–1866.* Manchester: University of Manchester Press, 1974.

Royle, Edward. *Radicals, Secularists and Republicans: Popular Freethought in Britain, 1866–1915.* Manchester: University of Manchester Press, 1980.

Secord, James A. *Victorian Sensation: The Extraordinary Publication, Reception, and Secret Authorship of Vestiges of the Natural History of Creation.* Chicago: University of Chicago Press, 2000.

Smith, Graeme. *A Short History of Secularism.* London: I. B. Tauris, 2008.

Southwell, Charles. *Confessions of a Freethinker.* London, circa 1850.

Southwell, Charles and William Carpenter. *The Trial of Charles Southwell: (editor of "the Oracle of Reason") for Blasphemy, Before Sir Charles Wetherall [i. e. Wetherell] Recorder of the City of Bristol, January the 14th, 1842.* London: Hetherington, 1842.

Taylor, Barbara. *Eve and the New Jerusalem: Socialism and Feminism in the Nineteenth Century.* Cambridge, MA: Harvard Univ. Press, 1993.

Taylor, Charles. *A Secular Age.* Cambridge, MA: Belknap Press/Harvard University Press, 2007.

The Oxford English Dictionary. Accessed September 4, 2014. http://ezproxy.library.nyu.edu:2181/view/Entry/174621?redirectedFrom=Secularism#eid.

Warner, Michael, Jonathan VanAntwerpen, and Craig J. Calhoun, *Varieties of Secularism in a Secular Age.* Cambridge, MA: Harvard University Press, 2010.

White, Paul. *Thomas Huxley: Making the "Man of Science."* Cambridge: Cambridge University Press, 2003.

Philip Kitcher
Secularism as a Positive Position

The loudest contemporary voices advocating a secular world-view offer a purely negative message. They identify religion as a repository of primitive superstitions to be expunged as thoroughly and as quickly as possible. Whether or not this is a politically astute strategy for transforming contemporary societies so that the frequency of religious belief is diminished, it is, to my mind, at least intellectually incomplete. Alongside the evils to which zealous atheists point – often gleefully – there are valuable functions served by religious attitudes and religious institutions. A fully satisfying secular position must provide some account of how these functions are to be discharged in a post-religious world.

Seen as a positive position, secularism faces two distinct tasks. The first is to address doubts that particular ways of thinking can be preserved once the religious perspective has been abandoned. The second is to understand how there can be secular surrogates for religious institutions. Would secular *life* inevitably be diminished? How can we craft a fully satisfying secular *society*? Today, I want briefly to address both types of question.

One extremely popular concern about the replacement of religious understandings with a secular perspective – voiced eloquently by Dostoyevsky's Ivan Karamazov – is the complaint that religion is essential for the grounding of value.[1] Despite Plato's incisive attacks on founding ethical commands in the divine will, and the subsequent conviction of most philosophers in the western tradition that the source of value must lie elsewhere, a tight connection between religion and ethics is perennially popular. To my mind, the enduring power of this highly problematic idea testifies to the remoteness of the philosophical abstractions that have been proposed as alternatives. Concrete substitutes, such as Bentham's aggregation of pains and pleasures across sentient beings, are not only insensitive to issues of distribution, but they also appear crass and inadequate. Invocations of principles of practical reasoning, of non-natural properties, of relations of supportive reasons inherent in nature, of moral sentiments that can be reliably triggered in us by particular events or states of affairs, while they evade the charge of falling far short of accounting for what is valuable,

---

1 Fyodor Dostoyevsky, Susan McReynolds Oddo, Constance Garnett, and Ralph E. Matlaw, *The Brothers Karamazov: A Revised Translation, Contexts, Criticism* (New York: W.W. Norton & Co., 2011).

do so at the cost of transporting ethics to a nebulous realm in which our ethical dilemmas and our ethical debates have no chance of convincing resolution.

A better approach, I suggest, is to recognize the long history of our ethical practices, a history that must ultimately terminate in pre-ethical ancestors. Anthropologists and primatologists offer well-grounded conjectures about their social lives: they lived in relatively small groups, mixed by age and sex. Judging by the predicaments of our surviving evolutionary cousins, those groups would have been held together by limited dispositions to mutual responsiveness. Our ancestors could respond to one another enough to live together, but their psychological capacities were not sufficient to enable them to live together easily. Their societies were tense and fragile, often on the edge of breaking-up and demanding lengthy processes of making-up.

How did we get from there to here? Through the invention of a social institution, agreed-on rules for joint living, passed on across the generations and refined in continued conversation. Ethics began as a social technology, whose function was to overcome the limits of our responsiveness to others. Along the way, the egalitarian conversations of the beginnings – still evident in the lives of those groups that live closest to our ancestors' way of life – were distorted by the idea of ethical expertise, initially conceived in terms of inspired access to some external, transcendent, source for which philosophical theorizing has offered its typically pallid substitutes.

That perspective on ethics, and on values more generally, articulates Dewey's pregnant assertion that *"[m]oral conceptions and processes grow naturally out of the very conditions of human life."*[2] If I am right, ethics is not an attempt to fathom some set of truths grounded in any external source. Ethical truth is generated from human attempts to construct life together. We seek solutions to the problem posed for us by our limited responsiveness to others, and "truth" is a label we attach to the precepts that emerge as elements in enduring problem-solutions: "truth *happens* to an idea," as William James says.[3] The resources for continuing the ethical project are our interlocutors in the conversation, their demands and aspirations, and our commitment to terms of mutual engagement. There is nothing more.

I have only sketched a position elaborated in much greater detail elsewhere, but I propose that these are the lines along which a response to Ivan Karamazov's assertion is to be found. When ethics is viewed as an evolving project, per-

---

2 John Dewey and Jo Ann Boydston, *The Later Works, 1925–1953* (Carbondale: Southern Illinois University Press, 2008), 308.
3 William James, *The Meaning of Truth* (Rockville, MD: Arc Manor, 2008), 5.

manently unfinished, the connection with religion is seen as a distorting accident in the history of our practices, one introduced when ancestral societies gained greater ability to secure compliance with their agreed-on rules by supposing a transcendent policeman, a being able to monitor human conduct even when none of the group is around. That apparently fruitful idea paved the way for a later phase at which individuals could claim that they had special access to the policeman's will. Then, and only then, did the idea of an external source displace that of an egalitarian conversation.

I want to extend this outline of an account of ethical values to address a second question, legitimately posed by those who worry that secularism diminishes human life. Many religious people see their lives as obtaining meaning in virtue of a relation to something larger than themselves, something permanent and transcendent. How can a secular perspective provide a substitute?

In a characteristically thoughtful essay, Thomas Nagel has posed this question with especial clarity, and he rightly sees that issues about the meaningfulness of human lives have been skirted in Anglophone philosophy.[4] Yet those issues are at the core of the western philosophical tradition: the well-born young men who flocked to the schools of the ancient world wanted to learn how to live well. The answers they received remain pertinent today: virtue, social activity, friendship, and understanding remain worthy goals. The Enlightenment added the idea that the worthwhile life is centered on a self-conception that is freely chosen – your life must be your own, your "project" or "life-plan" something you find satisfying.

I want to develop this general conception by adding what I take to be a necessary condition. No project is worthwhile unless it is directed towards contributing positively to the lives of others. Lives matter because they matter to other people. My condition does not entail the elitism of the ancient conceptions, for mattering to others does not only happen on a grand scale. You do not need to "forge the uncreated conscience of your race."[5] It is enough to nurture and sustain those who live after you, to preserve something you have inherited, to contribute to a larger human enterprise.

This approach to what makes lives valuable grows out of my conception of ethics as a human project whose central focus is the extension of our responsiveness to others. Instead of the religious thought that we are participants in a transcendent enterprise that is permanent and inexpressibly grand, I propose a con-

---

4 Thomas Nagel, *Secular Philosophy and the Religious Temperament: Essays 2002–2008* (New York: Oxford University Press, 2010), 3–18.
5 James Joyce, *A Portrait of the Artist as a Young Man* (New York: B. W. Huebsch, 1917), 299.

ception of the meaningful human life as one that extends connections to other human lives. As Nagel sees it, there is a link to something beyond the individual, but, in my version, the traces left by a meaningful life need not be permanent, nor need the collective venture itself endure forever. Our planet will eventually become uninhabitable – and we can only hope that "eventually" is the right word here; sooner or later, our species will become extinct. That does not diminish the meaningfulness of what we do.

If our lives go well they leave traces, welcome after-effects, in the lives of others. Like the ripples in a pool produced by a stone, those effects will, sooner or later, fade away and vanish. Their impermanence does not matter to their mattering. It is important that they have been – just as at the close of *King Lear*, "cheerless, dark and deadly" as it is, it remains important that Cordelia *has been*.

To a certain type of religious sensibility, this approach to the value of human lives may appear inadequate. Only a contribution to something permanent would be genuinely worthwhile. Longer would apparently be better, and an eternal effect would be best of all. Yet, under the religious perspective, permanence comes at the cost of incomprehensibility. Through religious devotion we are to play our infinitesimal part in an unfathomable cosmic scheme. The ends are allegedly permanent, but our labor is thoroughly alienated. By contrast, the secular perspective restores our autonomy, our agency, and our understanding of what we do.

I want to close by relating what I have said to the second type of question I initially posed. A positive secularism must not only account for valuable attitudes, but it must also provide institutions to replace those of religious societies. To see ethical life as bound up with the development of responsiveness, to recognize meaningful lives as those that matter to others, already points to an important social function of religious institutions. Temples and mosques, churches and synagogues have brought people together on common ethical endeavors. They have offered spaces in which the reflective choice of meaningful life-plans can be undertaken. At times, they have advanced the ethical project itself. That was most evident in the civil rights movement of the 1960s, but it endures, on a smaller scale, week by week, in religious assemblies of minority groups throughout this city.

In a society with pronounced tendencies to reduce people to atomized individuals, versions of *Homo economicus*, substitutes for these modes of community-formation are not easy to find. Building them is difficult, for the major religions have enjoyed centuries of experimentation in their rites and rituals, and, in consequence, the counterpart secular ventures often appear pallid and derivative. Yet finding ways in which community can be fostered in a post-religious world is central to securing the possibilities of meaningful lives on as wide a scale as possible.

In the end, I believe, a fully-articulated secular perspective will need to rethink large aspects of our accepted institutions, dedicating itself more resolutely to fashioning social (and economic) relationships that allow an ever wider circle of people to have the opportunity to live meaningful lives. Today I can only gesture in that direction. I hope, however, that I have said enough to prod discontent with that form of atheism that regards religion as simply rubbish to be carted away. A satisfying secularism must be secular humanism – with the accent on the human.

Works Cited

Dewey, John, and Jo Ann Boydston. *The Later Works, 1925–1953.* Carbondale: Southern Illinois University Press, 2008.

Dostoyevsky, Fyodor, et al. *The Brothers Karamazov: A Revised Translation, Contexts, Criticism.* New York: W.W. Norton & Co., 2011.

James, William. *The Meaning of Truth.* Rockville, MD: Arc Manor, 2008.

Joyce, James. *A Portrait of the Artist as a Young Man.* New York: B. W. Huebsch, 1917.

Nagel, Thomas. *Secular Philosophy and the Religious Temperament: Essays 2002–2008.* New York: Oxford University Press, 2010.

Özlem Uluç Kucukcan

Religion and Post-Secularity: New Perspectives on the Public Sphere

1 Introduction: Re-reading Secularism, Citizenship, and Claim Making

A widely shared understanding of modernity identifies secularism as a pre-requisite for political systems to qualify as democratic regimes. This, of course, does not suggest that all secular governments are inherently democracies and promote democratic policies. For example, the secular regimes in Iraq and Syria subscribed to a Ba'athist nationalist ideology over democracy. North Korea and China, although secular, are far from democratic countries. Democracy's functioning and legitimacy depends upon opening the public sphere to all views and the representation of citizens' opinions in politics. In the context of discussions regarding relations between democracy, the public sphere, and religion, the question arises as to whether matters of religion can be expressed in the public sphere of a democratic regime. In particular, the widely held view is that democratic regimes should be secular. When religious matters are brought into the public sphere, then, a question arises as to whether or not limitations should be placed on how religious rights and claims are expressed, managed, or governed. In order to understand the "functionality of the public sphere" in addressing the demands of religion in a modern democratic and political regime, the differentiation of secularity of the society and secularity of the state is helpful.

In order to appreciate the status of religion in modern society, examining relations between religion and the emergence of modernization and the modern nation state is essential. Theoreticians and founders of sociology, such as Max Weber, Emile Durkheim, and Karl Marx, have drawn attention to the social presence of religion and examined its impact on society. From their analyses, the dominant scholarly view and widely held assumption that modernization has brought on the erosion of religion emerged. They claimed that religion would gradually fade away from the lives of individuals in modernized societies. This expectation, referred to as the "secularization theory," has become a leading theory in studies on the status of religion in modern societies.[1]

---

1 For further readings on secularization theory, see David Martin, *A General Theory of Secula-*

Thus, the majority of sociologists have espoused the view that modernization necessarily pushes religion out of social life. The natural outcome of this
process is the emergence of a secular social structure, in addition to secular governing institutions. Especially in Europe, sociologists and political scientists
have argued that the European experience is a universal one and all countries
undergoing a process of modernization will experience a similar transformation.
In defiance of its clerical authority, the French style of secularism, known as laïcité, has removed religion from the public sphere and isolated it within the pe-
rimeter of citizens' private lives. This reform emerged mainly as a reaction to Europe's experience with a socially dominant and politically hegemonic religion
and church, especially during the Middle Ages. The French laïcité, which developed as an anti-clerical movement and a hostile ideology opposed to the church
establishment, illustrates well the underpinning of secularization theory as it
emerged in Europe. However, this theory relies heavily on the French experience
and fails to explain the developments in other countries, both in Europe and beyond. In other words, the theory generalizes the French experience as the dominant example of modern secularism, without taking into account other historical and national contexts.

Although scholars have debated the developments regarding religion and
the public sphere in Europe for many decades, the issue has recently come to
a head. Social and political dynamics around the world are constantly changing,
and new, troubling formations are emerging as a result of developments in globalization, democratization, migration, and international relations. On the one
hand, religion retains a powerful influence, especially outside of Western coun-

---

rization (Oxford: Blackwell, 1978); Bryan Wilson, *Contemporary Transformations of Religion*
(Oxford: Oxford University Press, 1976); *Religion in Sociological Perspective* (Oxford: Oxford
University Press, 1982); Karel Dobbelaere, *Secularization: An Analysis at Three Levels* (Bruxelles:
P. I. E.-Peter Lang, 2002); Steve Bruce, *God is Dead* (Oxford: Blackwell, 2002); Peter Berger, *The
Sacred Canopy: Elements of a Sociological Theory of Religion* (New York: Doubleday, 1967); "A
Bleak Outlook is Seen for Religion," *New York Times*, 25 April 1963, 3, "Secularism in Retreat,"
National Interest (Winter 1968), 3–12; Rodney Stark, "Secularization: R. I. P.," in *The Secula-
rization Debate*, ed. William H. Swatos and Daniel V. Olson, (New York: Rowman and Littlefield,
2000,. 41–66); Rodney Stark and William Sims Bainbridge, *The Future of Religion: Seculari-
zation, Revival and Cult Formation* (Berkeley: University of California Press, 1985); Daniel Bell,
"The Return of the Sacred," *British Journal of Sociology* 28.2, 419–19; Jeffrey K. Hadden,
"Desacralizing Secularization Theory," in *Secularization and Fundamentalism Reconsidered*, ed.
J. K. Hadden and A. Shupe (New York: Pragon House, 1989) 3–26; Jeffrey K. Hadden, "Religion
and the Quest for Meaning and Order: Old Paradigms, New Realities," *Sociology Focus* 28.1, 83–
100; Anthony Gill, "Secularization and the State, The Role Government Policy Plays in De-
termining Social Religiosity," in *The Role of Religion in Modern Society*, ed. Detlef Pollack and
Daniel V. A. Olson (New York & London: Routledge, 2008), 115–39.

tries; on the other hand, many ethnic and religious groups are migrating to European countries and forming new communities that are changing the countries' demographic and cultural compositions. This situation forces modern, secular governments to respond to the demands of their new religious populations.

This increasing diversity has led to great conflicts and tensions, suggesting that the founding ideals of these modern nation states are incompatible with the recognition of difference. The power of democracy depends upon the freedom to promote one's views, even those that might not receive government approval. Thus, democracy is stronger when minorities are permitted to express their ideas. Because of the existence of oppressed minorities in certain countries, many have criticized the nation state structure as suppressing democracy and failing to deliver freedom, justice, and equality.

Ancient Greece exemplifies a system of an early form of democracy, from which the modern nation state seems to have departed. Among the Ancient Greeks, the public sphere served as the mechanism through which citizens – at that time, property-owning males – were able to participate in politics. This open public sphere enabled citizens' participation in direct democracy. However, over centuries, global views of the public sphere, and its role in civil affairs, have undergone many changes, in keeping with social and political trends. The public-oriented democratic tradition of the Ancient Greeks declined during the Roman period, and disappeared in the Middle Ages.

As scientific, commercial, and economic advances in Europe brought the Middle Ages to an end, political groups strengthened and demanded greater participation in political and economic systems. During this period of transformation, some political actors declared the need to liberate society from the domination of religious institutions that had pervaded Europe in the Middle Ages. These sentiments remained prominent throughout the Renaissance, the Reformation, and the Enlightenment, and contributed to the birth of bourgeois society and the eruption of the French Revolution. This revolution signaled a turning point in the debate about the nature of the state, the political system, and public participation. This revolution also exemplified a major response to the entrenched hegemony of religion. Thus, revolutionaries attached secular assumptions to the concepts of state, power, citizenship, and representation during the nation-building process. Such secularist leanings spread across Europe along with other political ideas of the revolution. The concept of the public sphere also gained a new definition, as people began to view it as a platform for the expression of views about the state, and to debate their rights and liberties.

Today, in the post-secular, postmodern period, religion has become increasingly relevant socially. The public sphere represents a domain where religious groups might seek representation and recognition. Political demands have begun shifting from broad social and political rights to the rights of cultural expression.[2] This development signals a transition from the modern, secular period to the postmodern, post-secular period. As in the case of the French Revolution, this new emphasis indicates the shortcomings of the existing political system, a system incapable of addressing the challenges of increasing pluralism and political participation.

The United Nations Convention on Human Rights, the European Convention on Human Rights, and other such conventions, have raised awareness about instances of rights oppression, and have facilitated the institutionalization of protective mechanisms. In addition, they have strengthened the self-awareness of citizens. Groups, communities, and religious bodies, who feel disadvantaged in the modern nation-state, or who believe that the state or the political majority has curtailed their rights, continue to advocate for religious and cultural rights within the framework of a human rights discourse. Claims such as group recognition, group equality, justice, freedom and representation continue to be the focus of large-scale debates. While vested with rights in some countries, religious and cultural minorities were denied them in others, on several grounds. In the West, religious minorities in particular demanded official religious recognition so as to have the same legal public status enjoyed by the dominant religious communities. Such demands have often been denied – either by an assertive and hostile secularism, or by the protectionism accorded the dominant religion(s). Islam, for example, is officially and legally recognized as a religion in some countries, while remaining unrecognized in others. Further, demands for the representation of religious symbols in the public sphere have sometimes resulted in lawsuits when denied by public authorities and state officials.

Hanging a cross on a public school wall in Italy, wearing religious attire in public schools and government offices in France, the demand for religious recognition posed by Scientology in Germany, requests for permission to build mosques in Sweden – these emblems of religious expression pose challenges to modern secular nation states and indicate the shortcomings of existing secular-

---

2 T. H. Marshall defines citizenship rights as civil (equality before the law), political (the right to vote and elect representatives) and social (welfare rights). Turner, however, argues that the modern conception of citizenship fails to explain such questions as ethnicity and nationalism, and also claims that the assimilationist dimension in the construction of modern nation state citizenship has been ignored. In addition to civil, political and social rights, Turner also treats cultural rights. For detailed discussion, see: T. H. Marshall, *Citizenship and Social Class and Other Essays* (London: Cambridge University Press, 1950); Bryan S. Turner, "The Erosion of Citizenship," *British Journal of Sociology* 52.2 (2001): 191, 197; and Bryan S. Turner, "Outline of a Theory of Citizenship," *Sociology* 24.2 (1990): 189–214.

isms. In terms of the freedom of religious expression, minority religious and cultural groups represent needs that demand attention, needs with which the social order is often unfamiliar – for the inclusion of religious courses in private and public school curricula, for the partial implementation of religious law, for the right to purchase foods produced according to Islamic (Halal) or Jewish (Kosher) dietary rules, for permission to circumcize Muslim and Jewish boys, and others that I will illustrate below. Such issues pose new challenges for particular versions of the secular public sphere in secularity-related debates.

2 Post-Secularism as the New Social and Political Reality

In recent discussions, Jürgen Habermas offers a new, albeit contested, conception of the public sphere for the post-secular age. As I discuss below, Habermas aims to expand the public sphere, providing a sketch of a method composed of a set of rules and principles in order to enable the participation of different interest groups and communities in the process of negotiations with each other and with the state. A number of new social and political trends have motivated Habermas to reflect on the public sphere. First, globalization has introduced new circumstances, including the growing association of western secularism with economic, political and military hegemony, in turn contributing to increasing opposition figured in religious terms. Second, as mentioned above, the persistence and/or revival of religiosity has produced new problems for state secularity, while also introducing changing dynamics that challenge the terms of existing social relations. Third, a rising awareness of human rights discourse and the ideals of citizenship, which often run counter to the old notion of secularism and the secularized public sphere, has provided religious minorities a new political instrument. The secular state traditionally disallowed or limited the access of faith groups to political and social discourse, figuring them as irrational and incompatible with liberal values of Western modern nation-states. Along with other theorists, Habermas argues that secularization theory, and the forms of secularism that it has produced, have severe limitations. He does so by demonstrating that the prophesies of modernization theories were not realized, and that in the post-secular era, religion has remained dynamic and socially relevant. Moreover, Habermas and a number of sociologists contend that the secularization thesis has failed to explain the ongoing role and influence of religion in non-European societies, including the US, where religion is a vibrant aspect of social and political reality. Several sociologists even argue that different forms of religiosity have emerged, including "believing without belonging."[3] Moreover, immigration from Mediterranean regions and Catholic Central European countries has altered the European demographic and cultural landscape. Habermas refers to these developments as post-secular, and the period during which they are occurring as the post-secular age. The post-secular age is one during which religion remains a vital basis of identity for many, who likewise aspire to have their interests represented and their claims for religious rights made on equal footing vis-à-vis the dominant social and political actors within the state. The vitality of minority religiosities, and the claims made for their recognition and representation within the modern, secular nation state introduce new questions regarding the proper integration and response to such emerging demands, and their claims on legitimacy.

Scholars have conceptualized the re-emergence of religion in public life in various ways.[4] Habermas posits a series of transformations – from pre-modern religious times to modern secular times, and, presently, to post-secularism. He proposes that with the third stage of this historical development, the notion that religion will disappear as individuals become increasingly rational has been or should be abandoned.[5] This approach closely resembles the critique of the secularization thesis that other thinkers have developed over the past two decades. The post-secular public sphere, Habermas suggests, differs from

---

3 Grace Davie, *Religion in Britain Since 1945: Believing Without Belonging* (Oxford: Blackwell, 1994).

4 When the failure of secularization theory was accepted, it was claimed that religions in the modern period were privatized and individualized. This view claims that under the forces of modernity, all religions lost their collective dimensions and religiosity evolved from ritually based phenomena to a personal matter. Faith and practice started to express an identity. Lastly, religious attachment became a voluntary act based on preference rather than a fate. For further information on these lines of discussion, see Detlef Pollack and Gert Pickel, "Religious Individualization or Secularization, An Attempt to Evaluate the Thesis of Religious Individualization in Eastern and Western Germany," in *The Role of Religion in Modern Societies*, eds. Detlef Pollack and Daniel V. A. Olson (New York & London: Routledge, 2008): 191 – 220; Veit Bader, *Secularism or Democracy? Associational Governance of Religious Diversity* (Amsterdam: Amsterdam University Press, 2007). On the "privatization" of religion, see: Thomas Luckmann, *The Invisible Religion: The Problem of Religion in Modern Society* (New York: Macmillan, 1967). Jose Casanova uses the concept of "deprivatization" of religion to explain the new reality. Religion, to him, participates in the public sphere of civil society and raises normative questions and also engages in the process of formation of normative rules. This means that religious institutions started to play important roles when religions and political initiative changed their roles. Jose Casanova, Public Religions in the Modern World (Chicago: The University of Chicago Press, 1994), 5 – 6.

5 Lasse Thomassen, *Habermas: A Guide for the Perplexed* (London & New York: Continuum Books, 2010), 155.

the pre-post-secular (secular) public sphere, in that the latter has been demonstrated to be incompatible with the broadened sense of democracy and law that has emerged with the participation of non-elite, political agents. The pre-post-secular public sphere is by no means open to the expression and representation of competing worldviews, but rather is dominated by a hegemonic secular political ideology. The hegemonic secular political ideology either blatantly favors a dominant religiosity; tacitly demonstrates bias toward the dominant religion(s), even while posing as equally indisposed to all; or evinces an equal indisposition to all, but effectively eliminates the expression of difference from the public sphere by virtue of the differing standards for religious expression of minority religious groups – namely, more stringent and/or further-reaching demands for overt religious expression from believers and/or the more "exotic" and thus conspicuous features of religious representation of minority religious communities. Given a critical posture with reference to religion and its potential influence on society and politics, the pre-post-secular public sphere presents itself as putatively religion-free. It is figured as closed to religion and religious groups, or of providing only limited space for their representation. The pre-post-secular public sphere is also marked by an assertion of its rationality and an affirmation of the Enlightenment stance toward religion, which does not recognize the legitimacy of religious views, or their justification. Thus the pre-post-secular public sphere favors an exclusively secular, rational worldview, necessarily resulting in the exclusion of other kinds of convictions.

According to Habermas, the pre-post-secular public sphere suffers from several weaknesses. For one, even in relation to majority concerns, the state has become the dominant force, weakening the potential influence and foreclosing the impact of the contributions of all citizens within the public sphere. In addition to this consolidation of state hegemony, the disintegration of public rationality or a rational public, and the rise of competitive capitalism, have all, to varying degrees, contributed to the degeneration of public sphere in the pre-post-secular era. Such considerations seem to have motivated Habermas to look beyond such a restrictive notion of public sphere, and to introduce a new conceptual model that might be called the post-secular public sphere.

By focusing on what he calls post-secular age, Habermas proposes a post-secular public sphere that takes the social and political transformations of modern societies into account, in order to address challenges posed by the visible presence, and in some cases unexpected revival, of religion.

Although providing for the recognition and representation of religion, the Habermasian notion of a post-secular society is not meant to suggest the survival of religion despite widespread and intensive secularization; nor does it point to expectations for the inevitable presence of religious communities. Furthermore, post-secular society cannot be viewed as representing the public approval of religious communities for their functional contributions to the reproduction of desired instincts and attitudes. Rather, secular and religious tendencies do not disappear in post-secular societies, but merely enter different stages. Post-secular society features an ever-modernizing collective consciousness, which reflects normative ideas that shape and transform both secular and religious notions, and affect political relations between believers and non-believers. According to this collective consciousness, secular and religious approaches complement each other in society's secularization process and compel one another to contribute to controversial public issues. Religious and non-religious individuals and groups, therefore, have equal status in post-secular societies. For post-secular society does not assume a position about the veracity of religion's truth claims. Nor does it consider the positive or negative connotations of such claims. Post-secular society, similarly, neither endorses nor opposes the philosophy of Enlightenment that views religion as an obstacle to progress. However, it maintains that the common denominator between religious and non-religious groups ought to be fundamentally secular in nature. As a matter of fact, Habermas believes that claims of validity derive from three elements: (1) scientific knowledge; (2) secular government; and (3) a multitude of notions of "the good life," including the recognition of other faiths. Religions that refuse to be constrained by the above elements, in turn, are viewed as fundamentalist in post-secular societies.[6]

The content and attributes of public space, which facilitate the functioning of democracy in post-secular societies, in turn, remains in dire need of reshaping, deliberation, and definition within the context of modernization and secularism. Two competing sets of criticisms and comments about public space based on traditional models of the nation-state remain intact.[7] Accordingly, what we could term the modern approach regards the changing nature of the public space as the degeneration of bourgeois public space (i. e. ideal public space) by the corruption-driven forces of capitalism. Meanwhile, the postmodern view identifies the emergence of multiple public spaces, each of which reflects a different form of communicative organization, and each of which acts as a contributing factor to democracy's progress. Both approaches, as a matter of fact,

---

6 Jürgen Habermas, "On the Relation Between the Secular Liberal State and Religion," in *The Frankfurt School on Religion: Key Writings by the Major Thinkers*, ed. Eduardo Mendieta, trans. Mattias Fritsch (New York & London: Routledge, 2005), 346–47; Thomassen, 155–56.

7 Benjamin Lee, "Textuality, Mediation and Public Discourse," in *Habermas and The Public Sphere*, ed. Craig Calhoun (Cambridge, MA & London: The MIT Press, 1996): 416; Alan McKee, *An Introduction to the Public Sphere* (Cambridge: Cambridge University Press, 2005), 16–17 and19.

transmit and explain the progress of Enlightenment values, such as equality, liberty, justice, and prosperity. The fundamental difference between them, however, relates to the postmodern perspective's suggestion that different groups think in different ways, communicate among themselves accordingly, and, therefore, deserve respect. The postmodern approach acknowledges secondary (i. e. regional, national, international) public spaces where forms of communication, domains of conflict, and subjects of deliberation constantly evolve. This new collective consciousness, however, features various avenues through which extremely diverse groups, such as elites and the masses, or clergymen and non-believers, can communicate and work together, despite tensions. The body of listeners, readers and members of audiences – that is, all participants of public space – expand by disassociation with time and space, and thereby help public space assume an intangible character. After all, the emergence of new technologies, most notably social media platforms such as Twitter, Facebook, and Instagram, in addition to traditional public space and face-to-face communication, has given rise to anonymous public spaces that supersede individual differences, and theoretically attribute an equal level of validity and value to all diverse notions. This transformation has effectively entailed a shift from the classical public space, with its emphasis on fundamental truths, to a relativistic understanding of public space.[8]

One of the other differences between modern and postmodern definitions and interpretations regarding the attributes and contents of the public sphere is observed in discussions on the kinds of questions addressed in the public realm. Those who define and interpret the public sphere using a modernist approach argue that making familial, emotional, and private matters part of public negotiations implies the trivialization of the public sphere. The postmodern approach, on the other hand, underlines and emphasizes the political dimension of such private issues. For example, in line with the postmodern approach, a marriage contract may be considered a tool for the legalization and institutionalization of women's abuse and/or their enslavement. Therefore, familial, emotional, and private matters are issues wherein the state, i. e. the political establishment, may interfere in private life.[9] The modern approach to the public sphere argues that issues brought into the public sphere tend to lose their significance and value; the media bombards and shapes the public sphere with sensational

---

8 Erik Oddvar Eriksen, "Conceptualising European Public Spheres: General, Segmented and Strong Publics," in *The European Union and the Public Sphere, A Communicative Space in the Making?*, eds. John Erik Fossum and Philip Schlesinger (New York: Routledge, 2007), 26; McKee, 17.

9 Alan McKee, 47 – 8.

news and stories; public culture is fragmented as a consequence of claims and demands by different identities in the public sphere. This results in the emergence of a new but commercialized, fragmented, and trivialized form of the public sphere.

The functionality and effectiveness of this new public sphere, whether negative or positive, can be identified by asking three major questions. First and foremost, fundamental attributes of the public sphere should be identified in order to discover its analytical dimensions; second, contributions of the public sphere to democracy and its current value should be evaluated; third, challenges that the new public sphere faces should be identified; finally, research on the public sphere should focus on emerging problematic fields.[10] Citizens and members of the political community should be able to participate in the public sphere, enabling them to raise their agendas as equal citizens through the medium of open communication. While they engage in such an activity, citizens should leave their "ideal" status behind, liberate themselves from their affiliations, and subscribe to objective positions so that they can communicate with other citizens on mutually approved grounds.[11] This field of open deliberation and negotiation which empowers members of political community is a prerequisite for the realization of people's sovereignty, since it emerged to test governments and the established system. The said public sphere has been a space where citizens found a common ground for coming together and claimed its ownership by facing and objecting to the public/state authorities.[12] Therefore, identification of what kind of public sphere can contribute to the process of democratization requires, in the first place, looking at objectifying/concretizing problems and problems experienced on the ground. In this context, the following questions will facilitate the problematization of issues that should be addressed: Who can participate in the public sphere and under which situations? What should be the content and form of contributions to the public deliberations

---

10 John Erik Fossum and Philip Schlesinger, "The European Union and the Public Sphere, A Communicative Space in the Making?" in *The European Union and the Public Sphere, A Communicative Space in the Making?*, ed. John Erik Fossum and Philip Schlesinger (New York: Routledge, 2007), 3.

11 Jürgen Habermas, *Kamusallığın Yapısal Dönüşümü*, translated by T. Bora and M. Sancar. (İstanbul: İletişim Yayınları, 1997), 107; Pauline Johnson, *Habermas: Rescuing the Public Sphere* (London and New York: Routledge, 2006), 2.

12 Jürgen Habermas, *Between Facts and Norms: Contributions to a Discourse, Theory of Law and Democracy* (Cambridge: MA: MIT Press, 1996), 359–60; Eriksen, 23–30.

by participants? How do participating actors communicate with each other? What are the expected results from the process?[13]

Open public deliberation, participation, and naturally, freedom of expression among rational speakers, who are socially equal and can reason independently and individually in the Habermasian model of the bourgeoisie public sphere, constitute the foundations of democratic tradition – one of the inalienable and invaluable values of the states and societies in our age. Moreover, open public deliberation is the raison d'être for the existence of the public sphere. Sufficiency of the public sphere for a democratic policy, however, depends on the quality of debates and deliberations and the level of participation. The public sphere in modern societies is a democratic domain in which "everyone influenced by general social norms and collective political decisions" can participate and take part in the process of decision-making and its acceptance.[14]

Outcomes and conclusions stemming from deliberations and negotiations in the public sphere should be compatible with fundamental freedoms and should respect basic rights. The egalitarian aspect of the negotiation environment that depends on mutual understanding of values requires the following opportunities: participants should have equal rights and a chance to be part of the conversation; to initiate a debate; to raise an issue; to question matters debated; to make proposals; to share their own desires, demands, and feelings; and to open power relations to the debate on an equal footing. Therefore, all theories concerning the public sphere should place the model of deliberative democracy[15]

---

13 Myra Marx Feree, William A. Gamson, Jürgen Gerhards and Dieter Rucht, "Four Models of the Public Sphere in Modern Democracies," *Theory and Society* 31.1 (June 2002): 289–324; Birte Siim, "Gender and Diversity in the European Public Spheres," Eurosphere Working Paper Series, Online Working Paper No. 17, (February 2009): 1–19, http://eurosphere.uib.no/knowledge base/workingpapers.htm, p. 2. Accessed August 2014.

14 Laura Graham, "A Public Sphere in Amazonia? The Depersonalized Collaborative Construction of Discourse in Xavante," *American Ethnologist* 20.4 (November 1993): 717; Craig Calhoun, "Introduction: Habermas and the Public Sphere," in *Habermas and the Public Sphere*, ed. Craig Calhoun (Cambridge, MA & London: The MIT Press, 1996), 2; Meral Özbek, "Kamusal Alanın Sınırları," in *Kamusal Alan*, ed. Meral Özbek (İstanbul: Hil Yayınları, 2004), 62.

15 For more details on deliberative democracy, see John Elster, ed., *Deliberative Democracy* (Cambridge: Cambridge University Press, 1998); James Bohman, *Public Deliberation* (Cambridge: MIT Press, 1996); Amy Gutmann and Dennis Thompon, *Democracy and Disagreement* (Cambridge, MA: Harvard University Press, 1996); and C. Nino, *The Constitution of Deliberative Democracy* (New Haven: Yale University Press, 1996).

– which is at the core of phenomenon of the public domain – at the heart of the theoretical approach, and should defend it.[16]

If there is no powerful opportunity for deliberation and negotiation in a democracy, it will be difficult for citizens to defend constitutional rights and object to controversial laws, even temporarily. Democratization takes place when the bureaucratic nation-state transforms its legal and rational way of functioning into participatory democratic governance on the basis of communicative rationality. In this context, there is a correlation between the level of democracy and the degree to which problems can be identified correctly and dramatized. Questions and issues that are dealt with become the thoughts and a will that set the formal decision-making institutions into motion. However, at this point, Habermas argues that widening the domain in question and increasing the degree of its inclusiveness result in degeneration in the quality of the language of discourse and rhetoric. In his opinion, the public sphere today, which has acquired an elitist quality, cannot deliver the requirements of democracy.[17]

One can identify four principles or rules that define the relationship between the public sphere and democratic governance. The first is the norm of an action, i.e. the law in whose formation process everyone who will be affected by the application and implementation of such a rule should participate. These rules should become valid after such a process. The public sphere can only deliver its functions if such steps are followed. Second, the recognition by other participants of all individuals and persons as independent and rational agents is a precondition for the functioning of the public sphere in the realization and implementation of democracy. Third, the legitimacy of the norm resulting from the consensus derived from the common participation of people who "know" each other depends on participation of everyone in the process of dialogue on equal conditions. The fourth rule for the public sphere in the realization/actualization of democracy is the right, opportunity, and requirement that the participants participate in rational discourse by virtue of liberating themselves from

---

16 Gürcan Koçan, "Models of Public Sphere in Political Philosophy," Eurosphere Working Paper Series, Online Working Paper No. 02, (February 2008): 1–30. http://eurosphere.uib.no/knowl edgebase/workingpapers.htm. Accessed August 2014. Fossum and Schlesinger, 5; Eriksen, 23, 25; James Gordon Finlayson, *Habermas: A Very Short Introduction* (Oxford: Oxford University Press, 2005), 60; Özbek, 62.

17 Fossum and Schlesinger, 5; Calhoun, 3.

such qualities as power, wealth, tradition, or authority that could be turned into a taboo.[18]

At this juncture, the law emerges as one of the most important factors and tools that guarantees the formation, protection, and consolidation of a democratic public sphere. The law regulates and paces the system and functions to hold together independent subsystems. The law, however, should be the product of the process of democratic will and opinion formation; therefore, there is a need for a communicative space that would enable the checking and reviewing of legal rules and their implementation, as well as for providing an opportunity to participate in decision making processes. The dynamic structure of the public sphere and its diverse nature serves democracy by providing the need for a free environment. Thus the principle of rule of law is put into practice and realized. The legitimacy of the power of the modern state is achieved through an understanding of the communicative rationality of the democratic public sphere and normative principles based on rational understanding. Therefore, for Habermas, the legitimacy of the law depends on the existence of the public sphere. The rule of law, on the other hand, is the concretization of public reason. Political and legal institutions can function as means of negotiation and deliberation and can reflect demands coming from the public only when a sufficient level of democracy is achieved. Providing and granting religious freedom are integral parts of the framework of the postmodern/post-secular period, subject to the formation and emergence of the law from negotiations in a libertarian public sphere.[19]

3 State-Religion Relations in the Post-Secular Era

The postmodern society is not a unified monolith. Rather, it is diverse and plural, in which competing worldviews are present and represented. Therefore, ensuring an equal level of religious freedom for all is only possible by the adoption and practice of the principle of neutrality toward competing worldviews. Habermas claims that this principle – even while insufficient – can only be practiced

---

18 Levent Köker, "Radikal Demokrasi," *Diyalog* 1 (1996): 101–08 Cited by E. Fuat Keyman, "Kamusal Alan ve 'Cumhuriyetçi Liberalizm': Türkiye'de Demokrasi Sorunu," *Doğu Batı: Yıl 2, Sayı* 5 (1998–9): 61–62.
19 Jürgen Habermas, "Kamusal Alan," in *Kamusal Alan*, ed. Meral Özbek (İstanbul: Hil Yayınları, 2004), 95; Aykut Çelebi, "Kamusal Alan ve Sivil Toplum," in *Kamusal Alan*, ed. Meral Özbek (İstanbul: Hil Yayınları, 2004), 273–75; Keyman, 59; Calhoun, 6; Fossum and Schlesinger, 5; Thomassen, 47.

and implemented by a state system, which is of a secular character. More precisely, the secularity of the state, according to Habermas, is a precondition to guaranteeing religious freedom for all. It is a precondition for the state to remain neutral with reference to "competing world views." However, the degree of tolerance shown towards minorities by the authorities of the secular state is unreliable. With the process of secularization, a legitimacy vacuum emerged for state authority, as states had previously derived their legitimacy from religion. This legitimacy gap can be filled only by a democratic constitution. This democratic constitution, which would guarantee neutrality of the state authorities toward religious lifestyles and worldviews, should not place on the shoulders of the state's religious citizens an asymmetric and additional burden. Likewise, citizens should be able to freely decide whether or not to use religious language in the public sphere. Yet, the post-secular approach of Habermas draws attention to the distinction between faith and knowledge. For Habermas, if or when citizens use religious language, such religious statements should be translated into a secular language that can be generally understood. Such a translation or rendering would enable parliament, the courts, and other administrative authorities to take into account the possible reality of situations that such statements might represent. This practice would also be congruent with the ethics of multicultural citizenship.[20]

The principle of secularism in a post-secular age compels citizens to strike a balance between religious and secular beliefs. Just as proponents of secularism view religion as a threat, the religious deem their alienation from the divine as a threat to their identity and existence. A better understanding of this problem and additional research into various aspects of the question, however, could help secularism evolve in order to address the concerns and fears of the religious and meet their social needs.[21]

However, taking the principle of secularism out of its institutional frameworks to allow the expansion of its influence with reference to the opinions

---

20 Jürgen Habermas, Between *Naturalism and Religion: Philosophical Essays*, trans. Ciaran Cronin (Cambridge: Polity Press, 2009), 120–21, 128–29; Jürgen Habermas, "'The Political,' The Rational Meaning of a Questionable Inheritance of Political Theology," in *The Power of Religion in the Public Sphere*, eds. Eduardo Mendieta and Jonathan VanAntwerpen (New York: Columbia University Press, 2011), 25; Eduardo Mendieta and Jonathan VanAntwerpen, "Introduction, The Power of Religion in the Public Sphere," in *The Power of Religion in the Public Sphere*, ed. Eduardo Mendieta and Jonathan Vanantwerpen (New York: Columbia University Press, 2011), 3–4; Finlayson, 103.

21 Philip Kitcher defines it as secular humanism. Philip Kitcher, "Challenges for Secularism," in *The Joy of Secularism: 11 Essays for How We Live Now*, ed. George Levine (Princeton and Oxford: Princeton University Press, 2011), 33.

and statements of citizens and institutions operating in the public sphere would represent an undue generalization of this principle of secularism. Habermas claims that this type of laicism, which restricts the reach of religion to private life, appears to resolve the paradox of the secularization of society as a social process, in connection with laicism or secularization of the state as a legal process, by treating the two as referring to two distinct processes.

However, such a notion of secularism implies that religious ideas are bound to disintegrate in the face of scientific criticism and that faith groups will inevitably lose ground to cultural and social modernization. Such a perception of secularism prevents people from taking seriously the contributions of religion and religious authorities regarding controversial political issues. Still, all citizens, regardless of their worldviews and differences of opinion in terms of religious affiliation, should respect each other as equal and free members of the political community in order for democracy to prevail. In fact, citizens should pursue a rationally motivated consensus in controversial political issues.[22]

According to Habermas, the principle of secularism compels politicians and civil servants to formulate laws, court rulings, decisions, and precautions in ways that all citizens can understand. However, citizens, including representatives of political parties, social institutions, churches, other religious organizations, and other individuals who lead their lives according to religious principles, might not be able to make the same, "artificial" distinction between religious and rational discourse. In an attempt to tackle this challenge, Habermas proposes that instead of forcing all citizens to refrain from religious rhetoric when making public claims and demands, a filter may be established. The filter, he claims, can mediate the gap between unofficial communications and discussions in public, and official negotiations between political authorities who make binding decisions. As such, the religious claims and opinions of religious participants should be translated into a universal language so that religious participants might assume legitimate roles in public decision-making processes. Otherwise, defending a certain view on the basis of religious convictions would be inadequate. Therefore, such religious claims and arguments require support from political instruments. Religious reasoning, thus, ought not to be excluded from the public space. Government officials alone can be expected to engage

---

22 Charles Taylor, "Why We Need a Radical Redefinition of Secularism," in *The Power of Religion in the Public Sphere*, eds. Eduardo Mendieta and Jonathan VanAntwerpen (New York: Columbia University Press, 2011), 41; Habermas, *The Political*, 24; Habermas, *Between Naturalism and Religion*, 121, 127–29, 130–31, 138–39.

in this type of secular-minded legitimization, since they have an obligation to remain impartial toward different and competing worldviews.[23]

With regard to the state's official language, Habermas argues for the exclusion of religious references. However, he also proposes that it would not be abnormal that faith groups reflect religious references, at least indirectly, in the process of expressing their positions.[24] At this point, however, the means by which religious references are to be removed from the state's official language represents a serious problem. For it is not guaranteed that politicians will approach the demands of secular or religious citizens with parity, despite the separation of religion and the state, and various constitutional arrangements. In this regard, what matters is the establishment of a structure that ensures equality and justice for all.

4 Conclusion

As state-religion relations have become increasingly complex in the context of the rising visibility of religious individuals and communities in the public sphere and their claims deriving from human-rights-based discourse, the trajectory and rationale of responses to the new social and political reconfiguration need to be reconsidered. In particular, since the dominant (pre-post-secular) intellectual discourse for representation in the public domain is under heavy criticism, Jürgen Habermas undertakes the critical task of developing a new conceptual and theoretical framework to redefine conditions of participation in the public sphere. He does so, not only by examining the dominant actors that shape political culture and authority, but also by looking at other actors, including religious individuals and groups previously sidelined or isolated by the predominately secular guardians of governing ideologies.

Habermas neither challenges secularism nor the claims of religious groups in the public sphere, but notes that democratic governance requires actors in the public sphere to adopt a language accessible to all, so that common ground can be established without undue burden on any side. This is also the grounds on which cultural and religious diversity and plurality might be fostered in an inclusive political order. The filter system that Habermas constructs as a mech-

---

23 Habermas, *The Political*, 26; Habermas, *Between Naturalism and Religion*, 122, 127–28, 130; Thomassen, 155.
24 Roger Trigg, *Religion in Public Life, Must Faith Be Privatized?* (Oxford: Oxford University Press, 2007), 111–12; Habermas, *The Political*, 27, 33; Habermas, *Between Naturalism and Religion*, 119–20; Mendieta and Vanantwerpen, 4.

anism for mediating secular and religious languages and discourses is based on a rationale within which diverse, and at times, opposing views can be expressed freely, as long as defenders and contenders subscribe to the premise that everyone has the right to voice their views and that this right should be respected and protected. This filter mechanism has the potential to prevent not only the marginalization of religious individuals and groups but also the instrumentalization of sacred values and beliefs for political purposes, since a common ground would emerge as the culture of negotiation leads to deliberative democracy. Although Habermas encourages us to reconsider the public sphere in the post-secular age, he does not engage in the elaboration of normative and institutional formations that would enable states to resolve emerging challenges on the ground – especially when it comes to equal treatment of religious groups and their members as citizens in modern nation-states.

Habermas acknowledges limits of his own theoretical framework, as he argues that the post-secular public sphere in the modern period is degenerated and needs to be re-considered to return to its ideal type. He asserts that the state and its apparatuses have become so powerful and invasive that the modern period has experienced a decay and decline in the public sphere tantamount to "refeudalization." This process has weakened civil society and led it to take refuge in the state itself, a situation that contradicts pluralism, the substantive presence of competing worldviews, and equal representation. Moreover, in the course of this process, public opinion has become a tool of manipulation used as an intervention strategy by elites. This situation risks the loss of rational debate on emerging issues, such as claims for new, specific rights. Such challenges remain to be dealt with, especially when it comes to the presence, expression, and representation of religion and religious groups in the secular public sphere. However, the notion of post-secular public sphere offers some hope for inclusion of the religious in the process.

Works Cited

Bohman, James. *Public Deliberation*. Cambridge: MIT Press, 1996.

Calhoun, Craig. "Introduction: Habermas and the Public Sphere." In *Habermas and the Public Sphere*, edited by Craig Calhoun, 1–48. Cambridge, MA & London: The MIT Press, 1996.

Casanova, Jose. *Public Religions in the Modern World*. Chicago: The University of Chicago Press, 1994.

Çelebi, Aykut. "Kamusal Alan ve Sivil Toplum." In *Kamusal Alan*, edited by Meral Özbek, 237–83. İstanbul: Hil Yayınları, 2004.

Davie, Grace. *Religion in Britain Since 1945: Believing Without Belonging*. Oxford: Blackwell, 1994.

Elster, John, ed. *Deliberative Democracy*. Cambridge: Cambridge University Press, 1998.

Eriksen, Erik Oddvar. "Conceptualising European Public Spheres: General, Segmented and Strong Publics." In *The European Union and the Public Sphere, A Communicative Space in the Making*? Edited by John Erik Fossum and Philip Schlesinger, 23–43. New York: Routledge, 2007.

Feree, Myra Marx, William A. Gamson, Jürgen Gerhards and Dieter Rucht. "Four Models of the Public Sphere in Modern Democracies." *Theory and Society* 31.3 (June 2002): 289–324.

Finlayson, James Gordon. *Habermas: A Very Short Introduction*. Oxford: Oxford University Press, 2005.

Fossum, John Erik and Philip Schlesinger. "The European Union and the Public Sphere, A Communicative Space in the Making?" In *The European Union and the Public Sphere, A Communicative Space in the Making?*, edited by John Erik Fossum and Philip Schlesinger, 1–19. New York: Routledge, 2007.

Graham, Laura. "A Public Sphere in Amazonia? The Depersonalized Collaborative Construction of Discourse in Xavante." *American Ethnologist* 20.4 (November 1993): 717–41.

Gutmann, Amy and Dennis Thompson. *Democracy and Disagreement*. Cambridge, MA: Harvard University Press, 1996.

Gutmann, Amy and Dennis Thompson. "Democracy and Disagreement." In *The Democracy Sourcebook*, edited by Robert Dahl, Ian Shapiro and Jose Antonio Cheibub, 18–24. Cambridge: the MIT Press, 2003.

Habermas, Jürgen. "On the Relation Between the Secular Liberal State and Religion." In *The Frankfurt School on Religion, Key Writings by the Major Thinkers*, edited by Eduardo Mendieta, translated by Mattias Fritsch, 339–48. New York & London: Routledge, 2005.

Habermas, Jürgen. *Kamusallığın Yapısal Dönüşümü*, trans. T. Bora and M. Sancar. İstanbul: İletişim Yayınları, 1997.

Habermas, Jürgen. *Between Facts and Norms: Contributions to a Discourse, Theory of Law and Democracy*. Cambridge: MA: MIT Press, 1996.

Habermas, Jürgen. "'The Political,' The Rational Meaning of a Questionable Inheritance of Political Theology." In *The Power of Religion in the Public Sphere*, edited by Eduardo Mendieta and Jonathan Vanantwerpen, 15–33. New York: Columbia University Press, 2011.

Habermas, Jürgen. *Between Naturalism and Religion: Philosophical Essays*, trans. Ciaran Cronin. Cambridge: Polity Press, 2009.

Habermas, Jürgen. "Kamusal Alan." In *Kamusal Alan*, edited by Meral Özbek, 95–102. İstanbul: Hil Yayınları, 2004.

Johnson, Pauline. *Habermas, Rescuing the Public Sphere*. London and New York: Routledge, 2006.

Keyman, E. Fuat. "Kamusal Alan ve 'Cumhuriyetçi Liberalizm': Türkiye'de Demokrasi Sorunu." *Doğu Batı*, Yıl 2, Sayı 5 (1998–9): 57–73.

Kitcher, Philip. "Challenges for Secularism." In *The Joy of Secularism, 11 Essays of How We Live Now*, edited by George Levine, 24–56. Princeton and Oxford: Princeton University Press, 2011.

Koçan, Gürcan. "Models of Public Sphere in Political Philosophy." Eurosphere Working Paper Series, Online Working Paper 2, (February 2008): 1–30. http://eurosphere.uib.no/knowl edgebase/workingpapers.htm. Accessed August 2104.

Köker, Levent. "Radikal Demokrasi." *Diyalog* 1 (1996): 101–08.

Lee, Benjamin. "Textuality, Mediation and Public Discourse." In *Habermas and The Public Sphere*, edited by Craig Calhoun, 402–18. Cambridge, MA & London: The MIT Press, 1996.

Marshall, T. H. *Citizenship and Social Class and Other Essays*. London: Cambridge University Press, 1950.

McKee, Alan. *An Introduction to the Public Sphere*. Cambridge: Cambridge University Press, 2005.

Mendieta, Eduardo and Jonathan Vanantwerpen. "Introduction, The Power of Religion in the Public Sphere." In *The Power of Religion in the Public Sphere*, edited by Eduardo Mendieta and Jonathan Vanantwerpen, 1–14. New York: Columbia University Press, 2011.

Nino, C. *The Constitution of Deliberative Democracy*. New Haven: Yale University Press, 1996.

Özbek, Meral. "Kamusal Alanın Sınırları." In *Kamusal Alan*, edited by Meral Özbek, 19–89. İstanbul: Hil Yayınları, 2004.

Schwarzmantel, John. *Citizenship and Identity*. London: Routledge, 2003.

Siim, Birte. "Gender and Diversity in the European Public Spheres." Eurosphere Working Paper Series, Online Working Paper No. 17, (February 2009): 1–19. http://eurosphere.uib.no/knowledgebase/workingpapers.htm. Accessed August 2014.

Taylor, Charles. "Why We Need a Radical Redefinition of Secularism." In *The Power of Religion in the Public Sphere*, edited by Eduardo Mendieta and Jonathan Vanantwerpen, 34–59. New York: Columbia University Press, 2011.

Thomassen, Lasse. *Habermas: A Guide for the Perplexed*. London & New York: Continuum Books, 2010.

Trigg, Roger. *Religion in Public Life, Must Faith Be Privatized?* Oxford: Oxford University Press, 2007.

Turner, Bryan S. "The Erosion of Citizenship." *British Journal of Sociology* 52.2 (2001): 189–209.

Turner, Bryan S. "Outline of a Theory of Citizenship." *Sociology* 24.2 (1990): 189–214.

Patrick Loobuyck
Religious Education in Habermasian Post-Secular Societies

Jürgen Habermas is one of the main points of reference in the debate on post-secularism. Since 2001, he joined the debate about the role of religion in current day societies.[1] Somewhat surprisingly for those familiar with his earlier work on the rationalization of modern society, Habermas advances a rather positive view of religion and its possible contributions in the public sphere. Rejecting the secularist and reductive view of religion as a disappearing relic of pre-modern times, he recognizes the ongoing presence and importance of religion in what he calls "post-secular" societies. On the other hand, Habermas argues that the post-secular perspective requires a complementary learning process in terms of an adequate transformation of both traditional orthodox religious traditions and the secular(ist) mentality. Religions have to go through a learning process to cope with the normative starting points of a liberal democratic society; secular worldviews have to go through a learning process to open themselves for the potential meaning of religious discourses.

After a short presentation of Habermas's ideas about the post-secular society, I analyze the consequences of the post-secular perspective for the place of religious education in regular school curricula. Although I have sympathy for Habermas's nuanced approach to the place of religion in a secularized public sphere, I do not agree with him in all the details.[2] But this is not the subject of this chapter. The question here is: If we agree with Habermas's idea of post-secularism, both as a descriptive and a normative concept, what are then the consequences of his insights for the current debates on religious education in Western countries?

---

1 Jürgen Habermas, "Faith and Knowledge," in *The Future of Human Nature* (Cambridge: Polity, 2003), 101 – 115; Jürgen Habermas and Joseph Ratzinger, *The Dialectics of Secularization: On Reason and Religion* (San Francisco: Shambala, 2006); Jürgen Habermas, *Between Naturalism and Religion: Philosophical Essays* (Cambridge: Polity, 2008 [2005]); Jürgen Habermas, "Notes on a post-secular society," *New Perspectives Quarterly* 25.4 (2008): 17 – 29.
2 Patrick Loobuyck and Stefan Rummens, "Beyond Secularization? Notes on Habermas's Account of the Postsecular Society," in *Discoursing the Post-Secular: Essays on the Habermasian Post-Secular Turn*, ed. Peter Losonczi and Singh Aakash (Münster-Wien-London: LIT Verlag, 2010), 55 – 74; Patrick Loobuyck and Stefan Rummens, "Religious Arguments in the Public Sphere: Comparing Habermas with Rawls," *Religion in the Public Sphere*, Ars Disputandi Supplement Series, vol. 5. (2011): 237 – 49.

1 Habermas's post-secular perspective

According to Habermas, a post-secular society is in the first place a secular society – both in the sociological and normative senses of the term. The former implies that the term can only be applied to these societies where people's religious ties have lapsed in the post-War period.[3] Moreover, Habermas's concept of the post-secular society is also not in contradiction to ongoing sociological secularization. Against the spokesman of the so-called desecularization thesis,[4] Habermas acknowledges that "the data collected globally still provides surprisingly robust support for the defenders of the secularization thesis."[5] He does not predict a religious comeback in the western countries, but he warns against the idea that religion is dead. Habermas also agrees with authors such as José Casanova[6] that in secularized societies, religious groups and discourses are still relevant in the political arena and the public culture. The post-secular conditions have nothing to do with a numerical growth of religion, but with a change in public consciousness. The society is post-secular to the extent that it has to adapt and to adjust itself "to the fact that religious communities continue to exist in a context of ongoing secularization."[7]

Also, on the normative level, the Habermasian post-secular society is secular: the political order in a post-secular society is still legitimized on secular values such as freedom and equality. In line with Rawls's political liberalism,[8] Habermas argues that political solutions should always be based on a democratic common sense, which remains neutral toward both secularist and religious (truth) claims. Democratic legitimacy has nothing to do with theology or religion, but depends on a reasonable agreement between all citizens, and will, therefore, depend on "cognitive resources of a set of arguments that are inde-

---

3 Habermas, "Notes on a post-secular society," 17.
4 E.g. Peter Berger, ed., *The Desecularization of the World: The Resurgence of Religion in World Politics* (Grand Rapids, Mich.: Wm. B. Eerdmans Publishing, 1999); John Micklethwait and Adrian Wooldridge, *God is Back: How the Global Revival of Faith is Changing the World* (New York: The Penguin Press, 2009).
5 Habermas, "Notes on a post-secular society," 19.
6 José Casanova, *Public Religions in the Modern World* (Chicago: University of Chicago Press, 1980).
7 Habermas, "Faith and Knowledge," 104; see also Habermas, "Notes on a post-secular society."
8 John Rawls, *Political Liberalism* (New York: Columbia University Press, 1993); John Rawls, "The Idea of Public Reason Revisited," in *The Law of Peoples* (Cambridge Mass.: Harvard University Press, 2001), 129–80.

pendent of religious or metaphysical traditions."[9] This autonomous and immanent grounding of legitimacy is based on the rational dialogue and consensus between free and rational citizens. The secular character of the state implies that the government has to assume a neutral stance. It has to remain at an equal distance from all traditions and worldviews and abstain from prejudging political decisions in favor of one side or the other.

Typical for Habermas's post-secularism now is his argument that, in the public sphere, passive, indifferent tolerance between (religious) groups is not enough. Habermas's post-secularism insists on a willingness to learn from others in terms of their possible contributions concerning basic moral and political intuitions. This means that those holding religious and secularist worldviews should take each other's contributions to controversial public debates seriously. Where possible, the discourse of religious citizens should be translated into a secular language, and secular citizens must remain sensitive to the force of articulation inherent in religious languages.[10]

More generally, from the post-secular perspective, the modernization of public consciousness requires a *complementary learning processes*.[11] On the side of religion, the modernization of religious consciousness consists of the development of a *reflexive religion*.[12] This development does not require religions to abandon their religious beliefs. Instead, it demands, first, that religious citizens accept and agree with the fact of pluralism and acknowledge freedom of religion as a universal right. Secondly, religious citizens must accept the independent validity of scientific knowledge. They must conceive the relationship of sacred and secular knowledge in such a way that faith cannot contradict with the progress of scientific knowledge. Finally, religious citizens must acknowledge the secular character of the constitutional state and give priority to secular over religious reasons in public debate. They have to accept that the exercise of political authority must be neutral toward competing worldviews and that, therefore, in the formal political sphere, only neutral, secular reasons may count. This requires the epistemic ability to consider one's own faith reflexively from the outside and to relate it to secular views. This means that they have to connect the egalitarian individualism and universalism of modern law and morality with the premises of their own religious doctrine. Only when religions meet these

---

9 Habermas, *Between Naturalism and Religion*, 104.

10 Habermas, "Faith and Knowledge," 109.

11 Habermas, *Between Naturalism and Religion*, 111; Habermas, "Notes on a post-secular society."

12 Habermas, "Faith and Knowledge," 104; Habermas, *Between Naturalism and Religion*, 136–37.

three normative and epistemic expectations can they be taken seriously in the political sphere. In Western culture, the required processes of religious rationalization can be observed in the evolution of religious consciousness of Christianity since the Reformation and Enlightenment. This on-going process has not been easy, and, in the case of the Catholic Church, the Second Vatican Council in 1965 finally brought about an open acceptance and confirmation of the liberal political values of modern society. And, according to Habermas, it seems fair to say that many Muslim communities still have a large part of this often painful learning process before them.[13]

On the secular side, the complementary learning process consists in the development of a *post-metaphysical thinking*.[14] Like religious citizens, secular citizens need to assume a cognitive burden which goes beyond the political virtue of mere tolerance as a *modus vivendi*. Something more is called for. What is expected of religiously tone-deaf citizens is a "self-reflexive overcoming of a rigid and exclusive secularist self-understanding of modernity," and thus, the rejection of a form of secularism that is solely based on hard naturalism and radical scientism. This requires, first, that these citizens accept the idea of a "multi-dimensional concept of reason" according to which reason is not simply reduced to scientific rationality but also applies to moral, legal and religious judgments. Secondly, secular citizens should accept that religions are not necessarily irrational relics of pre-modern times. Instead, they should accept that religious discourse might contain morally and politically relevant meanings which could perhaps be translated and introduced into secular political discourse. Secular citizens should not, *a priori*, exclude the semantic contents of religion, and they should be aware that many philosophical insights are secular, reasonable translations of earlier religious discourse. "Secular citizens, in their role as citizens, may neither deny that religious worldviews are in principle capable of truth nor question the right of their devout fellow citizens to couch their contributions to public discussions in religious language."[15] Moreover, from the Habermasian post-secular perspective, secular citizens are expected "to enter into a political discussion of the content of religious contributions with the intention of translating potentially morally convincing intuitions and reasons into a generally accessible language."[16] What is at stake here is more than a respectful sensibility for the possible existential significance of religion for other persons. The

---

13 Habermas, *Between Naturalism and Religion*, 136–37; Habermas, "Notes on a post-secular society," 27–8.

14 Habermas, *Between Naturalism and Religion*, 112–3, 138–43.

15 Habermas, *Between Naturalism and Religion*, 113.

16 Habermas, *Between Naturalism and Religion*, 139.

post-secular perspective requires that religious contributions to contentious political issues can be taken seriously and that secular citizens in the public sphere must be able to speak with their religious fellow citizens as equals.

2 Religious education in post-secular societies

The focus of Habermas on the issue of religion does not stand on itself. In political philosophy, we could speak of a "religious turn," because within and beside the so-called multiculturalism debate, religion became an important topic in liberal political theory. The debate focuses especially on the interpretation of the separation of church and state, and the place of religion in the public sphere and in the political decision making process.[17] This "religious turn," however, did not introduce the topic of religious education as a substantial issue in political philosophy. This is remarkable when we take into consideration that in the last decades, religious education became a prominent issue of public, political and academic debate in many (post-) secular societies. There is an extensive literature about political liberalism and citizenship education,[18] but religious edu-

---

[17] Among others, see Robert Audi and Nicolas Wolterstorff, *Religion in the Public Square* (London: Rowman and Littlefield, 1997); Rawls, "The idea of public reason revisited," in *Religion and the Obligations of Citizenship*, ed. Paul Weithman (Cambridge: Cambridge University Press, 2002); Veit Bader, *Secularism or Democracy? Associational governance of religious diversity* (Amsterdam: Amsterdam University Press, 2007); Geoffrey Brahm Levey & Tariq Modood, eds., *Secularism, Religion and Multicultural Citizenship* (Cambridge: Cambridge University Press, 2008); Tariq Modood et al., eds., *Multiculturalism, Muslims and Citizenship: A European Approach* (London: Routledge, 2005); Tariq Modood, *Multiculturalism* (Cambridge: Polity Press, 2007); Martha Nussbaum, *Liberty of Conscience: In Defense of America's Tradition of Religious Equality* (Cambridge Mass.: Basic Books, 2008); Martha Nussbaum, *The New Religious Intolerance. Overcoming the Politics of Fear in an Anxious Age* (Cambridge Mass.: Harvard University Press, 2013); Jocelyn Maclure and Charles Taylor, *Secularism and Freedom of Conscience* (Cambridge Mass., Harvard University Press, 2011).

[18] Among others, see Amy Gutmann, *Democratic Education* (Princeton, Princeton University Press, 1987); Terence, H. McLaughlin, "Citizenship, Diversity and Education: a Philosophical Perspective," *Journal of Moral Education* 21.3 (1992): 235–250; Eamonn Callan, *Creating Citizens: Political Education and Liberal Democracy* (Oxford: Oxford University Press, 1997); Meira Levinson, "Liberalism, Pluralism, and Political Education: Paradox or Paradigm?" *Oxford Review of Education* 25.1–2 (1999): 39–58; Stephen Macedo, *Diversity and Distrust: Civic Education in a Multicultural Democracy* (Cambridge Mass: Harvard University Press, 2000); Kevin McDonough and Walter Feinberg, *Education and Citizenship in Liberal Democratic Societies* (Oxford: Oxford University Press, 2003); M. Victoria Costa, *Rawls, Citizenship and Education* (New York: Routledge, 2011); Michael Waltzer, "Moral Education, Democratic Citizenship, and Religious Authority," *Journal of Law, Religion & State* 1 (2012): 5–15.

cation and the possible link between religious education and citizenship education has been neglected so far.

The work of Habermas provides an interesting opportunity to enter the religious education debate from the perspective of political philosophy. Habermas is
not only one of the leading political philosophical voices on religion in the public sphere, but his ideas of post-secularism and the complementary learning
processes easily pave the way for some thoughts on the role and importance
of religious education for/in these learning processes. However, while there
seems to be an evident link between the post-secular perspective and religious
education, neither Habermas nor any other author has elaborated on this
issue. In the rest of this article, I make a first attempt to think about religious
education from a Habermasian post-secular perspective.

2.1 Teaching about religion

A first relevant observation is the difference between Habermas's post-secularism and the secularist perspective of so-called fundamentalists of the Enlightenment. The latter try to get rid of religion – especially in the public sphere and
education – because it is irrational, dangerous, divisive, backward, anachronis-
tic and contentious. The more religion is privatized, the better for society. Habermas's perspective on religion is much more nuanced. Religions should not
be considered as "an obstinate survival of pre-Modern modes of thought;"[19] religious discourse is an important historical building block of our western societies and, according to Habermas, we can still not dismiss the possibilities of dis-
covering semantic contents in religious discourse. It is noteworthy that
Habermas emphasizes that a careful reconstruction of the genesis of reason
and philosophy makes clear that philosophy is a translation program that did
a lot of work by translating and recovering meaning from religion. In some respect, the history of philosophy is a history of liberating "cognitive contents
from their dogmatic encapsulation" into the melting pot of rational discourse,
a history of rescuing "the profane significance of interpersonal and existential
experiences that have so far only been adequately articulated in religious language." And precisely because it would be unreasonable to reject out of hand

---

19 Habermas, "Notes on a post-secular society," 27.

the possibility that religions still bear semantic potentials, Habermas now believes that the cognitive substance of religions has not yet been exhausted.[20]

All of this implies that sociological secularisation does not mean that religion should be expelled from education and the public realm in general. Different from the secularist, laicistic perspective, the post-secular perspective seems to be much more open to religious education courses on regular school curricula. It is unclear if Habermas's post-secularism implies that confessional religious education (teaching *into* religion) should be part of the school curricula of official schools (cf. *infra*); however, there are good reasons to argue from Habermas's post-secularism that non-confessional religious education should be part of the curriculum of all the schools. The post-secular conscience pays attention to religion as an interesting human fact (with its positive and negative elements), to the religious genealogy of western societies, and to the continued presence and meaning of religions today. Together, with courses in art history or literature, religious education can help children and students to develop this post-secular conscience by improving their religious literacy. This implies not only knowledge about several religions and about differences within religious traditions and world views but also knowledge of the religious roots of our societies, arts and cultures. All of this is, in the words of the British educator Michael Grimmitt, teaching *about* religion.[21]

However, from the Habermasian perspective, this teaching about religion may not be merely understood as teaching the history of religion. For Habermas, religious traditions and communities should not be seen as "archaic relics of premodern societies persisting into the present." And thus religious education should not be seen as the equivalent of courses about "species threatened with extinction."[22] Sure, teaching about religion should have a historical component, but it should also make place for the phenomenological approach that gives students a better understanding of the meaning of religious rituals, festivals, texts and (dress) codes for people today.

---

20 Habermas, *Between Naturalism and Religion*, 142; Habermas, "Faith and Knowledge,"111; Jürgen Habermas, *Religion and Rationality* (Cambridge Mass.: MIT, 2002), 164.
21 See Michael Grimmitt, "Contemporary Pedagogies of Religious Education: What are They?" in *Pedagogies of Religious Education* (Great Wakering: McCrimmons Publishing, 2000), 24–52.
22 Habermas, *Between Naturalism and Religion*, 138.

2.2 Learning processes

A secondly relevant observation is Habermas's focus on the complementary learning processes that secular and religious citizens should go through. However, while this learning process is central to Habermas's post-secularism, he does not mention *how* this learning process should be realized. In his book *Secularism or Democracy*, Veit Bader defended three different ways in which religions can learn to accept the normative value of liberal democracy. First, there is the level of practical institutional learning: living under and participating in liberal institutions contributes to the acceptance of a liberal political design. This is the story of the Christian democratic political parties and civil society in Europe. Secondly, there is the dimension of what Bader has called theoretical, theological and doctrinal learning. This is what happened for instance with the Catholic Church at the Second Vatican Council around 1965. Thirdly, Bader mentions practical attitudinal learning: toleration and democratic attitudes as a result of concrete interactions among people with different worldviews.[23]

Neither Bader nor Habermas explicitly mention the potential role that religious education can play in the learning processes. However, it seems evident that religious education can and should contribute to Bader's third dimension of practical attitudinal learning. Therefore, schools should not (only) organize separated confessional religious education, but rather, what Wanda Alberts has called integrative religious education,[24] keeping pupils with different religious and non-religious backgrounds together in a common, non-confessional religious education class. More than is the case that separate, confessional religious education, integrative religious education gives students the opportunity to understand what other people think and to learn from each other. It also gives students occasion to discuss with each other and to disagree on important issues in a decent way. Students can learn how to live together, despite different religions and worldviews. As such, this kind of integrative religious education seems to be a promising and appropriate way to facilitate and establish complementary learning processes, wherein the secular student can learn from religious students, the religious student can learn from the secular one, and both can experience the right to disagree and develop an attitude of reciprocity.

---

23 Bader, *Secularism or Democracy?*, 118.
24 Wanda Alberts, *Integrative Religious Education in Europe. A study-of-religions approach* (Berlin/New York: Walter de Gruyter, 2007).

2.2.1 Learning from religion

The Habermasian learning process for the secular citizens has to do with openness for the potential meaning of religious discourses and their willingness to translate religious contents into a secular, generally accessible, language. The religious voice should be heard, and, so we could add, studied, "for it cannot be sure that secular society would not otherwise cut itself off from key resources for the creation of meaning and identity [...] Religious traditions have a special power to articulate moral intuitions, especially with regard to vulnerable forms of communal life."[25]

To foster this learning process and to make the secular citizen more open to the potential semantic content of religious discourse, nuanced religious education should be a compulsory part of the school curriculum. However, what comes to the fore here is that teaching about religion is not enough: the learning process of the non-religious side implies also what Grimmitt has called learning *from* religion[26].

2.2.2 Democracy and the science of religion

According to Habermas, religious people should learn to cope with the possible tensions between certain religious discourses, on the one hand, and a secular, liberal democratic discourse, on the other hand. Religions have to connect the liberal values of individual freedom, equality and reciprocity with the premises of their own religious doctrine. Here again, it seems that integrative religious education can contribute to this learning process to change the religion in what Habermas has called a reflexive religious attitude. Religious education can contribute to the epistemic ability to consider one's own faith reflexively and to relate it to secular views and the moral premises of modern, democratic law. If this is indeed a task of religious education, it should be linked with liberal citizenship education wherein (religious) students can learn how and why they should accept the moral values of a liberal democracy as the best way so far to organize a stable society.[27]

---

25 Habermas, *Between Naturalism and Religion*, 131.
26 Michael Grimmitt, *Religious Education and Human Development* (Great Wakering, McCrimmon Publishing, 1987).
27 About the link between religious and civic education, see Andrew Wright, "Religious Education, Religious Literacy and Democratic Citizenship," in *The Fourth R for the Third Millenium: Education in Religion and Values for the Global Future*, eds. Leslie J. Francis, Jeff Astley and

Habermas mentions also another element in the learning process: religious citizens must accept the independent validity of scientific knowledge. They must conceive the relationship of sacred and secular knowledge in such a way that faith cannot contradict the progress of scientific knowledge. Agreeing with this condition does not only mean that religious education cannot make room for Intelligent Design or Creationism, it implies also that religious education should not be based on theology (alone). Like all the other school subjects, religious education should inform the students and it should give them our best academic knowledge to date, in this case especially regarding religions and worldviews. Therefore, religious education should, in the first place, be based on the academic discipline of religious studies, not on theology.[28]

2.2.3 Compulsory integrative religious education

The conclusion so far is that from a post-secular perspective, it would be wise to facilitate religious education that can contribute to the complementary learning process of secular and religious citizens. Taking Habermas's post-secularism seriously gives, therefore, a strong argument in favor of integrative, religious studies based religious education. This course should not only be focused on learning *about* religion but also on citizenship education and learning *from* (the study of) religion. In the context of religious studies based integrative religious education, people can learn about and from religion, they can meet each other and they can learn how to discuss important issues in a context of religious pluralism and fundamental rights. Secular students are encouraged to listen and to learn from religious discourses, and religious students to learn how to accept liberal democracy from their own religious viewpoint. More than separated confes-

Mandy Robbins (Dublin: Lindisfarne, 2001), 201–19; Siebren Miedema and Gerdien Bertram-Troost, "Democratic Citizenship and Religious Education: Challenges and Perpectives for Schools in the Netherlands," *British Journal of Religious Education* 30.2 (2008): 123–32; Siebren Miedema, "Maximal Citizenship Education and Interreligious Education in Common Schools," in Religious Schooling in *Liberal Democracies: Commitment, Character, and Citizenship*, eds. Hannah A. Alexander and Ayman K. Agbaria (London/New York: Routledge, 2012), 96–102; Ian Mac Mullen, *Faith in Schools? Autonomy, Citizenship and Religious Education in the Liberal State* (Princeton: Princeton University Press, 2007).
28 Cf. Tim Jensen, "Why Religion Education, as a Matter of Course, ought to be Part of the Public School Curriculum," in *Religious Education in a Plural, Secularised Society: A Paradigm Shift*, eds. Leni Franken and Patrick Loobuyck (Münster: Waxmann, 2011), 131–150; Tim Jensen, "RS based RE in public schools: a must for a secular State," *Numen* 55.2–3 (2008): 123–50.

sional and theology-based religious education, integrative religious education can stimulate the post-secular attitude of reciprocity of all the students.

Habermas's normative idea of post-secularism also makes an important argument for making this kind of integrative, religious studies based religious education a compulsory course for all children and students. In a secular society based on freedom and equality, parents have the right to raise and to educate their children in the religious way they prefer. This is not the government's business. The only place where the government can intervene with this personal education is at school. Without adequate information about the world, without reflection about the different alternatives on how to live, and without the development of the capacity to think autonomously, children are not free at all. Therefore, respect for freedom implies a government's duty to guarantee that children get adequate information – (especially) also about world views and religions. The aim of school education is not to make people good Catholics, Muslims, Jews or atheists, but to make them well-informed, self-reflexive Catholics, Muslims, Jews or atheists. The duty of the school is not to destroy nor to confirm to the particular religious education of the parents, but to put the particular education of the parents into a broader perspective and to give children the possibility to think about their parents' education in a reflexive and autonomous way. So, even if we start from the normative position of a secular society, based on freedom and equality as political values that should be protected by the government, we have already a convincing argument to put integrative, religious studies based religious education on the school curriculum of all children and students.[29] Starting from the descriptive and normative idea of the post-secular society and adding the importance of the complementary learning processes makes this argument for compulsory, religious studies based, integrative religious education even stronger.

2.3 Teaching into religion

While teaching about religion and learning from religion can be understood as a post-secular duty of all schools,[30] the post-secular perspective is inconclusive

---

29 Patrick Loobuyck and Caroline Sägesser, *Le vivre-ensemble à l'école. Plaidoyer pour un cours commun d'Éthique, de Citoyenneté et de Culture religieuse et philosophique* (ECCR) (Brussels: CAL, 2014).

30 And indeed, the European Court of Human Rights has admitted the possibility of compulsory teaching about religion in state schools once the principles of pluralism, criticism and objectivity are fully respected. See the judgments in Kjeldsen, Busk Madsen and *Pedersen v. Denmark* of

about the issue of teaching into religion in separate confessional, theology-based religious education. Post-secularism does not exclude it, but it has not the same priority as religious studies based, integrative religious education. It is clear that official recognized confessional schools in post-secular societies have – besides the duty to organize religious studies based religious education – the freedom to organize confessional religious education.[31] These courses can but should not necessarily be paid for by the government[32].

The question about confessional religious education in public schools is more complex. Unlike the secularist perspective, it seems that the post-secular perspective also can allow that official schools offer confessional courses. However, the post-secular perspective does not give public schools a duty to organize them. But when confessional religious education is organized in public schools, it should be done in such a way that different religions can offer their religious educations, and nobody is obliged to follow a confessional course. If not (as in the case of Turkey),[33] the state is not neutral and secular any longer and does not equally protect the freedom of conscience of every citizen. Moreover, it should be guaranteed that confessional courses are in line with the normative building blocks (freedom and equality) of liberal democracy and that they do not contra-

---

December 1976; Folgerø and *Others v. Norway* of June 2007; *Hasan and Eylem Zengin v. Turkey* of October 2007 and *Appel-Irrgang and others v. Germany* of October 2009. There is similar jurisdiction about teaching about religion in the US (*Abington School District versus Schempp*, 374 US 203, 1963) and in Québec and Canada (*S.L. v. Commission scolaire des Chênes*, SCC 7, 2012). All of these courts seem to agree that there is no such a thing as a "right not to be exposed to convictions other than one's own" (*Appel-Irrgang and others v. Germany*; see also *Mozert versus Hamp* in the US 1987). Cf. Ian Leigh, "Objective, critical and pluralistic? Religious education and human rights in the European public sphere, in Law, State and Religion in the New Europe," *Debates and Dilemmas*, eds. Lorenzo Zucca and Camil Ungureanu (Cambridge University Press, Cambridge, 2012), 192–214; Ian Leigh, "The European Court of Human Rights and Religious Neutrality," in *Religion in a Liberal State*, eds. Gavin D'Costa, Malcolm Evans, Tariq Modood and Julian Rivers (Cambridge: Cambridge University Press, 2013), 38–66.

31 For discussion, see Walter Feinberg, *For Goodness Sake: Religious Schools and Education for Democratic Citizenry* (New York, Routledge: 2006).

32 Unlike in France or Quebec, the different confessional religious courses in recognized religious schools are paid for by the government in, for instance, the Netherlands and Belgium. See Patrick Loobuyck and Leni Franken, "Religious Education in Belgium: Historical Overview and Current Debates," in *Religious Education in a Plural, Secularised Society: A Paradigm Shift*, eds. Leni Franken and Patrick Loobuyck (Münster, Waxmann: 2011), 35–54.

33 Exemption from the (Islamic) religious course appears to be available only to parents of children who have identified themselves as Christian or Jewish. Parents from the Alevi stream of Islam do not have the possibility for exemption. This has been condemned by the European Court of Human Rights in the case *Zengin v. Turkey*, appl. No. 1448/04 (2007).

dict scientific knowledge. Because of the separation of church and state, the contents of confessional religious education is not the government's business. However, the government still has the right to decide whether or not these courses are reflexive enough and do not contradict freedom, equality and scientific knowledge. Confessional religious education is not "a lawless zone" and as a "manager of pluralism;"[34] the state is the protector of the fundamental rights of every individual. When these criteria are met, school curricula in post-secular societies can make room for facultative confessional religious education in addition to a compulsory course about religion and civic education.

3 Two policy trends

These theoretical considerations about religious education in post-secular societies have also a practical counterpart in concrete religious education policies. An increasing post-secular consciousness in many western countries resulted in a "shift in paradigm" concerning religious education.[35] For a long time, the main aim of religious education was, without any discussion, to respond to parents' wishes to educate their children in their own denominational interpretation of the Christian tradition. However, currently, in our post-secular societies, the aims of religious education are much broader: learning about different religions, contributing to pupils' personal development, developing intercultural

---

34 Alessandro Ferrari, "Religious education in a globalized Europe," in *Religion and Democracy in Contemporary Europe*, eds. Gabriel Motzkin and Yochi Fischer (London: Van Leer Jerusalem Institute and Network of European Foundations, Alliance Publishing Trust, 2008), 113–24, at 121.
See also Walter Feinberg, "Religious Education in Liberal Democratic Societies: The question of accountability and autonomy," in *Education and Citizenship in Liberal Democratic Societies*, eds. Kevin McDonough and Walter Feinberg, (Oxford: Oxford University Press: 2003), who argues convincingly that the more religious education and more general religious schools are paid for by the government, the more it is legitimate for the state to organize some significant public control.
35 Leni Franken and Patrick Loobuyck, eds., *Religious Education in a Plural, Secularised Society: A Paradigm Shift* (München: Waxmann, 2011); Luce Pépin, *Teaching about Religions in European School Systems: Policy Issues and Trends – NEF Initiative on Religion and Democracy in Europe* (London: Alliance Publishing Trust, 2009); Robert Jackson, Siebren Miedema, Wolfram Weisse and Jean-Paul Willaime, *Religion and Education in Europe: Developments, Contexts and Debates* (Münster : Waxmann, 2007); Robert Jackson, *Rethinking Religious Education and Plurality: Issues in Diversity and Pedagogy* (London: RoutledgeFalmer, 2004).

skills, attaining religious literacy, and preparing students for participation as citizens in a multicultural society.[36]

This shift in paradigm has different consequences in countries without confessional religious education (like France and the USA), on the one hand, and countries with confessional religious education, on the other. In those secular countries where religion was, until recently, missing from the school curriculum, the post-secular paradigm shift made it possible for religious education to become a more visible part of regular school curricula. In France, for instance, knowledge about *le fait religieux* became more important after the Debray Report in 2002. The idea of a *laïcité* of ignorance (*laïcité d'incompétence*) has been replaced by the idea of a *laïcité* of understanding (*laïcité d'intelligence*),[37] and religious literacy is now part of the curriculum, especially in history and literature courses.[38]

In countries where separate, confessional religious education was the norm, the post-secular perspective is an incentive in favor of a process of de-confessionalizing religious education. A post-secular society is characterized by increasing forms of secularization *and* religious diversity, which makes non-confessional, integrative religious education more appropriate than separate confessional religious education classes.[39] The introduction of ERC (Ethics and Religious Culture/ *Éthique et Culture Religieuse*) on the school curriculum in Québec is a good ex-

---

36 Cf. John Keast, ed., *Religious Diversity and Intercultural Education: a Reference Book for Schools* (Strasburg: Council of Europe Publishing, 2007); Council of Europe, White paper on intercultural dialogue: "Living together as equals with dignity" (Strasburg: Council of Europe Publishing, 2008); Pille Valk, Gerdien Bertram-Troost, Markus Friederici, Céline Béraud, eds., *Teenagers' Perspectives on the Role of Religion in their Lives, Schools and Societies: A European Quantitative Study* (Münster: Waxmann, 2009); Thorsten Knauth et al., eds., *Encountering Religious Pluralism in School and Society: A Qualitative Study of Teenage Perspectives in Europe* (Münster: Waxmann, 2008).

37 Régis Debray, *L'enseignement du fait religieux dans l'école laïque* (Paris, 2002), 22. For the US, see for instance Stephen Prothero, *Religious Literacy: What every American Needs to Know – and Doesn't* (New York: Harper Collins, 2007); Diane Moore, *Overcoming Religious Illiteracy: A Cultural Studies Approach to the Study of Religion in Secondary Education* (New York: Palgrave Macmillan, 2007).

38 Dominique Borne and Jean-Paul Willaime, dir., *Enseigner les faits religieux. Quels enjeux ? Préface de Régis Debray* (Paris: Armand Colin, 2009); " *Laïcité et enseignement des faits religieux en France* " 4th part of Jean-Paul Willaime, dir., *Le défi de l'enseignement des faits religieux à l'école: Réponses européennes et québéqoises* (Paris : Riveneuve éditions, 2014).

39 Alberts, Integrative *Religious Education in Europe*; Loobuyck and Sägesser, *Le vivre-ensemble à l'école*; Leni Franken and Patrick Loobuyck, "The Future of Religious Education on the Flemish School Curriculum: A Plea for Integrative Religious Education for All," *Religious Education* 108.5 (2013): 482–98.

ample here.[40] Until 2008, pupils had to choose between Catholic religious education, Protestant religious education, or ethics. These courses are replaced now by one compulsory, non-confessional ERC course. The ERC program has three important components: religious studies, ethics and dialogue. All this is in line with the post-secular perspective. What happened in Québec is only one example. There are other countries, like Sweden, Denmark and Norway,[41] where integrative religious studies based religious education is already the norm, and we can expect that other countries will follow when they take the post-secular consciousness seriously.

Works Cited

Alberts, Wanda. *Integrative Religious Education in Europe. A study-of-religions approach.* Berlin/New York: Walter de Gruyter, 2007.

Audi, Robert and Wolterstorff, Nicolas. *Religion in the Public Square.* London: Rowman and Littlefield, 1997.

Bader, Veit. *Secularism or Democracy? Associational governance of religious diversity.* Amsterdam: Amsterdam University Press, 2007.

Berger, Peter L. *The Desecularization of the World: Resurgent Religion and World Politics.* Washington, D.C.: Ethics and Public Policy Center, 1999.

Borne, Dominique and Willaime, Jean-Paul (eds.). *Enseigner les faits religieux. Quels enjeux? Préface de Régis Debray.* Paris: Armand Colin, 2009.

Callan, Eamonn. *Creating Citizens: Political Education and Liberal Democracy.* Oxford: Oxford University Press, 1997.

Casanova, José. *Public Religions in the Modern World.* Chicago: University of Chicago Press, 1980.

Costa, M. Victoria. *Rawls, Citizenship and Education.* New York: Routledge, 2011.

---

40 Mireille, Estivalèzes, "The Teaching of an Ethics and Religious Culture Programme in Quebec: A Political Project?," in *Religious Education, Politics, the State, and Society,* ed. Ansgar Jödicke (Würzburg : Ergon, 2013), 129–47; Mireille Estivalèzes and Solange Lefebvre, *Le programme d'éthique et culture religieuse. De l'exigeante conciliation entre le soi, l'autre et le nous* (Quebec: Les Presses de l'Université Laval, 2012); George Leroux, *Éthique, culture religieuse, dialogue. Arguments pour un programme* (Quebec: Fides, 2007); Richard Rymarz, "Teaching Ethics and Religious Culture in Québec High Schools: An Overview, Contextualization and Some Analytical Comments," *Religious Education* 107.3 (2012): 295–310; Bruce Grelle and Tim Jensen, eds., *Religion & Education* 38.3 (2011) (special issue devoted to the ERC program).

41 Wanda Alberts, "Religious Education in Norway," and Denise Cush, "Without Fear of Favour: Forty Years of Non-confessional and Multi-faith Religious Education in Scandinavia and the UK," in *Religious Education in a Plural, Secularised Society: A Paradigm Shift,* eds. Leni Franken and Patrick Loobuyck (Münster: Wawmann, 2011), 99–114 and 69–84.

Council of Europe, *White paper on intercultural dialogue: 'Living together as equals with dignity'*. Strasburg: Council of Europe Publishing, 2008.

Debray, Régis. *L'enseignement du fait religieux dans l'école laïque*. Paris, 2002.

Estivalèzes, Mireille. "The Teaching of an Ethics and Religious Culture Programme in Quebec: A Political Project?" In *Religious Education, Politics, the State, and Society*, edited by Ansgar Jödicke, 129–147. Würzburg : Ergon, 2013.

Estivalèzes, Mireille and Lefebvre, Solange. *Le programme d'éthique et culture religieuse. De l'exigeante conciliation entre le soi, l'autre et le nous*. Quebec: Les Presses de l'Université Laval, 2012.

Feinberg, Walter. "Religious Education in Liberal Democratic Societies. The question of accountability and autonomy." In *Education and Citizenship in Liberal Democratic Societies*, edited by Kevin McDonough and Walter Feinberg. Oxford: Oxford University Press: 2003.

Feinberg, Walter. *For Goodness Sake: Religious Schools and Education for Democratic Citizenry*. New York, Routledge: 2006.

Ferrari, Alessandro. "Religious education in a globalized Europe." In *Religion and Democracy in Contemporary Europe*, edited by Gabriel Motzkin and Yochi Fischer, 113–124. London: Van Leer Jerusalem Institute and Network of European Foundations, Alliance Publishing Trust, 2008.

Franken, Leni and Loobuyck, Patrick (eds.). *Religious Education in a Plural, Secularised Society. A Paradigm Shift*. Münster, Waxmann: 2011.

Franken, Leni and Loobuyck, Patrick. "The Future of Religious Education on the Flemish School Curriculum. A Plea for Integrative Religious Education for All." *Religious Education* 108.5 (2013): 482–98.

Grelle, Bruce and Jensen, Tim (eds.), *Religion & Education* 38.3 (2011) (special issue devoted to the ERC program).

Grimmitt, Michael. "Contemporary Pedagogies of Religious Education: What are They?" In *Pedagogies of Religious Education*, Grimmitt, Michael, 24–52. Great Wakering: McCrimmons Publishing, 2000.

Grimmitt, Michael. *Religious Education and Human Development*. Great Wakering, McCrimmon Publishing, 1987.

Gutmann, Amy. *Democratic Education*. Princeton, Princeton University Press, 1987.

Habermas, Jürgen. "Faith and Knowledge." In *The Future of Human Nature*, Jürgen Habermas, 101–15. Cambridge: Polity, 2003.

Habermas, Jürgen. *Between Naturalism and Religion. Philosophical Essays*. Cambridge: Polity, 2008.

Habermas, Jürgen. "Notes on Post-Secular Society." *NPQ: New Perspectives Quarterly* 25.4 (2008): 17–29.

Habermas, Jürgen and Ratzinger, Joseph. *The Dialectics of Secularization: On Reason and Religion*. San Francisco: Shambala, 2006.

Jackson, Robert. *Rethinking Religious Education and Plurality: Issues in Diversity and Pedagogy*. London: RoutledgeFalmer, 2004.

Jackson, Robert; Miedema, Siebren; Weisse, Wolfram and Willaime, Jean-Paul (eds.) *Religion and Education in Europe. Developments, Contexts and Debates*. Münster : Waxmann, 2007.

Jensen, Tim. "RS based RE in public schools: a must for a secular State." *Numen* 55.2–3 (2008): 123–50.

Jensen, Tim. "Why Religion Education, as a Matter of Course, ought to be Part of the Public School Curriculum." In *Religious Education in a Plural, Secularised Society. A Paradigm Shift*, edited by Leni Franken and Patrick Loobuyck, 131–50. Münster: Waxmann, 2011.

Keast, John (ed.). *Religious Diversity and Intercultural Education: a Reference Book for Schools.* Strasburg: Council of Europe Publishing, 2007.

Knauth, Thorsten et al., (eds.), *Encountering Religious Pluralism in School and Society. A Qualitative Study of Teenage Perspectives in Europe.* Münster: Waxmann, 2008.

Leigh, Ian. "Objective, critical and pluralistic? Religious education and human rights in the European public sphere." In *Law, State and Religion in the New Europe. Debates and Dilemmas*, edited by Lorenzo Zucca and Camil Ungureanu, 192–214. Cambridge University Press, Cambridge, 2012.

Leigh, Ian. "The European Court of Human Rights and Religious Neutrality." In *Religion in a Liberal State*, edited by Gavin D'Costa, Malcolm Evans, Tariq Modood and Julian Rivers, 38–66. Cambridge: Cambridge University Press, 2013.

Leroux, George. *Éthique, culture religieuse, dialogue. Arguments pour un programme.* Quebec: Fides, 2007.

Levey Geoffrey Brahm and Modood, Tariq (eds.), *Secularism, Religion and Multicultural Citizenship*, Cambridge: Cambridge University Press, 2008.

Levinson, Meira. "Liberalism, Pluralism, and Political Education: Paradox or Paradigm?" *Oxford Review of Education* 25.1–2 (1999): 39–58.

Loobuyck, Patrick and Rummens, Stefan. "Beyond Secularization? Notes on Habermas's Account of the Postsecular Society," In *Discoursing the Post-Secular: Essays on the Habermasian Post-Secular Turn*, edited by Peter Losonczi and Singh Aakash, 55–74. Münster-Wien-London: LIT Verlag, 2010.

Loobuyck, Patrick and Franken, Leni. "Religious Education in Belgium: Historical Overview and Current Debates." In Religious Education in a Plural, Secularised Society. A Paradigm Shift, edited by Leni Franken and Patrick Loobuyck, 35–54. Münster, Waxmann: 2011.

Loobuyck, Patrick and Sägesser Caroline. *Le vivre-ensemble à l'école. Plaidoyer pour un cours philosophique commun.* Brussels : Espace de Libertés (Éditions du Centre d'Action Laïque), 2014.

Loobuyck, Patrick and Sägesser Caroline. "Religious Arguments in the Public Sphere: Comparing Habermas with Rawls," *Religion in the Public Sphere, Ars Disputandi Supplement Series* 5 (2011): 237–49.

Macedo, Stephen. *Diversity and Distrust: Civic Education in a Multicultural Democracy.* Cambridge, MA: Harvard University Press, 2000.

Maclure, Jocelyn and Taylor, Charles. *Secularism and Freedom of Conscience.* Cambridge, MA: Harvard University Press, 2011.

Mac Mullen, Ian. *Faith in Schools? Autonomy, Citizenship and Religious Education in the Liberal State.* Princeton: Princeton University Press, 2007.

McDonough Kevin and Feinberg, Walter. *Education and Citizenship in Liberal Democratic Societies.* Oxford: Oxford University Press, 2003.

McLaughlin, Terence, H. "Citizenship, Diversity and Education: a Philosophical Perspective." *Journal of Moral Education* 21.3 (1992): 235–50.

Micklethwait, John and Wooldridge Adrian. *God is Back. How the Global Revival of Faith is Changing the World*. New York: The Penguin Press, 2009.

Miedema, Siebren. "Maximal Citizenship Education and Interreligious Education in Common Schools." In *Religious Schooling in Liberal Democracies: Commitment, Character, and Citizenship*, edited by Hannah A. Alexander and Ayman K. Agbaria, 96–102. London/New York: Routledge, 2012.

Miedema, Siebren and Bertram-Troost, Gerdien. "Democratic Citizenship and Religious Education: Challenges and Perspectives for Schools in the Netherlands." *British Journal of Religious Education* 30.2 (2008): 123–32.

Modood Tariq et al. (eds.). *Multiculturalism, Muslims and Citizenship: A European Approach*. London: Routledge, 2005.

Modood Tariq. *Multiculturalism*. Cambridge: Polity Press, 2007.

Moore, Diane. *Overcoming Religious Illiteracy: A Cultural Studies Approach to the Study of Religion in Secondary Education*. New York: Palgrave Macmillan, 2007.

Nussbaum, Martha. *Liberty of Conscience: In Defense of America's Tradition of Religious Equality*. Cambridge, MA: Basic Books, 2008.

Nussbaum, Martha. *The New Religious Intolerance. Overcoming the Politics of Fear in an Anxious Age*. Cambridge Mass.: Harvard University Press, 2013.

Pépin, Luce. *Teaching about Religions in European School Systems: Policy Issues and Trends – NEF Initiative on Religion and Democracy in Europe*. London: Alliance Publishing Trust, 2009.

Prothero, Stephen, *Religious Literacy. What every American Needs to Know – and Doesn't*. New York: Harper Collins, 2007.

Rawls, John. *Political Liberalism*. New York: Columbia University Press, 1993.

Rawls, John. "The Idea of Public Reason Revisited," In *The Law of Peoples*, John Rawls, 129–80. Cambridge, MA: Harvard University Press, 2001.

Rymarz, Richard. "Teaching Ethics and Religious Culture in Québec High Schools: An Overview, Contextualization and Some Analytical Comments." *Religious Education* 107.3 (2012): 295–310.

Valk, Pille; Bertram-Troost, Gerdien; Friederici, Markus and Béraud Céline (eds.), *Teenagers' Perspectives on the Role of Religion in their Lives, Schools and Societies. A European Quantitative Study*. Münster: Waxmann, 2009.

Waltzer, Michael. "Moral Education, Democratic Citizenship, and Religious Authority." *Journal of Law, Religion & State* 1 (2012): 5–15.

Weithman, Paul (ed.). *Religion and the Obligations of Citizenship*. Cambridge: Cambridge University Press, 2002.

Willaime, Jean-Paul (ed.), *Le défi de l'enseignement des faits religieux à l'école. Réponses européennes et québéqoises*. Paris : Riveneuve éditions, 2014.

Wright, Andrew. "Religious Education, Religious Literacy and Democratic Citizenship." In *The Fourth R for the Third Millenium: Education in Religion and Values for the Global Future*, edited by Leslie J. Francis, Jeff Astley and Mandy Robbins, 201–19. Dublin: Lindisfarne, 2001.

Rajeev Bhargava
We (In India) Have Always Been Post-Secular

The term "a post-secular age" suggests that we have moved to a condition or per-spective after or subsequent to the secular. But this begs the question: what is a "secular age?" The mainstream conception of the age of the secular is (a) that it is marked by a process that effects the marginalization, if not the disappearance, of religion. But the term "secular" also has value connotation. As a value-laden term, secular suggests (b) an age of truth and liberation, one that has left behind the dark period of religion, of superstition, falsehood, obscurantism and oppres-sion. The persistence of religion is a burden, the vestigial presence of unfree-doms; its return would be a disaster. What are the features of the state and the broader public sphere in such a secular age? The distinguishing feature of a secular state and a secular public sphere is that religion is conspicuous by its absence. If, by force of habit or design, it enters official or non-official public spaces, then attempts are made to expel it. A secular political theory offers a nor-mative view in which religious reasons should be excluded from the public jus-tification of law and public policy.

What then is connoted by the term "post-secular?" First, (a) an age in which religion has returned or in which the realization has dawned that it had never, in the first place, disappeared, that it was always around but lay unnoticed. A post-secular age is one where the non-religious must learn to exist with the religious. Second, as a value-laden term (b) it characterizes an age, which marks the return of the significance of religion, and is marked, therefore, by the realization that religion also has wisdom and insights and therefore something that we shun at our own peril. Hence, religion should not be ignored for it too has its own dis-tinctive cognitive and moral value. The religious and the non-religious *should* co-exist and because both have their distinctive value, people do and ought to have *meaningful* options between them. In a sense, post-secular marks a stage on way to a condition where the religion-secularity bipolarity is overcome and both are treated as species of the same, at present unnamed, genus. The post-secularist, therefore, seeks a rectification of hitherto mistaken or lop-sided secularist self-understanding and moves to a stage that recognizes religion's immanence and the transcendental qualities of the secular. Two other meanings of "post-secular" also follow: (c) that it is an age where multiple religions do and should coexist with multiple non-religious perspectives. Here a predominantly single-religion society is replaced by a society that copes with a variety of religions and secular worldviews and when that happens this development is viewed as enriching. Crossovers in both directions are permissible and have wider public and moral legitimacy. And finally: (d) that it is marked by the necessity of a state that is designed to cope with, indeed to value, the coexistence of multiple religious and non-religious perspectives. A post-secular theory questions the main secularist assumption: How can a state be liberal and presuppose at the same time the intrinsic, overall superiority of any non-religious perspective over religious ones? Also: How can the public sphere and the decision-making process in a state be democratic if religious voices are excluded and religious reasons entirely left out? A purely secular public sphere and state create a democratic deficit if religiously motivated people are still around in the society in question.

All that is mentioned above can then be embedded within a historical narrative. The secularist claimed or still claims that we have steadily moved from a general condition of belief in the past to an equally general condition of unbelief in the present. The post-secularist does not deny that such a process occurred at one time but then adds that it is now enfeebled and secular societies are currently retracting their steps and without abandoning unbelief completely are also embracing religious belief(s), or at least taking them seriously. A post-secular society is one that is moving towards the cohabitation of religious and non-religious perspectives, where there exists both a self-reflexive secularity and an equally self-reflexive religiosity, and every member of the society has a meaningful option between the two, because there are no political biases in favor of one or the other. The state is as impartial as it can be between all these perspectives and life-experiences.

Now Charles Taylor has famously challenged these conceptual and historical accounts of the secular and the post-secular. At the most important level, they fail to reach and appreciate the depth of modern secularity, the fact that everyone, in Europe and North America, regardless of their beliefs, lives their lives within what he calls the "immanent frame." But even at the levels at which they do manage to grasp the social world, the secular cannot be directly identified with what he calls "exclusive and self-sufficient humanism." The secular, instead, is the site of the meaningful option between religious and non-religious beliefs and practices. Despite the emergence of a powerful, de-transcendentalized secular humanism, i.e. exclusive humanism and the eclipse of early and traditional religions, new forms of religiosities and spiritualities continue to sprout. This is certainly true of the United States, if not Europe. But for the purposes of this chapter, I shall ignore Taylor's important challenge. If the post-secular refers to the acknowledgment of the continuous presence of religion, indeed of multiple religions, to the recognition of their positive value, to their coexistence with non-religious perspectives, and to the imperative that state be designed to cope with and value this plural condition, then, I argue, India has always been post-secular. Though I have the sense that at virtually no point of time in its history has the condition been absent – I say this despite the fact that there have been occasions where it has been challenged and in recent times, violently – I don't wish to be taken literally. "Always" must be taken with a little pinch of salt. This is not a historical demonstration of the continuing existence of post-secularity over thousands of years in India. Rather, my point is that there is a perfectly valid sense in which post-secularity existed in ancient India as it exists in our own times, and, therefore, it would not be an implausible conclusion to draw that it might have existed from time to time in India. Thus, this chapter questions not only the validity in India of the relevance of a historical narrative more suited to Europe and North America but also the relevance of terms such as "post-secular."

In Part I, I argue that, in the first millennium before the common era, the Indian subcontinent saw the birth of both Gods- or God-related and God- or Gods-denying perspectives; that overall, despite conflict and mutual recriminations, all of these were valued and sought to be valued even by political rulers. I then come in Part II, to the modern post-colonial era, where the same "post-secular" condition continues to exist.

1 Ancient India

The India of early religions was not monolithic. There were varieties of religious experience in ancient India. Multiple Indian secularities were also available. The sheer diversity of ethical perspectives is breathtaking.

Early religion, Charles Taylor tells us, was embedded in three different senses. First, human agency was embedded in society. Second, society was embedded in the Cosmos, and finally, the Cosmos incorporated the divine.[1] It is hard to disagree with Taylor. Each of these is true of Rig Vedic religion. (1500 – 1000 B.C.E.). First, for an individual to view himself or act outside the social matrix was inconceivable. For the Rig Vedics (henceforth referred to merely as Vedics), an individual was the social role he inherited. The Brahmin or the Kshatriya was nothing but a Brahmin or a Kshatriya. To use these terms somewhat anachronistically, their social identity was their personal identity. A second sense in which agency was socially embedded had to do with the primary reli-

---

1 Charles Taylor, *A Secular Age* (Cambridge, MA: The Belknap Press/Harvard University Press, and London: 2007), 152.

gious act, ritual sacrifice. No sacrifice could be performed by any agent all by himself. The sacrifice was offered by the Kshatriya, the primary householder, but it had to be executed by the Brahmin, who alone had the knowhow, and, thereby, the authority, to do so. Ritual sacrifice was then jointly performed by the two social agents, each complementing the other: one caused the ritual to be performed, the *yajaman*, and, therefore, was the primary recipient of the benefits accruing from it; and the other actually performed it, for which he received a gift/fee (*dakshina*). And why did the yajaman perform it? For the sake of society? As its protector and benefactor? Not really. The routine wishes of a Vedic householder, to be fulfilled by the performance of the sacrifice, were "sons, rain, cattle, superiority within his clan and tribe, living for the proverbial 100 years, and then finding his way to heaven."[2] In short what Vedic men hoped to achieve through sacrifice were very much goods of this-worldly human flourishing.[3] There was little that was supra-mundane about their ambition. This is underlined by the fact that life in heaven was a further continuation of a pleasant life on earth.[4] The idea of the *sanyasi* was yet to be conceived.[5] Nor was the normative idea yet born that one should strive to escape life in this world.[6] Indeed, in the *Rig Veda*, Richard Gombrich tells us, "man is born and dies only once."[7] There is no rebirth. *Eveamratva* (immortality) in some passages of the *Rig Veda* appears to be nothing but the continuation of a long life on earth.[8] Would it be wrong then to say that ritual sacrifice was the nodal point through which transactions occurred between socially constituted men? Was this too a moral order (like the modern moral order) constructed for mutual benefit, for the reciprocal exchange of goods and services? This would not be entirely correct, for there were also others who benefitted secondarily or indirectly from the *yajna* – for the sacrifice also sustained the entire social and cosmic order (*Rta*).[9] Since everyone benefitted, albeit differentially, from it, one could say that it was performed on behalf of and for the sake of all, for the entire society.

---

2 S. W. Jamison and M. Witzel, *Vedic Hinduism*, Unpublished text, 1992, 38.

3 B. Nakamura claims that in doing so the "Brahmins became strongly this-worldly." See Hajime Nakamura, *A Comparative History of Ideas* (Delhi: Motilal Banarsidass Publishers Private Limited, 1992), 38.

4 Richard Gombrich, *Theravada Buddhism: A Social History from Ancient Benares to Modern Colombo* (London: Routledge & New York: Kegan, 1988) 30. Also see Nakamura, 39.

5 S. W. Jamison and M. Witzel, *Vedic Hinduism*, 47.

6 S. W. Jamison and M. Witzel, *Vedic Hinduism*, 76.

7 Richard Gombrich, *Theravada Buddhism*, 30.

8 On this see Brian Black, *The Character of the Self in Ancient India* (Albany: SUNY Press, 2007), 11.

9 S. W. Jamison and M. Witzel, *Vedic Hinduism*, 67.

Perhaps this alone made the act sacred and lent it the religiosity it would not otherwise possess.

Even this Durkheimian account does not get it right, however. The impression it creates that men associated with one another for the sake of mutual benefit and largely for ordinary human flourishing, though not incorrect, misses out on two crucial points. First, there were two more clearly specified participants in the ritual act which we have failed thus far to mention: ancestors and gods. Second, the Vedic world of here and now was nevertheless thoroughly enchanted. In short, a sociology of ritual sacrifice will simply not do. We need rather a Cosmo-sociology. Relations between men were thoroughly implicated with and mediated by relations of men to their ancestors and gods.[10] These latter were the other participants in rituals, for gods and ancestors were invited to the sacrifice too. Except for Agni and Soma, all remained invisible. Yet a formal meal was offered to all these worthy dignitaries. A ceremonial offering of food (including animals) was made to fire so that Agni could carry it to other gods who ate it as smoke and aroma (*medha*). The leftovers were the more immediate and reciprocal gift of gods to the *yajaman*. The food offerings made to the Brahmin, in addition to his *dakshina*, were meant to go to the ancestors. Somehow the food consumed by Brahmins was transmitted to them. Hence, the importance of ritual feasts. A failure to do so would starve the ancestors and wreck the sacrifice. Thus, ritual sacrifice connected men not only to other men but also to gods and ancestors who lived either in heaven or somewhere between heaven and earth. As Taylor rightly puts it, society is embedded in the cosmos and the cosmos incorporates the divine (gods).[11]

Thus, reciprocity and mutual benefit were certainly key to ritual sacrifice but the system of mutual exchange crucially involved gods and ancestors. Gifts, mainly food, were offered to gods in order to procure mundane goods and for ultra-mundane, quite instrumental-looking reasons, in order to get something in return. The Vedic mantra was: "Give me, I give you." Of course even in the Rig Vedic period this must not be understood as a simple and true exchange or return of favours. The logic of reciprocity implied the principle of different and deferred returns. Equivalences were never sought by humans. Reciprocity entailed longterm relationships in which giving and receiving was never really over. If the sacrifice was performed exclusively for self-interest and without a sense of genuine gratitude, it was bound to fail.[12] Thus it doesn't appear entirely

---

10 S. W. Jamison and M. *Witzel*, 74.

11 Charles Taylor, *A Secular Age*, 26.

12 For a good discussion of these issues though in a different context see Daniel C. Ullucci, *The Christian Rejection of Animal Sacrifice* (Oxford: Oxford University Press, 2012), 26.

correct to say that "these were not then offerings to the almighty out of gratitude." Nor were they given out of "celebratory exuberance."[13] They were, as Witzel and Jamison admit, "mandated by the reciprocal system."[14] But the thoroughly enchanted world of porous Vedic selves has enough elements to keep the secularist and the humanist interested: There is no other world. No rebirth. One is born once and one dies only once. The only ends to be sought are this-worldly. There is no higher goal of human flourishing.

Much in this early religion then comes close to what Taylor calls "fully exclusive humanism." Three features mark his characterization of it. First, there is no other world but this, the only one we have. Second, following straight from the first, no human flourishing exists except in this world – nothing beyond and higher than flourishing here and now. Finally, it is achieved by human agency without help from or grace of God or gods. Exclusive humanism is self-sufficing. Early Vedic religion appears to meet the first two requirements but not the third. For Taylor, enchantment and exclusive humanism simply do not go together. Exclusive humanism is possible only for buffered selves. But Vedic selves are porous through and through.

Or are they? Matters are much too complicated in the Vedic world. In some passages, gods are manipulated and not just propitiated by humans, implying a power struggle between the two.[15] In others, sacrifice acquires coercive power to which gods submit. At least some of the power of gods is usurped by ritual sacrifice performed by humans. The sacrifice yields the desired result regardless of the wishes of gods. As Gombrich says, "In the early Vedic period, when gods were powerful supermen it was up to them to grant or withhold the benefits for which the sacrificer asked. Later it did not depend upon divine caprice. Sacrifice must work unless badly performed."[16] The correct performance of ritual, independent of gods, achieves everything desired in this world. This is socially embedded agency that works on its own, without help or hindrance from any other power. This indeed is self-sufficing, exclusive humanism as far as I can see in a relatively disenchanted world, for gods and spirits are inconsequential even if they exist. (Their existence is compatible with disenchantment as long as their role is negligible.) The causal efficacy resides in the power of skilled men, in this case Brahmins, who, by putting into words a significant and non-self-evident truth, acquire spiritual force.[17]

---

13 S. W. Jamison and M. Witzel, *Vedic Hinduism*, 63.
14 S. W. Jamison and M. Witzel, 65.
15 S. W. Jamison and M. Witzel, *Vedic Hinduism*, 1992, 60.
16 Richard Gombrich, *Theravada Buddhism*, 33.
17 S. W. Jamison and M. Witzel, *Vedic Hinduism*, 66.

This existence of something akin to exclusive humanism is not unique or entirely surprising, for Taylor acknowledges the presence of exclusive humanism in Greece, represented by Epicureanism, a tradition that admitted gods but found them "irrelevant to humans."[18] And what was possible in Greece is conceivable in India too. In fact, two of the major Indian "religions" in the first millennium before the Common Era, though very distant from Epicureanism, do not admit gods in their ontology. The original "asocial Buddhism" (a term used by Greg Bailey and Ian Mabbett) certainly took the same view on the relevance of gods.[19] M. Carrithers makes the same point, "Neither Socrates nor Buddha was much interested in God, gods or the supernatural, but both were passionately concerned with the ends and the conduct of human life."[20] The Jaina teachings, of greater antiquity than the teachings of the Buddha,[21] but which certainly came to fruition at the same time as the Buddha, also show little interest in "God, god and the supernatural." They do, of course, believe in the cycle of rebirth and the impact of a person's *karma* on the possibility of escaping it; but liberation is to be achieved exclusively by human agency, in this case by complete cessation of all action, by a state of complete motionlessness of both mind and body.[22] This actionlessness is the only answer to the problem of rebirth because on the Jaina view all karma results in demerit and, therefore, in rebirth. Karma sticks to the soul like dirt in objects.[23] One is born with the demerit of the karma of previous births. The only way out of this predicament is self-mortification, massive physical austerities to get rid of bad karma of past actions and births and henceforth to cease acting.[24] The only way to break the cycle is by attaining a condition of motionlessness and thoughtlessness and to move gradually and eventually to death.[25] Very different, perhaps even the opposite of Epicureanism, but exclu-

---

18 Charles Taylor, *A Secular Age*, 19 – 27.

19 Greg Bailey and Ian Mabbett, *The Sociology of Early Buddhism*. (Cambridge: Cambridge University Press, Cambridge, 2006).

20 M. Carithers, *The Buddha* (Oxford: Oxford University Press, 1983).

21 Louis Renou, *Religions of Ancient India* (Jordan Lectures, 1951) (London: The Antholone Press, 1953), 120.

22 Renou, *Religions of Ancient India* 132.

23 As Renou puts it, "Karman is a real substance, a sort of *poison* that infects the soul and renders it liable to be invaded by the other substances, space and time." *Religions of Ancient India*, 132

24 "The procedure is to destroy former karman and ward off the approach of new karman; this is accomplished by aceticism and the other methods of purification, both ritual and mental." Renou, *Religions of Ancient India*, 132.

25 Renou, *Religions of Ancient India*, 124 – 27.

sively humanist all the same and like other non-Vedic soteriologies, extremely focussed on individual *karma* and responsibility in the extreme.

Something in these accounts throws up the temptation then to introduce here the idea of an ancient post-secular age (parts of the late Vedic or early Upanishadic period that overlaps with a disappearing Rig Vedic, an emergent Buddhist and a continuing Jaina perspective). Recall that for our purpose, here, post-secularity is characterized by the presence of (a) exclusive humanism – a conception of human flourishing with no reference to anything beyond here and now, and a belief in the self-sufficiency of human agency along with the denial of life-worlds that presuppose the existence of God or Gods and Goddesses or their relevance, and (b) the equally easy availability of life worlds (presupposing the existence of God or Gods and Goddesses , an enchanted world, a conception of human flourishing beyond here and now). This diversity is accompanied by (c) a condition that allows for viewing these different outlooks as meaningful options with a freedom of movement across both Gods-affirming and Gods-denying perspectves and life-experiences. A person could move from one to another or simultaneously partake of many, indeed, in principle, could participate in all of them.

It's quite clear, since at least the early Rig Vedic period continuing well into a much later period, that large sections of Indian people have practiced some form of ritual sacrifice and committed themselves to the existence of multiple gods and goddesses. From the later Rig Vedic period there has, from time to time, also been a discourse of some form of inclusive monotheism, for example, prayer to *Ishwara*. However, in the entire first millennium before the Common Era, possibly earlier and quite certainly later, the Indic world has also witnessed three varieties of exclusive humanisms in roughly the sense outlined above. First, regardless of the existence and propitiation of gods, the correct performance of the ritual act by a specially qualified group of people can result in both the achievement of all the goods crucial to human flourishing and to maintain the entire cosmic order. Second, at least on one interpretation, for the Jain view, the ultimate end of human life, the complete cessation of thought and action, can be achieved by self-sufficing, austere and disciplined human action. Finally, a third view was prevalent among the Buddhists – that the ultimate goal of human flourishing can well be achieved by following the middle path, that is, acting in a way that is neither self-indulgent nor excessively austere and one that gives at least equal weight to self-related ethic as it does to other related morality. Each of these outlooks satisfies the conditions of exclusive humanism.

It is hard to tell whether exclusive humanism was restricted to a small group of Brahmans and Shramanas. But both the teachings of Buddha and Jaina were available to non-Brahmans and non-Kshatriyas, especially to *vis* (ordinary people). Indeed, there was free movement of Brahmans and Kshatriyas from one outlook to another. Recall that exclusive humanists do not have to deny the existence of gods. They presuppose the self-sufficiency of their own acts and find gods irrelevant to achieving their main goals. Some Vedic Brahmans were quite certainly exclusive humanists in this sense, but like the Epicureans who must have been small in numbers, these Brahmanic exclusive humanists must have been a tiny minority. However, the same cannot be said of the Jainas and the Buddhists. In my view, they too are exclusive humanists – although Buddha had an epistemic and ethical notion of transcendence.

I am trying to make a case then that different forms of exclusive humanisms (Vedic Brahmanical, Buddhists, Jainas and philosophical traditions of Charvaka) existed in India. All but one of them rejected ritual sacrifice as central to their worldview. And the one for which ritual sacrifice was pivotal does not appear to think of gods as relevant. These perspectives existed with life worlds that presupposed the existence of Gods and Goddesses, so that a meaningful option existed between these. What in India were the broader contexts within which religions/secularities were chosen, entered into, exited from? How could people cohabitate amidst such diversity? What did it mean to have an option or choice between rival worldviews? What did it mean to choose a religion? And to exit one?

I begin this discussion by reference to Richard Gombrich's characterization of religion in India.[26] According to him, "religion" might refer to (1) *Marga*, a path, providing an answer to the question: "what must I do to be saved." In short, religion might be a soteriology, a meaning-endowing perspective specifying ultimate goals, which gives individual life its point and direction, especially when confronted with the certainty of death. Equally, it refers to (2) those embedded beliefs and practices which structure the social life and normative expectations of individuals, particularly in relation to one another. Rituals, rites of passage, rules of hygiene and traditional norms can also be subsumed under this conception of religion. Gombrich calls it communal religion.

This distinction is important because it enables us to see how it is possible in India and more generally in Asia for many individuals to belong to two or more religions, for they can be attached at once to one of the many soteriologies (religion 1) and to a quite different set of communal practices (religion 2). They could continue to follow the set of practices they participated in before the new attachment. Hinduism has over time spawned many soteriologies but with minor regional variations has tended to keep a stable set of communal prac-

---

26 Richard Gombrich, *Theravada Buddhism*, 25 – 6.

tices. These communal religious elements have sometimes been so entrenched that even conversion to other religions, those which claim to perform both soteriological and communal functions, has not unsettled them. Thus, many converts to Islam and Christianity continued for long time with "communal" aspects of Hinduism, despite a change in their soteriology. Many Buddhists believe in gods but claim that this has nothing to do with and therefore is not inconsistent with their religion (soteriology). Gods, for them, have much to do with their this-worldly concerns and but have no bearing on their pursuit of *Nibbana*. This also allows a ruler to respect all "faiths." Since one might without contradiction follow the soteriological beliefs of one religion and the communal practices of another, one must respect both, and so must the ruler who himself may follow one or many "religions." It is clear that one should not view Hinduism and Buddhism as two mutually exclusive religions. To do so would be to utterly distort both.

1.1 Conditions of Mobility: Theological, social, political

What are the conditions of the possibility of moving easily from one religion (soteriology) to another (soteriology)? Three immediately come to mind. First, the religion or philosophy in question must not impose heavy costs or forbid movement across different worlds and their views and experiences. It should contain conceptual resources of ideological freedom rather than unfreedom. This is primarily a cognitive but also an emotional matter. Second, closely related to the first, it must not possess an internal institutional structure with enormous social power. This is a matter of social organization, of loose or tight internal social relations, of openness and flexibility within. Third, it must not provide direct legitimation to political power, and not become too closely aligned to it. Neither political rule nor political violence must be sanctioned by religion. This is an issue of the relationship between religion and political power, a matter of toleration or political secularity. I shall call these the theological, the social and the political conditions of free movement across religions.

The theological condition (the term is my own) can be discerned in the writings of several scholars, and in particular in the writings of Jan Assmann.[27] Several quite distinct ways of meeting this condition exist. First, the implicit or explicit theology of a religion must allow for translation of gods.[28] In virtually all

---

27 J. Assmann, *Of Gods and Gods* (Wisconsin: The University of Wisconsin Press, 2008); J. Assmann, *The Price of Monotheisim* (California: Stanford University Press, 2010).
28 On the distinction between implicit and explicit theology, see J. Assmann, *Of Gods and Gods*, 13.

cultures of classical antiquity, each god performed a function based on his cosmic competence. Thus, there are gods of love, war, knowledge, craftsmanship. Likewise, each god embodied an entity of potentially cosmic significance. Hence, gods of fire, rain, earth, time, sun, moon, sea or primal gods who create, destroy, preserve and so on. The god of love in one culture could then also acquire the name of the god of love from another culture. This way differences continue to be viewed as irreducible and yet translatable.[29] One might even call this feature of translatability, a theology of recognition – the gods of each culture are recognized within the background of a common semantic universe. Eventually, this theological mode of coping with diversity can be enlarged to include soteriologies that do not depend on gods. One can deploy the more general term "ethic of self-realization" that includes both god-dependent and god-free ethics pertaining to humans and even non-human selves. Each of these ethics can be treated as a way of being or relating to the ultimate, in whichever way the latter is defined or understood. Certainly, this inclusive monotheism or perhaps globalism of ethics permits easy movement across religions. If the different names refer to the same god or the same god has different cultural backgrounds, then why create too much fuss about leaving one and embracing another? Indeed, why not embrace both?

A second strategy, widely practised in ancient Egypt, involves the collocation of two or three gods leading to hyphenated cosmic deities such as Amun-Re.[30] The two, Re and Amun, Assmann tells us, do not merge. They retain their individuality, quite like in the mode of translation. But here each becomes a crucial aspect of the other. Thus Re becomes the cosmic aspect of Amun and Amun becomes the local and cultic aspect of Re. Each aspect complements the other, without subsumption or domination. This strategy was also available and practised in India.

Finally, a strategy even more common in all ancient cultures involves ontological subordination of one god to another god.[31] Thus one god becomes the supreme deity of which all other are gods are manifestations, as Ram and Krishna become avatars of Vishnu. Or we might have a pantheon of equal gods with very diverse primal functions, while others are but his manifestations or relations.

Each of these strategies meets the theological condition of free movement across different cultures and religions. Freedom of conversion would not be the appropriate term here. Conversion implies one's permanent departure from

---

29 J. Assmann, *Of Gods and Gods*, 54 – 8.
30 J. Assmann, *Of Gods and Gods*, 58.
31 J. Assmann, *Of Gods and Gods*, 58 – 62.

the worship of one god to the exclusive worship of another. But this goes against the very point of these strategies of translation, hyphenation and hierarchical assimilation. For here there can be free movement back and forth and indeed the simultaneous commitment to all. This is true both when unity is explicitly claimed (inclusive monotheism) or when it is merely implied as in polytheism.

This brings me to the second, social condition. Cantwell Smith has a very interesting discussion of how modern religions were formed. A glimpse of the portrait he draws might go somewhat like this. If you view the formation of religion as a process, you might find that in the beginning there is a teacher, often a dissenter from an existing outlook, who begins to attract a set of followers. These loyalists are attracted by his teachings and his example, and begin to see themselves first as wandering followers of a certain set of teachings and then as community. But this may or may not happen. When such a community becomes large, it acquires an institutional structure. Such institutionalized, rule-bound communities might be called a church. This too is not inevitable, and, therefore, may or may not happen. This happens more or less side by side with the formulation of an intellectual doctrine. So we now have a well demarcated community distinguished from others by its founder, his teachings, reflected in a scripture, possessing an organizational structure and an explicit theology. At the completion of this process, one might say that we have the birth of religion proper. Now clearly much depends on how much the Buddhist *sangha* resembles a church, and when Buddhist teachings become "Buddhism," a religion.

Now, one of my tentative proposals here is that the formation of a church places enormous restrictions on freedom of movement across *margas* or faiths and that such "churches" did not exist in ancient India. The *sangha* appears to have come closest to a church, but is not the same thing. It is, as Gombrich points out, "a body of men who meet regularly and in their face to face relations have some of the qualities of the family."[32] Furthermore, the function of the *sangha* is to help its members lead a disciplined life to achieve goals prescribed by the Buddha. Members are not gate keepers scrupulously watching whether other members reappear, or laws of entry or exit are observed, but rather follow each other's example to lead disciplined lives within the order. Moreover, as Cantwell Smith points out, Buddhism is a missionary religion but "Buddhist missionaries, in all their compassionate zeal, as they moved across all of Asia, did not expect that those who listened and responded to their message should abandon what other religious involvements they might already have [...] The result has been that from Ceylon to Japan those whom Westerners call 'Buddhists' are in almost

---

32 R. Gombrich, *Theravada Buddhism*, 90.

every case also and simultaneously participants in at least one other religious complex [...]"[33]

It follows that some of the key steps after the formation of *margis* may not have been taken in the ancient period. Even Buddhist *sanghas* were different from churches and did not place social restrictions on the free movement of *margis*. A third condition is the absence of political restrictions on religious and philosophical dissent, formation of opposing alternatives to mainstream faiths and philosophies or on movement from one philosophical/religious outlook to another. This condition seems to be frequently present in ancient India. A glorious illustration is to be found in the edicts of Asoka, the builder of a large empire in third century BCE.

Two Asokan edicts are particularly relevant for our purpose. The 7th edict begins with "The beloved of the gods wishes that 'all Pasandas'[34] must dwell everywhere, in every part of his kingdom."[35] This seems like a simple, quite inconsequential statement but, in fact, it articulates a normatively defensible response to religious coexistence and freedom.[36] To begin with, as already indicated above, many outlooks in that period were deeply opposed to one another. Vedic Brahmanism that centred around animal sacrifice in order to propitiate the gods and get their assistance to secure this-worldly goods was still pervasive. This was deeply offensive to the Jainas who rejected a this-worldly soteriology and believed in the principle of *ahimsa*. The teachings of the Buddha disagreed deeply both with the indulgences of Vedic Brahmanism as well as with the radical asceticism of the Jainas. Buddha introduced an other-related ethics that was as concerned with self-fulfilment as with right conduct towards others, especially the poor, the needy and the vulnerable. This morality encompassed all living be-

---

33 W. Cantwell Smith, *The Meaning and End of Religion*, Minnesota, 1991, 29–30.

34 This is one of the most difficult terms to translate. Its standard meaning is "heretic," but clearly Asoka does not use it in this sense. The standard translation is "sect," which is unsatisfactory because of its Christian association. There is an imaginative suggestion, now rejected, that it might be linked to *prasha*, a term in *avestha* and similar to *prashna* in sanskrit, meaning "question." An imaginative translation could then have been a group of questioners or enquirers. But there is no strong evidence to support this view. Radha Kumud Mookerjee links it to *Parishad*, meaning assembly. But that too is not accepted by everyone. Perhaps, the best translation would be "followers of a school of thought or teachings." I here use it to mean this and will continue to use the prakrit word *"Pasanda"* in the main text.

35 The identification of King Priya-darshi with Ashoka was confirmed by an inscription discovered in 1837.

36 For a detailed discussion see Rajeev Bhargava, "Beyond Toleration: Civility and Principled Coexistence in Asokan Edicts," in *The Boundaries of Toleration*, Alfred Stepan and Charles Taylor (eds.) (New York: Columbia University Press, forthcoming).

ings – not only humans but animals too. It required enormous political courage and imagination to build an inclusive polity where different religious groups could coexist and publicly debate their differences. After all, a number of morally dubious responses were also conceivable –extermination, expulsion or back-to-back neighbourliness rather than face-to-face discussion.

In edict 12, we find a discussion of the basis of such coexistence. For Asoka, *Dhamma* constitutes the all-important common ground, the essentials, of all *pasandas* and the fundamental content of *dhamma*, its core principle, *vacaguti*, variously interpreted as restraint on speech or control of tongue. We do not have much evidence of the verbal battles and the agonistic energies that were expressed in these vitriolic tongue lashings. But the edicts imply that verbal wars in that period were intense and brutal. They simply had to be reined in. But what kind of speech must be curbed? Edict 12 says that speech without reason that disparages other *pasandas* must be restrained. Speech critical of others may be freely enunciated only if we have good reasons to do so. However, even when we have good reasons to be critical, one may do so only on appropriate occasions, and, even when the occasion is appropriate, one must never be immoderate. Critique should never belittle or humiliate others. Thus, there is a multi-layered, ever deepening restraint on one's verbal speech against others. Let us call it *other-related self-restraint*. However, the edicts do not stop at this. They go on to say that one must not extol one's own *pasanada* without good reason. Undue praise of one's own *pasanda* is as morally objectionable as unmerited criticism of the faith of others. Moreover, the edicts add that even when there is good reason to praise one's own *pasanda*, it too should be done only on appropriate occasions and even on those occasions, never immoderately. Undue or excessive self-glorification is also a way to make others feel small. For Asoka, blaming other *pasandas* out of devotion to one's own *pasandas* and unreflective, uncritical, effulgent self-praise can only damage one's *pasanda*. By offending and thereby estranging others, it undermines one's capacity for mutual interaction and possible influence. Thus, there must equally be multi-textured, ever deepening restraint for oneself. Let this be *self-related self-restraint*.

Elsewhere, in the 7th edict, Asoka emphasizes the need not only for self-restraint – *samyama* – but also *bhaavshuddhi*, again a self-oriented act. *Bhaavshuddhi* is frequently interpreted as self-purification, purity of mind. However, this term is ambiguous between self-purification within an ethic of individual self-realization or one that at least includes cleansing one's self of ill-will towards others. My own view is that in the context of the relevant edicts, the moral feeling of good will towards others or at least an absence of ill will towards others must be a constitutive feature of what is meant by *bhaavshuddhi*. Self-restraint and self-purification are not just matters of etiquette or prudence. They have moral significance.

Given all this, and in order to advance mutual understanding and mutual appreciation, it is better, the edict says, to have *samovaya*, that is, concourse or assembly of *pasandas* where they can hear one another out, communicate with one another. They may then become *bahushruta*, that is, one who listens to all, the perfect open-minded listener. This way they will not only have *atma-pasandavraddhi*, the growth in the self-understanding of one's own *pasanda*, but also the growth of the essentials of all. The edicts here imply that the ethical self-understanding of *pasandas* is not static but constantly evolving and such growth is crucially dependent on mutual communication and dialogue with one another. Blaming others without good reason immoderately disrupts this process, and, apart from damaging dhamma, diminishes mutual growth.

The edicts add that no matter how generous you are with gifts and how sincere your devotion to rituals, if you lack *samyama*, *bhaavshuddhi* and the quality of *bahushruta*, then all the liberality in the world is in vain. Conversely, one who is unable to offer gifts but possesses the aforementioned virtues lives a *dhammic* life. Thus, one whose speech disrespects no one, who has no ill will towards others and who does no violence to living beings is truly *dharmic*. *Dharma* is realized not by sacrifice but by right speech and conduct.

Both these edicts point to political encouragement of civility across religious and non-religious worldviews, but the more general point that I wish to convey through this discussion is that no single philosophia[37] legitimated a political rule and, therefore, that the distance between state power and religion/philosophy was always maintained. I believe this point is of a piece with Sheldon Pollock's view that nothing compels us to believe that "legitimation, or its higher form, ideology, have anything like the salience in non-capitalist non-modernity that scholars have attributed to them."[38] In conjunction with other conditions, a continuing tradition of refusal to use any religious outlook for political legitimation helped both religious diversity and accommodation as well as freedom of movement from one religion or philosophy to another.

I hope to have shown that in this ancient period in India, multiple secular life-worlds independent of God or Gods/Goddesses and religious – life-worlds

---

37 For an explication of this term see Wilfred Cantwell Smith, *The Meaning and End of Religion*, 1991.

38 See Sheldon Pollock, *The Language of the Gods in the World of Men Sanskrit, Culture and Power in Premodern India* (Berkeley: Permanent Black, University of California Press, 2006), 517. Pollock's account is far more complex than suggested here and it is not my wish to get any further into its details.

that made god or gods and goddesses central – perspectives existed, and that there were meaningful options between them that existed, and that whatever form public power took, it permitted and sometimes even encouraged this plurality. In short, all the features of post-secularity appear to have been present then.

2 The Modern Period

My strategy for the modern period will be somewhat different. I will not try to establish the existence of multiple religious and non-religious perspectives. Apart from the many different kinds of Hindus (Hinduism has been described by the sociologist T. N. Madan as a "federation of faiths"),[39] India has a substantial presence of many varieties of Sikhs, Muslims (Shias, Sunnis, Ahmedias), Christians (early Syrian as well as Roman Catholic, Anglican and evangelists), Zoroastrians, Jains, the many Adivasi worldviews, Buddhists, and both ancient and modern western secularities. This rich diversity of Modern India has been well documented and I need not spend much time on it. I will focus instead on how the modern Indian state has evolved political perspectives to encourage the respectful coexistence of all these perspectives and life-worlds. Two conceptions are noteworthy, one that continues or revives an ancient pluralism and the other developed more recently that is inscribed in the Indian Constitution.

2.1 Two conceptions of modern Indian secularism

2.1.1 The communal harmony model

Perhaps the best way to begin articulating it is by sketching two broad and contrasting pictures of the socio-religious world. In the first, a persistent, deep, and pervasive anxiety exists about the Other, both the Other outside of one's religion and the other within. The Other is viewed and felt as an existential threat. So doctrinal differences are felt not as mere intellectual disagreements but are cast in a way that undermines basic trust in one another. The Other cannot be lived with but simply has to be expelled or exterminated. This results in major wars and a consequent religious homogenization. Though admittedly skewed,

---

39 T. N. Madan, "Religion in India," in *A Handbook of Indian Sociology*, Ed. Veena Das (New Delhi: Oxford University Press, 2006).

this picture approximates what happened in Europe in the sixteenth century.[40] One might then add that this constitutes the hidden background condition of European ideas of toleration and even its political secularism.

Consider now an entirely different situation. Here different faiths, modes of worship, philosophical outlooks, and ways of practicing co-exist customarily. Deep religious and philosophical diversity is accepted as part of the natural landscape. To feel and be secure is a basic psychosocial condition presupposed by these groups. All exhibit basic collective self-confidence, possible only when there is trust between communities. In short, the presence of the Other is never questioned. There is no deep anxiety; instead a basic level of comfort exists. The Other does not present an existential threat. This is not to say that there are no deep intellectual disagreements and conflicts, some of which even lead to violent skirmishes, but these do not issue in major wars or religious persecution. There is no collective physical assault on the Other on a major scale. This approximates the socio-religious world of the Indian subcontinent, at least till the advent of colonial modernity, and constitutes the background condition of civility and coexistence, perhaps even a different form of "toleration" in India. Indeed, it is not entirely mistaken to say that it was not until the advent of colonial modernity and the formation of Hindus and Muslims as national communities that this background condition was unsettled. Religious coexistence could no longer be taken for granted, doubts about coexistence forced themselves upon the public arena and religious coexistence became a problematic issue to be spoken about and publically articulated. An explicit invocation and defense of the idea became necessary that all religions must be at peace with one another, that there should be trust, a basic level of comfort among them, and, if undermined, mutual confidence must be restored. And trust and confidence requires that everyone, particularly the state, has equal regard for all religions. This was put sometimes normatively and sometimes merely affirmed, and might be called communal harmony or the "*sarva dharma sambhaava*" model; but if it is to be a variant of secularism, it is imperative to underline that it is derived entirely from its strong link with home-grown traditions. India had, therefore, worked out its own conception of secularism that is neither Christian nor western.

---

40 Religious homogenization was not absolute in Europe, of course, which is why I have used the term "predemoninantly single-religion societies" above. I say this also keeping in mind the presence of Jews in Europe. It should not be forgotten that the end of the 15th century witnessed waves of expulsion of Jews in many parts of Europe. Although members of the Jewish community subsequently remigrated, by "the 1570s, there were few openly professing Jews left in western or central Europe." See Benjamin Kaplan, *Divided by Faith* (Cambridge, Harvard University Press, 2010), 314.

The source of this conception can be found in Gandhi.[41] Gandhi begins by accepting religious pluralism as the inevitable and healthy destiny of human kind.[42] "There is endless variety in all religions and 'interminable religious differences.'" "Some go on a pilgrimage and bathe in the sacred river, others go to Mecca; some worship him in temples, others in mosques, some just bow their heads in reverence; some read the Vedas, others the Quran [...] some call themselves Hindus, others Muslims [...]" There is, for Gandhi, not only diversity *of* religions but also diversity within them. "While I believe myself to be a Hindu, I know that I do not worship God in the same manner as any one or all of them."[43] Given this deep religious diversity, "the need of the moment is not one religion, but mutual respect and tolerance of the devotees of different religions," indeed to entertain "equal regard for other religions and their followers."[44] The inescapability of religious diversity morally requires inter-religious toleration and equal respect for all religions. It also necessitates that every religion is viewed from the point of view of the religionists themselves. [45] Eventually, this theological mode of coping with diversity can be enlarged to include soteriologies that do not depend on gods. One can deploy the more general term "ethic of self-realization" that includes both god-dependent and god-free ethics pertaining to humans and even non-human selves. Each of these ethics can be treated as a way of being or relating to the ultimate, in whichever way the latter is defined or understood.

Gandhi did not find any inconsistency between demanding toleration and equal respect. It is of course true that in the classical seventeenth century meaning of the term, to tolerate is to refrain from interference in the activities of others

---

41 M. K. Gandhi, *The Way to Communal Harmony,* Ahmedabad: Navajivan Publishing House, 1963).

42 Building on the work of Arvind Sharma, Kenneth Ross has helpfully articulated a view of inclusive pluralism that, to my mind, fits Gandhi's views. Ross says "Given the long experience of the religions of India with the demands of religious pluralism, I will in this chapter look to Hinduism, and particularly to the Upaniṣads, for clues on how to proceed toward articulating a non-exclusive pluralism. The principle underlying non-exclusive pluralism is that of a non-exclusive both/and approach rather than an exclusive either/or approach, an approach that includes within pluralism the possibility that either inclusivism or exclusivism may be true and that pluralism may be false – a view brilliantly articulated as the central Hindu view of religious pluralism by Arvind Sharma." See Kenneth Ross, "Religious Pluralism and the Upanishads," in the *Journal of Vaishnava Studies* 19.1 (Fall 2010): 23–48. Also see Arvind Sharma, "Can There Be More than One Kind of Pluralism?" in *The Myth of Religious Superiority*, ed. Paul F Knitter (Indiana: Orbis Books, 2005), 59–60.

43 Gandhi, *The Way to Communal Harmony*, 39.

44 Gandhi, *The Way to Communal Harmony*, 40–1.

45 Gandhi, *The Way to Communal Harmony*, 41.

even though one finds them morally disagreeable, even repugnant and despite the fact that one has the power to do so.[46] Here one puts up with, even suffers, the morally reprehensible activities of others. The powerless Other escapes interference of the powerful because the latter shows mercy towards them, a virtue in the powerful exercised in relation to those who do not really deserve it. Let's call this a hierarchical notion of toleration, given the asymmetry of power between the two groups and the attitude of superiority that one has towards the other. Gandhi did not use the word "toleration" in this sense. His notion of toleration is different. Parents often put up with the blemishes of their children which they would not suffer in others. We choose to overlook a fault in our lover, even in our close friends that we would not excuse in others. We might endure deep difference in worldviews in fellow citizens because we value fraternity. In all such cases, we put up with dislikeable states of doing or being in others even if we have some power to do something about them simply because we have love or love-like feelings for them. Here one tolerates not despite hate but rather because one loves the other. A mixture of love, friendliness and fellow-feeling is in the background or becomes the ground of a different conception of toleration. So suppose that *A* accepts the value of many but not all of *B*'s beliefs and practices but recognizes that beliefs and practices he does not accept follow from some of those he does or that some beliefs and practices he is unable to endorse follow inescapably from *B*'s different background, then out of respect for some of his beliefs and practices, *A* would put up rather than interfere with those with which he disagrees

Unlike other conceptions which presuppose the idea that oneness with significant Others as well as with God is achieved by abolishing/ignoring/belittling the radical other, i.e. by eliminating plurality, here, in the second conception, oneness is attained by accepting all radical others as equally significant because they variously manifest one supreme being or concept. Thus, to tolerate is to refrain from interfering in the life of others not despite our hatred for them, or because we are indifferent to them, but because we love them as alternative manifestations of our own selves or deeply care for some basic norm common to all of us. We may not be able to do or be what they are, we may even dislike some of their beliefs and practices, but we recognize that they are translations of our own selves or of gods within each of us. This binds us together in a relationship of lasting affection.

Thus, the moral-practical attitude of equal regard for all religions is a (practical) entailment of a deeper epistemic grasp of the fundamental unity of all re-

---

46 See, for example, Susan Mendus, *Toleration and the limits of Liberalism* (Macmillan, 1989).

ligions. [47]" For Gandhi, "The soul of religion is one, but it is encased in a multitude of forms. The latter will persist to the end of time. Wise men will ignore the outward crust and see the same soul living under a variety of crusts."[48] The basic reference of all religions is the same: God or Truth. "All religions are true and also that all have some error in them and that whilst I hold by my own, I should hold others as dear as Hinduism, from which it logically follows that we should hold all as dear as our nearest kith and kin and that we should make no distinction between them."[49]

This move towards inclusive monotheism flows directly from the most ancient aspects of Indian polytheistic traditions, as mentioned above, a trait they share with other religious traditions of the ancient world.[50] Thus, "all worship the same God although under different names."[51] He illustrates this by a striking verse from the *Grantha Sahib* wherein Guru Nanak says that God may be called by the name of Allah, Rahim and so on. The name does not matter if he is enshrined in our hearts.

Although, Gandhi drew the opposite conclusion – that the move from to another religion or spirituality is redundant – this inclusive monotheism also permits easy movement across religions. If different names refer to the same god or the same god has different cultural backgrounds, then why create too much fuss about leaving one and embracing another? Indeed, why not embrace both, even all?[52] Two more things follow. First, "to revile one another's religion, to make

---

47 "Amidst the endless variety in all religions, one can discern a fundamental unity." Gandhi, *The Way to Communal Harmony*, 41.

48 Gandhi, *The Way to Communal Harmony*, 41.

49 Gandhi, *The Way to Communal Harmony*, 57. "My Hindu instinct tells me that all religions are more or less true. All proceed from the same God but are imperfect because they have come down to us through imperfect human instrumentality."

50 Gandhi, *The Way to Communal Harmony*, 58.

51 Gandhi, *The Way to Communal Harmony*, 42.

52 On multiple allegiances in India, see Margaret Chatterjee," Reflections on Religious Pluralism in the Indian Context," *Journal of Hindu-Christian Studies*, Vol. 7:5 [1994] http://digital commons.butler.edu/jhcs/vol7/iss1/5 Accessed in October 2014. This is possible not only in what might be called the "Indian family of religions" but due to what she calls "behavioural pluralism" among religions outside the Hindu community. She says, "When we come to the relation of Hindus to communities outside the Hindu fold we find here too a largely behavioural adjustment. Hindus in north India often prefer to have their family weddings solemnized in gurdwaras (Sikh temples), for Guru Nanak, the founder of the Sikh faith, is much revered by all communities. Hindus and Muslims visit the shrines of saints and pirs alike. Muslim workmen in some parts of India make the 'idols' used in Hindu worship. Again, the musicians who accompany dancers of classical dance forms (which usually have themes from Hindu mythology) are commonly Muslim." Chatterjee also discusses Indian henotheism, which supports pluralism.

reckless statements, to utter untruth, to break the heads of innocent men, to desecrate temples or mosques *is* a denial of God." Second, "it is wrong for anyone to say that his God is superior to that of another's. God is one and the same for all."[53] At one level, there is a fundamental unity among all religions and precisely because of it they must be regarded as equal. If so, movements of conversion or purification are pointless. "The real Shuddhi movement consists in each one trying to arrive at perfection in his or her own faith. In such a plan character is the only test. What is the use of crossing from one compartment to another, if it does not mean a moral rise?"[54] The political implication of this is that "it is the duty of the government to offer protection to all who look up to it, wherever they are and to whatever religion they belong."[55]

Soon after Independence, this idea found articulation in public discourse as secularism – strictly speaking, political secularism. The state must show *sarvadharma sambhāv* (be equally well disposed to all paths, god, or gods, all religions, even all philosophical conceptions of the ultimate good). But this should not be confused with what is called multiple establishment, where the state has formal ties with all religions, endorses all of them, and helps all of them, and where it allows each to flourish in the direction in which it found them, to let them grow with all their excrescences, as for example, in the Millet system and the imperial British rule. Rather, the task of the state as an entity separate from all religions was to ensure trust between religious communities, to restore basic confidence if and when it was undermined. This happens under conditions when there is a threat of interreligious domination, and when a majority religion threatens to marginalize minority religions. So here secularism is pitted against what in India is pejoratively called communalism – a sensibility or ideology where a community's identity, its core beliefs, practices and interests are constitutively opposed to the identity and interests of another community.

To generalize even more, secularism came to be used for a certain comportment of the state, whereby it must distance itself from all religious and philosophical conceptions in order to perform its primary function, that is, to promote a certain quality of fraternity or sociability, to foster a certain quality of relations among religious communities, perhaps even inter-religious equality under conditions of deep religious diversity.

---

53 Chatterjee, 43
54 Chatterjee, 58.
55 Chatterjee, 58.

2.1.2 The principled distance model

A second conception developed, too, even more ambitious, that tried to combine the aim of fostering better quality of social relations among all religious and non-religious perspectives with an emancipatory agenda driven by a critique from the outside (from a secular, non-religious perspective) of all religions, to not only respect all religions and philosophies but to protect individuals from the oppressive features of their own religions or religious communities – or to put it differently, to confront and fight both inter-religious, intra-religious domination, the domination of the secular by the religious and of the religious by the secular – all of these simultaneously. This is the constitutional secularism of India.

Several features of this model, found in the Indian Constitution read appropriately, make it distinctive, of which I mention a few. *First*, the presence of deep religious diversity and the simultaneous availability of secular perspectives is taken to be a natural part of the social landscape. Second, because it was born in a deeply multi-religious society, it is concerned as much with inter-religious domination as it is with intra-religious domination. Thus, it recognizes community-specific, socio-cultural rights. Although community-specific political rights (special representation rights for religious minorities, such as Muslims) were withheld in India for contextual reasons, the conceptual space for it is present within the model. At the same time, secular perspectives are not forgotten. Parliamentarians or state officials taking oath of office can do so either by invoking their religion or their own conscience. Third, its multi-value character. Indian secularism more explicitly registers its ties with values forgotten by western conceptions – for example, peace between communities – and interprets liberty and equality both individualistically and non-individualistically. It has a place not only for rights of individuals to profess their religious or non-religious beliefs, but, as mentioned above, also for the rights of religious communities to establish and maintain educational institutions crucial to the survival and sustenance of their religious traditions. These religious educational institutions coexist with those that are purely secular. Individuals may choose their community-specific personal laws or opt for a non-religiously grounded common civil code. *Fourth*, it is committed to the idea of principled distance,[56] poles apart from one-sided exclusion, mutual exclusion and strict neutrality or equidistance.

This feature needs further elucidation. For mainstream western secularisms, separation means mutual exclusion, one-sided exclusion or distance that supports one kind of secularity and one particular, preferred religion. The idea of

---

56 See section below.

principled distance unpacks the metaphor of separation differently. It accepts a disconnection between state and religion at the level of ends and institutions, but does not make a fetish of it at the third level of policy and law. (This distinguishes it from all other models of secularism, moral and amoral, that disconnect state and religion at this third level.) How else can it be in a society where religion frames some of its deepest interests? Recall that political secularism is an ethic whose concerns relating to religion are similar to theories that oppose unjust restrictions on freedom, morally indefensible inequalities, intercommunal domination and exploitation. Yet a secularism based on principled distance is not committed to the mainstream Enlightenment idea of religion. It accepts that humans have an interest in relating to something beyond themselves including God and that this manifests itself as individual belief and feeling as well as social practice in the public domain. It also accepts that religion is a cumulative tradition[57] as well as a source of people's identities. But it insists that even if it turned out that God exists and that one religion is true and others false, then this does not give the "true" doctrine or religion the right to force it down the throats of others who do not believe it. Nor does it give a ground for discrimination in the equal distribution of liberties and other valuable resources. Similarly, a secularism based on principled distance accepts that religion may not have special public significance antecedently written into and defining the very character of the state or the nation, but it does not follow from this that it has no public significance at all. Sometimes, in some versions of it, the wall of separation thesis assumes precisely that.

But what precisely is principled distance? The policy of principled distance entails a flexible approach on the question of inclusion/exclusion of religion and the engagement/disengagement of the state, which at the third level of law and policy depends on the context, nature or current state of relevant religions. This engagement must be governed by principles undergirding a secular state, that is, principles that flow from a commitment to the values mentioned above. This means that religion may intervene in the affairs of the state if such intervention promotes freedom, equality or any other value integral to secularism. For example, citizens may support a coercive law of the state grounded purely in a religious rationale if this law is compatible with freedom or equality.[58] Equally,

---

57 W. C. Smith, *The Meaning and End of Religion*, 1991, 154–69.
58 Principled distance rejects the standard liberal idea that the principle of equal respect is best realized only when people come into the public domain by leaving their religious reasons behind. Principled distance does not discourage public justification. Indeed it encourages people to pursue public justification. However, if the attempt at public justification fails, it enjoins religiously minded citizens to abandon restraint and support coercive laws that are consistent with

the state may engage with religion or disengage from it, engage positively or negatively; but it does so depending entirely on whether or not these values are promoted or undermined. This is one constitutive idea of principled distance. This idea is different from strict neutrality, that is, the state may help or hinder all religions to an equal degree and in the same manner, so that if it intervenes in one religion, it must also do so in others. Rather, it rests upon a distinction explicitly drawn by the American philosopher, Ronald Dworkin, between equal treatment and treating everyone as an equal.[59] Treating people as equals entails that every person or group be treated with equal concern and respect. It may sometimes require equal treatment – say equal distribution of resources –but it occasionally also dictates unequal treatment. Thus treating people or groups as equals is entirely consistent with differential treatment. This idea is the second ingredient in what I have called principled distance.

I said that principled distance allows for differential treatment, crucial in multi-religious societies and consistent with non-religious, secular worldviews. What kind of treatment do I have in mind? First, religious groups have sought exemptions from practices in which states intervene by promulgating a law to be applied neutrally to the rest of society. For example, Sikhs demand exemptions from mandatory helmet laws and from police dress codes to accommodate religiously required turbans. Muslim women and girls demand that the state not interfere in their religiously required chador. Principled distance allows then that a practice that is banned or regulated in one culture may be permitted in the minority culture because of the distinctive meaning it has for its members. For the mainstream conception, this is a problem because of their simple, somewhat absolutist morality that gives overwhelming importance to one value, particularly to equal treatment, equal liberty or equality of individual citizenship. Religious groups may demand that the state refrain from interference in their practices but they may equally demand that the state give them special assistance so that these groups are also able to secure what other groups are able to routinely get by virtue of their dominance in the political community. For example, it may grant authority to religious officials to perform legally binding marriages or to have their own rules of obtaining a divorce. Principled distance allows the possibility of such policies on the grounds that it might be unfair to hold people accountable to an unfair law.

---

freedom and equality based purely on religious reasons. See Christopher Eberle, *Religious Conviction in Liberal Politics* (Cambridge: Cambridge University Press, 2002).

59 Ronald Dworkin, *Taking Rights Seriously* (Cambridge, MA: Harvard University Press, 1978), 125.

However, principled distance is not just a recipe for differential treatment in the form of special exemptions. It may even require state intervention in some religions more than in others, considering the historical and social condition of all relevant religions. For the promotion of a particular value constitutive of secularism, some religions, relative to other religions, may require more interference from the state. For example, suppose that the value to be advanced is social equality. This requires, in part, undermining caste hierarchies. If this is the aim of the state, then it may be required of the state that it interferes in caste-ridden Hinduism much more than say Islam or Christianity. However, if a diversity-driven religious liberty is the value to be advanced by the state, then it may have to intervene in Christianity and Islam more than in Hinduism. If this is so, the state can neither strictly exclude considerations emanating from religion nor keep strict neutrality with respect to religion. It cannot antecedently decide that it will always refrain from interfering in religions or that it will interfere in each equally. To want to do so would be plainly absurd. All it must ensure is that the relationship between the state and religions is guided by non-sectarian motives consistent with some values and principles.

Fourth, it is marked by a unique combination of active hostility to some aspects of religion (a ban on untouchability and a commitment to make religiously grounded personal laws more gender-just, from a perspective that stands outside religion altogether) with active respect for its other dimensions (religious groups are officially recognized, state-aid is available non-preferentially to educational institutions run by religious communities, no blanket exclusion of religion as mandated by western liberalism). This is a direct consequence of its commitment to multiple values and principled distance. The Indian model accepts the view that critique is consistent with respect; that one does not always have to choose between hostility and respectful indifference. In this sense, it inherits the tradition of the great Indian social reformers who either attacked their religion or tried to change their religions precisely because they meant so much to them.

I have claimed that, in modern India, multiple religious and secular world views coexist, and that among religiously diverse views within the a very broadly defined Hindu fold, an option exists to move from one to another and the modern state in India supports this plurality of multple religiosities and secularities. Though I have not discussed this in this chapter, there are many social and even political restrictions now on free movement across religions that were born in India and those which were born elsewhere. Even so, a healthy tradition of multiple allegiances is still alive, with Hindus and Muslims visiting the same shrine in different parts of the country. Much of this and what I discuss in Section 1, substantiates my claim that in India, people can plausibly say that "we have always been post-secular."

In a symposium held in 1986, Wilfred Cantwell Smith posed a deeply interesting question: "Shall the next century be secular or Religious?" His own answer to that question was "no."[60] He adds, "I hesitate to affirm that the polarity between the two will not in fact last another hundred years. I feel that it should not last; but what I am saying for the moment is that we should not perpetuate it." Smith believed that the terms "secular" and "religious" were pushed upon us by thinkers who understood the world and the human condition within it poorly, and that "our endeavors to think by means of these terms has been proven misleading. We must forge new concepts with which to analyse these matters."[61] With statements such as these, Smith, I believe, inaugurated the post-secular age in the western world, a condition long prevalent in places such as India.

Works Cited

Assman, J. *Of Gods and Gods.* Wisconsin: University of Wisconsin Press, 2008.

Assman, J. *The Price of Monotheism.* Stanford: Stanford University Press, 2010.

Bailey, Greg and Ian Mabbett. *The Sociology of Early Buddhism.* Cambridge: Cambridge University Press, 2006.

Bhargava, Rajeev. "Beyond Toleration – Civility and Principled Co-Existence in Asokan Edicts." In *The Boundaries of Toleration*, edited by Alfred Stepan and Charles Taylor. New York: Columbia University Press, Forthcoming.

Black, Brian. *The Character of the Self in Ancient India.* Albany: SUNY Press, 2007.

Carithers, M. *The Buddha.* Oxford: Oxford University Press, 1983.

Chatterjee, Margaret. "Reflections of Religious Pluralism in the Indian Context." In *Journal of Hindu-Christian Studies.* 7:5 (1994). http://digitalcommons.butler.edu/jhcs/vol7/iss1/5. Accessed in October 2014.

Dworkin, Ronald. *Taking Rights Seriously.* Cambridge, MA: Harvard University press, 1978.

Eberle, Christopher. *Religious Conviction in Liberal Politics.* Cambridge: Cambridge University Press, 2002.

Gandhi, M.K. *The Way to Communal Harmony.* Ahmedabad: Navjivan Publishing House, 1963.

Gombrich, Richard. *Theravada Buddhism – A Social History from Ancient Benaras to Modern Colombo.* London: Routledge and New York: Paul Kegan, 1988.

Jamison S. W. and M. Witzel. *Vedic Hinduism,* Unpublished Text, 1992.

Kaplan, Benjamin. *Divided by Faith.* Cambridge: Harvard University Press, 2010.

Madan, T.N. "Religion in India." In *A Handbook of Indian Sociology*, edited by Veena Das. Page Numbers n.a. New Delhi: Oxford University Press, 2004.

Mendus, Susan. *Toleration and the Limits of Liberalism.* Macmillan, 1989.

---

60 W. C. Smith, "Shall the next century be Secular or Religious?," Tenri International Symposium '86: *Cosmos, Life, Religion: Beyond Humanism* (Tenri, Japan: Tenri University Press, 1988), 125–51. Reprinted in W. C. Smith, *Modern Culture from a Comparative Perspective* (Albany: State University of New York Press, 1997), 65–84.

Nakamura, B. *A Comparative History of Ideas.* Delhi: Motilal Banarsidass Publishers, 1992.

Pollock, Sheldon. *The Language of the Gods in the World of Men–Sanskrit, Culture and Power in Pre-Modern India.* Berkeley: Permanent Black. University of California Press, 2006.

Renou, Louis. *Religions of Ancient India.* Jordan Lectures 1951. London: The Anthlone Press, 1953.

Ross, Kenneth. "Religious Pluralism and the Upanishads." In *Journal of Vaishnava Studies,* 19.1 (Fall 2010), 23–48.

Sharma, Arvind. "Can There Be More Than One Kind of Pluralism?" in *The Myth of Religious Superiority,* edited by Paul F. Knitter, 59–60. Indiana: Orbis Books, 2005.

Smith W.C. "Shall the Next century be Secular or Religious?" Tenri International Symposium '86 and in *Cosmos, Life, Religion: Beyond Humanism,* 125–51. Tenri, Japan: Tenri University Press, 1988. Reprinted in W.C. Smith. *Modern Culture from a Comparative Perspective.* 65–84. Albany: SUNY Press, 1997.

Taylor, Charles. *A Secular Age.* Cambridge, MA: Belknap Press/Harvard University Press, 2007.

Ullucci, Daniel. *The Christian Rejection of Animal Sacrifice.* Oxford: Oxford University Press, 2012.

George Levine
The Troubles of An Unrepentant Secularist

As an unrepentant secularist, I want to insert into these two days of complex and learned discussion of a problem with deep global ramifications, an obvious, simple fact that may not otherwise get discussed: that there are people like me who are secular with a lot more than intellectual conviction, who feel down to their finger tips, in a way that is virtually coterminous with their own sense of being, that there is nothing transcendent anywhere ever and that believing that does not rob the world of its joys. Not taking such belief into account can lead to underestimation of how very difficult it is for secularism to reach that accommodation with religion in the public sphere that *post-secularism* aims for. Secularism is not the last part of the "subtraction story" that Charles Taylor has wanted to belie.[1] It is not just the last step down from belief in God to disbelief; it has, for many of us, at least, become a positive condition, affirmed not as a denial of something, of the supernatural and divine, but as the expression of something we might call the natural human condition. Certainly, secularism has significant historical roots, as Taylor has explored them most famously. But the history, focusing so hard on modes of belief, tends not to take into account the point at which secularity has become not strictly a conscious alternative to religion but a condition rather like breathing.

For the sake of capturing the sense of the secularism I'm talking about, I want to co-opt one of the great sentences of nineteenth-century prose. In the extraordinary last chapter of his *Apologia Pro Vita Sua*, John Henry Newman, accused of deviousness and rhetorical trickery, tries to convey the fullness and authenticity of his belief: he writes that "If I looked into a mirror, and did not see my face, I should have the sort of feeling which actually comes upon me, when I look into this living busy world, and see no reflexion of the Creator."[2] Neither Newman nor I find those "reflexions" in the "living busy world," but for him the absence is shattering, and implies – given his absolute faith – some great aboriginal calamity, out of which he brilliantly builds virtually the whole of Roman Catholic theology. But if things were reversed and I *were* to find such reflexions as intelligent design in the world that Newman so powerfully describes a bit later, with its "conflicts," its "random achievements," its "blind evolution," its disappointments, "the success of evil, physical pain, mental anguish," "cor-

1 Charles Taylor, *A Secular Age* (Cambridge: Harvard University Press, 2007).
2 John Henry Newman, *Apologia Pro Vita Sua* (London: W. Scott Pub. Co., 1864), 157.

ruptions,"[3] then I would be shattered; it would be like not seeing my face in the mirror.

I begin with this sort of existential representation of secularism because I think its visceral strength and its positive conditions need to be on the table if I am to explain why I stick doggedly and unrepentantly to secularism in the face of brilliant cultural critiques from around the globe and from the left. It is not that I oppose the post-secular efforts at accommodation and recognition of the crucial part religions play in politics and the public sphere, but that there is a firm ground, both profoundly felt and, I believe, politically essential that secularists find it extremely hard to yield. Secularism can make claims for itself, not just as the neutral referee among competing sectarianisms, which I believe strongly it must try to be, but as a way of being in the world.

It is unembarrassedly and even at times unreflectingly – if paradoxically – a visceral and moral commitment to modern Western assumptions about reason and evidence, caught in the tradition that sees scientific truth as a crucial human value, taking that as a condition for sustaining globally a livable human society. Although I am concerned that these values might be taken, in the polemics surrounding secularism these days, as provincial and even chauvinistically western, it is difficult for me not to think that such secularism is, by and large, a very good thing. One doesn't have to accept the idea that science is the world's cure-all, but it would be worse than folly not to accept as a standard test of truth the kinds of procedures that have brought science such enormous success across the last three centuries.

Yet this kind of secularism is not now so easy a position to sustain. Secularists like me are under siege from the right (we are used to that) and from the left (we are getting used to that), as we seem to accept parts of the narrative of secularism that sophisticated critics have spent the last few decades exploding: the one in which, in its naiveté, secularism assumes that religious fantasies will finally be worn away by true scientific knowledge, and in which its moral superiority to the various sects whose threats to democracy and civil order it disinterestedly tries to resolve, leads it to subtle assertions of its own power. Secularism, the critique goes, in reality, provides a cover for some pretty bad stuff that has even been theorized into the idea that a war of civilizations is necessary and inevitable. So what is a poor old left-leaning secularist to do?

Secularism is regularly defined (and has often defined itself) as what Charles Taylor calls "a subtraction story," nothing but a paring away from religion its claims about the immanent world. Taylor tries to demonstrate that it is itself,

---

3 Newman, *Apologia Pro Vita Sua,* 157.

if ironically, very much a Christian phenomenon, and in this respect, his analysis conforms to many analyses coming from predominantly non-Christian countries that have had to come to terms with secularism. Secularism is not an unmarked and disinterested force but has a distinct and positive charge, he argues. Since I too am claiming for it a positive charge, though not exactly of the same sort, it would seem that I am undercutting secularism's primary claim to political importance, that it is in a position to adjudicate without prejudice, among contending religions.

The excellent anthology, *Rethinking Secularism*, makes the case that "however one defines secularity and secularism [...] it involves religion. It is either the absence of it, the control over it, the equal treatment of its various forms, or its replacement by the social values common to a secular way of life."[4] But the secularism I've described is no longer just half of a binary with religion. It is not simply a self-important facing of the hard facts of life – Henley's "Invictus," claiming mastery of his fate – but a condition of "meaning," in the broadest sense of that word.

William Connolly has complained that secularism has lacked a "visceral register,"[5] but it is in such a register that I came to this talk, feeling it urgent – in this moment of almost catastrophic religious influence on national politics – to reconsider some of Connolly's critique, the negative implications of the accusations that secularism can be characterized as an enterprise of the left side of the brain. The reign of the amygdala, intellectuals' favorite body part these days, is not new, except as a name provided by neuroscientists for the new intellectual community of lovers of cognitive science. But the recent burst of interest in "the visceral register" recalled to me not the amygdala but the image of George Eliot, in the process of abandoning Christianity, studying the Higher Criticism, translating Strauss's *Das Leben Jesu*, with an image of Thorwaldsen's Christ over her desk. And all of that reminds me of the ethical urgency with which secularism affirms itself, even as the urgency is so largely expounded in commitment to rational argument and empirical evidence.

Beginning with such a manifesto, I am not describing a kind of secularism that fits neatly the role as rational and pragmatic arbiter that many secularists (like me) have claimed for it. In fact, while on the one hand, it seems to give to the secular stance a force of humane engagement that transcends simple rational argument, on the other, it threatens to undercut its assumed role as the

---

4 Craig J. Calhoun, Mark Juergensmeyer and Jonathan VanAntwerpen, *Rethinking Secularism* (Oxford, N.Y.: Oxford University Press, 2011), 5.
5 William E. Connolly, *Why I Am Not a Secularist* (Minneapolis, MN: Univ. of Minnesota Press, 1999), 19–46.

essential condition for a democratic society that seeks space for all sectarianisms while resisting the full claims of any of them.

But it is just here that the real struggles of unrepentant secularism come in. Connolly, who seeks admirably to theorize the incorporation of "deep plurality into existing political pluralism," claims that such a deep plurality is consonant with democracy "if and when an ethos of engagement is negotiated between numerous constituencies honoring different assumptions and moral sources." And this requires "reciprocal acknowledgment by a significant set of partisans of the uncertainty and profound contestability of the metaphysical suppositions and moral sources they honor most."[6] It may be that such acknowledgment will come some day, and that people will reasonably engage across deep cultural and metaphysical divides. But I am dubious about participating in this "ethos of engagement." I ask of anyone sitting at the table with me the willingness to put this-worldly ends first; politically, this means taking the welfare of the state and its people over any other transcendent value. If not, I would see no point in sitting down at the table.

Current history suggests that Connolly's is a utopian imagination. Not least, just because the secular imagination that I am invoking, however much it marks itself as secular by claiming the possibility and the necessity of doubt and self-criticism, is indeed where Connolly puts it, that is, based in profound and unshakeable metaphysical assumptions that have the immediate practical consequence of putting this world first. Making this metaphysical case is fundamental to modern science and to the possibility of our seeing ourselves in the mirror: it is very hard indeed to imagine accommodation to an alternative metaphysics.

Secularism exists in a vast range of paradoxes. On the one hand, it has a felt commitment to the priority of worldly things, and to a rational pursuit of the most humanly satisfying conditions of life. Recognizing that humans are fundamentally social creatures, its highest value is the human success constituted, yes, by life, liberty and the pursuit of happiness, and by a capacity for cooperation and mutual aid, achieved in a natural world that seems otherwise to be red in tooth and claw. And on the other, it comes up against places where it is very hard to imagine participation in an overlapping consensus, where being cooperative, and where compromise becomes something like suicide. How much is lost when transcendent values displace the values of the immanent world? Too much for a secularist, and too dangerous for the survival of a democratic society.

Somewhere, in the secularist's continuing effort to remain open and to recognize the convictions of non-secular groups, a line has to be drawn, despite our

---

6 Connolly, *Why I Am Not a Secularist*, 154.

well justified deep distrust of drawing lines. How does a secularist accommodate to the world's vast majority and the preponderance of diverse religious beliefs in this world? Admirably, post-secularism, up against this kind of problem, seems to be trying to negotiate accommodation. But I worry that it is, in the accommodation, in danger of giving away the store.

The crude American individualist assertion that everyone has a right to his opinion, of course, fogs over the reality that some opinions really are better than others within a context in which we take seriously the fundamental strategies of reason and empiricism. With the greatest respect, I have trouble with the conciliations we talk about these days as post-secular, of the sort that have come in many varieties from distinguished theorists like Taylor and Connolly and more assertively post-secularist and anti-secularist thinkers like Assad and Mahmood. Drawing a firm line around any given issue, like evolution or global warming, as we take as proven what vast scientific consensus argues, makes the "right" opinion as intransigent as the wrong one. The stakes are very high.

What could be more plausible to the intellectual left than the argument that secularism is just one more religion in the contest among religions, not unmarked – for no position can be unmarked – but one of the combatants, and one that has rather shamefully enforced oppression of the West against the East? Secularism, in some of these readings, becomes little more than a tool of Western imperialism. While I grew up thinking that proselytizing Christianity in the form of missionaries, for example, was a tool of Western imperialism, the Mr. Kurtz of the pure faith, recent critiques not only do not exempt secularism, but make it the dominant imperial force. "The whole constellation" of the kind of secularism I have been describing, Taylor says, "generates disastrously ethnocentric judgments."[7] So what I took to be morally innocent, or rather hyper-virtuous secularism is now often taken as a mere disguise for forces I thought I was repelled by. Why, then, as a secularist, remain so suspicious of so democratic an ideal, one that honors cultural diversity, digs deep into history, and asks for more seats at the table for religion, at least proportionate to its overwhelming majority around the world?

Religion's role in making morality central in any discussion in the public sphere remains a vital myth. "According to post-secularist theory," Nadia Urbinati has noted, "under secularism democracy becomes an empty shell," but

---

7 Charles Taylor, "Religion Is Not the Problem: Secularism and Democracy," *Commonweal* (February 25, 2011): 18.

we know quite well "that democratic rules are thick with moral principles."[8] The energy driving most secular thinking is intensely moral: secularists share a deep and for the most part democratic sense of the values of the immanent world. Despite the number of alternate forms secularism has taken, it builds on a deep sense of the overriding value of a stable and diverse society, a deep sense of the value for human fullness according to the best possible understanding of how the world works.

My greatest trouble as unrepentant secularist comes just where Connolly admirably calls for "a deep pluralism:" I am very grudging about welcoming religion to certain parts of the table. I worry about such things as the budgets for the NIH and NSF, about how and what students learn in public schools, about the way states have instituted laws about abortion or closed down abortion clinics, or about how immense problems like global warming get deferred, ignored, or denied. Some of the temper of this chapter follows from an item in the newspaper on the day I began writing, emerged in response to the fact that on the day before the debt crisis was scheduled to hit, "House Republicans began their closed-door meeting [...] with an impromptu rendition of "'Amazing Grace.'"[9] It is very hard to imagine accommodation to actions that flow from the stories that religions tell themselves about the immanent world, which are, to put it simply, not true if one accepts the criteria of evidence with which not only science but most normal worldly activities are conducted. It feels awkward to put it so crudely, but insofar as they are taken literally, religious stories are, or have become, obstructions to the democratic, multi-cultural, economically just ideals of a secular society even if we recognize that ostensibly secular societies have not themselves been able to live up to these ideals. It does not feel coincidental that evangelical religion in North America has become politically synonymous with rejection of the state. Under current conditions in the United States, many religious stories help provide moral cover for destructive behavior. So, while as secularists we are also committed to a more democratic public sphere, I find it hard to imagine how in matters that touch on anything religious the secularist can find that consensus.

---

8 Nadia Urbinati, "The charm of dangerous postsecolarismo," *Revelation Secular.* http://apoc alisselaica.net/en/focus/libri/il-fascino-pericoloso-del-postsecolarismo. Accessed August 3, 2014.
9 Ashley Parker and Jeremy W. Peters. "With G.O.P. Badly Divided, Boehner Is Left 'Herding Cats,'" *The New York Times.* (October 15, 2013). http://www.nytimes.com/2013/10/16/us/poli tics/as-deadline-looms-boehner-herding-cats-in-bid-for-deal.html?pagewanted=all&_r=0. Accessed August 21, 2014.

Had Stephen J. Gould been right in formulating his idea that science and religion occupy what he rather pretentiously called two non-overlapping magisteria, there would be little problem.[10] But history and the daily newspapers seem to belie that argument every day. From the point of view of the American secularist, it feels as though religion constantly inserts itself in matters that would seem to belong in the "magisterium" of science. Some matters of belief don't seem to allow compromises.

At the risk of repeating the obvious, I offer some old news. More people in America believe in the Virgin birth than in evolution; many people believe that if a woman is "really raped," she won't have children by the rapist; 46% of Americans believe that God created humans in their present form within the last 10,000 years. In some religiously oriented cultures – we read about this every day in the papers – women, even as they apparently acquiesce in and thrive in their cultures, are, from the Western point of view, diminished, subjected to sometimes horrifying abuse, under man's control. In Petersburg, Kentucky, there's a very prosperous young earth creation museum, with the motto, "Prepare to Believe," which gets an annual attendance of over a quarter million people. There's an intelligent design think tank in California, "The Discovery Institute," with an income of over four million a year, most from donations from religious institutions and most with distinctly far right political leanings. Just as I thought I should be closing down the list I came across an op-ed piece in the *New York Times* reporting on a poll that showed that eight out of ten Americans believe in angels. So aside from avowedly theocratic states, America is one of the most religious countries in the world. It is hard to get post-secularist here, where we have never really been secular. And as long as I have brought up politics, I'll conclude this litany with the pretty safe opinion that the chances of anyone who isn't avowedly a believer getting elected president here are nil.

"The post-secularist's premise," Bruce Robbins says, "must be that the particular content of the belief is irrelevant. If it is held by enough of those with whom he cohabits, then however grotesque it may seem, the deep pluralism Connolly seeks seems to decree that he must readjust his position on the belief or at least be ready to enter into open-minded dialogue about it."[11] The limits I am talking about in democratic accommodation are just there – *in the particular content of belief.* Despite the widespread view among contemporary intellectuals that in the triumphantly secular world, religion has not been allowed a represen-

---

10 Stephen Jay Gould, *Rocks of Ages: Science and Religion in the Fullness of Life* (New York: Ballantine Pub. Group, 1999).
11 Bruce Robbins, "Why I am Not a Post-Secularist," *boundary 2* 40:1 (2013): 57.

tative place in the public sphere, the American evidence seems to me pointing all in the other direction. Certainly, the United States *is* secular in the sense that everyone realizes that one has the choice to believe or not, but secular in the sense that I have been talking about, it most certainly is not. The constitutional requirement that church and state be separated has not diminished public debate about abortion, or gay marriage, or public morals, or assisted suicide, or children's vaccinations, or public education – all of which topics are almost always addressed from religious perspectives.

My argument here has been far too deeply inflected by the American experience, but I stand by the point that remaining an unrepentant secularist entails a reconsideration of that wonderfully reasonable ambition of Connolly's post-secular stance. In the end, the questions are not ultimately about the religion/secular binary to which we almost always return, but about how we manage to induce the world politically and economically to become more fair, more just. Our priorities must be in the immanent world and our ethical and legal practices, however much we might be willing to agree that they have developed out of religious traditions, have to be worked out outside of those religions in the very difficult here and now.

Works Cited

Calhoun, Craig J., Mark Juergensmeyer and Jonathan VanAntwerpen. *Rethinking Secularism*. Oxford, N.Y.: Oxford University Press, 2011.

Connolly, William E. *Why I Am Not a Secularist*. Minneapolis, MN: Univ. of Minnesota Press, 1999.

Gould, Stephen Jay. *Rocks of Ages: Science and Religion in the Fullness of Life*. New York: Ballantine Pub. Group, 1999.

Newman, John Henry. *Apologia Pro Vita Sua*. London: W. Scott Pub. Co., 1864.

Parker, Ashley and Jeremy W. Peters. October 15, 2013. "With G.O.P. Badly Divided, Boehner Is Left 'Herding Cats.'" *The New York Times* http://www.nytimes.com/2013/10/16/us/politics/as-deadline-looms-boehner-herding-cats-in-bid-for-deal.html?pagewanted=all&_r=0. Accessed August 21, 2014.

Robbins, Bruce. "Why I am Not a Post-Secularist." *boundary 2* 40:1 (2013): 55–76.

Taylor, Charles. *A Secular Age*. Cambridge, MA: Belknap Press/Harvard University Press, 2007.

Taylor, Charles. "Religion Is Not the Problem." *Commonweal*, February 25, 2011: 17–21.

Urbinati, Nadia. *Revelation Secular*. "The charm of dangerous postsecolarismo." http://apocalisselaica.net/en/focus/libri/il-fascino-pericoloso-del-postsecolarismo. Accessed August 3, 2014)

Bruce Robbins
Atheists in Foxholes

In the summer of 2013, I had the good fortune to witness a good secular death. The man who was dying, an 88-year-old optometrist named Jerry Stein, did not believe in any sort of afterlife but was gentle and loving toward the daughter who tried to offer him that consolation as he had been gentle and loving to everyone with whom I ever saw him interact. There was a large crowd at his funeral.

Atheism is not the same thing as secularism; it's not a political doctrine concerning the desirability (and, of course therefore, the possibility) of a separation between church and state. I will ignore the distinction for a moment in order to declare my personal, visceral convictions with a certain crudeness. It is often asserted that secularism's claim to neutrality is false, that secularism is as much a transcendent, dogmatic authority as the religious dogmas it wants to replace. When I hear such assertions, I think of how Jerry Stein died. He died knowing he left behind people he loved and who loved him, but without transcendent consolation of any kind. If to say this is to espouse secularism as "subtraction," a concept we are told (by Charles Taylor and others) that we should shun like the plague, then so be it.[1] Yes, transcendence had been subtracted from his life. And no, it had not been replaced. No secular authority filled the hole left by the absence of religious consolation. The hole stayed empty, and stays empty; for those who remain, the loved one is gone and stays gone. What was secular, as I am now using the word, was Jerry facing the emptiness with honesty and courage. He may have thought, as I think, that his courage and honesty were setting a valuable example for the next generation. But if so, this belief was not the same thing, not even the same kind of thing, as belief in an afterlife, or belief in a higher providential intention behind all pain and suffering, or belief in an omnipotent being who wants to protect you from all harm. All of these had been subtracted, and nothing like them took their place. Jerry died a secular death, and (in my opinion) a good one.

The truism about there being no atheists in foxholes is intended to suggest that in the face of mortality, no one can resist belief in an omnipotent being who wants to protect you from all harm or that everything that happens is intended to happen. This seems to me factually untrue as well as ingeniously misleading. The saying refers to a very particular situation – not just death but violent death, in fact (since people who find themselves in foxholes tend to be quite

---

1 Charles Taylor, *A Secular Age* (Cambridge: Harvard University Press, 2007).

young), violent and premature death. To be still more precise: it refers to death that is violent, premature, and preventable. From this very particular situation it draws, falsely, a universal conclusion about the supposed human need for religion or for "meaning" (whatever that means). I am not at all sure people have any such need.[2] To my mind, a better conclusion would address not the very speculative universal but the undeniable particular: the context of war.

When I looked up the expression "no atheists in foxholes" on Wikipedia, I found the following quotation: "'There are no atheists in foxholes' isn't an argument against atheism; it's an argument against foxholes."[3] Call this a mere debater's point, if you like, but I think it contains the germ of a serious hypothesis. For anyone who wants to speak of secularism in a global or geo-political context, the more pertinent issue is not mortality but war: war, an unpleasantness we could potentially do something about rather than mortality, one about which we can do nothing. This hypothesis would enrich our discussion of secularism in at least two ways. First, as concerns secularism's global dimension: it is the ongoing and predictable pervasiveness of military violence between and within nations that generates those many, many face-to-face confrontations with mortality, confrontations whose consequence, at least sometimes, probably quite often, is a desperate sense of helplessness and vulnerability and a reaching-out for divine help. And second: reference to war would lead us to consider the etymological branch of the word "secular" – a line of meanings that does not set the word against religion but rather is concerned with long periods of time, centuries or generations or ages.

In his recent book on debt, Richard Dienst retells a modern fable by Alexander Kluge called "Strategy from Below."[4] A German schoolteacher is in

---

2 The "meaning" that we think we need is, of course, open to change. Witness the breathtakingly premature deaths of significant, likable characters on recent TV series (*The Wire*, *Game of Thrones*, *Deadwood*, *Boardwalk Empire*, and others). This development is just as striking as the rise of ethically problematic protagonists. Until recently, the deaths of these characters would have seemed totally unacceptable to TV audiences. They challenge the general understanding of the meaning that audiences demand from their entertainment. People watching television no longer seem to need or even want the assurance that everything will work out in the end for those they care about. On this evidence, at least, providential schemes of the "it was meant to be" sort are among those elements that can be subtracted. And we should be glad that they can.

3 The source given is James Morrow, interviewed by Faith Justice, *Strange Horizons*, December 3, 2001.

4 Richard Dienst, *The Bonds of Debt: Borrowing Against the Common Good* (London and NY: Verso, 2011).

a cellar with her three children as Allied bombs begin to fall. What can she do? Which buildings are least likely to collapse or burn? Does she have time to seek a more reliable shelter? The moral of the story, as Dienst paraphrases it, is that "it is too late. Her only chance to develop an effective strategy against the bombers did not occur that morning or even the night before, or in 1939, or in 1933 ... but in 1918, at the end of the previous war, when she would have had to join with thousands of other teachers, to organize and 'teach hard,' in order to build lasting social relationships that might have blocked the rise of Nazis. But Gerda learns the lesson of November 1918 in April 1945: Once upon a time, it would have been possible to turn history around."

Where temporality is concerned, secularism has a bad rap. It is, of course, associated with the process of secularization or modernization. Hence it is also associated with the illusion of modernity as a universal rupture and the naïveté of progressive temporality that goes with that illusion. By now I think we can all recite in unison the phrase from Walter Benjamin taken over by Benedict Anderson: "homogeneous, empty time." Secular chronology is taken to offer an impoverished contrast to the richness of cyclical repetition and meaning-laden kairos. It seems to follow, then, that a secularist must espouse an over-simplified notion of the free, autonomous subject who wills and chooses, thus propelling this temporality forward in a neat linear fashion. When Judith Butler spoke at a 2013 Columbia University event honoring Edward Said ten years after Said's death, she rejected Said's description of criticism as "secular." Said, she said, was too much of a humanist. He believed we create ourselves. Butler declared herself less optimistic about self-knowledge and will. Her own idea of subject formation was (I quote from memory) "more tragic."

There are, of course, versions of secularism that take a relatively positive view of the autonomous, self-knowing subject – I think for example of Stathis Gourgouris's *Lessons in Secular Criticism*, a book which identifies the secular with a radically autonomous self in the present-tense act of choosing. But Gourgouris also claims for the secular the adjective "tragic," and I think the Kluge story backs up that claim by laying out an apprehension of time that is both secular and tragic.[5] "Once upon a time, it would have been possible to turn history around." This sentence is not in the present tense of clear, decisive willing and choosing. It sends us into a richer and more uncertain temporality, full of prolepsis and conditionality. The idea is that in order for young men not to find themselves in foxholes now, in order that mothers trying to protect their children from falling bombs should not find themselves with no good choices, better

---

5 Stathis Gourgouris, *Lessons in Secular Criticism* (New York: Fordham University Press, 2013).

choices had to have been made in the past. You could call this an exhortation about how to act and choose in the present, how to learn from the past so as to make better choices now. Or you could find in it the fatalism of "now, alas, it's too late." Or you could find both. Which is to say, you could call the situation tragic. The bombs were not the will of God. The missing of the opportunity for things to have turned out differently was not foreordained. The opportunity missed was real, and though it was located in a linear and irreversible sequence of events, it must also be considered available to instruct us about our present and about alternative futures. That's what allows us to describe the failure to seize the opportunity as tragic. This passage is secular in the sense of encouraging us to control what it is in our power to control, but it does not make the hubristic error of pretending that everything is always under our power to control.

Those who dislike secularism also tend to dislike modernity. It is because of their quiet disciplinary prejudice against modernity that literary critics have largely given the critics of secularism a free ride. Once upon a time, literary criticism made a case for itself as a disciplinary site of critique by leaning on the romantic/modernist protest against the techno-commercial wasteland that modernity was supposed to have made of the world. This logic automatically invested literature with value as a repository of the values of a neglected cultural past. The discipline has moved on since then, but it has never quite cured itself of its originary weakness for idealizations of past periods. For example, the idealization of the medieval period as a "sea of faith" in Charles Taylor's *A Secular Age* or in *All Things Shining: Reading the Western Classics to Find Meaning in a Secular Age*, by Hubert Dreyfus and Sean Kelly.[6] I recently talked to a medievalist from Northern Ireland. Like me, he was horrified by these idealizations of the Middle Ages and by the empirically unjustified assumption that in that period, or before it, unbelief was simply impossible. But coming from Northern Ireland, he was especially horrified because he has personal and up-to-date knowledge of the sort of religious-inspired bloodshed that the political doctrine of secularism was invented in order to discourage.

Had I more time, I would have liked to talk more about secular time – for example, geological time, which did so much to shake faith in the Biblical account of the creation in the nineteenth century, and about the astronomical or cosmological time-scale, the scale on which suns flicker and go out. The prospect

---

6 Hubert Dreyfus and Sean Dorrance Kelly, *All Things Shining: Reading the Western Classics to Find Meaning in a Secular Age* (NY: Free Press, 2011). I have expressed myself at length on these matters in "Why I Am Not a Post-secularist," *boundary* 2, 40:1 (2013): 55 – 76 and in "Enchantment? No, Thank You" in George Levine, ed., *The Joy of Secularism: 11 Essays for How We Live Now* (Princeton: Princeton University Press, 2011), 74 – 94.

of the sun's extinction (or, as the newspaper informs me this morning, that another galaxy will collide with ours in about two billion years) suggests to me that ultimate meaning, properly considered, ought not to be decisive in the conversations we are having here and now about activism and the humanities. On the contrary, it is perhaps something we might learn to do without. Ultimately, life on earth will disappear, most likely without a trace. I would also have liked to talk about the period that is coming to be called the Anthropocene, which is secular again in the sense that it claims a very extended time-scale but also, I would argue, in the sense that is defined by human action (on the environment) without in the least flattering the ability of human action now to undo the combined effects of past actions and natural processes. There is a considerable number of American voters who believe we need not worry about global warming because God can turn the Earth's thermostat up and down at will. I hope you agree that it would be a good thing if we could subtract from that number, and even (here I am less sure of agreement) if by our actions as teachers of the humanities that belief itself could be subtracted.

What does the adjective "global" add to our reflections on secularism? It reminds us, of course, of the existence of secularisms, plural – especially non-European or "native" secularisms, modes of cohabitation (as between Hindus and Muslims in South Asia) that emerged without any help or hindrance from European colonialism, and that, therefore, cannot be disposed of by the crude but not infrequent charge that secularism is simply European imperialism in a new guise. Those who think that secularization never really happened, that secularism is only Christianity lording it over other religions by pretending not to be a religion, like my colleague Gil Anidjar, are in particularly acute need of this more global perspective.[7] I, for one, would like to see imperialism taken out of this discussion. This might be another advantage of expanding our time-scale. If we could add to the discussion pre-modern, non-European versions of colonial conquest, it would do something to discourage the chain of invective that leads back and forth between secularism, secularization, and Europe as the sole source of the world's evil.

From a global perspective, the elephant in the room on topics like ours is the implicit charge that anyone defending secularism is endorsing Eurocentrism – that is, taking Europe as the standard of judgment and disrespecting the majority of the world's people, who continue to practice their traditional religions. There

---

7 See Gil Anidjar, "Secularism," *Critical Inquiry* 33.1 (Autumn 2006): 52 – 77. I comment on this essay in "Said and Secularism," eds., Mina Karavanta and Nina Morgan, *Edward Said and Jacques Derrida: Reconstellating Humanism and the Global Hybrid* (Cambridge: CSP, 2008), 140 – 57.

are all sorts of ironies in this argument, which is less democratic than demographic. One of these ironies is named China, which has the demographics but not the secularism problem. But I'll cut to the chase. We all recognize the geo-political tact dictating that, faced with someone whose life is harder than yours or who is otherwise deprived, disadvantaged, and suffering, you should not add to those sufferings by saying that she or he holds beliefs that are false or harmful to others. There are, no doubt, occasions when we will all want to practice this tact. But we should also try to expand the number of occasions on which it need not be practiced. The present context (conference and volume) is surely one of them. Is there anyone here who wants to claim epistemological immunity for their beliefs? (Raise your hands.) This seems a time and a place to remind ourselves that we can respect people perfectly well without respecting all of their beliefs; in fact, it's more respectful to be forthright about the belief, or unbelief. Even in a global discussion of a global issue, it seems relevant to say that the characteristic American "I'll respect your beliefs, and you respect my beliefs, and we won't say anything more about it" is not an ideal formula for strenuous democratic or academic self-scrutiny or the kind of upsetting of the status quo that would lead to fewer military adventures.

People who work in institutions of higher education have a responsibility to teach. This means a responsibility to teach something that our students don't already know, don't already think, and won't necessarily like to hear. In the US, those who vilify secular humanism from the Christian Right think that the university is already a bastion of it. I'm not sure. I'd like to see a conversation about whether what we teach is secular. What should we teach at a moment when respect for other people's beliefs threatens to become a new excuse for sending young people, British as well as American, to dig foxholes on other people's territory? Yes, secular nationalism is also a danger. But more atheists will mean fewer foxholes, and fewer foxholes will mean more atheists. Do what you can to prevent foxholes – do what you can to satisfy people's non-metaphysical needs, including the need for respect and physical security, needs that for most of the world's peoples are not currently fulfilled, and then wait and see how vociferous the so-called metaphysical needs still are.

What we call secularism at any given moment will, of course, not be the remainder left by a series of subtractions; it will be the sum of a long history of words and images, concepts and practices, all of them tainted and imperfect. About the necessary taintedness and imperfection, the musty smell of the do-it-yourself materials we bring up from history's basement to do our home improvements and our suddenly urgent repair jobs – always a little too late and not quite the right thing – there is a surprising intimacy between Derridean deconstruction and Anglo-Saxon common sense. In other words, secularism is, of course, tainted and imperfect. But to describe it as tainted and imperfect in this way is not to refuse the responsibility of subtracting from it, whenever and wherever possible, the theological vestiges that can be subtracted and that deserve to be subtracted.

Works Cited

Anidjar, Gil. "Secularism." *Critical Inquiry* 33.1 (Autumn 2006): 52 – 77.

Dienst, Richard. *The Bonds of Debt: Borrowing Against the Common Good.* London and NY: Verso, 2011.

Dreyfus, Hubert, and Sean Dorrance Kelly. *All Things Shining: Reading the Western Classics to Find Meaning in a Secular Age.* NY: Free Press, 2011.

Gourgouris, Stathis. *Lessons in Secular Criticism.* New York, Fordham University Press, 2013.

Morrow, James. *Strange Horizons.* Interview by Faith Justice. December 3, 2001. http://en.wiki pedia.org/wiki/There_are_no_atheists_in_foxholes. Accessed July 2014.

Robbins, Bruce. "Enchantment? No, Thank You." In *The Joy of Secularism: 11 Essays for How We Live Now,* edited by George Levine, 74 – 94. Princeton: Princeton University Press, 2011.

Robbins, Bruce. "Said and Secularism." In *Edward Said and Jacques Derrida: Reconstellating Humanism and the Global Hybrid,* edited by Mina Karavanta and Nina Morgan, 140 – 157. Cambridge: CSP, 2008.

Robbins, Bruce. "Why I am Not a Post-Secularist." *boundary 2* 40:1 (2013): 55 – 76.

Taylor, Charles. *A Secular Age.* Cambridge, MA: Belknap Press/Harvard University Press, 2007.

Part II: **Case Studies: Global Secularisms**
A **The Political Sphere**

Rochelle Almeida
Secularism and 'Gazetted' Holidays in India

I begin by noting that the word "secularism" has entirely different connotations in India and in the West. According to Larry A. Hickman, in the US, secularism designates "the ascendency of political control over the public activities of religious institutions (which has in many quarters had the effect of rendering religion a matter of individual choice rather than social conscription)."[1] It connotes neutrality regarding religious belief and requires that human activities and decisions, especially political ones, be unbiased in terms of religious influence. This interpretation of the term "secularism" is to be expected in a country that was perceived, especially during colonial times, as a haven for religious freedom, and which has attracted generations of pilgrims, Huguenots and Jewish settlers, among others.

In India, on the other hand, Secularism means "no religion is to be privileged over any other in the sphere of political life, including education [...] By *legislating* the place of religion in society, secularism in fact provides a safe harbor for religious diversity."[2] Thus, unlike the western concept of secularism that envisions a separation of church and state, the concept of secularism in India involves the acceptance of religious laws (known as Personal Law) as binding on the state, and the equal participation of the state in different religions. In India, Personal Law governs family matters such as marriage and divorce. For non-personal issues, such as commercial matters, the statutes of a uniform civil code prevail. As Flavia Agnes explains in *The Crisis of Secularism in India,* the continuance of Personal Law in India, following the removal of the British in 1947, was intended to ensure all minorities (not just Muslims but Christians and Parsees, as well) "their separate religious and cultural identities."[3]

Secularism's *raison d'etre* in India was the baptism of the nation in blood that flowed between its rival communal groups, divided primarily on the basis of religion, with Hindus, the predominant religious majority, outnumbering minority factions, composed of Muslims and Sikhs. The sub-continent exploded into a bloodbath that broadly coincided with the revelation of Sir Cyril Radcliff's

---

1 Larry A. Hickman, "Secularism, Secularization and John Dewey," *Education and Culture* 25:2, (2009): 21–33.

2 Larry A. Hickman, 21–33, emphasis added.

3 Flavia Agnes, "The Supreme Court, the Media and the Uniform Civil Code Debate in India," in *The Crisis of Secularism in India,* eds. Anuradha Dingwaney Needham and Rajeswari Sunder Rajan (Durham: Duke University Press, 2007), 295.

plan for its partition into the two nation states of India and Pakistan in August of 1947.[4] In this context, Secularism was introduced by its founding fathers as part of India's ideology, mainly as a result of their own introduction to western liberal humanism through higher education in Britain. As liberal humanists, they envisioned an India that would flourish through religious harmony based on the principles of equality. As Anuradha Dingwaney Needham and Rajeswari Sunder Rajan state in *The Crisis of Secularism in India*, the implication was that "[t]he nation is above and apart from religion; religious belief is a matter of private faith; and this secular spirit will bring into being the 'nation' as a viable, homogeneous, governable entity."[5]

Thus, the non-communal leadership of India at the time of the country's independence ensured a non-theocratic state. Although interpretations of the term "secularism" varied, the one sense upon which the country's leaders could agree unequivocally, and which formed the cornerstone of the constitution, was the freedom to practice any religion and to be certain that no discrimination would exist in terms of those religious beliefs and practices in the eyes of the law. Such an ideology, it was hoped, would eliminate Hindu hegemony in a country of diverse, subaltern creeds. It would create security for religious minorities, no matter how minuscule those minorities. It would foster the equality that is intrinsic to a parliamentary democracy.

Nowhere is this ideology of religious freedom more ostentatiously manifest than in India's list of federal holidays – known colloquially, in keeping with British colonial tradition, as "Bank Holidays." An examination of the list of the current Bank Holidays in India shows that they far outnumber those in other secular democracies. Since Bank Holidays (also known as Public Holidays in India) vary from state to state, it is impossible to put a number on them. Suffice it to say, however, that while the USA provides 11 national federal holidays, India has no less than 17 –- based on what are known as 'Gazetted' Holidays, that is, national holidays that keep federal offices shut.[6] Singapore, an equally diverse former British colony, gives its people 10 public holidays.[7]

---

4 Dominic Lapierre and Larry Collins, *Freedom at Midnight* (New York: Simon and Schuster, 1975) provides a detailed account of the manner in which the geographical partitioning of the sub-continent led to a mass migration that resulted in unprecedented communal violence, bloodshed and loss of life.

5 Anuradha Dingwaney Needham and Rajeswari Sunder Rajan, *The Crisis of Secularism in India* (Durham: Duke University Press, 2007), 6.

6 See Government of India's National Portal website: http://india.gov.in/calendar/2014 – 12 for a list of Gazetted Holidays. (July 28, 2014)

In addition to national Gazetted Holidays, at its discretion each state may add a number of holidays based on the particular traditions of its people. Thus, in the state of Kerala, Onam is a holiday, while the people of Tamil Nadu celebrate Pongal (both holidays are associated with the customs and rituals of harvest and are restricted to the states that celebrate them). This provision makes the Indian calendar read like a Farmer's Almanac. Indeed, in some cases, holidays associated with the seasons are also Gazetted Holidays. For example, Holi (known as Baisakhi in the predominantly-Sikh Punjab), celebrated in the north of India at the onset of spring is marked by a national public holiday throughout the country.

The official government website of India divides the possible Indian holidays into Gazetted and Restricted Ones. Various other categorizations of holidays exist. For example, *Patriotic Holidays* are Gazetted Holidays. They mark dates associated with the country's history. Thus Independence Day (August 15) is a Gazetted Holiday, as is Republic Day (January 26), the date on which India's Constitution was implemented (in 1950). Patriotic Holidays mark the birth of India's national heroes and martyrs, such as October 2, Gandhi Jayanti, birthday of the Father of the Nation. The birthday of Netaji Subhas Chandra Bose, associated with freedom-fighting, especially among the Bengalis of West Bengal from where he hailed, is marked as Bose Jayanti. Compare India's plethora of holidays to Singapore, for example, which has none other than National Day. It grants no holidays associated with individual patriots.

My point of departure in this chapter, however, is the allocation of *Religious Holidays* – ironically, as an indication of a nation's commitment to secularism. I focus on those holidays that relate to the births or deaths of the founders of individual religions. For example, the birthday of Guru Nanak, founder of Sikhism, is celebrated in India with a national public holiday called Guru Nanak Jayanti, while the birthday of Jesus Christ is celebrated throughout India on December 25 as Christmas. The dates on which practitioners of various religions celebrate New Year also feature on this list. Thus, Diwali, the Hindu festival of Lights, celebrated with pomp and splendor all across India as the Hindu New Year, appears on the list with Navroz, traditionally celebrated in Iran (formerly Persia) as the Spring Equinox, but associated in India with the New Year of Zoroastrians, also known as Parsees, who fled to India to escape persecution following the Muslim conquest of Persia. The fact that Parsees are a small minority in India

---

7 See Singapore Government's Ministry of Manpower website: http://www.mom.gov.sg/employment-practices/leave-and-holidays/Pages/public-holidays-2014.aspx for a list of Public Holidays. (July 28, 2014)

matters little in the allocation of their New Year as a national holiday. The fact that their numbers have been dwindling in India (as indeed in the rest of the world) does not signify either.[8] In keeping with India's secular ideology, all religions (theoretically) merit equal recognition in terms of allocation of Gazetted Holidays.

It is interesting to note that whereas in the "secular" USA, Good Friday is not a federal holiday, despite the fact that Christianity is the dominant religion among the US population, in India it is a Gazetted Holiday, with both national and state administrative offices shutting down completely. Indian Christians, not accustomed to the American ideology of separation of church and state and educated under a British colonial Christian tradition that kept the country closed on Good Friday, consider it sacrilegious, on first arriving in the USA, to find that on Good Friday, it is business as usual in America. Having noted this, it is curious that although Judaism arrived in India as long as 2,500 years ago, when the Cochin Jews are first known to have settled in Kerala in south India, neither Gazetted nor Restricted Holidays give a nod to Judaism in India. The fact that most of India's Jews have relocated to Israel since its formation in 1948 probably has much to do with the omission of Jewish holidays on the gazetted list. But given its commitment to a particular form of secularism, Jewish holidays should technically feature on the calendar in the same way that Parsee ones do. Supposedly, the allocation of Gazetted Holidays should not depend on the size of the religious population. Daniel J. Elazar of the Jerusalem Center for Public Affairs puts the current population of India's Jews at between "seven to eight thousand, according to the official estimates, most of Bene Israel origin."[9] Compared to the Parsees, who currently number 69,000, the Jewish presence in India is tiny, which partly explains why lobbying for Jewish rights in India remains largely ineffective.

On the other hand, India maintains an array of Gazetted Holidays related solely to Islam (Bakhri Eid, Ramzan Eid and Muharam). Although a minority, Muslims have been a vocal segment of India's population since India's independence. The inclusion of no less than three Gazetted Islamic holidays on the Indian calendar clearly indicates a desire on the part of the nation's founding fathers to placate minority insecurities and demands by making their concerns a federal

---

8 See Dean Nelson, "Indian's Dwindling Parsi Population to Be Boosted by Fertility Clinics." *The Telegraph*, New Delhi, October 16, 2012. http://www.telegraph.co.uk/news/worldnews/asia/india/9612009/Indias-dwindling-Parsi-population-to-be-boosted-with-fertility-clinics.html. Accessed September 15, 2014.

9 Daniel J. Elazar, "The Jewish Community of India". Jewish Community Studies. Jerusalem Center for Public Affairs. http://www.jcpa.org/dje/articles2/india.htm. Accessed July 28, 2014.

priority. Most likely, any attempt to curtail Muslim holidays in India would meet with vociferous protests from a well-mobilized, organized minority, whose members would brook no interference in their observance of religious practices.

Interestingly, it was not until 1976, in the midst of a state of emergency imposed by then Prime Minister Indira Gandhi, that the word "secular" first entered the Indian vocabulary in terms of rights, freedoms and responsibilities enshrined within its Constitution. By the Forty-Second Amendment to the Constitution, enacted in 1976, attempts were made to reduce the powers of India's High Courts and Supreme Court. It declared India to be a "socialist" and "secular" republic – these words were added to the Preamble of the Constitution of India presumably to ensure the "unity" and "integrity" of the country. The Forty-Second Amendment to the Constitution is still considered to be the most momentous ever enacted. In outlining the fundamental duties of the citizens and achieving the kind of widespread changes that it did, it has come to be known as a mini-constitution, and more sarcastically, as "the Constitution of Indira." Subsequent amendments (the Forty-Third and the Forty-Fourth), achieved through the intervention of the Janata Government that followed Indira Gandhi's Emergency in 1977, sought to reverse these changes, and did, to some extent, achieve their objectives.

The reason that secularism as a concept had not featured in India's Constitution prior to this date is attributed to the fact that no particularly significant national case concerning religious rights had emerged until then to upset the status quo, that is, to take precedence over the statutes that would govern a uniform civil code. However, just after the inclusion of the term "secular" in India's Constitution, a number of high-profile cases concerning women and minorities brought attention to the particular provisions of the Constitution and highlighted the fact that despite its professed secularism, only very precarious protections existed for these segments of India's population in the eyes of the law.

For instance, the Shah Bano case of the 1980s threw light on the subaltern status of Muslim women in India with regards to divorce and alimony when governed by Muslim Personal Law. Disregarding its restrictions that bestowed upon Shah Bano a one-time lump sum payment, the Supreme Court ruled that she could receive monthly alimony payments. India's orthodox, male-dominated, Islamic leadership challenged the ruling. This caused the elected Congress Government to play into the hands of India's Muslim patriarchy by overturning the Supreme Court ruling and depriving the petitioner of monthly alimony payments, thus leaving Shah Bano virtually destitute.

Needless to say, the ruling Congress Party, which then enjoyed a majority in Parliament, was perceived as severely curtailing the rights of Muslim women in India. In his book, *Altered Destinations: Self, Society and Nation in India*, Makarand Paranjape sees the overruling of the Supreme Court verdict in the Shah Bano case as one of the examples of the Congress Party's pseudo-secular tactics which allowed "cynical manipulation of religion for political ends."[10] Flavia Agnes agrees. She states: "[t]his move by the ruling Congress Party headed by Rajiv Gandhi came to be projected as the most glaring instance of the defeat of the principle of gender justice for Indian women as well as the defeat of secular principles within the Indian polity."[11]

Thus, what becomes evident from this instance of the Congress government's gendered response in the Shah Bano case and by the presence of three Islamic holidays on the Indian calendar is that every attempt is made to acknowledge and placate the Muslim minority in India – or at least the male members of its hierarchy. Repeatedly, in complex matters intertwined with the workings of Personal Law in India, ruling governments cave under pressure exerted by minority religious clergy and, in displaying concern for electoral results rather than for safeguarding women's rights, err on the side of caution. Herein lies the dilemma that Partha Chatterjee examines in his essay entitled, "The Contradictions of Secularism."[12] Here was the Congress confronted with two facets of the term "minority" – for Shah Bano was a Muslim *and* a woman. Whose rights should the Congress have prioritized under the circumstances? Those of women? Or those of Muslims? She clearly had rights as a woman; but what was made clear by the manner in which the controversy was resolved was that, as a Muslim woman, her entitlement was limited. Evidently, the Congress Party was caught between a rock and a hard place; having historically represented itself as a champion of Indian minority rights through its secular ideology, it displayed what came to be perceived as fear of loss of the Muslim vote over the Shah Bano issue. Thus, although feminists protested vehemently at the time in their efforts to protect her interests and that of all Indian Muslim women, the Indian government took the course of bowing to the demands of Islamist theocracy. Chatterjee quotes from a letter by a female Muslim journalist, who in another context involving the challenge to Islamic orthodoxy in India, had written, "[h]ow much longer will political leaders succumb to the imams and put a lid on reforms within Muslim society?"[13]

---

10 Makarand Paranjape, *Altered Destinations: Self, Society and Nation in India* (New Delhi: Anthem Press, 2009), 50.

11 Agnes, 307.

12 Partha Chatterjee, "The Contradictions of Secularism," In *The Crisis of Secularism in India*, eds. Anuradha Dingwaney Needham and Rajeswari Sunder Rajan (Durham and London: Duke University Press, 2007), 153.

13 Chatterjee,153. Quoted from a letter by Fatema Begum, Bagnan, Howrah, in *Anandabajar Patrika*, February 28, 2002.

In reacting as it eventually did, the Congress allowed secularism in India to move quickly, as Dingwaney and Sunder Rajan put it, "from its basis in arguments about national unification to legitimizing the state's regulation of 'difference.'"[14] Repeated demands by the Supreme Court for the enactment of a Uniform Civil Code in India had led to debates about how secularism and multiculturalism are played out within the communally vitiated political climate. Agnes is therefore right in questioning whether the enactment of a Uniform Civil Code can in itself guarantee gender and minority equality in the Indian context.[15]

The Shah Bano debate served to unearth the startling dichotomies that exist in contemporary, post-colonial India. It underscored the binaries that dwell amidst the modernist ethos between secularism and nationalism on the one hand and chauvinism and orthodoxy on the other, aspects that innumerable commentators believe to be the natural outcome of a nation that has become so rapidly globalized, affluent and populated by a restless upwardly mobile middle class. As Agnes explains:

> As the debate progressed, the media projected two insular and mutually exclusive positions: those who opposed the bill and supported the demand of a UCC [Uniform Civil Code] were represented as modern, secular, and rational, while those on the opposing side were viewed as fundamentalist, orthodox, male chauvinist, communal and obscurantist. To be progressive, modern and secular was also to be nationalist; conversely the opposing faction could be labeled as antinational.[16]

As the controversy escalated, many Muslims were mobilized into viewing the situation as yet another threat to their tenuous security in India. The rigid stance of Muslim leadership provided right-wing Hindu forces with the fuel they craved for their anti-Muslim propaganda. Meanwhile, the Muslim intelligentsia, states Agnes, "distanced itself from the opinion of the Muslim religious leadership and approached the government with a petition supporting the Judgment and opposing the proposed bill."[17] Although of Muslim heritage themselves, they sided with the Supreme Court ruling because, as they saw it, it set a precedent that would protect the rights of divorced Muslim women in India. As Agnes explains, the Congress's dilemma stemmed from the tension that periodically surfaces in India between two constitutional guarantees: that of equality and non-

---

14 Dingwaney Needham and Rajeswari Sunder Rajan, *The Crisis of Secularism in India* (Durham: Duke University Press, 2007), 8.

15 Agnes, 294.

16 Agnes, 308–9.

17 Agnes, 308–9.

discrimination (under Articles 14 and 15 of the Indian Constitution) on the one hand, and of religious freedom and cultural plurality (under Articles 25–28) on the other.[18] The raging crisis was terminated when Shah Bano made a public statement renouncing her claim. She stated that if the entitlement was against her religion, she would rather be a devout Muslim than a woman spared financial worry. Agnes states that Shah Bano's stance "strengthened the popular misconception that Islam subverts the economic rights of women."[19] Although the hastily drafted statute that followed was full of contradictions that led to prolonged responses challenging its constitutionality rather than examining its viability, the act acquired tremendous historical significance as it represented the first attempt made in independent India to codify Muslim Personal Law. It opened up the field for even more concern about the rights of India's minorities in a country that, at the end of the twentieth century, became rapidly dichotomized on all sorts of issues—not just those that exclusively concerned women.

The question of the rights of India's minorities within the secular framework of the country was also challenged by the Mandal Commission Report of 1980. Set up by then Prime Minister Morarji Desai, the report was a sincere attempt to incorporate India's Backward Classes (known as Scheduled Castes and Scheduled Tribes or SCSTs) into the mainstream, by offering the kind of affirmative action programs that exist in many countries where social and economic disparities prevail. By the terms of the report, underprivileged segments of India's society were entitled to "reserved" seats in educational institutions and jobs in government-run institutions (the public sector). Aimed at boosting the literacy levels of the underprivileged, and, in doing so, preparing them for improved job opportunities, as opposed to the menial jobs they had traditionally undertaken as India's Untouchables, attempts to implement the Mandal Commission's Report – so-called because B.P. Mandal chaired it – backfired badly.

When then Prime Minister V.P. Singh tried to implement the recommendations of the report in 1989, the nation was rocked by protests led mainly by students of Delhi University, who alleged that reservation of seats on the basis of birth rather than meritocracy was unconstitutional, indeed that it represented reverse discrimination. Faced with resolving the issue, as in the Shah Bano case, the Congress Party (at that time in the opposition) fanned the political flames, fueling protests in an attempt to bring down the coalition opposition government of V.P Singh. Once again, the question of whether India's political parties were really interested in safeguarding the rights of its unfortunate minorities or inter-

---

18 Agnes, 294.
19 Agnes, 308.

ested only in securing power at the polls became the controversy of the day. These responses from the Congress bred cynicism about its oft-articulated, secularist mandate.

Yet another historical occurrence that brought aspects of India's secularism sharply to the forefront was the storming and subsequent demolition of the Babri Masjid in Ayodhya in the Faisalabad district of Uttar Pradesh in 1992. Built in 1527 by Babar, the first Moghul emperor of India and named after him, the Babri Masjid became the target of right-wing Hindu fundamentalists primarily from the Bharatiya Janata Party (BJP), through the creation of the Ram Janmabhoomi Movement in the early 1990s. Having advocated the ideology of Hindutva (a belief in Hindu supremacy) and attempting to force minorities such as Muslims to accept a position of inferiority in India, they alleged that the mosque was forcibly built on the legendary birth place of the Hindu Lord Rama, and therefore, that it ought to be razed to the ground. When dissent on this issue flared up, their state government assured Uttar Pradesh's 31 million Muslims that any attempt to destroy the mosque would be immediately thwarted by the authorities. However, when a rally of 150,000 Hindu protestors quickly escalated into a riot at the site of the mosque that led to a systematic razing of the building, the authorities did nothing but watch helplessly as the mosque was destroyed. The destruction of the Babri Masjid has become an enduring symbol of the erosion of minority rights in India and the national rise of Hindutva power which over time, has become synonymous with nationalism.

The destruction of the Babri-Masjid, more than any other issue in India since Partition, pitched Hindus against Muslims in ways that augured poorly for the decade to follow. Yet, rumblings about the origins of the Babri Masjid are by no means recent. Roger W. Stump states that, "Attempts by Hindus to reclaim possession of it in 1949 led to widespread violence between Hindus and Muslims that forced the government to close the site to both religious groups"[20] The destruction of the Babri Masjid was a watershed moment in India's re-shaping because it provided Hindu nationalists the opportunity to boast publicly of the direction in which they intended to steer the nation. In his book entitled *India After Gandhi*, Ramachandra Guha quotes the polemicist public intellectual Arun Shourie who said, "the Ayodhya movement has to be seen as the starting point of a cultural awareness and understanding that would ultimately result in a complete restructuring of the Indian public life in ways that would be in con-

---

[20] Roger W. Stump, "Religion and the Geographies of War," in *The Geography of War and Peace: From Death Camps to Diplomats*, ed. Colin Flint (New York: Oxford University Press, 2005), 165.

sonance with Indian civilizational heritage."[21] Guha interprets Shourie's pronouncement as "a somewhat roundabout way of saying that the demolition of the Babri Masjid should, and perhaps would, be a prelude to the reshaping of India as a Hindu nation."[22] Indeed, the demolition of the Masjid triggered a court case that dragged on for over a decade, during which time the right-wing Hindutva element in India became more militant, more brazen, and less fearful. Taking refuge in their majority status, they repeatedly challenged minority rights in India, striking fear in the hearts of the county's religious minorities.

The precariousness felt by minorities in India continued through the 1990s. Leaders of Sikh, Muslim and Christian communities watched helplessly through the media hype stirred by Lal Krishna Advani's 'rath yatras' – chariot rides that spanned vast territory of northern India designed to bring urgent national attention to the need for building a Hindu temple to Lord Rama on the site of the mosque. Between 1990 – when he led the first such *yatra* (literally 'journey'), even before the Masjid was demolished – and 2011, when the last *yatra* was held, Advani made a spectacle of Hindu hegemony in India, displaying costumes (saffron robes) and repeating slogans to underscore nationalism. From the rhetoric that accompanied his campaigns, it appeared that his main objective was to assert Hindu supremacy in India through gaudy showmanship and courting of the media.

However, it was finally the incident at Godhra in Gujarat on February 17, 2002 that brought new focus to what Needham and Sunder Rajan call "the Crisis of Secularism"[23] in India. It was alleged that some Muslims had attacked Hindu pilgrims by torching the Sabarmati Express at Godhra railway station upon their return from Ayodhya, site of the Ram Janmabhoomi dispute. Hindus retaliated by brutally targeting Muslims throughout India, but primarily in Gujarat. Although Hindu-Muslim disharmony was by no means historically uncommon in India, what particularly distinguished the communal violence in Gujarat in 2002 from traditional Hindu-Muslim disagreements was the perception of the attacks "as a Hindutva strategy deployed to garner electoral gains and the state's participation in this violence."[24] Reports circulating ever since about the terrible loss of life and destruction of property wrought by the rioting has pointed to the collusion of the state's administrative machinery in the action, even the tacit approval of then Chief Minister of the state, Narendra Modi, who, despite being held

---

[21] Ramachandra Guha, *India After Gandhi: The History of the World's Largest Democracy* (London: Macmillan, 2007), 640.

[22] Guha, *India After Gandhi*, 640

[23] Dingwaney Needham and Rajeswari Sunder Rajan, *The Crisis of Secularism*, 2007.

[24] Dingwaney Needham and Rajeswari Sunder Rajan, *The Crisis of Secularism*, vii.

responsible for genocide by many Indians, emerged as the hero of the hour. Absolving himself of any role in the genocide, Modi attempted to allege that Pakistan was responsible. Indeed, a renowned historian from the Sub-Altern Studies Group, Gyanendra Pandey, writes that in a press note issued by the state government, the incident was described as a "pre-planned inhuman collective violent act of terrorism" conducted by Pakistan.[25] Pandey states that Chief Minister Modi spoke of Pakistan's proxy war and its "clandestine role [...] behind the Godhra genocide."[26] Recurrently, Muslim-instigated communal disharmony in India is conveniently blamed on neighboring Islamic Pakistan.

Indeed, Modi and his government have grown in stature with every claim his party (the BJP) has made on behalf of the Hindu mainstream. Modi has been hailed as "the Sardar opposed to terrorism,"[27] a moniker that refers to Sardar Vallabhai Patel, a highly revered and much respected Hindu Gujarati, prominent in India's achievement of Independence. For the national elections of May 2014, Modi became the likely candidate for India's next Prime Minister, in direct opposition to the ruling Congress Party and its candidate Rahul Gandhi, Nehru's great-grandson. Much to the consternation of the United Progressive Alliance (UPA) headed by the Congress Party, Modi's autocratic style – which allowed him to produce massive infrastructural development, a tax-free industrial haven, and, subsequently, significant economic gains for Gujarat – only served to endear him to his (largely young) supporters, who, far more entrepreneurial than their counterparts in the rest of India, saw him as the country's Next Great Hope. Given Modi's alliance with Gujarat, he was swept into victory in a dramatic electoral landslide in May 2014, making him India's fifteenth Prime Minister.

The tragedy of Godhra underscored more dramatically than ever the helplessness of India's minorities in a supposedly secular environment. In highlighting the rise of Hindu fundamentalism in India, achieved primarily through the popularity of the BJP, Godhra elicited widespread questions about the adequacy of the Constitutional guarantees offered by secularism to the safety and rights of India's minority communities. It is no coincidence that among Christian minorities, for example, doubt is escalating regarding the acceptance and toleration of their largely westernized cultural traditions. Although no official mandates have been issued regarding clothing (unlike that for their Pakistani Christian counter-

25 Quoted by Gyanendra Pandey: "The Secular State and the Limits of Dialogue," In *The Crisis of Secularism in India*, Durham: Duke University Press, 2007, 173.
26 Quoted by Pandey, 173.
27 Quoted by Pandey, 173, from Aakar Patel et al: "Rights and Wrongs: Ordeal by Fire in the Killing Fields of Gujarat". Editors, Guild Fact Finding Mission Report, New Delhi: May 2002, 13.

parts, who decades ago, felt compelled to give up Western clothing and to adopt the traditional *salwar-khameez*), restrictions have been imposed upon Indian Christians in terms of their religious and social practices. The annual 13-hour Adoration, for instance, honoring the Feast of Christ the King, which once wound its ways through multi-creed urban neighborhoods where public altars were erected for the celebration of Mass, are now relegated to Church-owned premises. Similarly, Holy Week services, including Good Friday, usually held in the open-air in church premises in major Indian cities, must now be conducted within the confines of churches. In the city of Mumbai (formerly Bombay), the regional political party known as the Shiv Sena, a rabidly anti-minority body openly vocal about its hatred of Muslims, discouraged Christmas Midnight Masses. The municipal authorities maintained that the public address systems disturb non-Christian residents. Therefore, it is now mandatory for Midnight Masses to conclude before 10.00 PM. Christmas, Easter and New Year gala balls held in Catholic social clubs called "gymkhanas" may no longer continue till the early morning hours, as they had in the decades immediately following Independence. Aside from the "anti-secular" implications of these restrictions, social commentators see such curbs on social freedom as a means by which essentially unique cultural aspects of India's religious minorities will die a quick and unnatural death.

The curtailment of Christian forms of worship and entertainment are the least of the ways in which this small westernized minority feels threatened in India. As early as 1998, four nuns in the Jhabua district of Madhya Pradesh were raped by tribals from the neighboring area. Digvijay Singh, then Chief Minister of the State, faced a defamation civil suit for remarking that Hindu organizations had been involved in the incident. When the issue acquired communal overtones, pitching local Hindus against local Christians, a BJP leader named Uma Bharati stated that some of the alleged rapists were Christians themselves, a matter that is still under dispute.[28] Thus, politics and political leaders rear their heads to court religious majority voters each time minority rights are breached or minority citizens are violated.

Hostility towards Christians was also evident in the horrific case of Dr. Graham Staines, an Australian Protestant missionary. He and his two young sons Phillip (10) and Timothy (6) were burned to death while sleeping in their van in Manoharpur in Odisha in 1999. The incident rocked the country, as the heinous crime not only involved a clergyman (and his children), but appeared to

---

28 "Warrant Against Digvijay Cancelled." *The Hindu.* December 27, 2003, http://www.the hindu.com/2003/12/27/stories/2003122711491300.htm. Accessed September 2014.

be completely unprovoked. Although Bajrang Dal activist Dara Singh was convicted of the crime and is currently serving a life sentence, the incident severely shattered any Christian sense of security. In the debates that followed, right-wing Hindu spokespersons alleged that Staines had been responsible for the forcible conversion of scores of tribals, which played on local Hindu prejudice. Staines's widow, Gladys, vehemently denied the allegation, but her denial faded into the background. Although Staines had been working with the tribal poor of Odisha (particularly leprosy patients) since 1965, anti-Christian politicians called for the cessation of visa issuances for foreign missionaries so as to stop the proselytizing, and the alleged luring of the rural poor to Christianity with material incentives.[29] In commenting on Staines' repugnant death, Guha wrote: "Hindus were a comfortable majority in India, yet the RSS insisted that their pre-eminence was threatened on the one hand by Christian proselytization and on the other by the larger family size of Muslims, this in turn attributed to the practice of polygamy."[30]

In the lengthy and passionate discourse that filled the press at the time, instead of drawing attention to the need for the authorities to ensure the safety of minority citizens in a country that advocates secularism, the focus shifted to the need for missionaries to leave India. This was not a recent development in itself. Since the 1970s, the number of visas granted to foreign Christian clergy had dropped dramatically. Jesuit Spaniards and Italian nuns, who once routinely served as principals and teachers in Catholic convent schools in India's metropolitan cities, have been consistently replaced by Indian clergy and lay teachers.

What message does India send when it honors Good Friday and Christmas as Gazetted Holidays, yet looks the other way, or worse, vilifies the victims, when those who celebrate these holidays are persecuted? Is it any coincidence that since the 1990s, thousands of Indian Christians, mainly from metropolitan cities such as Bombay and Madras (now Mumbai and Chennai), have been applying for immigrant visas, with the opening of New Zealand as a possible site of emigration? Voluntary exoduses *en masse*, provoked by religious insecurity, are not unheard of on the Indian sub-continent. Such an exodus, when it occurs, depletes a country of its diversity.

Gyanendra Pandey sees a co-relation between the deterioration of the status of religious minorities in India and the aftermath of the terrorist attacks on the US on September 11, 2001. He states that the "war against terror has provided

---

29 See "Two Acquitted in Graham Staines' Murder Case," *Times of India*, February 27, 2014. http://timesofindia.indiatimes.com/india/Two-acquitted-in-Graham-Staines-murder-case/article show/31087879.cms. Accessed September 2014.
30 Guha, *India After Gandhi*, 649.

powerful non-secularist groups the opportunity to settle old scores against communities they wish to harass."[31] In the interests of national security, governments and bureaucracies have accumulated increasing powers by which minorities have been suppressed. Indeed, Pandey submits, that

> in many parts of the world, the area of religious belief and observance, and more generally that of cultural practice, is very much subject to this new, illiberal regime. These must now [...] conform to the definitions (and prescriptions) of the 'mainstream'. Instead of constitutionally guaranteed right to diversity of faith and worship and a struggle for tolerance and understanding based on that, what we have in India today is an *intolerance* not so much of particular religious practices or beliefs as of the simple fact of existence of people belonging to other religious denominations.[32]

To sum up the new politics of violence that has emerged from this intolerance, Pandey repeats the adage, *"Pahle Qasai, phir Isai"* (First the Butcher, that is, the Muslim, followed by the Christian). Indeed, if Indian Christians once thought that their informal policy of communal non-interference would grant them immunity from the politics of intolerance, they are increasingly made aware of how mistaken they were. Very recent "morchas" (processions) held in Mumbai have highlighted the plight of the Christian community, a plight that remains ignored because the community is perceived as docile and harmless. Except during elections, when they are regarded as a safe and valuable "vote bank," Christians have remained largely unacknowledged. The community has finally come to accept and adopt mobilization through politicization as a means of ensuring that its voice is heard in India. Although they have remained a largely invisible minority, India's Christians are increasingly uneasy about their future. They echo the fearful sentiments of Geoffrey Morehouse who, in an article in *The Guardian*, had written, "all who care about that country (India) must tremble for the future of its secular democracy."[33]

Despite the threats to security that minority communities face, as Guha writes, "In theory, if less assuredly in practice, India remains a secular state."[34] Because the writ of law still runs, however precariously, over most of India, religious and cultural pluralism has resulted in a country that still honors an extravagant number of public holidays. Indeed, an Indian employed in a state or central government office works much less than his western counterparts,

---

31 Pandey, 174.
32 Pandey, 174.
33 Geoffrey Morehouse, "Chronicle of a Death Foretold," *The Guardian*, March 10, 2001. Accessed September 2014.
34 Guha, *India After Gandhi*, 659.

given vacation and other generous leave policies, combined with the long list of Gazetted Holidays. Yet, attitudes regarding these liberal benefits are changing just as controversies rage regarding the erosion of minority rights. Although one does not wish to indulge in too much speculation, one can now imagine the annulment of some minority Gazetted Holidays as another aspect of the erosion of "secularism" in India.

Works Cited

Agnes, Flavia. "The Supreme Court, the Media, and the Uniform Civil Code Debate in India." In *The Crisis of Secularism in India*, edited by Anuradha Dingwaney Needham and Rajeswari Sunder Rajan, 294–315. Durham: Duke University Press, 2007.

Chatterjee, Partha. "The Contradictions of Secularism". In *The Crisis of Secularism in India*, edited by Anuradha Dingwaney Needham and Rajeswari Sunder Rajan, 141–156. Durham: Duke University Press, 2007.

Elazar, Daniel J. "The Jewish Community of India". Jewish Community Studies. Jerusalem Center for Public Affairs. http://www.jcpa.org/dje/articles2/india.htm

Guha, Ramachandra. *India After Gandhi: The History of the World's Largest Democracy.* London: Macmillan, 2007.

Hickman, Larry A. "Secularism, Secularization and John Dewey". *Education and Culture* 25 :2 (2009): 21–33.

Lapierre, Dominic and Larry Collins. *Freedom at Midnight.* New York: Simon and Schuster, 1975.

List of Indian 'Gazetted' Holidays. See Government of India's National Portal website: http://india.gov.in/calendar/2014–12 (July 28, 2014).

List of Public Holidays in Singapore. Government's Ministry of Manpower website: http://www.mom.gov.sg/employment-practices/leave-and-holidays/Pages/public-holidays-2014.aspx (July 28, 2014).

List of Countries by Zoroastrian Population", Wikipedia: http://en.wikipedia.org/wiki/List_of_countries_by_Zoroastrian_population (July 28, 2014).

Needham, Anuradha Dingwaney and Rajeswari Sunder Rajan, eds. *The Crisis of Secularism in India.* Durham: Duke University Press, 2007.

Morehouse, Geoffrey. "Chronicle of a Death Foretold". *The Guardian* (March 10, 2001).

Nelson, Dean. "India's Dwindling Parsi Population to be Boosted with Fertility Clinics". *The Telegraph*, New Delhi. October 16, 2012. http://www.telegraph.co.uk/news/worldnews/asia/india/9612009/Indias-dwindling-Parsi-population-to-be-boosted-with-fertility-clinics.html. Accessed September 15, 2014.

Pandey, Gyanendra. "The Secular State and the Limits of Dialogue". In *The Crisis of Secularism in India*, edited by Anuradha Dingwaney Needham and Rajeswari Sunder Rajan, 157–176. Durham: Duke University Press, 2007.

Paranjape Makarand. *Altered Destinations: Self, Society and Nation in India.* New Delhi: Anthem Press, 2009.

Stump, Roger W. "Religion and the Geographies of War." In *The Geography of War and Peace: From Death Camps to Diplomats*, edited by Colin Flint, 149–168. New York: Oxford University Press, 2005.

"Two Acquitted in Graham Staines' Murder Case". *Times of India* (February 27, 2014), http://timesofindia.indiatimes.com/india/Two-acquitted-in-Graham-Staines-murder-case/articleshow/31087879.cms Accessed in September 2014.

"Warrant Against Digvijay Cancelled". *The Hindu* (December 27, 2003). http://www.thehindu.com/2003/12/27/stories/2003122711491300.htm Accessed in September 2014.

Arolda Elbasani and Murat Somer[1]

Muslim Secularisms in the European Context

1 Introduction

This chapter contrasts the evolution of secular models in two post-Ottoman Muslim-majority countries in Europe – Turkey and Albania. Both countries, and their respective secular models, have historically developed under the heavy influence of European ideals. Their secular arrangements, established especially during their founding moments in the early twentieth century, reflected these new states' engagement with modern European concepts such as nation- and state-building, central-state authority, and rational differentiation between state and religion. They also reflected the urge the builders of these new states felt to secure their identities as European states by downplaying and controlling the contested role of Islam in a lukewarm, and predominantly Christian, European geopolitical context. Furthermore, secular arrangements in these countries were affected by their peculiar social-demographic, ideational and historical-institutional settings. For example, many Turkish practices simultaneously dismantled and built on late-Ottoman institutions, and Albanian practices tried to maintain interreligious equality. What kind of secular models did Turkey and Albania develop under the influence of Europe? How do these models relate to European secular ideals? What are the institutional devices to discipline and manage the role of Islam? And how have Islamic actors operated within these models – adapted to, contested but also benefited from existing institutional frameworks?

Our analysis follows in four parts. The first part summarizes the main features of contrasting secular traditions within European modernity – civic republican and liberal traditions. The empirical part investigates the founding arrangements and modification of secular systems since the creation of independent states in Albania and Turkey. The second part outlines the features of what we call the state-engineered republican model of secularism, which was institutionalized during the founding moment of both post-Ottoman independent states: 1) selective exclusion of religion from the public sphere; 2) state control of Islam through religious hierarchies; and 3) establishment of an official Islam at

---

1 Names listed in alphabetical order; both authors contributed equally.

home with secular, nationalist and reformist ideas. The third section traces differential modifications of foundational secular models after the Second World War, when communist Albania moved towards the ban of religion, while Turkey's plural politics led to increasing accommodation of Islam. The last part then investigates how revived Islamic actors, after liberalization of the religious sphere in Albania and the success of Islamic parties in Turkey since the 1990s, have navigated the secular system to expand their respective political claims.

By comparing these cases in a long-term perspective, we can, specifically, examine how organized Islamic actors in Turkey and Albania relate to state-engineered secularisms and how they contest, conform with, and try to transform these models. Since the pro-Islamic Justice and Development Party (AKP) assumed and consolidated its power in the 2000s, the case of Turkey gives us the opportunity to examine what Islamic actors do when they actually govern and enjoy the capability to reshape state-engineered secularism. The case of Albania, where the revived Albanian Muslim Community has established an alliance with state structures, allows us to analyze how centralized hierarchies work to maintain stagnant state-controlled features of secularism. In particular, we would like to know to what extent they try to dismantle, instrumentalize, or reform the inherited Republican model in a liberal or more pluralist direction.

2 Models of secularism

The extensive and growing empirical research on the actual practices of secularism indicates that very few countries have effectively realized, or, for that matter, pursued, a strict separation between religion and state.[2] Instead, the institutional and political arrangements that regulate the relation between state and religion reflect a mixture of separation, interaction, cooperation, and enmeshment between the two. Socio-political conditions of time and place inform various secular arrangements, which vacillate somewhere between two broad ideal-type traditions, each proposing different political projects and related institutional solutions within the context of European modernity: civic-republican and liberal traditions.[3]

The civic-republican tradition is rooted in Enlightenment ideas, which consider religion as a source of dogma and tutelage over individual reason and au-

---

2 Daniel Philpott, "Explaining the Political Ambivalence of Religion," *American Political Science Review* 101.3 (2007): 505–25; Jonathan Fox, *A World Survey of Religion and the State* (New York: Cambridge University Press, 2008).
3 Jose Casanova, *Public Religions in the Modern World* (University of Chicago Press, 1994).

tonomy. Constitutive ideas of the Enlightenment such as critique, emancipation, freedom and progress suggest the negation, and, to some extent, reformation of religion by reason. As a social model, the civic-republican tradition encourages secular modernization and heavy social engineering. In terms of the religion and state relationship, it inspires strictly separationist, hostile or reformist attitudes vis-à-vis religion. As a political-institutional model, it supports the emergence of a dominant and often interventionist state that monitors and controls expressions of faith, particularly in the emancipated and rationalized public arena.

By contrast, the historical origins of the liberal view of secularism lie at the post-Reformation religious wars and the way they were settled. In the context of religious conflict and struggle, it became necessary to find a ground for regulating the public domain in a way that allowed different sects to coexist peacefully. The liberal view claimed that such a ground could only be based on "an independent political ethic."[4] Accordingly, the state should safeguard this independent political ethic and, normatively speaking, should be neutral vis-à-vis different religions and sects. As a social model, the liberal tradition inspires a process of bottom-up rather than state-led modernization. In terms of the religion-state relationship, it induces neutral independence and mutually respectful relationships. And, as a political-institutional model, it engenders non-interventionist state institutions based on "twin tolerations" between state and faith.[5] In its liberal sense, secularism is associated with religious plurality and tolerance. Any attempt at putting society under the principles of a comprehensive doctrine would mean injustice to the plurality of ideas, beliefs and conceptions of the good life, which characterizes modern societies.[6] The basic principles for co-existence of plural ideas, therefore, should be state impartiality vis-à-vis particular religious doctrines.

These two traditions constitute "ideal types" and individual states may combine features of both. Furthermore, although these two traditions provide different justifications and formats of secularism, they also have commonalities. They claim to uphold freedom of conscience and both suggest that separation of the state from religious doctrine and some insulation of the public sphere from mutually exclusive and absolutist religious assertions are common goods. For the sake of tolerance and plurality, or for the sake of national homogeneity, state sovereignty and emancipation from dogma, there must be some regulation of

---

4 Charles Taylor, "Modes of Secularism," in *Secularism and Its Critics*, ed. Rajeev Bhargava (Oxford Univ. Press, 1998), 94–136.
5 Alfred Stepan, "Religion, Democracy and the 'twin tolerations,'" *Journal of Democracy* 11 (2000): 35–57.
6 John Rawls, *Political Liberalism* (Columbia University Press, 2005).

or at least voluntary self-restraint in public space so that religious dogmatism can be controlled and disciplined. However, whereas the civic-republican model would like to render religion a private matter and keep it outside the political realm altogether, the liberal model is more tolerant of public religions and seeks to promote a pluralist and tolerant political culture and civil society.

3 The republican model during the founding moment of independent states

From the eighteenth century on, the Ottomans launched a series of ambitious reforms to modernize and centralize the state and to move from indirect to direct rule in order to militarily and financially compete with other European powers.[7] These reforms were led by a new class of Ottoman military and civilian bureaucrats endowed with western-style education, whose powers expanded at the expense of the official Ulama class.[8] In the second half of the nineteenth century, the reforms increasingly took on the character of a top-down state-led modernization in addition to some autonomous societal modernization triggered by integration with global markets. Islam and the Islamic clergy adapted to these processes in various ways. At the same time, they were variably seen as barriers and at times as vehicles and agents of mobilization for modernization and for constructing an overarching identity.[9]

Ottoman modernization attempts, however, reinforced the centrifugal tendencies among the empire's vastly diverse people and regions. The weakening of the Empire in the nineteenth century made way for competing European concepts of the organization of modern nation-states, and related principles of religious organization, across the post-Ottoman political space. New entities that emerged out of former Ottoman territories became active in constructing national uniformity and consolidating central state authority as the basis of new modern

---

7 Kemal H. Karpat, *The Politicization of Islam: Reconstructing Identity, State, Faith, and Community in the Late Ottoman State* (Oxford, New York: Oxford University Press, 2001); Andreas Wimmer, *Waves of War: Nationalism, State Formation, and Ethnic Exclusion in the Modern World* (Cambridge: Cambridge University Press, 2013).

8 Carter V. Findley, *Turkey, Islam, Nationalism, and Modernity: A History, 1789–2007* (New Haven: Yale University Press, 2010).

9 Niyazi Berkes, *The Development of Secularism in Turkey* (New York: Routledge, 1998); Şerif Mardin, *Religion, Society, and Modernity in Turkey* (Syracuse: Syracuse University Press, 2006); Amit Bein, Ottoman Ulema, *Turkish Republic: Agents of Change and Guardians of Tradition* (Stanford: Stanford University Press, 2011).

nation-states in- the-making.[10] Attempts by post-Ottoman political entrepreneurs to agitate for national unity and to 'secure the state' were the liveliest in composite areas, where religious, ethnic and national belonging remained the most fluid. During the founding moment of post-Ottoman nation-state building, religion was thus used and sacrificed for the grand political project of demarcating new nations, enforcing state authority, consolidating borders, and excluding others.

In the cases of Albania and Turkey, which became the only Muslim-majority countries in a rather unfriendly European geopolitical context, managing reactionary Islamic impulses was another key pillar of the modern nation-state project. In the eyes of the nation- and state-building elites, Islam as the faith of the majority had to be curtailed, but also utilized in order to boost state legitimacy and national unity. Indeed, re-arrangement of the state-religion relations at the founding moment of independent states targeted particularly the privileged role of Islam.

The reorganization of the religious sphere in the function of the states' goals of ensuring national unity and a centralized authority led to the creation of a similar top-down republican model of secularism, which consisted of three pillars. First, state elites pursued large-scale reforms to separate and minimize, or banish religious influences from the public political sphere. Second, the envisioned differentiation between state and religion entailed close state supervision, particularly through the creation of nationalized state-controlled religious hierarchies operating under state regulations. Last but not least, state authorities, in line with the European modernization project, intervened to make sure that their religious intermediaries adapted to the new reality of "modern times" and pursued the path of state-led modernization.

The founder of the Turkish Republic, Kemal Ataturk (1881–1938), used the muscles of the authoritarian state to install the secular model. The main goal of the Kemalist project was selective exclusion and instrumentalization of Islam's public role and control of the clergy. To this end, reforms made during the 20s and 30s abolished the Caliphate, removed Islam as state identity, and replaced the latter with the constitutional principle of secularism. Kemalist elites also secularized the legal and educational system and marginalized religious education in an effort to educate "rational citizens."[11] A 1934 law prohibited the

---

10 Arolda Elbasani and Olivier Roy, "Islam in the post-Communist Balkans: Alternative pathways to God," Southeast European and Black Sea Studies (2015).
11 Metin Heper, "Does Secularism Face A Serious Threat in Turkey?" in *Secular State and Religious Society: Two Forces in Play in Turkey*, ed. Berna Turam (New York: Palgrave Macmillan, 2012): 79–94.

public use of certain outfits and titles signifying traditional religious authority. Religious courts were dissolved, and traditional religious foundations (vakfs) were brought under government supervision. A number of other changes followed, such as the westernization of the alphabet and calendar, universal suffrage for both sexes, and the adoption of secular civil and penal codes based on Swiss and Italian models. Kemalist reformers also capitalized on the former Ottoman millet system of organization to establish tighter controls over Islam.[12] The Ottoman office of *Sheikh ul Islam* was reorganized into the directorate of Religious Affairs (Diyanet), operating under close state supervision and indeed helping state elites to discipline "Islamic" impulses. Secularism thus entailed "the establishment of an official religious establishment in the form of a subordinate government agency."[13] By monopolizing the regulation and control of religion, Kemalists tried to minimize religious reactionary movements but also to utilize Sunni Islam to attain social cohesion and reinvent the new Turkish nation.[14] Indeed, Diyanet was tasked with the job of inculcating society with "correct" Islam, that is, a rational and nationalized official doctrine devoid of "superstition" and at home with a Turkish and secular, "civilized" European state.

In the case of Albania, the authoritarian regime, led by Zog (1922–1939), pursued similar reforms to marginalize Islamic influences from the public sphere; state jurisdiction was completely detached from Sharia or any religious influences; Islamic lawyers, *Kadis*, who for centuries had regulated family disputes, were abolished; religious authorities were stripped of any role in state structures; religious education was gradually nationalized and cleansed of religious courses; and the public wearing of religious symbols, including the veil, was banned by law.[15] Quite similar to the Turkish case, the post-Ottoman Albanian state also pressured religious communities to reorganize into easy-to-control central associations, operating under state jurisdiction and control. The Muslim community

---

12 Ali Kazancigil, "The Ottoman Turkish State and Kemalism," in *Ataturk: Founder of a Modern State*, eds. Ali Kazangil & Ergun Ozbudun (London: C. Hurst and Co, 1981): 37–52.

13 Ümit Cizre, "State and Religion in a Secular Setting: The Turkish Experience," *History of European Ideas* 20.4–6 (1995): 751–57.

14 Taha Parla and Andrew Davison, "Secularism and Laicism in Turkey," in *Secularisms*, eds. Janet Jakobsen and Ann Pellegrini (Duke University Press, 2008): 64. Also see Berna Turam, ed. *Secular State and Religious Society: Two Forces in Play in Turkey*. (New York: Palgrave Macmillan, 2012).

15 For a detailed account of large-scale reforms and the resulting bargains achieved between the state and the Sunni majority in the post-Ottoman Albanian independent state, see Roberto Della Rocca, *Kombi dhe Feja ne Shqiperi 1920–1944* (Tirana: Elena Gjika, 1994); Nathalie Clayer, *Ne Fillimet e Nacionalizmit Shqiptar: Lindja e nje Kombi me Shumice Myslimane ne Evrope* (Tirana: Botime, 2009).

of Albania (MCA), founded in 1924, was recognized by the state as the only agency with authority over all affairs pertinent to the community of Muslim believers. The organization adopted new statutes and bylaws in compliance with modern state legislation; severed all previous administrative and financial links with the supranational authority of *Sheikh-ul-Islam* in Istanbul; and dissolved old structures such as the *Sharia Council*, in favor of elected structures.[16] The state further controlled key religious appointments and approved their finances. Additionally, the Albanian state made sure that the Islamic community adapted to the demands of the new age, which meant the embracing of "modern principles" of European progress and civilization, where Albania now belonged.[17] State-led reforms thus contributed to consolidate what can best be called a state-controlled, national, patriotic and progressive Islam.

Despite similar secular arrangements to discipline and frame the role of religion, the different composition of population in Albania and Turkey informed various solutions to boosting the Muslim majority as a source of nation-state unity. In the case of Albania, whose population included a mixture of Muslim and Christian denominations, the state pledged religious neutrality and pressed for an ecumenical model as the only way to pacify and keep together separate religious communities. Accordingly, all religious communities present in the Albanian territory enjoyed the same rights and duties and were similarly restructured into central organizations working in collaboration with the state. In the case of Turkey, which by 1923 presided over a rather homogenous Muslim population, the state advocated Muslimness as a source of common national identity.[18] The tiny population of recognized non-Muslim minorities was given religious and cultural-educational autonomy, but suffered from severe discrimination – alongside non-Sunni Muslim Alevis – because they were perceived as not fully loyal to the Turkish state. A unitary state, unitary society,

---

16 Della Rocca, *Kombi dhe Feja*, 129; Clayer, *Ne Fillimet e Nacionalizmit*, 406–23.

17 Nathalie Clayer, "Adapting Islam To Europe: The Albanian Example," (Paper presented at a conference: Islam und Muslims in (Südost) Europa. Kontinuität und Wandel im Kontext von Transformation und EU-Erweiterung, Berlin. November 7–8, 2008).

18 Within the territory of contemporary Turkey, the share of Muslims increased from 80 to 98 percent and that of non-Muslims decreased from 20 to 2 percent between 1913 and 1927. This drastic demographical transformation resulted from wars, ethnic-religious cleansings and genocides, forced and voluntary migrations, and population exchanges, which led to major drops in the numbers of non-Muslims as well as to a massive influx of Muslims from the Balkans and the Caucasus, a development that had already begun in the nineteenth century. See Justin McCarthy, *The Ottoman Peoples and the End of Empire* (New York: Oxford University Press, 2001); Feroz Ahmad, *From Empire to Republic: Essays on the Late Ottoman Empire and Modern Turkey* (Istanbul: Bilgi Üniversitesi, 2008).

and unitary identity have been the backbone of the official secular ideology in Turkey.[19] Such diverging approaches toward existing religious communities and the place of an Islamic majority inculcated diverse socio-political attitudes toward religious diversity, pluralism and tolerance. Albania has upheld equal treatment and respect for religious diversity as the main value of its secular arrangements. Turkey, instead, has institutionalized a Sunni bias at the expense of religious plurality in its founding model of secularism.

4 Modifications of state-engineered secularisms

While both countries were launched on similar paths of secularism, state-engineered secularism was modified differently in Turkey and Albania in post-World War II. In the case of Albania, which in the period between 1949 and 1990 experienced one of the strictest communist regimes, state control mechanisms were reinforced in the direction of hostility, which went as far as the total ban of religion as a social and moral institution.[20] By contrast, after World War II, Turkey transitioned to a multiparty democracy, which led to the moderation of state-controlled secularism and more accommodation vis-à-vis Islam.[21]

In Albania, the communist regime built on the main pillars of the post-Ottoman independent state ideology – national unity, centralized state authority, and modernization – but it relied on extreme dictatorial means to ensure cooptation of religious communities into the totalitarian project of social and state engineering. Once in power, the communist regime assaulted all religious institutions as a threat to the party's ideology and its total monopoly of power, a process which managed to interrupt the evolution of religious life, thus halting and weakening rather than altering the arrangement of the religious sphere. During its first years, the communist government resorted to depriving religious actors of their properties and sources of revenue, forbidding religious education, appointing party cronies in all religious posts, and censuring religious publications.[22] In 1949, the government made mandatory for all religious bodies "to profess loyalty

---

19 Ahmet Insel, "Introduction," in *Modern Türkiye'de Siyasi Düşünce: Kemalizm*, ed. Ahmet Insel (Istanbul: İletişim Yayınları, 2001).
20 Ali Basha, *Islami ne Shqiperi gjate Shekujve* (Tirane: Dudaj, 2000).
21 Murat Somer, "Moderation of Religious and Secular Politics: A Country's 'Center' and Democratization," Democratization 21.2 (2014): 244–67.
22 Peter Prifti, *Socialist Albania since 1944: Domestic and Foreign Developments* (Cambridge: MIT Press, 1978)

to the party and People's Republic."[23] Any resistance on the part of the clergy provoked harsh retaliation, including indictment and sentencing to long years in prison for the highest hierarchy of the clergy. By the mid-60s, the regime launched a final attack to eradicate religion after the model of China's cultural revolution; religious institutions were banned by law, religious infrastructure was destroyed or converted to other uses, and even the practice of religion in the privacy of one's home was deemed a criminal act.[24] The 1976 constitution officially endorsed the statement that the state "supports atheist propaganda," an acknowledgement which signaled the total abrogation of religious organizations and closure of all objects of cults, until the collapse of the communist system in 1990.

With the first free elections in 1950, Turkey transitioned to multi-party politics, which opened up important opportunities for Islamic actors to participate in the political-economic process and demand modification of existing secular arrangements via engagement with government agencies, and even power-sharing in coalition governments.[25] It also brought about a moderation of secular actors and institutional controls, further differentiating the Turkish case from the civic-republican model.[26] Many of the religious communities, which had survived the struggle for national unity during the early years of the republic, flourished during the establishment of multi-party democracy. They eventually became the springboard of political Islamism, alongside the gradual emergence of an Islamic-minded conservative middle class, a process that gained momentum after the 1980 military coup and economic liberalization. Initially, Islamic communities had an ambiguous relationship with party politics, often shunning it as divisive and morally corruptive. But, with time they became politically active and allied with economically progressive and culturally traditionalist center-right parties, although they shunned organic links with one single party.

The influence of Islamist ideologies in the world, and dissatisfaction with what center-right parties had delivered for pious Muslims, led to the mobilization of openly political-Islamic parties, which further challenged the established contours of secularism, particularly regarding banishment of Islam from the public political sphere. Yet, bringing religion into the public sphere does not curtail state control over religious space or its restrictions on that religiosity. Neither does it liberalize the state-organized religious sphere. In fact, Diyanet, as the

23 Alexander Popovic, *Islami Ballkanik* [*Islam in the Balkans*] (Tirana: Toena, 2006): 67.
24 Basha, *Islami ne Shqiperi*, 163–67.
25 Michele P. Angrist, "Party Systems and Regime Formation in the Modern Middle East: Explaining Turkish Exceptionalism," *Comparative Politics* 36.2 (2004): 229–49.
26 Somer, "Moderation of Religious and Secular Politics."

main institution in charge of controlling and imposing religious morality, has been kept in place, with the same task of reproducing Sunni Islam.[27] The compulsory religious education introduced in the 1980s by the Junta regime as a means to educate society and neutralize leftist ideas has also been kept in place. The constitution upheld freedom of conscience, and religious worship remained free in general, but very little was done to alleviate discrimination and policy restrictions towards religious "others," particularly regarding non-Muslims and Alevis.[28] A more open and moderate secularism, therefore, meant only more freedom and visibility for Sunni versions of Islam. Hence, rather than a movement toward the liberal model, it produced more openness to and greater instrumentalization of the majority religion. Meanwhile, while the state apparatus and political system practically became more inclusive of the pious (and, in particular) Sufi communities, many Islamic communities continued to nurture a deep-seated sense of being oppressed, because the basic legal-ideological framework of secularism remained the same, and the accompanying restrictions, such as the infamous Islamic headscarf ban, continued on university campuses and in government offices.[29] The Turkish state, meanwhile, continued to control and regulate religious affairs, shape acceptable forms of religiosity, and oppress heterodox forms of belief, including anti-religious expression.

5 Revival of Islam and challenges to secularism

Since the early 90s, both countries have seen the revival of Islam as a social and political force. Organized religious actors have also capitalized on the mobilization of the power of faith to assert their claims and reconfigure the institutional limits of secularism. In Albania, the liberalization of the communist restrictions in the 1990s enabled the reorganization of the Albanian-Muslim Community (AMC), the successor of pre-communist central organization, which emerged as the main actor representing newborn Muslims impulses.[30] Turkey, meanwhile,

---

27 Non-Muslim religions recognized by the Lausanne Treaty have autonomous institutions but also face restrictions, which have been relaxed in recent years alongside EU-led legal reforms. Other religions need first to be recognized by the state in order to have legal protection.

28 John R. Bowen, "Secularism: Conceptual Genealogy or Political Dilemma?" Comparative Studies in Society and History 52.3 (2010): 687. Also see Şeriban Şahin, "The Rise of Alevism as a Public Religion," Current Sociology 53.3 (2005): 481.

29 Somer, "Moderation of Religious and Secular Politics."

30 Olsi Jazexhi, "The Muslim Community of Albania," Unpublished manuscript 2010, 1–18; Arolda Elbasani, "Islam and Democracy at the Fringes of Europe: The Role of Useful Historical

witnessed in the 1990s the growing experience and success of political Islamist actors within competitive politics, a process that culminated in the ascendance to power of the Justice and Development Party (AKP). The newborn dominant organizations in both countries – the weak state-controlled AMC organization that came out of the ashes of communism, and the well-organized AKP in a ruling party position – enjoyed different institutional capacities to assert their preferences and negotiate the main contours of the republican format of secularism. Both organizations, however, could capitalize on the existing secular arrangements to strengthen their hold within the system – AMC as the official voice of Islam, and AKP as a ruling Islamic party – and thus maintain the main contours of the state-engineered system.

5.1 AMC's alliance with the state to safeguard secular architecture

The secular arrangements that regulate state-church relations in post-communist Albania, by and large, replicate the institutional choices made during the founding moment of Post-Ottoman independent state. The post-communist reshuffling of the constitutional framework, however, was also a crucial moment to update the secular framework, with a range of religious freedoms guaranteed in democratic systems. The first constitutional amendments guaranteed that the state "respects religious freedoms and creates the conditions for their exercising."[31] The constitution further elaborates a range of individual rights: "all citizens enjoy freedom of conscience to choose or change one's religion and express it individually or collectively, in public or private space." [32] Additionally, "no one may be compelled or prohibited to take part or not in a religious community."[33] Similar to the previous pre-communist model, the post-communist state has no religion and instead "is neutral in questions of belief" and "recognizes the equality of all religious communities."[34]

Besides these hints of liberalism, the secular model continues the tradition of close state supervision and management of religious activity. First of all, reli-

Legacies," Politics and Religion (2015), FirstView: http://dx.doi.org/10.1017/S1755048315000012.

31 People's Assembly of the Republic of Albania, Law on Major Constitutional Provisions (1991), Article 7.

32 Albanian Parliament, Constitution of the Republic of Albania (1998), Article 24.

33 Albanian Parliament, Article 24

34 Albanian Parliament, Article 10.

gious communities enjoy independence in running their affairs, but are also required to "work for the good of each and all."[35] A set of institutional indices ensure that religious communities indeed work under the state's close political and juridical control; all religious organizations must be registered as judicial persons, a process which requires their screening for compatibility with state legislation. The Committee of Cults, a special state institution headed by a civil servant, is responsible for registering and documenting the activity of religious organizations, in addition to serving as a forum where the state and religious communities meet together to decide related policy initiatives.[36] The constitutional requirement that religious communities be organized as centralized hierarchies regulated by bilateral agreements entered into with the state further enables the latter to coopt the official Sunni organization, which in return works to advocate and transmit the official line of Islam in an organized manner. The AMC has indeed struck a deal with the state in order to safeguard the freedom of thought, conscience, and religion within the necessary restrictions "of a democratic society, public security and protection of third-party rights."[37] Accordingly, the new AMC, as the official structure of the Sunni community, has become the main pillar of the state-controlled religious sphere.

The liberalization of religious conduct has certainly created an open market of religion where foreign influences – migrants, students from abroad, humanitarian organizations and virtual internet networks – effectively compete with established institutions and traditional ideas for hearts and minds of post-communist Albanians.[38] Rich Arab associations have provided much-needed resources – funds for building necessary infrastructure, scholarships for students, Islamic literature and translations, religious missionaries and humanitarian assistance, mixed with proselytization activities – to help local Muslims find the way to "pure" faith.[39] Incoming alternative ideas and associations have upset the state-organized religious field, including its institutional infrastructure and tra-

---

35 Albanian Parliament, Article 10, point 4.

36 Council of Ministers, Decision on the Creation of The Committee of Cults, No, 459, adopted 23 September 1999.

37 Albanian Parliament, Law on the Ratification of Agreement of Mutual Understanding with the Muslim Community (i) Tirana: 2009.

38 Arolda Elbasani, "Rediscovering the Umma: Muslims in the Balkans between nationalism and transnationalism," Southeast European and Black Sea Studies 13 (2013): 471–73.

39 Rajwantee Lakshman-Lepain, "Albanian Islam – Development and Disruptions," In *Albania – A Country in Transition*, eds. Karl Kaser and Frank Kressing (Baden-Baden: Nomos, 2002): 34–65.

ditional interpretations developed around state concerns on national unity, state authority, and the embracing of European modernity. Yet, the AMC benefits from the alliance with the state to reinforce and protect its position within the system. Indeed, in the bilateral agreement, which regulates its relations to the state, AMC has required state authorities to support its actions "against any deformations, extremist tendencies, or other aggressive demonstrations in the spaces occupied by [its] believers."[40] The strong alliance between the two has enabled the consolidation of an official doctrine, which develops parallel to the country's socio-political expediencies and goals – democracy and European integration – but also maintains the institutional status quo.

Given its weak position as a subordinate state organization, the AMC has been confined to follow the state's generally restrictive attitude toward the presence of religion in the public sphere. The mushrooming links with the Islamic world in the first half of the 1990s has enabled a certain recovery of the role of the AMC and the presence of Islam in the public sphere. Faith became more obvious through the building of new imposing mosques, the opening of a wide range of private schools, the proliferation of humanitarian activities, and the upsurge of Islamic literature.[41] For a short time, the representative of AMC was placed as the chairman of the state institution in charge of administering religious affairs, showing its privileged role in the post-communist secular structure. This, however, came to an end soon afterwards as the Socialist Party, the successor of the former communist party, came to power in 1997 and moved to dismantle "Islamic fundamentalism." Most Arab "charities" were closed down, and different groups associated with terrorist movements and illegal activities were arrested. The AMC was reshuffled with new staff, and surveillance state mechanisms were reinforced.[42] Mainstream public debates, meanwhile, have been shaped around a certain hostility towards Islam as a remnant of the obscure Ottoman past and an obstacle to the country's European future. This has followed a widespread socio-political consensus to keep Islam out of state institutions, schools, arts, and the public sphere more generally. As Clayer puts it, "Albanian Muslims find themselves in the situation of a

---

40 Albanian Parliament, Law on the Ratification, article 3 f.
41 Lakshman-Lepain, "Albanian Islam," 49. Estimates show that in the early 1990 s foreign aid from Islamic countries was 50% of the foreign investment of well over 5% of GDP.
42 ICG, The State of Albania (Balkans Report No. 45, January 16, 2009): 6–8.

numerical majority, but [in an] intellectual, social and political minority situation."[43]

5.2 AKP: Utilization and challenge of secular model in function of power

With respect to secularism, the AKP's record can be divided into two terms. During its first term in government, roughly between 2002 and 2008, the party, in general, refrained from any policies that would affect secularism. However, it used a liberal discourse, and made some minor yet real changes, which upheld freedoms and opportunities for all religions, alongside general democratization and EU reforms.[44] In its second term, the AKP did not necessarily modify the institutional structure of state-engineered secularism, but expanded it with an enhanced Sunni-Islamic discursive and ideological emphasis. These changes served the majority Sunni Muslim believers, but did little to expand freedoms and opportunities for others. As its policies and discourse turned increasingly authoritarian, reflecting religious nationalism and a majoritarian perception of democracy, the party capitalized on state-engineered secularism in the service of Islamic social engineering.

During its first term, the AKP was checked and balanced by the EU-accession process, a watchful military, a secularist president, liberal-secular intelligentsia and civil society, and a critical and combative media. Short-lived attempts at criminalizing adultery and lifting the Islamic headscarf ban were quickly withdrawn after domestic and international skepticism; the party's priorities seemed to lie with distancing itself from its political Islamist roots. Accordingly, the party avoided a religious and nationalist discourse and made some changes, including reducing government involvement in religion – such as the right to leave blank the religious identity section in national identity cards, and easing legal procedures for establishing non-Muslim places of worship.[45]

During and after 2007–2008, the outcomes of various legal-political confrontations between the AKP and the secularist military and bureaucracy ena-

---

43 Nathalie Clayer, "God in the 'Land of the Mercedes,' The Religious Communities in Albania since 1990," in Österreichische Osthefte, Sonderband 17, Albanien, ed. Peter Jordan (Wien: Peter Lang, 2003): 277–314.

44 Arolda Elbasani and Beken Saatçioğlu, "Muslims' Support for European Integration: the Role of Organizational Capacities," *Democratization* 21 (2014): 458–79.

45 US Department of State, International Religious Freedom Report (Washington, DC: Bureau of Democracy, Human Rights and Labor, 2012).

bled the AKP to free itself from secular checks and balances, without replacing them with new and more democratic ones.[46] The AKP's room for maneuver was drastically expanded with a new and cooperative president, a subdued military, a gradually packed bureaucracy, a heavily pressured media, weak opposition parties, and a series of electoral victories.

The AKP could use its new mandate to reform Turkish secularism in a more liberal and post-secular direction, as many liberal and religious critics had long demanded; alternatively, the party could maintain the principle and interventionist institutional structures of Turkish secularism and instrumentalize them in the service of majority Sunni-Muslim interests.[47] A more liberal secularism would have meant that, for example, the Diyanet would be abolished, or reformed to be inclusive of more Muslim minorities and devoid of domineering roles – such as the regulation of the affairs of "the religion of Islam," and the promotion of "national solidarity and unity." In fact, the Diyanet retained its mandates and became larger and more powerful.[48]

Various policies considerably enhanced the freedoms and opportunities for pious Sunni Muslims, and, to some extent, non-Muslim minorities. The Islamic headscarf ban was practically eliminated for college students and civil servants, and a fundamental restructuring of the primary and secondary school system enabled students to attend a religious school more easily and at an earlier age. The number of government-subsidized Sunni Muslim mosques and Qur'an schools steadily increased, while mandatory religion courses remained in high schools.[49] The government began to compensate non-Muslim religious foundations for property confiscated during previous decades.

But attempts at open discussion for reforms that would secure equality for the Alevis – who constitute somewhere between 5 and 25 percent of the population – bore no tangible results. On the contrary, the government began to employ

---

46 See Murat Somer. "Moderate Islam and Secularist Opposition in Turkey: Implications for the World, Muslims and Secular Democracy," *Third World Quarterly* 28 (7) (2007): 1271-1289 and Arolda Elbasani and Beken Saatçioğlu, "Muslim Democracy in the Making! Of Pragmatism and Values of AKP's Selective Democratization Project," (Paper presented at APSA Annual Meeting, Washington, D.C., 2014).

47 For different criticisms of Turkish secularism and their policy implications, see Murat Somer, "Is Turkish Secularism Anti-Religious, Reformist, Separationist, Integrationist, or Simply Undemocratic?" Review Essay, *Journal of Church and State* 55.3 (2013): 585–97; Murat Somer, "Democracy-Secularism Relationship Revisited," *Today's Zaman*, January 25, 2009. http://www.todayszaman.com/news-165004-democracy-laicism-relations-revisited-by-murat-somer-.html

48 Somer, "Is Turkish Secularism Anti-Religious," 593–94.

49 Somer, "Is Turkish Secularism Anti-Religious," 593–94.

an increasingly religious-moralist, anti-secular, pro-Sunni, and anti-Alevi rhetoric. This gained momentum after the Arab uprisings in 2011–2012, when the AKP formed alliances with Egyptian and Syrian Muslim Brothers, and after the anti-government Gezi riots were disproportionately supported by Alevis and pro-secular groups. Meanwhile, new laws, regulations, and practices restricted abortion rights, alcohol consumption, and coed student housing, fueling secular concerns with Islamization and government restrictions on secular freedoms.

6 Conclusions

Both Albania and Turkey developed secular systems in which secularism was instrumental and subservient, first, to nation- and state-building based on European models, and, second, state-led social-political modernization in their respective social-demographic and historical-institutional contexts. Their state-engineered secularisms enabled the state to regulate and discipline Islam, with a view to subordinating as well as "reforming" and "rationalizing" it. Given Albania's greater religious diversity, more emphasis was placed on interreligious equality, while the Turkish state promoted selective aspects of Islam as a basis of national identity and social cohesion. In both cases, Islamic actors were flexible enough to contest but also to adapt to their secular environments in a competitive context.

Especially in the Turkish case, Islamic actors also helped to reshape secularism by using competitive politics. When Turkey's AKP acquired sufficient power and opportunity to do so, it tried to instrumentalize, and, to some extent, Islamize state-engineered secularism. This gives rise to an interesting observation and that Islamic actors may adopt and seek to Islamize the civic-republican model, rather than embrace the liberal model, for their own purposes. This is not to say, however, that Islamic political actors have a fixed orientation toward state-engineered secularism. On the contrary, our comparative cases show that they adapt to their political-institutional and demographic environments, as the AMC's orientation toward non-Muslims and AKP's relatively liberal orientation during its first period demonstrate. From this perspective, the recent endurance of Turkish state-engineered secularism with a more pro-Islamic bent is a product of politics rather than unchanging ideologies. It is an outcome produced by secular as well as Islamic political actors, who have so far failed to share power in pursuit of a more inclusive and pluralistic social and political-institutional order.

Works Cited

Ahmad, Feroz. *From Empire to Republic: Essays on the Late Ottoman Empire and Modern Turkey.* Istanbul: Bilgi Üniversitesi, 2008.

Albanian Parliament. *Constitution of the Republic of Albania,* 1998.

Albanian Parliament. *Law on the Ratification of Agreement of Mutual Understanding with the Muslim Community, Tirana, 2009.*

Angrist, Michele P. "Party Systems and Regime Formation in the Modern Middle East: Explaining Turkish Exceptionalism." *Comparative Politics* 36. 2 (2004): 229–49.

Basha, Ali. *Islami ne Shqiperi gjate Shekujve.* Tirane: Dudaj, 2000.

Bein, Amit. *Ottoman Ulema, Turkish Republic: Agents of Change and Guardians of Tradition.* Stanford: Stanford University Press, 2011.

Berkes, Niyazi. *The Development of Secularism in Turkey.* New York: Routledge, 1998.

Bowen, John R. "Secularism: Conceptual Genealogy or Political Dilemma?" *Comparative Studies in Society and History* 52.3 (2010): 687.

Casanova, José. *Public Religions in the Modern World.* University of Chicago Press, 1994.

Cizre, Ümit. "State and Religion in a Secular Setting: The Turkish Experience." *History of European Ideas* 20.4–6 (1995): 751–57.

Clayer, Nathalie. "God in the 'Land of the Mercedes.' The Religious Communities in Albania since 1990." In Österreichische Osthefte, Sonderband 17, Albanien, ed. Peter Jordan (Wien: Peter Lang, 2003): 277–314.

Clayer, Nathalie. "Adapting Islam To Europe: The Albanian Example." Paper presented at a Conference: Islam und Muslims in (Südost) Europa. Kontinuität und Wandel im Kontext von Transformation und EU-Erweiterung. Berlin, November 7–8, 2008.

Clayer, Nathalie. *Ne Fillimet e Nacionalizmit Shqiptar: Lindja e nje Kombi me Shumice Myslimane ne Evrope.* Tirana: Botime, 2009.

Council of Ministers. *Decision on the Creation of The Committee of Cults,* No. 459, adopted 23.09.1999.

Della Rocca, Roberto. *Kombi dhe Feja ne Shqiperi 1920–1944.* Tirana: Elena Gjika, 1994.

Diyanet: http://www.diyanet.gov.tr/turkish/tanitim/tanitimistatistik.asp. Accessed May 27, 2013.

Elbasani, Arolda and Beken Saatçioğlu. "Muslims' support for European integration: the role of organizational capacities." *Democratization* 21.3 (2014): 458–79.

Elbasani, Arolda and Beken Saatçioğlu. "Muslim Democracy in the Making! Of Pragmatism and Values of AKP's Selective Democratization Project." Paper presented at APSA Annual Meeting, Washington, D.C., 2014.

Elbasani, Arolda. "Rediscovering the Umma: Muslims in the Balkans between nationalism and transnationalism." *Southeast European and Black Sea Studies* 13.3 (2013): 471–73.

Elbasani, Arolda. "Islam and Democracy at the Fringes of Europe: The Role of Useful Historical Legacies." Politics and Religion (2015) , FirstView: http://dx.doi.org/10.1017/S1755048315000012.

Elbasani, Arolda and Roy, Olivier. "Islam in the post-Communist Balkans: alternative pathways to God." Southeastern Europe and Black Sea Studies (2015), FirstOnline: http://dx.doi.org/10.1080/14683857.2015.1050273.

Findley, Carter V. *Turkey, Islam, Nationalism, and Modernity: A History, 1789–2007.* New Haven: Yale University Press, 2010.

Fox, Jonathan. *A World Survey of Religion and the State*. New York: Cambridge University Press, 2008.

General Directorate of Budget and Fiscal Control, Republic of Turkey: http://www.bumko.gov. tr/. Accessed June 6, 2013.

Heper, Metin. "Does Secularism Face A Serious Threat in Turkey?" In *Secular State and Religious Society: Two Forces in Play in Turkey*, edited by Berna Turam, 79–94. New York: Palgrave Macmillan, 2012.

ICG. The State of Albania, Balkans Report no. 45, January 16, 2009.

Insel, Ahmet. "Introduction." In *Modern Türkiye'de Siyasi Düşünce: Kemalizm*, edited by Ahmet Insel. Istanbul: İletişim Yayınları, 2001.

Jazexhi, Olsi. "The Muslim Community of Albania." Unpublished manuscript: 1–18, 2010.

Karpat, Kemal H. *The Politicization of Islam: Reconstructing Identity, State, Faith, and Community in the late Ottoman state*. Oxford, New York: Oxford University Press, 2001.

Kazancigil, Ali. "The Ottoman Turkish State and Kemalism." In *Ataturk: Founder of a Modern State*, edited by Ali Kazangil and Ergun Ozbudun. London: C. Hurst and Co, 1981.

Lakshman-Lepain, Rajwantee. "Albanian Islam – Development and Disruptions." In *Albania – A Country in Transition*, edited by Karl Kaser and Frank Kressing, 34–65. Baden-Baden: Nomos, 2002.

Mardin, Şerif. *Religion, Society, and Modernity in Turkey*. Syracuse: Syracuse University Press, 2006.

McCarthy, Justin. *The Ottoman Peoples and The End of Empire*. New York: Oxford University Press, 2001.

Parla, Taha and Andrew Davison. "Secularism and Laicism in Turkey." In *Secularisms*, edited by Janet Jakobsen and Ann Pellegrini, 64. Duke University Press, 2008.

People's Assembly of the Republic of Albania. *Law on Major Constitutional Provisions* (1991), Article 7.

Philpott, Daniel. "Explaining the Political Ambivalence of Religion." *American Political Science Review* 101.3 (2007): 505–25.

Popovic, Alexander. *Islami Ballkanik*. [Islam in the Balkans]. Tirana: Toena, 2006.

Prifti, Peter. *Socialist Albania since 1944: Domestic and Foreign Developments*. Cambridge: MIT Press, 1978.

Rawls, John. *Political Liberalism*. Columbia University Press, 2005.

Somer, Murat. "Moderation of Religious and Secular Politics: A Country's 'Center' and Democratization." *Democratization* 21 (2014): 244–67.

Somer, Murat. "Is Turkish Secularism Anti-Religious, Reformist, Separationist, Integrationist, or Simply Undemocratic?" Review Essay, *Journal of Church and State* 55.3 (2013): 585–97.

Somer. Murat "Moderate Islam and Secularist Opposition in Turkey: Implications for the World, Muslims and Secular Democracy," *Third World Quarterly* 28 (7) (2007): 1271-1289.

Şahin, Şeriban. "The Rise of Alevism as a Public Religion." *Current Sociology*, 53.3 (2005): 481.

Turam, Berna, ed. *Secular State and Religious Society: Two Forces in Play in Turkey*. (New York: Palgrave Macmillan, 2012).

Ayşe Seda Müftügil
Education and Religious Minorities in Turkey: the Story behind the Introduction of Compulsory Religion Courses

The introduction of compulsory *religion education*[1] to the Turkish state education system via the 1982 constitution is generally attributed to the military junta. Although this is mostly correct as the final decision on the subject was taken by the junta, I argue that various civilian groups and academics also contributed to the process that led the way to the introduction of the course. Between 1980 and 1982, mainly by order of the junta, various commissions were formed to produce reports about the compatibility of the course with the existing secularism clause in the constitution. These reports assessed the necessity of the course, as well as the details of its proposed content.

It is my contention that the influence of these commissions on both the structure and content of the course has not yet attracted the attention of scholars. Yet this period reveals significant information as to which issues regarding the proposed compulsory religion course were deemed important by these civilian groups and consequently which were not considered as important. Therefore, a critical examination of this period is useful for explicating the blind spots in its exhausted debates about secularism.

Thus my first objective in this chapter is to look at the period between 1980 and 1982 in order to examine the preparatory phase of the course, its key actors and ideas. More specifically, this is a genealogy of the processes that would result in the course being made compulsory. I argue that a detailed scrutiny of the reports, the composition of the various commissions and finally, the junta's evaluative response, makes clear that the potential problems posed by the course to Turkey's existing religious minorities (Jews, Orthodox Christians, Armenians and Alevis[2]) were not deemed important by the state. This is partly due to the Lau-

---

1 Instead of deploying the term religious education typically used in English, I use the term religion education advisedly to refer to a course in religion, a course alongside other regular courses such as history, mathematics or literature. Not only is religion education an accurate translation of the Turkish din eğitimi, but the retention of the term can be read as an attempt to legitimize the existence of the course in a secular curriculum.

2 In this chapter, I refer to Alevis as a religious minority, although in fact, there is no consensus among Alevis or within academic circles as to whether Alevis should be regarded as a religious minority or not. In the EU Progress Reports, Alevis are also defined as a non-Sunni Muslim mi-

sanne Treaty, which granted non-Muslims educational rights, including the right to set up minority schools for the teaching of other religions. Thus, it is arguable that the problems of minority groups (particularly with regard to the compulsory course) became invisible and unimportant, especially given the diminishing population and economic power of non-Muslims. The Lausanne Treaty effectively gave the Turkish state immunity, an exemption from considering the problems of non-Muslims with respect to the compulsory religion education course. Thus, a critical gaze at this period, when the course became entrenched in the school curriculum, tends to confirm the existence of the asymmetrical relationship that the state had established with non-Muslims and Alevis.

Secondly, I will briefly examine the discussions that took place in the immediate aftermath of the junta regime in order to show how the course was applied. After 1982, under the civilian regime, there were some politicians who problematized the issue from a minority rights perspective and tried to introduce new regulations to handle the complicated situation of religious minorities who attended state school and, therefore, had to take this course. However, these measures were limited and could not alter the structure of a course that was in many ways discriminatory.

In subsequent years, Turkish school curricula have changed tremendously, but the compulsory religion education course has stayed in the constitution, and its existence remains relatively unchallenged. In 2008, I conducted an interview with Beyza Bilgin, as part of background research for this study. Bilgin, the first religious educator to achieve a professorship in religion education, was one of the most influential people in the move to make religion education compulsory in 1980. In general, her works approach the topic from a pedagogical point of view, focusing on the merits of the provision of religion education in a formal education system. My interview with Bilgin revealed important information about the internal dynamics of those processes that ended with the consolidation of the course, and more importantly, about subsequent modifications of the original course, especially with respect to its practical application. In addi-

---

nority, a label to which some Alevis are opposed. The minority concept in Turkey is strongly informed by the Lausanne Treaty in which only non-Muslims were considered as minorities. Due to this narrow definition, groups like Alevis and Kurds, who experience discrimination in Turkish society, may resist the term. My choice derives from Louis Wirth's approach to the term. Wirth defines a minority group as being composed of people, who, because of their physical or cultural characteristics, are singled out from other citizens for differential and unequal treatment, and, who, therefore, regard themselves as objects of collective "discrimination." See Louis Wirth, "The Problem of Minority Groups," in *The Science of Man in the World Crisis*, ed. Ralph Lindon (New York: Columbia University Press, 1945), 347.

tion, I analyzed various materials including textbooks, speeches by education ministers, government programs, legal documents and finally, scholarly debates about compulsory religion education which took place at the time.

1 History of Compulsory Religion Education

In the early Republican era in Turkey, all levels of religious education were officially banned for nearly two decades. After the Second World War, improving socio-economic relations with Western democracies and the initiation of a multi-party system influenced the educational structure. It was in this context that religious education in schools emerged as an important issue. After a long debate at the political level, religious education was introduced not only in primary schools (in 1949), but also in lower secondary schools (*orta okul*) (in 1956), and in upper secondary schools (*lise*) (in 1967).[3] It must be noted that during these years, the course was not compulsory insofar as anyone, Muslim or non-Muslim, could apply for exemption through a petition to the school government.

In September 1980, the Turkish military mobilized to prevent the erosion of state authority. There was a fear of social breakdown due to widespread political violence between leftist and rightist groups, particularly in high schools and on university campuses.[4] The state imposed a number of harsh measures, including strict control of the media and of universities and bureaucratic offices. Power was centered in the military, specifically in the *Milli Güvenlik Kurulu*/National Security Council (MGK) headed by the chief of staff, General Kenan Evren. The military was determined to de-politicize the urban youth, which since the 1960s had played an important role in the riots against state power. To that end, they sought to crush every manifestation of dissent from the left, including revolutionaries, social democrats and trade unionists. "The extreme right too, represented by the MHP (Milliyetçi Hareket Partisi/Nationalist Action Party), was crushed although its ideology was adopted in the form of the so-called 'Turkish Islamic Synthesis' (*Türk İslam Sentezi*) and designed by a group known as the 'Intellectuals' Hearth' (*Aydınlar Ocağı*)".[5] This ideology held that Turkishness and Islamism were com-

---

3 Recep Kaymakcan, "Christianity in Turkish Religion education," *Islam and Christian-Muslim Relations* 10.3 (1999): 279–93.
4 Sam Kaplan, "Religious Nationalism: A Textbook Case from Turkey," *Comparative Studies of South Asia, Africa and the Middle East* 25.3 (2005): 113–27.
5 Kaplan, "Religious Nationalism: A Textbook Case from Turkey," *Comparative Studies of South Asia, Africa and the Middle East* 25.3 (2005): 113–27.

plementary aspects of Turkish culture and that religious values should be emphasized in Turkish nationalism.[6] In the late 1970s, these views became very popular on the political right. Despite the secularist culture of Turkish military officers, the Turkish Islamic Synthesis also appealed to prominent military leaders. Subsequently, this ideology characterized the 1980s and was highly influential for the political mindset of those in power, even after the military withdrew from politics.

In the months following the coup, the junta generals made their views on education fairly clear. Within two years, the military endorsed a new constitution that mandated compulsory religious education in all primary and secondary schools. All school children from fourth grade until graduation from high school were required to take the Religion Culture and Morals Course (*Din Kütürü ve Ahlak Bilgisi Dersi*). The new course combined two previously separated subjects: the compulsory civics course and the optional religion courses. The military view was that if people accepted this new curriculum, greater social cohesion among the different populations in Turkey might be achieved. The 1982, a ministerial directive states, "Just as we cherish our national values, customs and traditions, we acknowledge that one of the important components of a nation is religion."[7] More than any other school subject, the state now viewed religious education as the means to introduce students to tradition, modernity and nationalism.[8]

The motives behind the introduction of compulsory religion courses by the military junta in 1982 were related to the presumption that teaching religion would mitigate the leftist communist movements that were prevalent at the time. After September 12, 1980, the generals tightened institutional links between the armed forces and the national education system. Before power was returned to civilian politicians approximately three years later, the military passed a series of education reforms that "sought to prevent at all costs the consolidation of identities that threatened to fragment nation into a politics of differences."[9] The promotion of Sunni Islam in the textbooks and the omission of information about Alevism were legitimized by the larger aim to foster social unity and prevent denominational fights within Islam, an argument that effectively marginalized Alevism and its believers.

---

6 Şule Toktaş, "Citizenship and Minorities: A Historical Overview of Turkey's Jewish Minority," *Journal of Historical Sociology* 18.4 (December 2005): 394–429.
7 Milli Eğitim Bakanlığı Tebliğler Dergisi, Din Kültürü ve Ahlak Bilgisi Programı [Religion and Morals Program] (March 29, 1982): 156.
8 Kaplan, 2005.
9 Kaplan, 2005.

2 Repercussions of the Commissions on Religion Education, 1980–1982

By the time religion courses became compulsory in 1982, religious education had already established a clear foothold in the state education system. Although the Ministry of Education showed some interest in structuring these courses according to pedagogical concerns, religious education was not yet regarded as a social scientific field. Apart from the work of Beyza Bilgin, no academic studies had been conducted on the topic of religious education in Turkey. Bilgin conducted her doctoral research at the Ankara University Theology Faculty in 1971; her topic was "Love as the basis of education in Islam." But her best-known work dealt with the issue of religious education in the Turkish formal education system and was titled *Religion Education in Turkey and Religion courses at High Schools*.[10] In this research, conducted between 1973 and 1976, Bilgin's objective was to identify current problems in religious education, the situation of the courses, and any possible improvements. She contacted various actors within religion education, including teachers, students and parents, all of whom were invited to discuss their views and expectations of the courses. Bilgin's findings were based mainly on the surveys she distributed to 1255 high schools in Turkey, of which 873 high schools were evaluated in her research.[11] Her principal conclusion was that religion education courses should be made compulsory and given a proper place in the school curricula. She argued that if the courses remained voluntary, they would eventually become less effective and various pedagogical problems would follow. Bilgin also argued that if certain legislative changes were made, religion education could be reconciled with the constitution.

A young assistant professor at the time, Beyza Bilgin had immense influence on the process of making the religion courses compulsory. Her controversial thesis was published in 1980. The dean of the university, Professor Hüseyin Atay, read the book and determined that Bilgin's ideas should be put before the MGK. Atay's written proposal received little support from other scholars, who, although in agreement with Bilgin's ideas, feared taking them to the military junta. The report was sent to the MGK on November 19, 1980, and contrary to expectations, Atay was invited to explain his proposal in detail. In addition, Atay offered his own ideas about why religion education was important for Turkish youth and how to conduct it without violating any freedoms.

---

10 Beyza Bilgin, *Türkiye'de Din Eğitimi ve Liselerde Din Dersleri*, (Ankara: Emel, 1980).
11 Beyza Bilgin, 1980.

As a consequence of Atay's report, Bilgin was appointed as a consultant to the Ministry of Education Religion Instruction Working Committee (*MEB Din Öğretimi Çalışma Grubu*), a committee also working on the improvement of religion education. Here, she repeated her arguments in favor of compulsory religion education. In February 1981, the committee produced a report that in its "Suggestions" section explained how the courses might be conducted.[12] Although favoring compulsory religion education, the report argued that in religion courses, children should not be compelled to practice their own religion. The report also stated that where a sufficient number of non-Muslim students attended a class, their religion should be taught. However, this number remained unspecified in the report. This suggestion shows an implicit awareness that if courses did not address non-Muslims, the secularism clause in the constitution might be compromised. On this same topic, again in February 1981, the Minister of Religious Affairs produced a fifty-page report titled *A Report about Religion Education in Turkey.* For the first time, there was a clear statement that "as a requirement of freedom of religion and conscience, non-Muslims must have the right to opt out from the course given that they submit a petition to the school administration at the beginning of the school year. If numbers of non-Muslims in a classroom exceed ten, then a special class for them could be opened where they could learn their religion."[13] However, no further research or work followed from that proposal.

There were other committees that proposed ideas similar to those suggested by Bilgin. The Ministry of Education Religion Education Consultation Committee (*Milli Eğitim Bakanlığı Din Eğitimi Danışma Kurulu*) was one of them. The purpose of this committee was to research the feasibility of the transition to compulsory religion education from the previous voluntary course. The committee met on May 28, 1981 and after two days of intense debate, agreed (with only two members opposing the idea) that religion education should be compulsory during primary and secondary education.

Another group, this one called The Science Committee with Respect to Atatürk's Ideas about Religion and Secularism (*Atatürk'ün Din ve Laiklik Konusundaki Görüşleri Hakkında Bilim Kurulu*), was set up by the Ministry of State Responsible for Religious Affairs.[14] The aim of this committee was to investigate whether

---

12 Turkey, "Din Eğitimi Çalışma Grubu Raporu" [Religion Instruction Working Committee]. Ankara: Milli Eğitim Bakanlığı (February 6, 1981): 7–21.
13 "Diyanet İşleri Başkanlığı, Türkiye'de Din Eğitim ve Öğretimi Hakkında Rapor" [Report about religion education and instruction in Turkey]. Ankara: Devlet Basımevi, 1981.
14 Din Öğretimi Genel Müdürlüğü, ed., *New Methodological Approaches in Religion education, International Symposium, Papers and Discussions* (Ankara: MEB, 2004): 686.

compulsory religion courses were compatible with Atatürk's idea of secularism, and to evaluate the issue in the context of contemporary needs. Years after his death, Atatürk remained *the* reference point, the accepted authority whose ideas were always referred to when it came to the issue of religion education. Yet Atatürk's ideas had not been crystal clear during his lifetime or beyond. Indeed, as the disagreements on this committee show, his views were appropriated and interpreted by opponents of religion education *and* by those in favor of it.

A final committee, the Religion Education Committee (*Din Eğitimi Komitesi*), was formed by the General Secretary of the National Security Committee. According to Bilgin, the most important discussions of the *pedagogical* transition to compulsory religion education took place in this committee.

There were two other important academic gatherings that preceded and informed the work of the committees.[15] In April 1981, the Ankara University Theology Faculty hosted the First Religion Education Seminar. And in May that same year, the Intellectuals' Hearth (*Aydınlar Ocağı*) held a National Education and Religion Education Science Seminar (*Milli Eğitim ve Din Eğitimi İlmi Semineri*). In both of these seminars, the main focus of the papers was on the need for compulsory religion education. As in previous decades, the question of the course's legitimacy received the greatest attention. This meant that other important issues, such as the content and actual program of the course, were not given much thought. Moreover, there was no discussion of the possible problems that the course might create or how those problems might be solved. There was a consensus among participating scholars that compulsory religion education would unite the polarized Turkish youth, especially along *mezhep* (denominational) lines.

The Constitution of 1982 was not arranged by an assembly that had legal representation or authority. A draft constitution was prepared by the Assembly of Consultation that consisted of appointed members as opposed to elected ones. The National Security Council had control of the overall project. The Assembly of Consultation consisted of 160 members and was formed in June 1981. The Commission on Constitution (a working party within the Assembly of Consultation) produced a proposal of 200 articles. Throughout most of August and September of 1981, the proposal was the subject of fierce debates prior to its submission to the National Security Council. Article 24 of the draft constitution came under particular scrutiny. It dealt with religion education, but in terms that remained unchanged from the 1961 Constitution. This ran counter to previous de-

---

15 Nurullah Altaş, "Türkiye'de Zorunlu Din Öğretimini Yapılandıran Süreç, Hedefler ve Yeni Yöntem Arayışları," in *Dini Araştırmalar Dergisi* (January-April 2002): 145–68.

cisions by both the government and the National Security Council to render religion education compulsory. As a result of public debates on this specific issue, the draft constitution was revised and eighteen different amendments were made. Finally, on September 1, 1982, the following wording was agreed for article 24:

> Religion and Morals (Ethics) education and instruction is compulsory during primary and secondary education and is done under the surveillance of the state. The participation in the course by people who do not belong to Islam depends on their volition; the international treaty clauses regarding minorities are reserved.[16]

After further discussion and rewriting, article 24 took final shape. The fourth clause of the article was changed to the following:

> Education and instruction of religion and morals (ethics) shall be conducted under state supervision and control. Instruction of "Religion Culture and Morals" course shall be compulsory in the curricula of primary and secondary schools. Other religious education and instruction shall be subject to the individual's own desire, and in the case of minors, to the request of their legal representatives.

In the 1961 Constitution, a non-Muslim student's situation with regards to the course was clearer because a statement was included stipulating, "the international treaty clauses regarding minorities are reserved." [17] However in the newly proposed constitution, this last premise, together with the statement that non-Muslims must have the right to opt out of the course, was removed. M. Fevku Uyguner, a Member of Parliament, explained the reasoning. In the Assembly, he argued that the term "minority" was not referred to in any other statutes.[18] To introduce the term would conflict with the main principles of the constitution that proclaimed all individuals equal before the law regardless of language, race, sex, political opinion, philosophical views, religion or religious sect. Clearly, some MPs did not see that the needs of non-Muslims might differ and, therefore, require specific regulations.

As a consequence of these various commissions and reports, the content of the religion course was being renewed and rethought. It seemed that in the new constitution, the courses would be made compulsory. At the same time, some of Evren's advisors informed him that the new religion course contained much repetitive information that could prove boring to children. Evren called a brief

---

16 Halis Ayhan, *Türkiye'de Din Eğitimi* (Istanbul: Dem, 2004), 300.

17 Ayhan, 300.

18 Ayhan, 313.

meeting with representatives of the commissions, in order to clarify the issue. After presentations by the Ministry of Education and the Board of Education and Discipline (*Talim Terbiye Kurulu*), a general took the floor and argued that there was no need to teach the course from fourth grade to the end of high school, and that religion could be learned in a period of three months. Bilgin, who was at the meeting, later explained that she and other members were hesitant to enter into discussion with the general but at the same time, were very eager to present their counter arguments. Finally, Bilgin stood up and was granted permission to speak on the matter. She explained that religion courses should not be seen only as a means to teach Islam, but as an opportunity for children to study their culture. This, according to Bilgin, could not be achieved in three months. She also asserted that not only Islam but also other religions and cultures must be included in the courses for students to gain a more thorough understanding of religion.

The next day, the constitution (as endorsed by the military) was voted upon and accepted by a large majority of the public. This meant that article 24 was approved; Bilgin and all those who supported religion education in schools were content with the outcome. In one of her articles, Bilgin notes that many people at the time thought that the religion courses became compulsory as a consequence of military imposition. By explaining the process in a detailed manner, she tries to show that theology scholars, in fact, initiated it. The significance of the scholars' involvement is undeniable, but it is also important to note that the generals approved many of the ideas emanating from the Intellectuals' Hearth (*Aydınlar Ocağı*). This gave added force to the process of making the course compulsory.

In my interview with Beyza Bilgin, she raised a number of important points. First of all, many theologians, including Bilgin, pushed for compulsory religion education to be included in the education system. However, once the course was accepted by constitutional amendment, the theologians' ideas about its content were not strictly followed. Thus, the course developed along different lines. For instance, Bilgin wanted the different *mezheps* of Islam, including Alevism, to be included in the curriculum. This was strongly opposed on the grounds that the issue was highly political and that it was preferable not to mention terms relating to Alevism or any other *mezhep*. Secondly, she argued that it was better to teach religious concepts that could be agreed upon by the different religions, or in the case of Islam, by every *mezhep*. But again, this did not materialize and according to Bilgin; the scholars did not have sufficient editorial control over the content of the textbooks. They were able to set topic headings, but not the material that appeared under those headings. She cited the example of books that illustrated *namaz* (ritual prayer).[19]. Illustrations were selected according to Sunni faith and did not contain the Alevi version of *namaz*. Although this was inaccurate, it was allowed to pass, as most of the teachers and textbook authors were Sunnis.

This evidence suggests that the views of Bilgin and other scholars were overlooked in the planning of the course. As such, the dominant Sunni-Hanefi branch of Islam played a strong role in the evolution of the course and its textbooks. In addition, the plan to teach non-Muslims their own religion was never put into practice, on the grounds that there were insufficient numbers of non-Muslims in the classrooms. There was a clear contradiction between the *ideal* of offering religion courses to non-Muslims and what actually occurred. Arguably, this constituted a failure on the part of the state to treat all citizens equally. Finally, despite proposals that the course content should consist of ethics, it is apparent that the final design was primarily intended for Sunni Muslims.

In the 1982–83 school year, the newly organized course finally appeared in the curriculum and was taught at every level. Nonetheless, various issues relating to the course continued to be debated. On March 7, 1986, Şeyhmus Bahçeci, an MP from the SHP (*Sosyaldemokrat Halk Partisi* /Social Democratic People's Party), put three written questions to the Minister of Education, Metin Emiroğlu.[20] Of these, the third question cast particular light on how the state viewed the relation between religion education and non-Muslims. Bahçeci asked, "How are the religion courses carried out in schools where non-Muslims are going?" The answer he received was:

> In line with the aims of the course, the Religion, Culture and Morals Course gives information about religion, culture and ethics. Among the aims of the course are: to bear always in mind and protect our state's secularism principle; not to cause any breach of freedom of thought and conscience; not to force anybody to practice religious teachings.[21]

---

19 Namaz is the word for prayer used by Muslims speaking Indo-Iranian, South Slavic, and Turkic languages; it comes from an Indo-European root meaning to bow, or prostrate.

20 Yasemin Gümüş, "TBMM Tutanaklarında Milli Eğitim Bakanlarının Din Eğitimi ve Öğretimi Hakkındaki Görüşleri, 1980–2003." MA thesis, Marmara University Social Sciences Institute (2007): 32.

21 TBMM Tutanak Dergisi 27 (March 17, 1986): 94.

This was a summary response, which can only be interpreted as a failure by the government to engage seriously with the needs and rights of non-Muslims in the context of religion education.

The fact that compulsory religion education included non-Muslims was again a subject of the parliamentary agenda during the 1987 budget discussions. The Minister of Education said at this time that the Ministry would send out a directive to school administrators, reminding them that non-Muslims had the right to opt out of the religion course, but must still take the ethics course. The Minister then repeated his previous assertions that the course, in his view, offered general ethical and cultural dimensions of religion, making it relevant to non-Muslims.

Thus, between the years 1982 and 1987, when the religion course was first introduced in a compulsory manner, non-Muslims were forced to take the course. During this period, the Ministry received a number of letters from non-Muslims demanding an end to this practice. In 1987, the Board of Education and Discipline (*Talim Terbiye Kurulu*) finally agreed to that demand.[22] The same decision was repeated in a decree passed in 1990 and signed by Minister of Education Avni Akyol, Minister of Culture Namık Kemal Zeybek, Minister of National Defense Sefa Giray, and Minister of Labor and Social Security İmren Aykut. The decree ordered that Christians and Jews would be exempt from religion courses, provided they gave proof of their religious status. However, if they wished to attend the courses, they were to provide a petition from their parents.[23] All of this evidence suggests that there was much ambiguity, especially between 1982 and 1990, about how to handle non-Muslims who attended state schools.

In 1988, the Ministry of Religious Affairs, the Ankara University Theology Faculty, and the Turkish Diyanet Foundation (*Türk Diyanet Vakfı*) put together a seminar.[24] Along with other topics, the plan was to discuss the quality of compulsory religion education in Turkey. Mualla Selçuk gave a presentation detailing the current problems in religion education.[25] According to her field evidence, the courses did not take into consideration individual and cultural differences among students. Although it did not result in a reconsideration of the course structure, this was an important piece of research. It is arguable that state confidence in the educational model/approach known as the "non-confessional approach" (*mezhepler üstü yaklaşım*), allowed these problems to continue without

---

22 Zaman Gazetesi. "Bakanlık'tan 'seçmeli' din dersi uyarısı," *Zaman Gazetesi* (September 28, 2007).
23 Hacer Yıldırım Foggo, "Çocuğa Zorunlu Ayrımcılık," *Radikal Gazetesi* (October 24, 2004).
24 Altaş, 2002, 147.
25 Altaş, 2002, 154.

further scrutiny. As Shephard notes, this model had been developed in England by Ninian Smart during the 1970s, but was applied rather erroneously in its Turkish version.[26] Smart distanced religious studies from traditional theology. He argued that evaluating truth claims and apology had no role, but that investigation into the "truth" and "worth" of religion *per se* was a valid academic enterprise in the public arena of state funded education.[27] Thus the key point was that religious education should be non-confessional. Moreover, according to Smart, religious education should transcend the informative and "engage in dialogue with the para-historical claims of religions and anti-religious outlooks."[28] He argued that it need not be hostile to the type of committed approach pursued in theology, "provided it is open, and does not artificially restrict understanding and choice."[29] The basic premise here was that religious education should not be concerned with evangelizing, but with elucidating understanding or meaning.

In its Turkish version, although the intentions of theologians such as Bilgin were in line with Smart's ideas, the application of the course was far from Smart's model. In Turkey, it became a model that effectively "Sunnified" the course, under cover of this term "non-confessional" (*mezhepler üstü*), which can be literally translated to English as *supra-sectarian*, a model originally intended to safeguard students against the imposition of a single religion or *mezhep*. In practice, however, the model was used both to foreground Islamic teaching and maintain the unity of Islam. In sum, the application of Smart's model to the Turkish context proved to be highly problematic for non-Sunnis. In 1992, as the presence of non-Sunni students in classrooms was an undeniable fact, the Ministry of Education added non-Islamic religions to the framework of the course. This decision was explained in the *Tebliğler Dergisi*,[30] a decree that was sent to all schools nationwide:

> During the preparation of the religion education curriculum the possibility of the existence of a small number of pupils who belong to Christianity, Judaism and other religions was taken into consideration. In line with this view, to support the national and general culture, commensurate with the proportion assigned to each religion, knowledge has been provided about Islam, Judaism, Christianity and other religions respectively. This knowledge will un-

---

26 John Shepherd, "İslam ve Din Eğitimi: Mezhebe/dine Dayalı Olmayan Yaklaşım," *Din Öğretimi ve Din Hizmetleri Semineri* (Ankara: DIB, 1988): 370–78.
27 Ninian Smart, *Secular Education and the Logic of Religion* (New York: Humanities, 1968), 105.
28 Ninian Smart, *Secular Education*, 105.
29 Ninian Smart, *Secular Education*, 105.
30 Tebliğler Dergisi is a biweekly journal that has reported all Ministry of Education decisions since 1939.

doubtedly extend the world of pupils' faith and culture and it will enable them to behave more tolerantly and sensitively (sympathetically) towards followers of other religions.[31]

The decree also stated that Jewish and Christian students should not be taught or made to recite the prayers and topics of *Kelime-i Şahadet, Kelime-i Tevhid, Besmele, Amentü, Ayet, Sure* and *Namaz.* Therefore, they must not be held responsible for these topics in determining their grades.[32] This decree marks a clear departure from the previous (1990) decree, which stated that Christians and Jews were to be exempted from the course. Unfortunately, there is little evidence to show why this change was introduced. It certainly added to the ambiguity about how to handle non-Muslims in religion courses, even if the larger state intention was to make the course more secular.

Kaymakcan argues that the secondary school curriculum prepared in 1982 did allow for teaching non-Islamic religions, and accordingly, textbooks have included material on Christianity, Judaism and other non-Islamic religions.[33] (In fact, these plans never progressed beyond a couple of pages in some of the textbooks. Moreover, Alevism was almost never mentioned.) Kaymakcan seeks to explain the lack of interest in the question of how non-Islamic religions should be presented and handled in religion education. He identifies three explanatory factors. The first one addresses the "theological understanding of other religions."[34] According to Kaymakcan, the inherited *medrese* understanding of religion has remained prevalent in contemporary religious studies in Turkey. This inherited (Islamic) understanding of religion defines non-Islamic religions as either corrupted divine religions or non-divine religions. And on the basis of this outlook, a confessional method has been adopted for the study of other religions. Thus, the main purpose of this method has been to assert the superiority of Islam over other religions. Certainly it is true that course textbooks almost always stress the "fact" that Islam is the only divine religion and that it has remained uncorrupted, unlike other religions.

Secondly, Kaymakcan cites what he calls the "'priorities in the study of religion education in Turkey."[35] He argues that as a result of many fluctuations in the role of religion, and the relatively late recognition of the importance of religion education in modern Turkey, the question of how to handle non-Islamic re-

---

31 Kaymakcan, 1999, 283.
32 Foggo, 2004.
33 Kaymakcan, 1999, 281.
34 Kaymakcan, 1999, 281.
35 Kaymakcan, 1999, 281.

ligions, particularly Christianity and Judaism, has received little attention from academic researchers.

The third factor, according to Kaymakcan, is the "Practical importance of the study of non-Islamic religions for Turks."[36] In this article, Kaymakcan argues that in comparison with Western Europe, Turkey cannot be considered a multi-faith society. He finds that because the majority of the Turkish population is Muslim and non-Muslims have their own community schools, Turkish theologians have felt little pressure to conduct research in this area.[37] Taken together, these three factors help to explain educators' reluctance to develop religion education for religions other than Sunni Islam.

The parliamentary debates between 1980 and 1997 revealed MPs' concerns about the religion course once it had come into full force. Many thought that the application of the course was not going as planned, and rumors surfaced that teachers were making the children learn the Koran in schools. There were MPs who thought that religious material should be kept to a minimum in the courses, and that parents who wanted their children to receive religion instruction had access to places outside school to do so.[38]

With time, it became obvious that the curriculum of the religion course developed by the Board of Education included the teaching of prayers and religious practices. The curriculum required students in the 4th grade to memorize prayers and at the 6th grade level, to perform daily prayers. Thus, it was clear that confessional religious instruction was being conducted within the compulsory courses.[39]

The courses have lasted to the present day and remain relatively unchallenged, due partly to a lack of debate or civic interest in the issue. Yet far from bringing peace to society and between the different *mezheps*, the courses seem to have created greater enmity, undermining public trust (especially that of the Alevis) in the impartiality of the state towards all religions.

3 Conclusion

This chapter has provided a detailed study of a period in the history of compulsory religion education that has been largely unexamined by Turkish scholars. It

---

36 Kaymakcan, 1999, 281.
37 Kaymakcan, 1999, 282.
38 Gümüş, 2007, 51.
39 "Religion and Schooling in Turkey: The Need for Reform," Education Reform Initiative. Istanbul: Sabancı University, 2005.

is my contention that this history holds important details as to how the course came into being, as well as its development in the context of various pedagogical and policy commissions that worked under the shadow of the military junta. Looking at specific debates throughout this period, one can see that the main point of controversy concerned the question of the compatibility of the course with the existing secularism clause of the constitution. As this question was addressed mainly through rather abstract legal discourses, the situation of religious minorities in relation to both the course and the secularism principle was largely ignored. More specifically, Alevism was ignored, with a kind of imposed "assimilation" occurring at the state level. The numbers of non-Muslims attending the state schools were diminishing, and so, the question of their longer-term situation was not seen as a major problem. These processes worked to reinforce the asymmetrical relationship that the Turkish state established in relation to minorities, one that effectively undermines the principle of secularism and state neutrality.

Works Cited

Altaş, Nurullah. "Türkiye'de Zorunlu Din Öğretimini Yapılandıran Süreç, Hedefler ve YeniYöntem Arayışları" [The Process, Aims and the Search for New Methods that Structure Compulsory Religion Education in Turkey]. *Dini Araştırmalar Dergisi* (January-April 2002): 145–68.

Ayhan, Halis. *Türkiye'de Din Eğitimi* [Religion Education in Turkey]. Istanbul: Dem, 2004.

Bilgin, Beyza. *Türkiye'de Din Eğitimi ve Liselerde Din Dersleri* [Religion Education in Turkey and Religion Courses at High Schools]. Ankara: Emel, 1980.

Din Öğretimi Genel Müdürlüğü, ed. *New Methodological Approaches in Religious Education, International Symposium, Papers and Discussions.* Ankara: MEB, 2004.

Foggo, Hacer Yıldırım. "Çocuğa Zorunlu Ayrımcılık" *Radikal Gazetesi* (October 24, 2004).

Kaplan, İsmail. "The Ideology of National Education in Turkey and Its Implications for Political Socialisation." PhD Diss., Boğaziçi University Institute of Social Sciences, 1998.

Kaplan, Sam. "Religious Nationalism: A Textbook Case from Turkey." *Comparative Studies of South Asia, Africa and the Middle East* 25.3 (2005): 113–27.

Kaymakcan, Recep. "Christianity in Turkish Religious Education." *Islam and Christian-Muslim Relations* 10.3 (1999): 279–293.

"Religion and Schooling in Turkey: The Need for Reform." *Education Reform Initiative.* Istanbul: Sabancı University, 2005.

Shepherd, John. "İslam ve Din Eğitimi: Mezhebe/dine Dayalı Olmayan Yaklaşım." Trans. Bekir Demirkol. *Din Öğretimi ve Din Hizmetleri Semineri.* Ankara: DIB, 1988. (Originally published as "Islam and Religious Education: A Non-Confessional Approach.")

Smart, Ninian. *Secular Education and the Logic of Religion.* New York: Humanities, 1968.

Toktaş, Şule. "Citizenship and Minorities: A Historical Overview of Turkey's Jewish Minority." *Journal of Historical Sociology* 18.4 (December 2005): 394–429.

Turkey. *Din Eğitimi Çalışma Grubu Raporu* [Religion Instruction Working Committee]. Ankara: Milli Eğitim Bakanlığı, February 6, 1981.

Turkey. Diyanet İşleri Başkanlığı. *Türkiye'de Din Eğitim ve Öğretimi Hakkında Rapor* [Report about religion education and instruction in Turkey]. Ankara: Devlet Basımevi, 1981.

Turkey. Milli Eğitim Bakanlığı Tebliğler Dergisi. *Din Kültürü ve Ahlak Bilgisi Programı* [Religion and Morals Program]. March 29, 1982.

Turkey. TBMM *Tutanak Dergisi* 27 (March 17, 1986): 94.

Wirth, Louis. "The Problem of Minority Groups," in *The Science of Man in the World Crisis*, edited by Ralph Linton, 347, New York: Columbia University Press, 1945.

Yasemin, Gümüş. "TBMM Tutanaklarında Milli Evğitim Bakanlarının Din Eğitimi ve Öğretimi Hakkındaki Görüşleri 1980–2003" [The views of Ministers of National Education about Religion Education as Reflected in the Parliamentary Reports]. Master's thesis, Marmara University Social Sciences Institute, 2007.

Zaman, Gazetesi. "Bakanlık'tan 'seçmeli' din dersi uyarısı" ['Voluntary' Religion Education Warning of the Minister]. September 28, 2007.

Jonathan R. Beloff
The Historical Relationship between Religion and Government in Rwanda

1 Introduction

Rwanda recently commemorated the twenty-first year anniversary of the 1994 Genocide Against the Tutsi, commonly known around the world as the Rwandan Genocide. The horrific massacres did not take place in concentration camps, in spaces removed from society, as in the Holocaust or the Cambodian Genocide. Rather, the killing of nearly one million Tutsis and moderate Hutus took place in schools, neighborhoods and most conspicuously of all, in religious establishments. The houses of God became saturated with the blood of a people who believed in the mercy of an all-knowing religious deity and the religious figures who represented their religious faiths. The cornerstone of the Rwandan Genocide was the erstwhile "infallible" Catholic Church, which had arrived with the colonization of Rwanda by Germans and Belgians in the early 20 century. The Church supported laws of "ethnic" division, influenced politics, and, ultimately, housed the genocide. With the infamous 100 days of genocidal killing, ending with an invasion by the Rwandan Patriotic Front (RPF) on July 4, 1994, the church faced something that it never had before – a great wall of secularity dividing it from the government of Rwanda. Based on the genocide, the new RPF-dominated government decided that religious institutions should have significantly less political power and influence in civil society, as opposed to its historically dominant role, and advanced a secular government free of subservience to religious leaders.

Rwanda is considered a Christian country. Around 57 % of Rwandans classify themselves as Roman Catholic, with Anglicans making up roughly 26 %. Other forms of Christianity, such as the Seven Day Adventists and Jehovah's Witnesses, also exist and are thriving. Islam has grown to over 5 %[1] since the end of the genocide, with the support of the RPF government that promotes freedom of religion. Agnosticism and atheism have also increased sharply among the community of genocide survivors, survivors who either question existing religious establishments or have basic fundamental problems of believing in an all-loving God

---

1 US Department of State, "2012 Report on International Religious Freedom," Last modified May 20, 2013 http://www.refworld.org/docid/519dd4963.html (Accessed February 1, 2014).

who allowed such cruelties to take place against them and their families. Given such religious diversity, and a very unpleasant history, this chapter examines the relationship of the Rwandan government and its citizens with religious institutions. It highlights how Rwandan history, played out in a contest between political and religious institutions, saw the new Rwandan government promoting a secular-based government.

This chapter will first examine the history of Rwanda's religiosity within three particular time periods. The first is during Rwanda's colonization from 1886 to 1962, when Christianity was introduced, "ethnic" divisions were created, and church-government relations were established, ultimately leading to the rise of Hutu genocide ideology. Secondly, the chapter examines the role of religion after independence, until 1994, including a historical section outlining the role of Christianity during the genocide. The chapter will then turn to the manner in which the new RPF-led Rwandan government crafted public policy that created separation of religious from the state. Rwanda is still a highly religious Christian country, but since the genocide, it sees its religious establishments as flawed and incapable of ruling within the political sphere. Further, Rwanda has created a government under which religious belief and practice is *plural* and government is ideally neutral with reference to religious doctrines and institutions.

2 The Saturation of Religious Influence in Rwandan Political History

2.1 The development of church-state influence in colonial Rwanda

Rwanda's religious history is structurally based on the role of the White Fathers and their missions in colonial Rwanda. Carney and Mbanda[2] have written in depth on the history of the White Father, the first religious priest in the region. In 1900, the first Catholic missionaries under Fr. Leon-Paul Classe entered the colony to try to spread Christianity after successful missions in Buganda, Uganda. Classe developed the strategic relationship between the White Fathers and the Rwandan monarchy. This close church-government relationship provided

---

2 J. J. Carney, *Rwanda Before the Genocide: Catholic Politics and Ethnic Discourse in the Late Colonial Era* (New York, NY: Oxford University Press, 2014), 16 – 22, 210 – 1; Laurent Mbanda. *Committed to Conflict: The Destruction of the Church in Rwanda* (London: Society for Promoting Christian Knowledge, 1997), 3 – 6.

the *Mwami*, the (usually Tutsi) King of Rwanda, with the full support of the Catholic Church.[3] It was under Classe's watch that Rwanda became a "Christian Kingdom in Africa."[4] As Classe was gaining more followers, he encountered conflict with the Mwami, Yuhi V Musinga, who decreed that Christian missionary centers could operate in his kingdom, but could not be established within the region's capital city of Nyzana, thus robbing Classe of access to political elites. However, he was able to establish missions in the east (Zaza), north (Rwaza), northwestern (Nyundo) and southwestern (Mibirizi) parts of Rwanda, which was were the poorer local populations resided.[5] Because of this geographical challenge, missionaries were only able to convert the poorest of the Hutu and Tutsi peasants rather than the desired Tutsi elites. In addition to its inability to convert the masses, the Catholic Church also faced competition from the Anglicans, and by 1908, from the Lutherans.[6]

The end of World War I led to the colonial transfer of governance of Rwanda and Burundi from Germany to Belgium. Under Belgian colonial rule, Christianity was finally able to gain political power. Three important figures came out of this time period. The first was Mutara III Rudahigqa, who became Mwami after Classe and Belgian colonial leaders conspired for Musinga's removal in 1931. Mutara's rise to power signaled the start of Rwanda becoming a Christian nation. In 1943, he was baptized into the Christian faith and, three years later, in 1946, he dedicated "Rwanda's allegiance to Jesus Christ." The conversion to Christianity sparked two results. The first was that many Rwandan elites saw no other choice but to convert to Christianity. Thus, conversion numbers grew rapidly, to the tens of thousands every year. The high conversion rate would continue well into independence. The second result was that many Rwandans saw the removal of Musinga as Belgium's official message to all potential opponents of its colonial governance. This event is now depicted as the point of no return for

---

3 Stephen Kinzer, *A Thousand Hills: Rwanda's Rebirth and the Man Who Dreamed It* (Hoboken, NJ: John Wiley & Sons, Inc., 2008), 27.
4 J.J. Carney, *Rwanda Before the Genocide: Catholic Politics and Ethnic Discourse in the Late Colonial Era*, 27 – 39; Gérard Prunier, *The Rwanda Crisis, History of A Genocide* (London: Columbia University Press, 1997), 30 – 33.
5 J.J. Carney, *Rwanda Before the Genocide: Catholic Politics and Ethnic Discourse in the Late Colonial Era*, 25, 210; Kinzer, *A Thousand Hills: Rwanda's Rebirth and the Man Who Dreamed It*, 27.
6 Carney, *Rwanda Before the Genocide: Catholic Politics and Ethnic Discourse in the Late Colonial Era*, 25, 210; Kinzer, *A Thousand Hills: Rwanda's Rebirth and the Man Who Dreamed It*, 36 – 43; Philip Gourevitch, *We Wish to Inform You That Tomorrow We Will be Killed With Our Families: Stories from Rwanda* (New York, NY: Farrar, Straus and Giroux, 1999), 590 – 601; Mbanda, *Committed to Conflict: The Destruction of the Church in Rwanda*, 8 – 26; Timothy Longman, *Christianity and Genocide in Rwanda* (New York, NY: Cambridge University Press, 2010), 33 – 82.

Rwandans, who became permanently affected by European colonization.[7] The third was the controversial figure of Andre Perraudin, who led the Catholic Church in Rwanda after the death of Classe in 1945.[8] Christian scholars credit Perraudin for making Rwanda a Christian nation. However, he is mostly known by Rwandans and particular the RPF as the priest who helped in the formation of "ethnic" identities through the publication of *Super Omni Caritas,* which is recognized as the document that shifted the Church's allegiance away from the Tutsi political order to the Hutu peasants, and which changed the socioeconomic classes into ethnicities with *ethnic* Hutus needing to raise themselves above *ethnic* Tutsis.[9] This support stemmed from religious pity for the poor conditions that non-elites endured as well as his fears over the fact that the pro-monarchy political party, the Rwanda National Union (UNAR), was also pro-communist.[10] The last person is Aloys Bigirumwami, who was able to foresee the future ethnic problems that the Catholic Church was propagating. Throughout his tenure as bishop, he tried to push for national unity and dismissed ideas of ethnic power.[11] His vision of a post-ethnic Rwanda became the unofficial norm for the RPF-led government, which has through legislation ended ethnicity in favor of a population of Rwandans rather than Hutus, Tutsis, or Twa.

The most significant aspect of the White Fathers was not the number of Rwandans they converted, nor making the nation into one of the most religiously Christian countries in Africa. It was how the Rwandans were converted. As mentioned before, the religious establishment utilized the previous socioeconomic conditions and mistakenly saw them as ethnic identities. In other words, the socioeconomic differences between the groups would later become "ethnicities" that the Belgians, with support from the Catholic Church, fostered with the introduction of ethnic identity cards in 1932 and 1933. There are historically three groups in Rwanda. The first is the Hutu, predominantly farmers. The historical and then the Belgian understanding of the Hutu was someone who owned

---

7 Prunier, *The Rwanda Crisis, History of A Genocide,* 30–2, 47–53.

8 Carney, *Rwanda Before the Genocide: Catholic Politics and Ethnic Discourse in the Late Colonial Era,* 64, 151–65.

9 Carney, *Rwanda Before the Genocide: Catholic Politics and Ethnic Discourse in the Late Colonial Era,* 98–9, and 167; Colin Waugh, *Paul Kagame and Rwanda: Power, Genocide and the RPF* (Jefferson, NC: McFarland & Company, Inc., 2004) e-ISBN: 978–14766–1315–4, 3825–33.

10 Carney, *Rwanda Before the Genocide: Catholic Politics and Ethnic Discourse in the Late Colonial Era,* 114, 30, and 44.

11 Carney, *Rwanda Before the Genocide: Catholic Politics and Ethnic Discourse in the Late Colonial Era,* 129–33, 49, 62–74; Longman, *Christianity and Genocide in Rwanda,* 68, 72–4.

less than 10 cows. For the White Fathers and especially Perraudin, they were considered the suffering masses that needed to be converted in order for them to reach "salvation." The Tutsi are classified as predominantly herders who owned more than 10 cows. The Tutsis were considered the unreligious bourgeoisie, who, by the late colonial period, aligned themselves more with wealth than with God. The last group, which comprises less than 1% of the country, is the Twa. They are predominantly hunter-gatherer nomads that are found in central Africa.[12] "Ethnicity" played a significant role in the access to education, when the German and Belgian colonial powers granted full control to the White Fathers. Education was the key mechanism for Rwandans to be able to escape poverty. However, education was restricted for only Tutsis, and a few lucky Hutus. Higher education was extremely exclusive, with the existence of only one university in the southern city of Butare, now currently called Huye.[13] Ethnic-based enrollment angered many Hutus, who felt that Tutsi elites were preventing them from access to education in order to maintain their own political and social supremacy. After independence, ethnic quotas continued, but educational restriction negatively affected the Tutsis rather than the Hutus.

During most of Belgian colonial rule, the Tutsi elites governed Rwanda under the orders of the Belgian colonial government. Resentment against the Tutsi political elite by the Hutu population grew with a growing desire for independence.[14] However, as Belgium was under pressure by the international community to withdraw from their colonies and institute democratic elections, the country switched its allegiance from the Tutsi elites to the Hutu general population. This began with Belgian colonial Governor Jean-Paul Harroy, who supported Hutu ethnic leaders, as would the future Rwandan president Gregorie Kayibanda.[15] In a similar fashion, the Catholic Church also switched its allegiance from the Tutsi population to Hutu parties. As previously mentioned, Perraudin was nervous that Tutsi aligned political groups such as UNAR would transform

---

12 Prunier, *The Rwanda Crisis, History of A Genocide*, 1–23; Kinzer, *A Thousand Hills: Rwanda's Rebirth and the Man Who Dreamed It*, 24–8.

13 Prunier, *The Rwanda Crisis, History of A Genocide*, 54; Longman, *Christianity and Genocide in Rwanda*, 103–5, 67–77, 201; John Rutayisire, John Kabano and Jolly Rubagiza, "Redefining Rwanda's Future: The Role of Curriculum in Social Reconstruction," in Tawil S. and Harley A. eds. *Education, Conflict and Social Cohesion* (Geneva: International Bureau of Education, UNESCO, 2004): 315–74.

14 Robert Gribbin, *In the Aftermath of Genocide: The U.S. Role in Rwanda* (Lincoln, NE: iUniverse, Inc., 2005). E-ISBN 978–0–5957–9170–5 (eBook), 372–3; Waugh, *Paul Kagame and Rwanda: Power, Genocide and the RPF*, 3818–9.

15 Carney, *Rwanda Before the Genocide: Catholic Politics and Ethnic Discourse in the Late Colonial Era*, 101–2, 125–8; Prunier, *The Rwanda Crisis, History of A Genocide*, 41–8, 81.

Rwanda into a communist society, thus ending the church's role in the country. Kayibanda previously worked for the White Fathers as an editor for their newspapers, the *L'Association des Amities Belge-Rwandaises* and the *Mouvement Politique Progressiste*. His writings and education helped him to create the pro-Hutu party named, *Parti du Mouvement de l'Emancipation Hutu*, or in English, the Party of the Hutu Emancipation Movement (Parmehutu).[16] This party had the unofficial support of Perraudin; however, he instructed his priests not to openly support any particular political party, although by its declarations Party of the Hutu Emancipation Movement thanked the Catholic Church and specifically the White Fathers for helping save the country from Tutsis.[17] Colonization resulted in Rwanda becoming one of the most Christian nations in the world. It also crafted a Hutu ideology that led to pogroms and the exiling of thousands of people, and eventually, genocide. This shift in loyalty on behalf of the Belgian colonialists and the Catholic Church in the country set the stage for future ethnic tensions, and for the positioning of the Catholic Church in a more politicized role.

2.2 Church-state partnership and reparation for the 1994 genocide

By 1962, Belgium departed from Rwanda, which was governed by a Hutu majority that seized political control from Kayibanda and his Parmehutu party. During the Kayibanda regime from 1962 to 1973, church-state relations remained strong. During colonization, governmental responsibilities to society, such as education and healthcare, were being completely or partially facilitated by the church. In particular, educational services were still restricted for Hutu students, and in particular, preference for southern Hutus allowed only them to attend.[18] Kayibanda continued to use the church to keep political dominance with the promise

---

16 Carney, *Rwanda Before the Genocide: Catholic Politics and Ethnic Discourse in the Late Colonial Era*, 48–55, 125–9, 56–7, 84–9; Mbanda, *Committed to Conflict: The Destruction of the Church in Rwanda*, 91.

17 Carney, *Rwanda Before the Genocide: Catholic Politics and Ethnic Discourse in the Late Colonial Era*, 114, 147, Mbanda, *Committed to Conflict: The Destruction of the Church in Rwanda*, 158–9.

18 Gribbin, *In the Aftermath of Genocide: The U.S. Role in Rwanda*, 572–5; Prunier, *The Rwanda Crisis, History of A Genocide*, 54–61.

of Rwanda continuing to be a Christian nation.[19] Religious leaders had access to alter laws that they believed threatened the church's power. Throughout this time period, Kayibanda would orchestrate pogroms against the Rwandan Tutsis in order to try to secure more of his Hutu political base. Unlike during the 1994 genocide, the churches were relatively left untouched by the violence.[20] However, the Parmehutu began to lose power as Kayibanda tried to push for new legislation that would grant him more authority.[21]

In 1973, Major General Juvenal Habyarimana seized political control in a military coup from Kayibanda. He and his wife were devout Catholics, who promoted religiosity in Rwanda. Unlike under the previous regime, the Habyarimana administration took over educational and health services from religious institutions. Even with these public policy changes, the role of religious institutions in government did not decrease, but shifted. Priests and religious leaders changed from being the predominant administrators of public services to the ones drafting laws and regulations. Many high profile priests and bishops became members of a small pro-northern Hutu association known as the *Akazu* or the *'little house'*, run by the President's wife, Agatha Habyarimana.[22] The shift which involved the Catholic Church crafting public policy had an impact on the continued anti-Tutsi ideology, anti-birth control methods, education, and anti-Muslim policies.[23] As during the Kayibanda regime, Habyarimana allowed religious influence into legislation with the unofficial agreement that religious leaders would support his administration and the *Akazu*.[24]

The Habyarimana administration experienced great difficulties during the late 1980s and during the 1990–1994 civil war in Rwanda, because of economic underdevelopment and newfound pressure by Rwandan Tutsi-refugees, who had been forced to flee over the previous thirty-year period, and who wished to return

---

19 Carney, *Rwanda Before the Genocide: Catholic Politics and Ethnic Discourse in the Late Colonial Era*, 160.
20 Mbanda, *Committed to Conflict: The Destruction of the Church in Rwanda*, 90; Romeo Dallaire, *Shaking Hands with the Devil: The Failure of Humanity in Rwanda* (New York: Carroll & Graf Publishers, 2004), 190.
21 Carney, *Rwanda Before the Genocide: Catholic Politics and Ethnic Discourse in the Late Colonial Era*, 189–90; Prunier, *The Rwanda Crisis, History of A Genocide*, 74.
22 Gourevitch, *We Wish to Inform You That Tomorrow We Will be Killed With Our Families*, 891–2.
23 Prunier, *The Rwanda Crisis, History of A Genocide*, 89, 132–3.
24 Carney, *Rwanda Before the Genocide: Catholic Politics and Ethnic Discourse in the Late Colonial Era*, 193; Margee Ensign, and William Bertrand, *Rwanda: History and Hope* (Lanham, MD: University Press of America, Inc., 2010), 5; Mbanda, *Committed to Conflict: The Destruction of the Church in Rwanda*, 60–1.

to their homes. By 1990, the church's pro-Hutu and anti-Tutsi ethnic ideology began to be questioned by some religious leaders. They questioned how the Catholic Church could spread the loving word of God and combine it with a hatred for God's creatures. Unfortunately, only five priests spoke out nationally, and most religious institutions did not support them.[25] Even though religious institutions were helping to spread a message that was becoming ever more genocidal against the Tutsi population, some Tutsis did view religious priesthood as a possible escape from the camps into opportunities for education and better jobs.[26] Post-independence Rwanda did not see a significant change in power for the Catholic Church or any other major denominations of Christianity. Perhaps the only change was the growth of ethnic hatred that was able to spread through the network of churches in a very religious country.

2.3 The "Big Genocide": church participation in the 1994 genocide

Many authors have written about the involvement of the church in the 1994 Rwandan Genocide, including Aguilar[27], Gourevitch[28], Longman[29], Kantongole and Wilson-Hartgove[30], and Rittner, Roth and Whitworth[31]. On the night of April 6, 1994, the presidential plane of President Habyarimana was shot down when he was returning from a regional conference in Arusha, Tanzania, attempting to end the Rwandan Civil War and facilitating the integration of the RPF into the Rwandan government. Pro-Hutu extremists, who believed in the fundamentals of Hutu supremacy of the Hutu Ten Commandments, established a new government that oversaw what was arguably one of the bloodiest genocides in the 20th century. In 100 days, an estimated 800,000 to one million Tutsis and mod-

---

25 Mbanda, *Committed to Conflict: The Destruction of the Church in Rwanda*, 73 – 4; Prunier, *The Rwanda Crisis, History of A Genocide*, 132 – 3.
26 Prunier, *The Rwanda Crisis, History of A Genocide*, 75.
27 Mario Aguilar, *Theology, Liberation and Genocide: A Theology of the Periphery*, (London: SCM Press, 2009).
28 Gourevitch, *We Wish to Inform You That Tomorrow We Will be Killed With Our Families*.
29 Longman, *Christianity and Genocide in Rwanda*.
30 Emanuel Katongole and Jonathan Wilson-Hartgrove, *Mirror to the Church: Resurrecting Faith after Genocide in Rwanda* (Grand Rapids, MI: Zondervan, 2009).
31 Carol J. Rittner, John. K Roth, and Wendy Whitworth, *Genocide in Rwanda: Complicity of the Churches?* (St. Paul, MN: Paragon House, 2004).

erate Hutus were butchered by their friends and neighbors.[32] Most of the massacres occurred within the walls of religious establishments, which had previously protected Tutsis during previous pogroms. Before 1994, priests protected their religious followers from the militias by publically declaring churches safe zones for all who sought refuge.[33] But in 1994, the churches predominantly worked with local governing institutions. Local government leaders told Tutsis to hide in the churches for protection, as they had during past violence. Priests would welcome the fleeing people and promise that the churches would be protected. Once the churches were filled to capacity, the priests called for the killing squads to enter the churches to butcher the refugees.[34] Not even the holy Christian city of Kibeho was spared the violence.[35] It is important to note that not all priests and nuns participated in these horrific acts. Some did try to save the refugees, but would be unsuccessful and usually faced the same threats, even if they were Hutus.[36] Nearly every church that existed in 1994 was used for some form of mass killing. Churches, such as the St. Famille church in central Kigali, which were not used in the massacres, were usually protected by United Nation's troops, but even such churches saw some violence.[37]

During the last few weeks of the genocide, two significant events occurred that later shaped the RPF-led Rwandan government's relationship with the country's religious institutions. The first was the undertaking of revenge killings by RPF soldiers in the Catholic Church Center outside of Gitarama known as Kabgayi. This was a specific location that Pope John Paul II formally requested that General Romeo Dollaire protect with UNAMIR troops; but they were ineffective. Most of the residents at the religious site decided to stay and wait for the

---

32 Carol J. Rittner, John. K Roth, and Wendy Whitworth, *Genocide in Rwanda: Complicity of the Churches*, 20–4; Kigali Memorial Centre, *Jenoside* (Kigali, Rwanda: Aegis Trust, 2004), 20; Kinzer, *A Thousand Hills: Rwanda's Reirth and the Man Who Dreamed It*, 1, 104; Melvern, Linda, Melvern, *A People Betrayed, the Role of the West in Rwanda's Genocide* (New York, NY: Zed Books Ltd, 2004), 1–6.

33 Dallaire, *Shaking Hands with the Devil: The Failure of Humanity in Rwanda*, 190; Mbanda, *Committed to Conflict: The Destruction of the Church in Rwanda*, 90.

34 Gourevitch, *We Wish to Inform You That Tomorrow We Will be Killed With Our Families*; 1768–80; Kinzer, *A Thousand Hills: Rwanda's Rebirth and the Man Who Dreamed It*, 160–1; Longman, 2001, 163–86, 181; John Rucyakana, *The Bishop of Rwanda* (Nashville, TN: Thomas Nelson, 2007), 106.

35 Jean-Pierre Bucyensenge, "Kibeho: When the 'Holy Land' Was Turned into 'Butcher Land,'" *The New Times* Last modified February 1, 2014. http://www.newtimes.co.rw/news/index.php?i= 15620&a=74201 (Accessed February 2, 2014).

36 Prunier, *The Rwanda Crisis, History of A Genocide*, 231.

37 Dallaire, *Shaking Hands with the Devil: The Failure of Humanity in Rwanda*, 348–9; Gourevitch, *We Wish to Inform You That Tomorrow We Will be Killed With Our Families*, 1756.

incoming RPF soldiers, even though the religious leaders were risking their lives after they participated in earlier genocide-related crimes. On June 3, a number of RPF soldiers, who invaded and secured the region, entered the monastery with the goal of butchering its religious leaders. At the time, there were more than 25,000 people seeking refuge at the church. A handful of RPF troops killed the archbishop with three of his bishops (Vincent Nsengiyumva, Thaddee Nsengiyuva and Joseph Ruzindana), ten priests, and some 1,500 other victims.[38] UNAMIR was able to coordinate with the RPF and the Rwandan government military known as the Rwanda Armed Forces (FAR) to have the bodies transferred to the interim government for proper burial.[39] The real cause for the killing might never be fully known. But this event did pave the way for the RPF to recommend new bishops, whom they wanted appointed by the Vatican. If Catholic leaders saw these murders as horrific, the RPF saw the final acts of fleeing religious leaders as equally reprehensible. Twenty-nine priests wrote an official letter to Pope Paul II, who had visited Rwanda in 1990, asking him to forgive the Hutus who had been killed by their Tutsi neighbors during the genocide. That is, they referred to the genocide as having been committed by the Tutsis against the Hutus. Pope Paul II blessed the Hutu refugees, and unbeknownst to him, also blessed the genocidaires from his Vatican office. This genocide denial was later corrected.[40] Many within the RPF were outraged that not only had the domestic Catholic Church participated in the massacres, but that Catholicism seemed to have blessed the killers.

The genocide finally ended on July 18 when the RPF liberated Rwanda from the genocidal government.[41] Many RPF fighters who liberated towns and villages across country saw churches not only as accomplices to the massacres, but also as the main warehouses of the genocide perpetrators. Some soldiers as well as survivors were affected by what they witnessed and used religious observance as a coping mechanism. However, others rejected religion altogether. This was likely because of their inability to accept a God that would allow such suffering in his own religious establishments, which is a common theme among survivors of the genocide.[42] Also, a number of these soldiers and survivors turned to other religions in order to worship God without being connected to the institutions that

---

38 Prunier, *The Rwanda Crisis, History of A Genocide*, 270 – 1; Gribbin, *In the Aftermath of Genocide: The U.S. Role in Rwanda*, 141.
39 Dallaire, *Shaking Hands with the Devil: The Failure of Humanity in Rwanda*, 414.
40 Rucyakana, *The Bishop of Rwanda*, 107.
41 Prunier, *The Rwanda Crisis, History of A Genocide*, 299.
42 This was gathered through research conducted at the Kigali Genocide Memorial of genocide survivors in June 2012.

participated in the genocide. Perhaps most significantly, the genocide effected state/religious relations as the post-genocide government broke away from religion-backed and shifted towards secular-based governance in order to reduce the Catholic Church's political power on civil society.

3 Post-Genocide Rwanda and Church and State Relations

3.1 RPF's trust in religious institutions

The Catholic Church could only speculate on what the future held for Rwanda. Most of the religious leaders, with the nearly two million Hutus, fled from the RPF to eastern Zaire.[43] While in self-exile, they continued religious services for their followers, who, during the genocide, had been either bystanders or perpetrators. The Sunday sermons contained a dual message. The first was a campaign to paint the RPF as perpetrators of the Civil War violence and genocide against Hutus. Thus, it became a religious duty for the exiled Hutus to pray to God for newfound strength to prepare to retake Rwanda from the 'un-Godly' RPF. The next message was for the congregation to continue to seek the return to their home villages back in Rwanda of priests as religious leaders. Many priests fully expected that once they returned to Rwanda, they would be able to regain their parishes, even though they participated in mass killings that took place within church walls. The remaining priests and religious officials were uncertain on how the RPF would govern Rwanda. Most of all, they were nervous about losing political influence in the new government especially with news of its promotion of a secular-based society.[44] Some Priests openly spoke out against the RPF immediately after the genocide, because of how the RPF's murdered the former Archbishop Nsengiyumva, its Marxist origins and suspected anti-religious beliefs, as well as the great loss of political power that the Priests were accustomed

---

43 Prunier, *The Rwanda Crisis, History of A Genocide*, 312.

44 Prunier, *The Rwanda Crisis, History of A Genocide*, 312–8; Mahmood Mamdani, *When Victims Become Killers: Colonialism, Nativism and the Genocide in Rwanda* (Princeton, NJ: Princeton University Press, 2001), 254–6; Ensign, Bertrand, *Rwanda: History and Hope*, 43–4, 8–50; Longman, *Christianity and Genocide in Rwanda*, 163–86, 181–2; Maria Rinaldo and Peter Rinaldo, "In the Name of God," http://www.youtube.com/watch?v=LQBmd4–5UEM. Accessed February 1, 2014.

to having under the Habyarimana that was now gone with the RPF in political power.[45]

The RPF's history with religious institutions reflects the origin of Tutsi refugees in Uganda. Religious education was one of the few vehicles for upward mobility in Uganda, as a result of xenophobic measures enforced by the Milton Oboto and Idi Amin Administrations. However, unlike in Rwanda, religious institutions were scarce in refugee camps.[46] This lack of religious exposure was one of the factors that influenced the RPF's rather dismissive attitude towards religion. At first, the RPF was a Marxist organization that upheld some of the principles of involved in ending religious domination over local populations. Many saw the church as one of the main reasons for underdevelopment and corruption on the African continent. Others saw the church as a player in public affairs that needed to be restrained in order to prevent religious corruption among government officials. Still others saw the church as a huge potential ally for the RPF once they gained political power. However, the genocide significantly altered most perceptions of the role of religion in society. After liberating Rwanda from the genocide forces and witnessing churches filled with dead bodies, many RPF members increasingly saw Christianity as nothing more than a political tool that needed to be restrained. The genocide heightened the need for a decreased role for the church in the new RPF-led government, through the creation and enforcement of a separation between church and state and the promotion of a secular nation that could be privately but not publically religious.[47] In addition, they questioned whether religion could play a positive role in preventing a future genocide; given that the religious had committed genocide themselves, how could the religious continue to follow religious leaders, and how could they use houses of worship that were sites of massacres? Overall, an internal debate raged within the new government regarding the role of Christianity in the Rwanda.

The RPF decided that the new government would enforce a new policy of separation of church and state in order to prevent future abuses of soft political church power on public policies.[48] Rwanda would allow churches and other religious establishments to influence public opinion but not public policy. Former Vice President and current President Paul Kagame supported the decision to continue to allow religious involvement in the civil society. The RPF's policies to-

---

45 Ensign, Bertrand, *Rwanda: History and Hope*, 45.
46 Ensign, Bertrand, *Rwanda: History and Hope*, 61–73; Kinzer, *A Thousand Hills: Rwanda's Rebirth and the Man Who Dreamed It*, 30, 9, 50.
47 Aguilar Mario, *Theology, Liberation and Genocide: A Theology of the Periphery*, 4–7.
48 Mbanda, *Committed to Conflict: The Destruction of the Church in Rwanda*, 114–5.

wards religion were to be modeled after Kagame's own religiosity.[49] He was born a Christian, yet was never publically religious. Religious leaders such as Rick Warren extols Kagame as an African visionary who strives for development through market-oriented principles and individual improvement. Pastor Warren calls Kagame a "great Christian" even though Kagame rarely express his religious beliefs in public ceremonies. Anglican Bishop John Rucyahana, a leading public religious official, writes that Kagame's religious beliefs are private and that they do not affect his decisions.[50] Kagame is still somewhat skeptical of religious institutions even though religious leaders have promoted the RPF's beliefs of social cohesion for economic development. Overall, Kagame's religious opinion represents the stance of the Rwandan government towards religious organizations. Openly, the Rwandan government is secular with no religious overtones in its public policies. The historical relationship of religion within government is seen in terms of ethnic divisions and violence. Thus, for a new conflict-free Rwanda, at least in terms of ethnicity, religion must come second to a secular-based society. Privately, government leaders and bureaucrats have a high level of religiosity. Unlike other past regimes that pledged to fully back the Kagame administration, the church does not have special access to the crafting and enforcing of public policy.

3.2 The formal separation of religious institutions and government

Before the RPF could fully transition into an established government with the ability to enact and enforce public policy, the state needed to draft a constitution that would prevent religious institutional abuses of government power. The internal decision from the prior RPF debate on the role of religion concluded with the beliefs upheld by President Kagame of a separation of religious affairs from state power rather than a religious-based government or religious exclusion from civil society. The new secular Rwandan government was implemented through the 2003 Rwandan Constitution that printed the new separation: that the RPF-led Rwandan government has with all religious institutions. Article One of the Rwandan Constitution simply states the strong stance of making Rwanda into a secular government, "The Rwandan state is an independent, sovereign, democratic,

---

49 Mbanda, *Committed to Conflict: The Destruction of the Church in Rwanda*, 4–7.
50 Kinzer, *A Thousand Hills: Rwanda's Rebirth and the Man Who Dreamed It*, 302–8.

social and secular Republic."[51] The separation between government and religion is extended in Article Fifty-Four with the government banning religious divisionism in the political process.[52] Thus, it is now illegal for religious organizations to become formally political. Earlier regimes used religion as a public mechanism to gain political power. The last section that mentions religion is Article Eleven, which attempts to prevent future ethnic divisions– a stance held and propagated by religious institutions. This section reinforces the concept of unity among the Rwandan population while specifically mentioning that religious preference cannot be a valid reason for the physical, psychological, social or economic harm of any Rwandan.[53] This is a dramatic step away from past Christian-sanctioned perpetration against the local Muslim population under the Habyarimana regime.[54] These few amendments in the Rwandan Constitution made political involvement by religious institutions almost illegal; but it still gives enough legal room for religion to play an informal role in society's operations. Religious institutions have worked with government officials in promoting reconciliation, national unity and in efforts to alleviate the prison population problem.[55] However, it has always been in the constraints as a member within civil society rather than a dominating political institution.

4 Conclusion: What is the Future Role of the Church in Rwanda?

Christianity and religious institutions have always played a significant role in Rwanda's history. Since the introduction of the White Fathers to Rwanda in the early 19th century, both colonial and post-independent governments have relied on Christianity to secure political power and influence. In particular, the Catholic Church used this political will for its own interest in converting the

---

51 Republic of Rwanda, "The Constitution of the Republic of Rwanda," Last modified, 2014. http://www.rwandahope.com/constitution.pdf, 2. Accessed February 1, 2014.
52 Republic of Rwanda, "The Constitution of the Republic of Rwanda," Last modified, 2014. http://www.rwandahope.com/constitution.pdf, 12. Accessed February 1, 2014.
53 Ibid. Republic of Rwanda, "The Constitution of the Republic of Rwanda," Last modified, 2014. http://www.rwandahope.com/constitution.pdf, 5. Accessed February 1, 2014).
54 Anne Kubai, "Walking a Tightrope: Christians and Muslims in Post-Genocide Rwanda," *Islam and Christian-Muslim Relations* (2007): 219–35.
55 TRIAL, "National Unity and Reconciliation Commission – Rwanda," Last modified 2014, http://www.trial-ch.org/en/resources/truth-commissions/africa/rwanda.html. Accessed February 1, 2014.

country away from traditional beliefs to Christianity. The Kayibanda (1962–1973) and Habyarimana (1973–1994) regimes utilized religiosity and the Catholic Church's desire for Rwanda to remain predominately Catholic in order to hold political power even when the country was underdeveloped. The Church's lasting effect turned the socioeconomic order of Hutu, Tutsi and Twa into "ethnicities" that would play a leading role in causing the 1994 genocide. The genocide proved to be the height of Catholic Church's political power as the country has reduced religion's power and influence in the now secular public society.

The RPF ended the genocide through the relatively rapid invasion of Rwanda. Historically, the RPF had a fractured opinion of the role of religion in any future Rwandan society. Some followed the belief that religion can be beneficial for the cohesion and development of a society. Others saw religion as one of the main causes for poverty, government corruption, and, worst of all, establishing ethnic hatred between Rwandans. Ultimately, the RPF adopted the same view that its leader, Paul Kagame, held with respect to religious institutions. This was manifested through the establishment of a separation between church and state affairs. Many government officials are privately religious, but their religiosity does not affect the work that they have been assigned to perform.

Most Rwandan religious leaders have accepted the current realities of their place in society. Rwanda is now a society that still wants religion, but only in private life. Despite other African nations that heavily use religious law and institutions to govern, Rwanda moved toward a secularization of government and social institutions in order to promote a more stable society. The promotion of a secular Rwanda allows for a religious pluralism, and minority religions such as Islam to be able to practice without state interference or persecution. Social issues, such as birth control, deemed taboo in the previous conservative Christian political culture, can now be openly discussed in public, due, in part, to the secular culture of political governance. The Rwandan government has the ability to promote health and public safety without fear of religious interference, unlike during the former regimes. The close-knit nature of the Church and the State during colonial rule and during Rwandan independence (before 1994) shows an abuse of powers that played a clear role in preparing and carrying out the genocide. However, twenty-one years after the genocide, religious affiliation and sentiment is still high in Rwanda.

Works Cited

Aguilar, Mario. *Theology, Liberation and Genocide: A Theology of the Periphery.* London: SCM Press, 2009.

Bertrand, Willian and Margee Ensign. *Rwanda: History and Hope.* New York, NY: University Press of America, Inc, 2010.

Bucyensenge, Jean-Pierre. "Kibeho: When the 'Holy Land' Was Turned into 'Butcher Land.'" In *The New Times.* Last modified February 1, 2014. http://www.newtimes.co.rw/news/index.php?i=15620&a=74201. Accessed February 2, 2014.

Carney, J. J. *Rwanda Before the Genocide: Catholic Politics and Ethnic Discourse in the Late Colonial Era.* New York: Oxford University Press, 2014.

Dallaire, Romeo. *Shaking Hands with the Devil: The Failure of Humanity in Rwanda.* New York: Carroll & Graf Publishers, 2004.

Gourevitch, Phillip. *We Wish to Inform You that Tomorrow We Will be Killed with Our Families: Stories from Rwanda.* New York, NY: Picador, 1998. (Ebook)

Gribbin, Robert E. *In the Aftermath of Genocide: The US role in Rwanda.* Lincoln, NE: iUniverse, 2005. (Ebook).

Katongole, Emanuel and Jonathan Wilson-Hartgrove, *Mirror to the Church: Resurrecting Faith After Genocide in Rwanda*, Grand Rapids, MI: Zondervan, 2009.

Kigali Memorial Centre. *Jenoside.* Kigali, Rwanda: Aegis Trust, 2004.

Kinzer, Stephen. *A Thousand Hills, Rwanda's Rebirth and the Man Who Dreamed It.* Hoboken: John Wiley & Sons, Inc, 2008.

Kubai, Anne. "Walking a Tightrope: Christians and Muslims in Post-Genocide Rwanda." *Islam and Christian-Muslim Relations* (2007): 219–35.

Longman, Timothy. "Church Politics and the Genocide in Rwanda." *Journal of Religion in Africa* 31.2 (2001): 163–86.

Longman, Timothy. *Christianity and Genocide in Rwanda.* New York, NY: Cambridge University Press, 2010.

Mamdani, Mahmood. *When Victims Become Killers: Colonialism, Nativism and the Genocide in Rwanda.* Princeton, NJ: Princeton University Press, 2001.

Mbanda, Laurent. *Committed to Conflict.* London: Society for Promoting Christian Knowledge, 1997.

Melvern, Linda. *A People Betrayed, the Role for the West in Rwanda's Genocide.* London: Zed Books, 2000.

Prunier, Gerard. *The Rwanda Crisis, History of A Genocide.* New York: Columbia University Press, 1997.

Republic of Rwanda. "The Constitution of the Republic of Rwanda." Last modified, 2014. http://www.rwandahope.com/constitution.pdf. Accessed February 1, 2014.

Rinaldo, Maria, & Rinaldo, Peter, "In the Name of God." Documentary, Web, http://www.youtube.com/watch?v=LQBmd4–5UEM. Accessed February 1, 2014.

Rittner, Carol, John Roth, and Wendy Whitworth. *Genocide in Rwanda: Complicity of the Churches?* St. Paul, MN: Paragon House, 2004.

Rucyakana, John. *The Bishop of Rwanda.* Nashville, TN: Thomas Nelson, 2007.

TRIAL. "National Unity and Reconciliation Commission – Rwanda." Last modified 2014. http://www.trial-ch.org/en/resources/truth-commissions/africa/rwanda.html. Accessed February 1, 2014.

Rutayisire, John, John Kabano and Jolly Rubagiza. "Redefining Rwanda's Future: The Role of Curriculum in Social Reconstruction." In Tawil S. and Harley A. eds. *Education, Conflict and Social Cohesion*, 315–74, Geneva: International Bureau of Education, UNESCO, 2004.

U.S. Department of State. "2012 Report on International Religious Freedom." Last modified May 20, 2013. http://www.refworld.org/docid/519dd4963.html. Accessed February 1, 2014.

Waugh, Colin. *Paul Kagame and Rwanda, Power, Genocide, and the Rwandan Patriotic Front.* Jefferson: McFarland & Company, Inc., 2004.

Jonathan Scott
Secularism from Below: On the Bolivarian Revolution

> We have begun to create a new geopolitics of oil that is not at the service of the interests of imperialism and big capitalists. – Hugo Chávez

Over the past fifteen years, a sea change has taken place in Latin America. Yet due largely to a pro-imperialist US media, the total scale of these developments has been, in North America, either deliberately misrepresented or not known about at all.[1]

The case of Ecuador is especially instructive. During the worst of the Great Recession (between 2008 and 2010), Ecuador experienced no rise in unemployment, a direct result of its government's robust economic stimulus package of 5 percent of GDP.[2] Ecuador's fiscal stimulus was twice that of President Obama's and the polar opposite of the European Central Bank's severe austerity measures, both of which have had crippling effects on the economies of the United States and Europe. In the case of the US, of the $16.4 trillion in household wealth that was destroyed in the financial crash of 2008, only half has, so far, been replaced: American families today have $7.7 trillion less than they had in 2007, which amounts to 8.5 million less jobs, and substantially reduced levels of investment in education, health care, housing, infrastructure, research and development.[3] As far as Europe goes, the Spanish unemployment rate remains around 25 percent.

Latin America's new economic and political independence, the enabler of Ecuador's astonishing success story, is one of the most important events of the twenty-first century, and its basic features go a long way toward explaining

---

1 Lauren Carasik, "The US Should Respect Venezuela's Democracy," *Al-Jazeera America*. February 25, 2014, http://america.aljazeera.com/opinions/2014/2/the-us-should-respectvenezuelasdemocracy.html. Accessed May, 26, 2014. Carasik, the Director of the International Human Rights Clinic, characterizes the US mainstream media's coverage of the Bolivarian Revolution as "deliberate misinformation." See also Keane Bhatt, "On Venezuela, the *New Yorker*'s Jon Lee Anderson Fails at Arithmetic," *NACLA*, March 15, 2013, https://nacla.org/blog/2013/3/15/venezuela-new-yorkers-jon-lee-anderson-fails-arithmetic. Accessed May 26, 2014.

2 Rebecca Ray and Sara Kozameh, *Ecuador's Economy Since 2007* (Washington, DC: Center for Economic and Policy Research, 2012), 1–4.

3 Chris Isidore, "America's Lost Trillions," *CNNMoney*, June 9, 2011, http://money.cnn.com/2011/06/09/news/economy/household_wealth/. Accessed May 26, 2014.

the muting and distortion of it in the US media. Not only was it completely unforeseen, but it also came as sharply discontinuous with two consecutive centuries of American colonialism in Latin America and the Caribbean. For the obvious fact is that it has been precisely *because of* the South's new political independence from the North that the nations of Latin American have been able to design and implement successful progressive economic programs – in the first instance, to counter the catastrophic effects of the US housing market crash, and, in the last, as a means by which to reconstruct their societies along egalitarian lines, from below. Under their new economic policies, the flow of wealth has been redirected from outgoing (into the investment banks of the US and Europe) to the basic projects of national development (the fight against extreme poverty and income inequality, the expansion of access to higher education, the building of key energy and transportation infrastructures, and the establishment of durable popular-democratic civic organizations). In short, it should come as no surprise that in the US, where the flow of wealth continues going straight to the top and the poverty rate is increasing, any developments in the opposite direction would get blocked from popular consciousness. For US elites, the Bolivarian Revolution is the threat of a good example.

But reducing US government hostility toward the Bolivarian Revolution to political economy – to the South's rejection of the Wall Street model of economic development, of using the state to radically redistribute wealth upward – would be a mistake. While it is true that had Argentina, Venezuela, Ecuador, and Bolivia continued to follow Washington's "free market" policy prescriptions (privatizing state-owned industries, deregulating the banking sector, lowering corporate taxes, and reducing social spending), their political relations with the US would have remained friendly, the Revolution's rejection of neoliberalism runs much deeper than the economy. It has introduced a new kind of secularism, popular-democratic in form and content, through which the European and North American secularization process – that of reason overcoming the irrationality of belief – can now be seen as the *first moment* of global secularism, instead of its ultimate fulfillment. As I will show, as a concrete synthesis of economics (technological and scientific development) and popular culture (the symbols, rituals, and cults of the majority), the Bolivarian Revolution is secularization's second moment. The Argentine philosopher Enrique Dussel framed the matter with clarity:

> Stalinist "economism," understood as the economic level as infrastructural base that determines the superstructure (the political and ideological), and "politicism" (of a Habermasian type, for instance), which gives absolute priority to the social or political relations over and above economics (relegated to a juxtaposed and secondary "system"), imagines that

"democracy," legitimation, and other essential levels of human survival are fundamental. However, it is forgotten that corporeality (which is hungry, and lives in misery, in the unjust distribution and productivity of the majority of humanity in the periphery) points to a relationship in the "products" of technological labor, which fulfill the needs of life. We are living beings who have a *logos*, that is, the *logos* is a condition of life and not vice versa. Human life, its corporeality, is not only the condition of possibility but the being itself and human existence as such. Reason (*logos*) is a moment of human life, and not life of reason. Still, to be a corporeality, to have needs (to eat, drink, dress, have a roof, need culture, technology, science, art, religion, and other things) is a practical moment because *a priori* we are part of a community, and productive because "bread" is eaten, and "clothing" is for dressing, as products of human labor. This articulation of the practico-productive is economics; it is ethics, anthropological realization par excellence.[4]

Important to stress is that Latin America's new economic populism, what Dussel calls "the practico-productive," is not at all new. Those familiar with the history of US intervention in Latin America and the Caribbean during the postwar period – beginning with the CIA bombing in 1954 of the Jacobo Arbenz administration in Guatemala, down to the recent US-supported right-wing coup against President Manuel Zelaya in Honduras in 2009 – know that virtually every government either directly overthrown or politically and economically undermined by Washington was not only democratically elected but on a political path of fundamental land reform and the improvement of union rights for workers.[5] The struggle to develop modern economies and participatory democratic political systems has a long history in Latin America and the Caribbean, going back to the Haitian and Mexican Revolutions. In the case of Venezuela, its late President Hugo Chávez was well known for arguing for a replication of Simón Bolívar's Third Republic, organized in Panama in 1826, the goal of which was the political unification of Latin America through the coordinated development of economic democracy in each country. And while it's true that Chávez's resurrection of the South American heroes of the nineteenth century, in particular Bolívar's revolutionary teacher Simón Rodriguez, as well as Ezequiel Zamora, who led landless peasants against the oligarchy in the Federal wars of the 1840s and 1850s, was squarely in the secular cult of Bolívar, his strong emphasis on their black heritage – on

---

4 Enrique Dussel, *The Underside of Modernity*, trans. Eduardo Mendieta. (Atlantic Highlands, New Jersey: Humanities Press International, 1996), 12.
5 William Blum, *Killing Hope: US Military and CIA Interventions Since World War II* (Monroe, Maine: Common Courage Press, 1995), 72–83.

their militant antislavery politics and radical economic populism – was definitely not, according to Richard Gott.[6]

This is a crucial point emphasized repeatedly by Latin American historian Gott in his valuable study of Chávez's political career: that it would be wrong to see in Chávez's invocation of the great nineteenth-century Latin American liberators a case of demagoguery, as simply *de rigueur* for anyone seeking political power in Venezuela or elsewhere in Latin America. He shows convincingly that Chávez's re-appropriation of the popular cult of Bolívar was both perspicacious and original, coming out of an intense period of study during a five-year post at the Venezuelan military academy in Caracas (1980–85), where Chávez was also an instructor of Latin American history, of new empirical research then being published in Venezuela and Colombia on Bolívar's concrete strategies and tactics.[7] My thesis here takes its lead from Gott's account of Chávez's intellectual formation: that the new economic populism now sweeping Latin America could not have happened without a prior transformation of the secular ideology of Bolívar, from a Europeanized secularism reflexively deployed by a numerically tiny elite, over more than a century and a half, to justify their oligarchic rule, to a national-popular secularism on behalf of the majority, of the many millions below.

1 Beginnings of the Break

In December of 2001, the government of Argentina, to get its nation out of a very severe and prolonged recession, defaulted on its debt, and, a few weeks later, it abandoned the currency peg to the dollar. For the next three months, the economy contracted sharply, but, from that point on, the Argentine economy grew 94 percent.[8] For the past ten years, it has been the most successful economy in the Western Hemisphere, and has one of the fastest growth rates in the world – all without any direct foreign investment, which it lost after the default. Nor has Argentina's impressive economic growth been due to the so-called "commodities boom."[9] Poverty has fallen by two-thirds, from almost half the population in

---

6 Richard Gott, *Hugo Chávez and the Bolivarian Revolution* (London and New York: Verso, 2005), 91–92.

7 Richard Gott, 38–39.

8 Mark Weisbrot, et al., *The Argentine Success Story and Its Implications* (Washington, DC: Center for Economic and Policy Research, 2011), 1–2.

9 David Rosnick and Mark Weisbrot, *Latin American Growth in the 21st Century: The "Commodities Boom" That Wasn't* (Washington, D.C.: Center for Economic and Policy Research, 2014), 3.

2001 to one-seventh in 2010; income inequality has been reduced by nearly 50 percent: in 2001, the richest Argentinians had 32 times the income of the poorest Argentinians, but by 2010 it was down to 17 times. Unemployment has been cut by more than half, from 20 percent to 8 percent, and social spending has tripled in real terms, much of it as part of the government's Universal Allocation per Child Program (*Asignación Universal Por Hijo*), the goal of which is to reduce poverty and improve the living conditions of children. There was inflation, a rise of 27 percent, but rather than sacrificing economic growth to fight it, by cutting these successful social programs, the government chose instead to depreciate the nominal exchange rate, which worked.[10] As economist Mark Weisbrot and his colleagues at the Center for Economic and Policy Research have pointed out, almost no attention has been paid in Europe and the United States to Argentina's remarkable story, the implications of which are extremely significant. They write:

> Argentina's experience calls into question the popular myth that recessions caused by financial crises must involve a slow and painful recovery... The Argentine government has shown that Europe's bleak current situation and projected scenario is just one possible outcome, and that a rapid recovery in output, employment, poverty reduction, and reduced inequality is another very feasible path that can be chosen.[11]

A few years after this successful economic reversal by Argentina, left-populist candidates running against neoliberal policies which had been imposed by the United States (through the so-called "Washington Consensus"[12]), as well as Washington-dominated institutions such as the IMF and World Bank, took the presidency not only in Argentina but Brazil, Ecuador, Uruguay, Venezuela, and Bolivia. The epic scale of the neoliberal disaster in Latin America had been impossible to miss – even political centrists were going on the warpath against it. For instance, at a conference in Bogotá, Colombia, in 2005, the mayor of Sao Paulo, José Serra, argued that the Washington Consensus had been a complete failure in Latin America, and that a new economic model had to be designed and implemented. He noted that Brazil during the 1960s

---

10 Weisbrot et al., *The Argentine Success Story and Its Implications*, 3 – 7.

11 Weisbrot et al, *The Argentine Success Story and Its Implications*, 2.

12 The theory behind the "Washington Consensus" policies that Latin American countries have been forced to accept in order to receive international loans is that trade liberalization, i.e. the elimination of tariffs and the abolition of restrictions on international investment flows will stimulate rapid economic growth. As a result, in the 1990s alone more than $178 billion of state-owned industries in Latin America were privatized. Governments were also compelled to adopt higher interest rates and tighter fiscal policies.

and 1970s had one of the fastest-growing economies in the world, but that, since 1980, its income per person had grown by less than one-half percent annually.[13] As far as Latin America as a whole goes, from 1980 – 2000, per capita GDP grew by just 7.7 percent, or 0.4 percent annually, compared to 91.5 percent growth, or an average annual rate of 3.3 percent, between 1960 and 1980. In his research, Weisbrot demonstrates that had Brazil and Mexico never adopted neoliberalism, they would have today a European standard of living.[14] In this environment, electoral victory for parties militantly opposed to the Washington Consensus was virtually guaranteed.[15]

The South's break with the North, then, came out of a situation free of ideology: fundamentally economic, it was the termination of two decades of failed neoliberal policies pushed by Washington and the US economics profession, crystallized in Argentina's 2001 default. This is crucial for two reasons. First, in all previous US attempts to crush Latin American national independence movements, recourse to anticommunism was decisive – for demonizing its leaders in the US media, such as Guatemala's Arbenz, Chile's Allende, the Dominican Republic's Juan Bosch, Cuba's Castro, among many others, contriving fake controversies and sectarian divisions on the ground, and creating counterrevolutionary paramilitary forces, such as the *Contras* in Nicaragua. Deprived of the bogeyman of Soviet Russia, the US today confronts, for the first time in history, the struggle for Latin American national independence at the level of basic economics. Second, at this level of basic economics, the Bolivarian Revolution has brought to the surface the underlying class war between rich countries and developing countries. That is, by funding opposition movements in Latin America

---

13 Quoted by Mark Weisbrot, "Latin America's Long Economic Failure Sparks Desire for Change." *Miami Herald*, October 15, 2005. http://www.cepr.net/index.php/op-eds-&-columns/op-eds-&-columns/latin-americas-long-economic-failure-sparks-desire-for-change/. Accessed May 26, 2014.

14 Weisbrot, "Latin America's Long Economic Failure Sparks Desire for Change."

15 Thomas Frank, *Pity the Billionaire: The Hard-Times Swindle and the Unlikely Comeback of the Right* (New York: Picador, 2012). A compelling parallel to the left-populist landslide electoral victories in Latin America in the mid-2000s is the right-populist victories in the US in 2010. As Thomas Frank has shown convincingly in his study of the Tea Party Movement, *Pity the Billionaire*, the surprising conservative takeover of the US House of Representatives in the midterm elections of 2010, during the worst of the Great Recession, could not have happened without the government bailout of failed Wall Street financial institutions, which was strongly opposed by the vast majority of Americans. Franks's overall argument in the book is savvy: had President Obama and liberal Democrats dropped their wispy "post-partisan" rhetoric and replaced it with a combative left-populist, FDR-style approach to the big banks, the political climate in the US would likely have shifted to the left, as it did in the 1930s.

whose goal is the overthrow of democratically elected governments, as the Obama administration is currently doing in Venezuela,[16] the rationale for this kind of regime change can only be economic: to replace governments that are reducing poverty and income inequality and increasing economic growth with those that will slow down these progressive changes and return control of economic policy to the leisure classes.

2 The Reality of the Impossible

The irrationality of capitalism is suffered by its periphery.
– Enrique Dussel

From the standpoint of contemporary US society, where economic policy has for the past thirty years been under the total control of Wall Street and big corporations, the prospect of an economic populism is utopian. Yet it should be recognized that Latin American intellectuals were a very short time ago in a similar position: searching for a viable path out of badly failed economic arrangements, that, while built upon a demonstrably false and ludicrously stupid theory of how modern economies work, had behind them the most powerful class interests in the world.

Writing in the 1990s, Enrique Dussel elaborated the terms of this distinctively American utopianism, in his work *The Underside of Modernity:*

> There is no need to create future projects, products of pure imagination and fantasy that are only "possible" for the ruling order. It has to be known how to discover in the transcendental exteriority of the oppressed the *actual* "presence" of utopia as actual reality of the impossible, which is impossible for the system of domination without the help of the Other.[17]

The thrust of Dussel's critique is that for Latin America to achieve liberation from imperial domination, from the exploitative relations built into global capitalism, its model of development must begin with those situated in what he calls "the Exteriority of the system": underdeveloped and exploited nations, women, oppressed classes, marginalized ethnic groups, people excluded from formal de-

---

16 Mark Weisbrot, "The Truth About Venezuela: A Revolt of the Well-Off, Not a 'Terror Campaign,'" *The Guardian*, March 20, 2014, http://www.theguardian.com/commentisfree/2014/mar/20/venezuela-revolt-truth-not-terror-campaign. Accessed May 26, 2014.
17 Dussel, 7.

mocracies.[18] In other words, the limits of beginning decolonization with a model of development centered on the interests and values of the middle and upper classes is that this can never be more than a mere negation of the old economic arrangements under colonialism – a case of setting out, in Dussel's terminology, "from out of the Totality."[19] Instead, the path of Latin American liberation must be an affirmation of "that-which-has-no-place" (which is the actual definition of utopia: *ouk-tópos*): the people who under capitalist and imperialist domination *have no being*, the many millions of poor and propertyless – the majority. In this precise sense is the reality of the Latin American laboring classes utopian; is it the horizon of a new secular order of reason and self-consciousness.

Charles Taylor's definition of secularism in *A Secular Age* is that it is a historical condition that requires the perfect tense: "a condition of 'having overcome' the irrationality of belief."[20] Considering the European Central Bank's disastrous austerity policies in response to the Great Recession, and the jobless recovery in the US, under which a generation of American workers have lost forever the opportunity for decent employment – which in both cases has been due to the irrationality of neoliberal economic doctrine – Taylor's definition would suggest that secularism in Europe and the US is a failed project. A compelling example from the Bolivarian Revolution sheds light on this question.

In April 2002, in collaboration with senior military officers, the oil business owners of Venezuela (through their political organization *Fedecámeras*) began a coup against the democratically elected government of Hugo Chávez. To achieve it, they needed the Venezuelan Workers' Confederation (CTV) to call a general strike, which they did, in December 2002, shutting down all oil production in the country for the next three months. The Venezuelan oil business owners were incensed over the Chávez administration's proposed structural reform of *Petróleos de Venezuela*, Venezuela's state oil company, under which it would have a 51 percent stake in all joint ventures with foreign companies, and establish a minimum royalty rate of 30 percent, to be paid by private oil companies to the government. The goal of the reform was to enable the state oil company to spend less on overseas investment and more on poverty reduction at home. Reporting on events as they were happening, journalist John Pilger wrote: "The crime of Hugo Chavez is that he has set out to keep his electoral promises, redistributing the wealth of his country and subordinating the principle of private

---

18 Dussel, 8.
19 Dussel, 7.
20 Charles Taylor, *A Secular Age* (Cambridge, MA: Harvard University Press, 2007), 269.

property to that of the common good."[21] Under the threat by coup leaders that he would be bombed in the Miraflores palace by tanks and planes, Chávez agreed to go to the military base of Fuerte Tiuna, where he was detained by the chief of the armed forces, General Lucas Rincón Romero, who demanded that he announce his resignation on television. Chávez, who hadn't slept in two days, asked for a night's sleep before continuing negotiations with the coup leaders. When he woke in the morning, he saw on television that newsreaders were stating over and over that he had resigned. Fortunately, several of the soldiers guarding him were seriously upset about the coup and were more than happy to comply with his request for a telephone, which he used to tell his wife and daughter to get the word out that he had not resigned. Meanwhile, the coup leaders had already staged a swearing-in ceremony in the Miraflores palace of Pedro Carmona as the new president, with Chávez watching on TV. But two days later, the coup was null and void, for, shortly after his phone call to his wife and daughter, tens of thousands came pouring down from the hilltop shantytowns surrounding Caracas and filled the city's streets and highways, demanding the return of their president. In response, the commander of President Chávez's Honor Guard, Colonel Jesus Morao Cardona, ordered his troops to seize the palace and arrest Carmona and the leaders of the coup. At three that same morning, Chávez returned to Miraflores palace, greeted by massive crowds chanting in unison: "*¡Ou, ah, Chávez no se va!*" (Chávez, Please Don't Go!)[22]

Writing in response to the latest upper class attempts to topple the left-populist government in Venezuela, Weisbrot notes:

> Back in 2003, because it did not control the oil industry, the government had not yet delivered much on its promises. A decade later, poverty and unemployment have been reduced by more than half, extreme poverty by more than 70 percent, and millions have pensions that they did not have before. Most Venezuelans are not about to throw all this away because they have had a year and a half of high inflation and increasing shortages. In 2012, according to the World Bank, poverty fell by 20 percent – the largest decline in the Americas. The recent problems have not gone on long enough for most people to give up

---

21 John Pilger, "Venezuela: The Next Chile?". *Coup Against Chávez in Venezuela,* ed. Gregory Wilpert (Caracas: Fundación por un Mundo Multipolar y Venezolana para la Justicia Global, 2003), 14.
22 See Gregory Wilpert's essay, in Wilpert, *Coup Against Chávez in Venezuela.* This collection of eyewitness reporting on the 2002 coup attempt in Venezuela and its aftermath is an invaluable resource; most of the facts and information referred to in my account come from it.

on a government that has raised their living standards more than any other government in decades.[23]

Here, the proposition that the Bolivarian Revolution is a new kind of secularism, and the second moment of global secularism, can be clarified and further substantiated. First to note is the politics of identification expressed in the spontaneous popular defense of the Chávez government: that what the masses of the Venezuelan poor saw in the attempted overthrow of President Chávez was far worse than the loss of their elected leader; it would have been the re-imposition of oligarchic rule, a return to the days of voicelessness, marginalization, and exclusion. Their militant identification with the government they put in place was a clear case of what Dussel has termed "liberating reason," which he considers the hallmark of real secularization. It is the discovery of a new "objectivity," he argues, the function of which is "to unify the historical 'tradition' of a people with the necessary technological and scientific development (according to the real exigencies of the nation, and not simply imitating foreign models)."[24]

Pace Dussel's concept of the reality of utopianism ("the praxis of liberation of the oppressed"), and consistent with Taylor's emphasis on secularism's "perfect tense," this new secular order in Venezuela – like its Bolivarian counterparts in Argentina, Ecuador, Bolivia, Uruguay, Nicaragua, and El Salvador – is both a divergence from Western modernity and postmodernity (and, hence, serves as an actually existing *alternative* modernity and postmodernity) and the historical fulfillment of each. Bolivarian secularism does this by, at one and the same time, negating the old totality (imperialism) and creating a new totality (economic populism) that cannot but affirm and develop the laboring people from which its structure is made.

---

23 Mark Weisbrot, "The Class Conflict in Venezuela," *CounterPunch*, March 5, 2014, http://www.counterpunch.org/2014/03/05/the-class-conflict-in-the-venezuela/. Accessed May 26, 2014.
24 Dussel, 11.

Works Cited

Bhatt, Keane. "On Venezuela, the *New Yorker*'s Jon Lee Anderson Fails at Arithmetic." *NACLA*. March 15, 2013. https://nacla.org/blog/2013/3/15/venezuela-newyorkersjon-lee-ander son-fails-arithmetic. Accessed May 26, 2014.

Blum, William. *Killing Hope: US Military and CIA Interventions Since World War II.*Monroe, Maine: Common Courage Press, 1995.

Carasik, Lauren. "The US Should Respect Venezuela's Democracy." *Al-Jazeera America*. February 25, 2014. http://america.aljazeera.com/opinions/2014/2/the-usshould-re spectvenezuelasdemocracy.html. Accessed May 26, 2014.

Dussel, Enrique. *The Underside of Modernity*, trans. Eduardo Mendieta. Atlantic Highlands, New Jersey: Humanities Press International, 1996.

Frank, Thomas. *Pity the Billionaire: The Hard-Times Swindle and the Unlikely Comeback of the Right*. New York: Picador, 2012.

Gott, Richard. *Hugo Chávez and the Bolivarian Revolution*. London and New York: Verso, 2005.

Isidore, Chris. "America's Lost Trillions." *CNNMoney*, June 9, 2011. http://money.cnn.com/ 2011/06/09/news/economy/household_wealth/. Accessed May 26, 2014.

Pilger, John. "Venezuela: The Next Chile?" In *Coup Against Chávez in Venezuela*, edited by Gregory Wilpert, 12–18. Caracas: Fundación por un Mundo Multipolar y Venezolana para la Justicia Global, 2003.

Ray, Rebecca and Sara Kozameh. *Ecuador's Economy Since 2007*. Washington, DC: Center for Economic and Policy Research, 2012.

Rosnick, David and Mark Weisbrot. *Latin American Growth in the 21st Century: The"Commodities Boom" That Wasn't*. Washington, DC: Center for Economic andPolicy Research, 2014.

Taylor, Charles. *A Secular Age*. Cambridge, MA: Belknap Press/Harvard University Press, 2007.

Weisbrot, Mark, Rebecca Ray, Juan A. Montecino and Sara Kozameh. *The Argentine Success Story and Its Implications*. Washington, D.C.: Center for Economic and Policy Research, 2011.

Weisbrot, Mark, Rebecca Ray, Juan A. Montecino and Sara Kozameh. "The Truth About Venezuela: A Revolt of the Well-Off, Not a 'Terror Campaign.'" *The Guardian*, March 20, 2014. http://www.theguardian.com/commentisfree/2014/mar/20/venezuela-revolt-truth-not-terror-campaign. (May 26, 2014).

Weisbrot, Mark, Rebecca Ray, Juan A. Montecino and Sara Kozameh. "Latin America's Long Economic Failure Sparks Desire for Change." *Miami Herald*, October 15, 2005. http:// www.cepr.net/index.php/op-eds&columns/opeds-&columns/latin-americaslong-econom ic-failure-sparks-desireforchange/. Accessed May 26, 2014.

Weisbrot, Mark, Rebecca Ray, Juan A. Montecino and Sara Kozameh. "The Class Conflict in Venezuela." *CounterPunch*, March 5, 2014. http://www.counterpunch.org/2014/03/05/ the-class-conflict-in-the-venezuela/. Accessed May 26, 2014.

Wilpert, Gregory, ed. *Coup Against Chávez in Venezuela*. Caracas: Fundación por un Mundo Multipolar y Venezolana para la Justicia Global, 2003.

Gregorio Bettiza

Post-secular Expertise and American Foreign Policy

The past decades witnessed a growing interest in religion among American scholars. This interest is not only confined to the field of international affairs, but is a much wider phenomenon that cuts across disparate fields and disciplines – from philosophy, to the humanities, the social and natural sciences, and medicine. So much so, that John Schmalzbauer and Kathleen Mahoney have talked about an increasingly "post-secular academy."[1] This post-secular turn in the academy, Schmalzbauer and Mahoney argue, has been spearheaded by a "religious resurgence movement," a heterogeneous and often uncoordinated group of scholars, who have both directly and indirectly "raised the profile of religion in American higher education."[2]

A similar movement has taken place in the field of international affairs, with the rise of what I call American post-secular expertise on international affairs.[3] The concept of post-secular here does not define who these experts are – whether they are religious or not, or whether they used to be secular in the private and public sphere and now religious – but what they do. That is, these experts are post-secular because they are closely tied to the production of a particular knowledge regime that seeks to challenge the dominant secular paradigms that underpin research and thinking on international affairs.

This article argues that much American scholarship challenging the secular premises of social scientific research on international affairs cannot be completely divorced from parallel efforts directed towards challenging the secular premises of American foreign policy. In other words, American scholarship seeking to bring a better understanding of religion into the social scientific study of international affairs is in many cases either explicitly or implicitly contributing – to paraphrase Schmalzbauer and Mahoney – to raising the profile of religion in American foreign policy.

---

1 John Schmalzbauer and Kathleen Mahoney, "Religion and Knowledge in the Post-Secular Academy" (New York: SSRC Working Papers, 2012). See also John Schmalzbauer and Kathleen A. Mahoney, "American Scholars Return to Studying Religion," *Contexts* 7.1 (2008).

2 Schmalzbauer and Mahoney, "Religion and Knowledge in the Post-Secular Academy," 24.

3 I use the term "international affairs" to include a broad range of fields and disciplines, such as international relations, comparative politics, peace and security studies, area studies, international law, and/or international and comparative sociology.

We can think of post-secular expertise and experts as constituting a particular kind of epistemic community. An epistemic community is "a network of professionals with recognized expertise and competence in a particular domain and an authoritative claim to policy-relevant knowledge within that domain or issue area."[4] Post-secular experts base much of their authority on their social scientific knowledge of religion(s), as well as – in many cases – on their firsthand religious belief, belonging, and experience.[5] These experts are challenging social scientists and policymakers alike to recognize and acknowledge the importance of religion as a social phenomenon, and, when speaking also from a religious perspective, as a way of knowing.[6] Thinking of American post-secular experts not simply as detached scholars, but also as taking part in a epistemic community – a heterogeneous and pluralist one with its internal debates, disagreements and often competing agendas – conceptually highlights their relationship and relevance to policy debates and policy-making.[7]

The post-secular epistemic community on international affairs is influential in American foreign policy debates and practices in three ways. First, it has been effective in discursively arguing that religion *matters* in world politics. In particular, it has highlighted the limits of standard secularization theories and secular knowledge paradigms, showing that religions are not only still alive and well in the modern world, but also that their social and political salience is on the rise globally.

Second, this epistemic community has been important in arguing not only that religion matters, but also in showing *how* it matters. In particular, it has challenged the premises of much social scientific research that understands religion exclusively as epiphenomenal and reducible to other factors – whether economic, political, or individual. It has put forward the case for treating religion, instead, as "an independent variable" or as an "autonomous force." A growing number of international events, especially when it comes to conflict and violence or peace and democracy, cannot be understood if one does not

---

4 Peter M. Haas, "Introduction: Epistemic Communities and International Policy Coordination," *International Organization* 46.1 (1992): 3.

5 I will use interchangeably the terms expertise, experts, and epistemic community. For a discussion about religious actors and organizations as an "epistemic community," see Nukhet A. Sandal, "Religious Actors as Epistemic Communities in Conflict Transformation: The Cases of South Africa and Northern Ireland," *Review of International Studies* 37.3 (2011).

6 Some, for instance, have a triple orientation – as committed religious individuals, as scholarly analysts of religion, and as policy-engaged actors on matters of religion.

7 Gil Eyal and Larissa Buchholz, "From the Sociology of Intellectuals to the Sociology of Interventions," *Annual Review of Sociology* 36 (2010): 129.

take religion – whether actors, communities, beliefs, or identities – seriously into account, these authors claim.

Third, drawing from the above arguments, post-secular experts have often concluded that American foreign policy cannot afford to ignore a world that is experiencing a revival in the social and political salience of religions. The point is made that, if America is to create a more peaceful and secure international order, its diplomats and security officials need to shed much of their secular biases and do a better job in understanding religion and including religious actors and resources in foreign policy. Hence, we often find that scholars and centers engaged in the social scientific study of religion and its effects on international societies and politics are also engaged in debates on two key issues which pertain to American foreign policy: religious engagement and faith-based approaches to conflict-resolution, and the promotion of international religious freedom.

An investigation into the connections between post-secular expertise and American foreign policy is warranted for a number of reasons. First, because there has been little research carried out so far on this relationship and what it means for the pursuit of social scientific knowledge about religion beyond the United States. The intent here is not to get involved in normative and policy debates about the necessity, or perils, of bringing religion into American foreign policy. Nor do I want to make any specific claims about the need for or impossibility of having a more clear distinction between objective, value-neutral social scientific research on religion, and subjective normative religious preferences and ethics. Furthermore, it is not my intention to engage in contentious debates about First Amendment interpretations regarding the establishment clause and the free exercise of religion when it comes to American foreign policy.

The point is, however, to generate a more self-reflective debate within the social scientific study of religion about the American-centric nature of much of this literature. Not only in terms of its origins in the American academy, but also because of its substantial proximity to America's national interest and foreign policy concerns. Put differently, the scope here is not to engage in policy debates, or to critique or praise post-secular expertise, nor to police the boundaries of what appropriate scholarship on religion should be. The intent here is largely of a sociological and analytical nature: to highlight and make more explicit, as others have done in other domains,[8] a phenomenon that has generally been underap-

---

8 For example, the heavy American footprint in terms of scholars, institutions, funding, and what type of research is being produced, and for what purposes, in international relations (IR) – the discipline I identify with – has long been recognized in the field itself. See Stanley Hoffmann, "An American Social Science: International Relations," *Daedalus* 106.3 (1977);

preciated and overlooked when it comes to scholarship on religion in international affairs.

Second, this investigation is warranted because scholarly research on the influence of religion in American foreign policy, so far, has generally ignored the place and role of elites and post-secular expertise. In fact, while interest in religion and American foreign policy has grown exponentially over the past decade, most of the literature has focused on the role of religious organizations and movements,[9] or on the personal religiosity of American people[10] and their presidents,[11] or on the religious – protestant and missionary – character of American exceptionalism and national identity.[12] Yet, that experts and epistemic communities can and do have an influence on foreign policy has been shown by an increasing number of studies:[13] None of these, however, has paid enough attention to *post-secular* expertise.

To be specific, this chapter does not offer any strictly causal or explanatory analysis. I will not trace the process nor identify the precise mechanisms through which the American post-secular epistemic community on international affairs has affected American foreign policy. Its scope is more modest. On the one hand, it maps the emergence of post-secular expertise on international affairs. It traces two novel phenomena. First, the development of new policy-oriented centers and initiatives in key universities, think tanks, and research institutes dedicated to the study of religion. Second, it traces the development of important faith-based "think and do tanks", which have contributed substantially to the rise of religion in scholarly and policy debates. On the other hand, this mapping is used to highlight the connections between academic and official narratives,

---

Ole Waever, "The Sociology of a Not So International Discipline: American and European Developments in International Relations," *International Organization* 52. 04 (1998).

9 See, among many, Stephen R. Rock, *Faith and Foreign Policy: The Views and Influence of U.S. Christians and Christian Organizations* (New York, NY: Continuum International, 2011).

10 See, among many, James L. Guth, "Religion and American Public Opinion: Foreign Policy Issues," *The Oxford Handbook of Religion and American Politics*, ed. James L. Guth, Lyman A. Kellstedt, and Corwin E. Smidt (New York/Oxford: Oxford University Press, 2009); Walter Russell Mead, "God's Country," *Foreign Affairs* 85.5 (2006).

11 See, among many, Andrew Bacevich and Elizabeth Prodromou, "God Is Not Neutral: Religion and US Foreign Policy after 9/11," *Orbis* 48.1 (2004).

12 Dennis R. Hoover, ed. *Religion and American Exceptionalism* (New York, NY: Routledge, 2014).

13 Emanuel Adler and Peter M. Haas, "Conclusion: Epistemic Communities, World Order, and the Creation of a Reflective Research Program," *International Organization* 46.1 (1992); Jeffrey T. Checkel, "Ideas, Institutions, and the Gorbachev Foreign Policy Revolution," *World Politics* 45.2 (1993); Jolyon Howorth, "Discourse, Ideas, and Epistemic Communities in European Security and Defence Policy," *West European Politics* 27. 2 (2004).

and the institutional links between key individuals and centers constitutive of the post-secular epistemic community, and the religious engagement and international religious freedom foreign policy agendas.

Third, and lastly, the neglect of research on post-secular expertise appears also rooted in a general portrayal of American elites as singularly secular, whether individually secularized (with little believing in or belonging to any religion), epistemically secular (with no interest in the study of religion), or ideologically secularist (with anti-religious sentiments). Such an understanding of the secular nature of American intellectual life is put forward, among many, by important American sociologists of religion, such as Peter Berger and Christian Smith.[14] This chapter contributes to challenging this dominant narrative of intellectual and scholarly elites, in general, and American ones, in particular, as overwhelmingly secular, secularized, and secularist.

The essay is organized around two main sections that follow each other in chronological order. The first section charts the early emergence of the post-secular epistemic community from the end of the Cold War up to around the year 2000. The second section traces the expansion of post-secular expertise in the American academy and among policy-oriented research institutions following the events of 9/11. These two sections highlight how post-secular expertise consolidated around a number of key themes as they became ever more important in the making and delivery of American foreign policy from the 1990s onwards, namely: producing better knowledge and understanding of religion, engaging religious communities abroad to resolve conflicts, promoting international religious freedom norms and arrangements.

1 1989 – 2000: The Emergence of Post-secular Expertise

With the end of the Cold War, debates in Washington DC about the Soviet threat, containment, balance of power, and mutually assured destruction increasingly petered out. The American foreign policy establishment was left in search of new paradigms and perspectives that would help interpret and explain the emerging post-Cold War world. One was Francis Fukuyama's optimistic account

---

14 Peter L. Berger, ed. *The Desecularization of the World: Resurgent Religion and World Politics* (Grand Rapids, MI: Ethics and Public Policy Center; Eermans Publishing, 1999); Christian Smith, *The Secular Revolution: Power, Interests, and Conflict in the Secularization of American Public Life* (London: University of California Press, 2003).

of the "end of history" and the emergence of a peaceful and prosperous era driven by the triumph of economic and political liberalism. Another was Samuel Huntington's famous "Clash of Civilizations" thesis. Huntington's thesis, which appeared on the influential pages of *Foreign Affairs* – the leading journal among American foreign policy elites, published by the Council on Foreign Relations (CFR), America's preeminent think tank on international politics – offered a rather different vision of world politics to come.

Huntington's reference to civilizations, which he largely defined on cultural and religious grounds, did more than just offer an alternative narrative to liberal cosmopolitan optimism. His thesis brought religion abruptly to the center of scholarly and foreign policy conversations, precisely at a time when many states appeared mired in sectarian conflicts and political Islam was spreading across the Middle East. Religion was no longer treated as irrelevant or epiphenomenal, as had become customary among social scientists. It was instead now seen, for better or worse, as key to understanding international dynamics and relations.

1.1 Religion matters

Huntington was not alone in bringing greater attention to the vastly unexplored and seemingly growing relevance of cultural and religious forces in international politics. The 1990s, in fact, saw the publication of a number of seminal sociological works that directly challenged the secularization thesis and highlighted the continued, if not expanding, public vibrancy of religions globally. The first volumes of the monumental *Fundamentalism Project*, edited by Martin Marty and Scott Appleby, were making their appearance at this time.[15] Sociologists of religion such as José Casanova were deeply challenging the privatization thesis embedded in secularization theories.[16]

What quite vigorously caught the attention of scholars and policy researchers at the time, in particular, was Peter Berger's recanting of the secularization thesis, which he had done much to advance in the 1960s–1970s.[17] In 1999, Peter Berger published an edited book suggestively titled *The Desecularization*

---

15 Martin E. Marty and R. Scott Appleby, *The Fundamentalism Project*, 5 vols. (Chicago: University of Chicago Press, 1991).

16 José Casanova, *Public Religions in the Modern World* (Chicago, IL: University of Chicago Press, 1994).

17 Peter L. Berger, *The Sacred Canopy: Elements of a Sociological Theory of Religion* (New York, NY: Anchor Books, 1969).

of the World: Resurgent Religion and World Politics.[18] The volume was published under the auspices of the Ethics and Public Policy Center (EPPC), a Washington-based think tank with a conservative and religious slant.[19] In it, Berger famously argued:

> [...] the assumption that we live in a secularized world is false. The world today, with some exceptions [...] is as furiously religious as it ever was, and in some places more so than ever. This means that a whole body of literature by historians and social scientists loosely labeled "secularization theory" is essentially mistaken.[20]

Berger's statement was groundbreaking. Religion had now reentered with a bang serious social scientific scholarly inquiry about world politics.

1.2 Religion, conflict and peace

Huntington's piece also tapped into conventional understandings of religion as powerful force for conflict and violence. This somewhat standard narrative about the dangers of religion was increasingly challenged by studies wishing to highlight religion's contribution to peace.

Around the time of Huntington's *Foreign Affairs* article, Douglas Johnston was working on the Religion and Conflict Resolution Project at the Center for Strategic & International Studies (CSIS), a Washington-based think tank. The project, which Johnston has described as "a complete novelty for a think tank devoted to hardnosed strategic issues and known for its realist Cold War mentality,"[21] culminated in the 1994 co-edited volume with Cynthia Sampson, *Religion: the Missing Dimension of Statecraft*. The volume was forwarded by former president Jimmy Carter and produced under the auspices of a major security-based think tank. It was also was one of the first and most prominent pieces of research intended to speak to a broader policy audience about the nexus between religion, violence, and peace-building.

---

18 Berger, *The Desecularization of the World: Resurgent Religion and World Politics.* (Grand Rapids, MI: Ethics and Public Policy Center, Eermans Publishing, 1999).

19 The EPPC was established in 1976 to "clarify and reinforce the bond between the Judeo-Christian moral tradition and the public debate over domestic and foreign policy issues." It is a think tank that brings together conservative Catholic, Evangelical, and Jewish intellectuals and analysts and straddles between secular and religious research. See http://www.eppc.org/about/

20 Berger, *The Desecularization of the World: Resurgent Religion and World Politics*, 2.

21 Douglas M. Johnston, 10 June, 2011, interview with the author.

The volume primarily sought to push for an intellectual paradigm shift by exposing both the epistemic and ideological secularist bias of the foreign policy and diplomatic establishment. Articles throughout complained that in a world increasingly abuzz with religious fervor, the intellectual traditions and statecraft practices that American diplomats and policy-makers were steeped in were stubbornly secularist. American statecraft suffered from an "enlightenment prejudice," some suggested,[22] or "dogmatic secularism," others lamented.[23] This secularist bias, the book argued, was problematic for two reasons. First, it led scholars, policymakers and diplomats to discount the growing salience of religion in international affairs. Secondly, if religion was to be brought back into the study and praxis of international diplomacy, it should not be seen solely as a cause of conflicts, but also as a way to foster nonviolent change, and preventing or resolving conflicts.

Upon leaving CSIS, Johnston founded the International Center for Religion and Diplomacy (ICRD) in 1999. This was an important turning point for the deeply secularized institutional and intellectual landscape on international affairs in Washington. The ICRD was the first and most prominent faith-based "think and do tank" entirely dedicated to conducting programs and research on the nexus between religion, violence and peace. ICRD was mainly created to practice what Johnston had preached in his edited volume *The Missing Dimension*. That is, "prevent and resolve identity-based conflicts that exceed the reach of traditional diplomacy by incorporating religion as part of the solution."[24] Since 1999, Johnston and ICRD have been at the forefront of debates about the necessity of integrating faith-based approaches to conflict resolution in American foreign policy.

A further seminal work on religion, conflict, and peace published in this decade was Scott Appleby's *The Ambivalence of the Sacred*.[25] The book was an outgrowth of a project hosted by the Kroc Institute for International Peace of the University of Notre Dame. The Kroc Institute was founded in 1986 out of a deep concern for nuclear weapons and the arms race. Here, in 2000, thanks to

---

22 Edward Luttwak, "The Missing Dimension," *Religion, the Missing Dimension of Statecraft*, eds. Douglas M. Johnston and Cynthia Sampson (New York, NY: Oxford University Press, 1994), 9.
23 Stanton Burnett, "Implications for the Foreign Policy Community " *Religion, the Missing Dimension of Statecraft*, ed. Douglas M. Johnston and Cynthia Sampson (New York, NY: Oxford University Press, 1994), 286.
24 http://icrd.org/.
25 R. Scott Appleby, *The Ambivalence of the Sacred: Religion, Violence, and Reconciliation* (Lanham, MD: Rowman & Littlefield Publishers, 2000).

Scott Appleby, a Program on Religion, Conflict and Peacebuilding was then launched.

1.3 International religious freedom

Concern for religious persecution and freedom internationally was another issue area at the intersection of faith and world politics gaining momentum in the 1990s. Michael Horowitz, a senior fellow at the Hudson Institute, a conservative think tank in Washington DC, published in 1995 an editorial in *The Wall Street Journal* entitled, "New Intolerance Between the Crescent and the Cross." The article, which echoed Huntington's controversial clash thesis, was responsible for raising the profile of alleged Christian persecution in Muslim-majority countries among the international affairs community. As the campaign against Christian persecution gathered momentum, vigorously pushed forward also by Nina Shea and Paul Marshall of the Center for Religious Freedom at Freedom House, a Washington-based research and advocacy institute, this led to the passage of the International Religious Freedom Act (IRFA) in 1998.[26]

IRFA made the promotion of religious freedom an explicit and organized objective of American foreign policy. This policy change increased the profile and importance of international religious persecution and freedom among American foreign affairs experts. When Robert Seiple, the first-ever U.S. Ambassador-at-Large for International Religious Freedom (between 1998–2000), left his post, he would go on to found further key institution in the faith-based "think and do tank" DC panorama. The Institute for Global Engagement (IGE).

Since 2000, IGE, which has been directed by Robert's son Chris Seiple, has pursued two important and parallel missions. First, it has directly worked for the promotion of international religious freedom through programs and initiatives on the ground. Second, it has sought to become a leading intellectual force at the intersection of American scholarly and policy debates on religion and religious freedom in international affairs. IGE's contribution to these debates and to American foreign policy will be explored in greater detail in the following section.

---

26 For different perspectives on the motivations animating the anti-persecution and religious freedom campaign, see Allen D. Hertzke, *Freeing God's Children: the Unlikely Alliance for Global Human Rights* (Oxford: Rowman & Littlefield Publishers, 2004); T. Jeremy Gunn, "The United States and the Promotion of Freedom of Religion and Belief," in *Facilitating Freedom of Religious Belief: A Deskbook*, ed. Tore Lindholm, et al. (The Hague: Martinus Nijhoff, 2004).

In sum, with the end of the Cold War, religion appeared to command a sporadic but growing attention among leading scholars in the social sciences and among certain areas of the Washington–based think tank and policy advocacy community. Huntington's *Foreign Affairs* article brought public attention to a range of issues as they pertained to the intersection of religion and international affairs.[27] Security-based think tanks such as the CSIS, more generalist ones such as the Hudson Institute and Freedom House, faith-based ones such as the long-established EPPC, and the newly created ICRD and IGE, along with Notre Dame's Kroc Institute, were all giving greater attention to the matter. These developments anticipated many of the issues and themes – from an interest in understanding global religious dynamics, to faith-based approaches to conflict-resolution, and international religious freedom – that would then be picked up, expanded and carried forward by an increasing number of scholarly and policy research projects and initiatives in the post-9/11 environment.

2 2001–2014: The Expansion and Consolidation of Post-secular Expertise

The public religiosity of President Bush, the attacks on September 11, 2001, and the religiously charged discourses that surrounded America's War on Terror thereafter, have had a dramatic effect in spurring greater attention to religion in American scholarly circles and foreign policy debates. Post-secular expertise expanded considerably, progressively consolidating in both secular and religious-based universities, secular and newly created faith-based think tanks, and other research centers. This development occurred along the intellectual tracks already laid out in the previous decade.

---

27 A fourth area where Huntington's article was seminal was in directing foreign policy attention towards Islam. This spurred important debates about the possibilities of clashes or dialogue with the Muslim world in the post-Cold War era. For reasons of space, this article focuses mostly on the issue of religion more generally and not Islam in particular. For a more detailed account of American post-secular expertise on Islam and foreign policy change, see Bettiza, Gregorio, "Constructing civilisations: Embedding and reproducing the 'Muslim world' in American foreign policy practices and institutions since 9/11," *Review of International Studies* 41.03 (2015).

2.1 Religion matters

Universities, often thought of as the bedrock institutions of secularism in America, started to open centers and offer new courses discussing the complex and apparently ever growing salience of religion in international politics. This section does not present a comprehensive list of all new courses and developments across the American academy.[28] It will focus on a number of changes in leading scholarly institutions, especially those with important links to the Washington foreign policy community.

A key development in post-secular expertise in the academic panorama has been the inauguration, in 2006, of the Berkley Center for Religion, Peace and World Affairs, at Georgetown University in Washington DC.[29] Georgetown has long been recognized as a leading training ground for America's security experts, diplomats, and foreign policy decision-makers. The Berkley Center is been organized around an ever-expanding number of programs that carry out research, organize conferences, and design university courses on religion in international affairs. As of 2014, the center featured such programs as Globalization, Religions, and the Secular, led by José Casanova; Religion and US Foreign Policy, led by Thomas Farr; the Religious Freedom Project, led by Thomas Farr and Timothy Samuel Shah; Religion, Conflict, and Peace led, by Eric Patterson; and Islam and World Politics, led by Jocelyne Cesari.

I will touch upon some of these programs in greater detail in a moment. What is interesting to note, at this stage, is that much of this knowledge produced by prominent scholars in the fields of sociology of religion, religion in comparative and international politics, and Islam in world politics, filters into policy-making world through two important channels. First, through teaching. In particular thanks to an optional certificate course on Religion, Ethics, and World Affairs, available to interested students, launched by the Berkley Center in 2011 in collaboration with Georgetown University's Edmund A. Walsh School of Foreign Service. Second, through a wide-ranging series of scholarly publications, courses, events, and seminars explicitly targeted to foreign policy and security officials in the State Department and the military.[30]

The Notre Dame Kroc Institute's Religion, Conflict and Peacebuilding program, under the direction of Scott Appleby, has continued to be a key center

---

28 For a good overview of courses in the United States see: http://globalengage.org/global-ed ucation/syllabi. Accessed October 14, 2014.

29 berkleycenter.georgetown.edu .

30 http://berkleycenter.georgetown.edu/publications and berkleycenter.georgetown.edu/events

in the production of social scientific, as well as theological[31] knowledge on religion and peace. Daniel Philpott, one of the leading and most prominent voices in the burgeoning field of religion in comparative politics and international relations, has long been associated with the Kroc Institute.

Other major universities, with more secular traditions than Catholic Georgetown and Notre Dame, have launched important projects. The Belfer Center, Harvard University's Center for international affairs, hosted between 2007–2012 the Initiative on Religion in International Affairs directed by Monica Duffy Toft, one of the foremost scholars of religion and conflict. Courses, seminars, executive training sessions, and research projects were offered, "focusing on the study of religion as it bears on international relations and foreign policy,"[32] with the goal to "integrate a sophisticated understanding of religion with international affairs in policymaking and scholarship."[33]

Johns Hopkins' School for Advanced International Studies (SAIS), in the heart of Washington DC, labeled its 2009–10 academic year the Year of Religion, and hosted a wide range of seminars, workshops and events on the topic.[34] A Global Politics and Religion Initiative was then launched in 2012. Its objectives included the mainstreaming of the study of religion and politics into the school's existing graduate-level international relations program; to promote new Master's degree courses, faculty and community research seminars; and to provide executive education training sessions. The initiative's goal is to "foster an appreciation and deeper understanding of religion and international affairs among students, scholars and practitioners who will shape and influence future policymaking."[35]

In terms of the academic environment, a further noteworthy development was the inauguration in 2007 of *The Immanent Frame* blog, sponsored by the Social Science and Research Council. The blog has been at the forefront of scholarly debates on religion and the secular in the humanities and the social sciences, hosting contributions by prominent social theorists and philosophers in the

---

31 http://kroc.nd.edu/research/religion-conflict-peacebuilding/theology-practice-just-peace
32 http://belfercenter.ksg.harvard.edu/project/57/religion_in_international_affairs.html?page_id=159
33 http://belfercenter.ksg.harvard.edu/project/57/religion_in_international_affairs.html?page_id=159
34 www.sais-jhu.edu/religion/index.htm
35 www.sais-jhu.edu/academics/functional-studies/global-theory-history/global-politics-and-religion-initiative.html

field.[36] The blog has also served as an important venue for a number of debates about the growing entanglement of religion in American foreign policy, especially on issues of global religious engagement and freedom.[37] Most of those taking part in these debates, such Elizabeth Shakman Hurd, have tended to be critical of the growing scholarly-policy nexus on religion. These discussions are participating in important ways in post-secular knowledge production. They are substantially raising the stakes as well as the attention around the operationalization of religion in American foreign policy far beyond the immediate circle of its most engaged advocates.

Interest in understanding religion, how it relates to international affairs and American foreign policy, has not been the concern of academics and universities alone. Policy-makers and think tanks are also increasingly turning their gaze towards God. That the intellectual mood among policy elites was increasingly changing became especially evident when the former Secretary of State Madeleine Albright published her autobiographical reflections on how the "Mighty and the Almighty" had become surprisingly relevant to America's security at the dawn of the twenty-first century.[38] In her memoirs, Mrs. Albright argued that in order "to anticipate events rather than merely respond to them, American diplomats will need to [...] think more expansively about the role of religion in foreign policy and about their own need for expertise."[39]

The Council on Foreign Relations (CFR) has wholly embraced and partly led this post-secular turn within the policy community. From 2003 to 2006, CFR launched a Religion and U.S. Foreign Policy Project, designed to address "one of the most important challenges facing U.S. foreign policy in the 21st century: the growing importance of religion in world politics."[40] The project was led by Walter Russell Mead, a historian and scholar of American foreign policy, and Timothy Samuel Shah, a political scientist. During this period, CFR became ever more active in engaging the Evangelical community and its leaders, such as Richard Land of the Southern Baptist Convention, and Rick Warren pastor

---

36 The blog, edited by Jonathan VanAntwerpen, has published contributions by Charles Taylor, Jürgen Habermas, Talal Asad, Robert Bellah, Craig Calhoun, José Casanova, William E. Connolly, Mark Juergensmeyer, and Saba Mahmood, among others.
37 http://blogs.ssrc.org/tif/2013/07/30/engaging-religion-at-the-department-of-state/   and http://blogs.ssrc.org/tif/the-politics-of-religious-freedom/
38 Madeleine K. Albright, *The Mighty and the Almighty: Reflections on America, God, and World Affairs*, Large print ed. (New York, NY: Harper Large Print, 2006).
39 Madeleine K. Albright, *The Mighty and the Almighty: Reflections on America, God, and World Affairs*, 99.
40 http://www.cfr.org/projects/religion-and-politics/religion-and-us-foreign-policy-project/ pr421

of Saddleback Church.[41] Mead's seminal 2006 *Foreign Affairs* article "God's Country?," charting the growth and influence of Evangelicals in American foreign policy, grew out of these initiatives.

Following this early and specific interest on Evangelicals, CFR then established in 2006 a broader Religion and Foreign Policy Initiative. Its stated scope is to provide a more structured "forum to deepen the understanding of issues at the nexus of religion and U.S. foreign policy." The initiative does so by collecting research, hosting conferences, and organizing events as a way to connect and serve as a resource for religious and congregational leaders, scholars, and thinkers on religion "whose voices are increasingly important to the national foreign policy debate."[42] A Religious Advisory Committee provides guidance for all aspects of the initiative. Along with boasting the presence of Madeleine Albright, it includes many of the most prominent American scholars and analysts on religion, as well as religious leaders across groups and denominations.[43]

A number of leading Washington-based think tanks covering both domestic and foreign affairs are also paying increasing attention to religion. Since the early 2000s, the Brookings Institute started widening its interest in religion and politics beyond the domestic sphere to include also international issues. In 2003, it organized its first major conference on religion and American foreign policy, which led to an edited volume, *Liberty and Power: A Dialogue on Religion and U.S. Foreign Policy in an Unjust World*. Through the work of scholars and fellows – such as E.J. Dionne on religion in America, Justin Vaisse on Islam and Europe, and Ömer Taşpinar on religion and secularism in Turkey and the Middle East – Brookings engagement with religious actors and issues has expanded considerably over the past decade.

The AEI has hosted discussions and commentary by Michael Novak and others on religion and American politics since the 1980s. Their frequency, however,

---

41 http://www.cfr.org/projects/world/evangelicals-and-foreign-policy-roundtable/pr1287; http://www.cfr.org/religion-and-politics/christian-evangelicals-us-foreign-policy/p11341
42 http://www.cfr.org/about/outreach/religioninitiative/mission.html
43 Among scholars and analysts, the committee includes Peter Berger, Boston University; Father Bryan Hehir, Harvard University; Scott Appleby, University of Notre Dame; Reza Aslan, University of California Riverside; Mark Noll, University of Notre Dame; Luis Lugo, Pew Forum on Religion and Public Life; and Paul Marshall, Hudson Institute. It counts among its religious leaders and activists the following: Richard Land, Southern Baptist Convention; Eboo Patel, Interfaith Youth Core; Feisal Abdul Rauf, Cordoba Initiative; David Saperstein, Religious Action Center of Reform Judaism; Chris Seiple, Institute for Global Engagement; Richard Stearns, World Vision; Jim Wallis, Sojourners; and Robert Wood, The Church of Jesus Christ of Latter-Day Saints. For the full list see www.cfr.org/about/outreach/religioninitiative/advisory_board.html

noticeably increased during the 1990s, as a quick glance at AEI's webpages reveals.[44] Following 2001, growing attention was directed towards international issues with a focus on the religious character of America and Middle Eastern politics.

An important post-secular development in the secularized intellectual and policy milieu of Washington DC was the creation of the well-funded Pew Forum on Religion & Public Life in 2001.[45] The PEW Forum on Religion is one of the largest of seven projects that make up the Pew Research Center, a non-partisan research and polling institute. The Forum started as a place for bringing religious leaders across traditions – mainly Christians, Muslims and Jews – to engage in dialogue and interfaith discussions in the tense post-9/11 atmosphere. When Louis Lugo joined as director in 2004, he turned the forum into a research center that, as the website states, seeks to "promote a deeper understanding of issues at the intersection of religion and public affairs." It does so through two main programs, one on Religion and American Society, and the other on Religion and World Affairs.

The following statement by Louis Lugo, explaining the rationale for re-directing the PEW Forum towards a research center on religion, captures perfectly the sentiment of many in the post-secular epistemic community:

> When I took my Ph.D. in political science at the University of Chicago most social scientific theories I was taught assumed the world to be secularizing. But already since the late 1970s with the Iranian revolution and Likud winning its first election in Israel I realized then that some kind of religious resurgence was occurring in the world... Peter Berger's admission that he was wrong about secularization in the 1990s was another turning point. Things were happening, religion was everywhere, but no one was noticing. With the Forum we attempted to fill that knowledge vacuum with solid social scientific research.[46]

Seiple's IGE and Johnston's ICRD faith-based "think and do tanks" have become, in the post 9/11 context, important fulcrums of research and debates on religion in international affairs. IGE's Center on Faith and International Affairs hosts a thriving research program that seeks to equip "scholars, practitioners, policymakers, and students with a balanced understanding of the role of religion in public life worldwide."[47] The Center has been involved in supporting and publishing a series of scholarly and policy-oriented books on the nexus between re-

---

44 www.aei.org/policy/society-and-culture/religion/
45 www.pewforum.org/
46 Louis Lugo, 24 June, 2010, interview with author.
47 www.globalengage.org/research/about.html

ligion, security, and international affairs.[48] The Center quite prominently features a recently published volume co-edited by IGE's Dennis Hoover and ICRD's Douglas Johnston, entitled *Religion and Foreign Affairs: Essential Readings*.[49] Since 2002, IGE publishes a quarterly journal, *The Review of Faith & International Affairs*. The Review is, to this day, the only peer-reviewed journal entirely dedicated to issues of religion and world politics.[50]

2.2 Religion, conflict and peace

Research at the intersection of religion, violence and conflict-resolution has expanded exponentially within the academic field, as well as in the think tank community. Much attention has been directed towards the issue of "religious engagement." Religious engagement is an umbrella term that encompasses two key concerns voiced by post-secular intellectuals and experts about American foreign policy: first, a critique of what is perceived to be an excessively secular approach to international affairs, which is blind to religious dynamics and conflicts; second, a call to understand religion and to include religious actors and factors more constituently in American diplomacy and conflict-resolution strategies.

Douglas Johnston and his ICRD have been at the forefront of these debates since the 1990s, and have continued to be throughout the 2000s.[51] A growing range of think tank initiatives and reports, including by the United States Institute of Peace (USIP) and CSIS, have joined Johnston and his efforts to bring greater attention to religious engagement in American foreign policy.[52]

---

48 http://globalengage.org/faith-international-affairs/books

49 Dennis Hoover and Douglas Johnston, eds. *Religion and Foreign Affairs: Essential Readings.* (Waco, TX: Baylor University Press, 2012). The book collects a wide-range of seminal articles and excerpts in the field by Madeleine Albright, Scott Appleby, Benjamin Barber, Peter Berger, Timothy Byrnes, José Casanova, Thomas Farr, Jonathan Fox, Jeffrey Haynes, Allen Hertzke, Samuel Huntington, Mark Juergensmeyer, Paul Marshall, Vali Nasr, Daniel Philpott, Timothy Shah, Chris Seiple, and Scott Thomas, among others.

50 Since 2010, *The Review* is being published by Routledge/Taylor & Francis, improving its scholarly quality and credibility, along with making it more widely available through the publisher's indexes.

51 Douglas M. Johnston, ed. *Faith-based Diplomacy: Trumping Realpolitik* (Oxford: Oxford University Press, 2003); Douglas M. Johnston, *Religion, Terror, and Error: US Foreign Policy and the Challenge of Spiritual Engagement* (Santa Barbara, California: Praeger Publishers, 2011).

52 The United States Institute of Peace (USIP) established a permanent Religion and Peacemaking Program in 2001. AT CSIS, religious-related initiatives are less well institutionalized. In

Particularly significant in this space has been the 2010 *Engaging Religious Communities Abroad: A New Imperative for U.S. Foreign Policy* report by the Chicago Council on Global Affairs, explicitly addressed to the Obama administration.[53] The report argued that "despite a world abuzz with religious fervor [...] the U.S. government has been slow to respond effectively to situations where religion plays a global role."[54] It urged President Obama and his national security staff to make religion and engaging with religious communities around the world "an integral part of our [American] foreign policy."[55]

The document was the result of a task force of thirty-two "experts and stakeholders" – former government officials, religious leaders, heads of international organizations, and scholars. The task force was co-chaired by Scott Appleby and Richard Cizik, President of the New Evangelical Partnership for the Common Good and former Vice President for Governmental Affairs of the National Association of Evangelicals (NAE). Key scholars and policy analysts directly or indirectly affiliated with Georgetown's Berkley Center were included in the task force, such as José Casanova, Thomas F. Farr, Timothy Samuel Shah, Katherine Marshall, and William Inboden. Douglas Johnston was also a member, along with a number of prominent Muslim scholars and activists, such as Radwan A. Masmoudi, Dalia Mogahed, and Eboo Patel.

It is within this intellectual context that a Religion and Foreign Policy Working Group was convened in the State Department by then Secretary Hillary Clinton as part of its wider Strategic Dialogue with Civil Society initiative launched in 2011. The working group was tasked with making recommendations on four issues: Religion in Foreign Policy and National Security, Religious Engagement and Conflict Prevention/Mitigation, International Religious Freedom: Advocacy to Combat Religious-Based Violence and Human Rights Abuse, and Faith-

---

2007, CSIS Post-Conflict Reconstruction Project hosted a series of events on religion in conflict settings and produced a groundbreaking 92-page report entitled *Mixed Blessings: U.S. Government Engagement with Religion in Conflict-Prone Settings* (Washington D.C.: Center for International and Strategic Studies, 2007). The report extensively surveyed – with the intention to improve – US government attention and approaches to religion abroad.

53 Chicago Council, "Engaging Religious Communities Abroad: A New Imperative for U.S. Foreign Policy," in *Report of the Task Force on Religion and the Making of U.S. Foreign Policy* (Chicago: Chicago Council on Global Affairs, 2010). The report was covered by major media outlets and further generated a lively and sometimes heated debate within the social scientific community in the pages of *The Immanent Frame*. See blogs.ssrc.org/tif/category/religious-freedom

54 Chicago Council, "Engaging Religious Communities Abroad: A New Imperative for U.S. Foreign Policy," .21

55 . Chicago Council, "Engaging Religious Communities Abroad: A New Imperative for U.S. Foreign Policy," 13

Based Groups and Development and Humanitarian Assistance. Chris Seiple of IGE was invited to be one of the two civil-society, non-governmental representatives of the working group. Following on the working group's recommendations,[56] Secretary of State John Kerry created an Office of Faith-Based Community Initiatives in 2013, later renamed the Office of Religion and Global Affairs.[57]

2.3 International religious freedom

Research and advocacy efforts on international religious freedom would expand substantially in the think tank community from 2001 onwards. Nina Shea and Paul Marshall moved the Centre for Religious Freedom from Freedom House to the Hudson Institute in 2007.[58] Chris Seiple of IGE went on to cofound the International Religious Freedom (IRF) Roundtable, a Washington-area consortium of NGOs concerned with the issue of religious freedom. The roundtable meets bimonthly to discuss how best to promote religious freedom in American foreign policy, Washington policy circles, and across countries worldwide.[59]

The *Global Restrictions of Religion* reports compiled by Brian Grim at the PEW Forum on Religion have become hugely popular.[60] The PEW reports have provided a vast array of empirical data and statistics that scholars, campaigners and interested policymakers have widely and regularly drawn upon in their research and advocacy efforts on international religious freedom. Grim has explored the relationship between religious freedom and violence in further scholarly publications with leading sociologists of religion,[61] and recently founded the Religious Freedom and Business Foundation.[62]

These efforts are joined by greater scholarly attention to the historical roots, normative and philosophical substance, as well as strategic value of religious freedom in promoting democratic practices, fighting religious fundamentalism, fostering peace, and supporting economic development in societies around the

---

56 IGE, "Inaugural Meeting of State Department Working Group on Religion and Foreign Policy," Institute for Global Engagement (IGE), http://www.globalengage.org/pressroom/releases/1236-video-now-available-from-the-working-group-on-religion-and-foreign-policy.html.

57 http://www.state.gov/s/fbci/#

58 http://crf.hudson.org/

59 www.aicongress.org/wp-content/uploads/2012/05/IRF-Roundtable-Web-Update.pdf.

60 http://www.pewforum.org/category/publications/restrictions-on-religion/

61 Brian J. Grim and Roger Finke, *The Price of Freedom Denied: Religious Persecution and Conflict in the Twenty-First Century* (Cambridge: Cambridge University Press, 2010).

62 http://religiousfreedomandbusiness.org/

world. Leading this scholarly effort has been Thomas Farr at Georgetown's Berkley Center, who has written about religious freedom on leading policy-oriented journals, such as *Foreign Affairs* and *Foreign Policy*.[63] Since 2011, Farr also directs, along with Timothy Samuel Shah, the Berkley Center's Religious Freedom Project. The Project counts among its associates scholars and prominent academics on religion in the social sciences, including José Casanova, William Inboden, Daniel Philpott, and Monica Duffy Toft.[64]

Parts of the post-secular epistemic community concerned with religious freedom are closely affiliated with the implementation, consolidation and expansion of America's international religious freedom policy. Robert Seiple served as first-ever U.S. Ambassador-at-Large for International Religious Freedom in the State Department (between 1998 to 2000). Thomas Farr served as first Director of the State Department's Office of International Religious Freedom (1999–2003). Nina Shea served as Commissioner of the United States Commission on International Religious Freedom (mandated by the 1998 International Religious Freedom Act). Moreover, Farr, Shea, Paul Marshall, Timothy Samuel Shah, Chris Seiple, and Brian Grim have all, in various occasions and capacities, testified before Congress on issues of international religious persecution and freedom in the past two decades.

In terms of foreign policy priorities and bureaucratic politics, religious freedom remains largely marginalized within the State Department.[65] However, post-secular experts critical of this agenda, mostly associated with the Politics of Religious Freedom project based at the University of California, Berkeley, and Northwestern University, are contributing to draw ever greater attention to this issue.[66] The power of American international religious freedom discourse and practices, these critiques suggest, can no longer be ignored, and its problematic nature needs to be urgently addressed. This is a further, somewhat paradoxical way that the heterogeneous, pluralist, and internally divided American post-secular epistemic community on religion in international affairs contributes to put, maintain, and raise the profile of religion in American and global scholarly and foreign policy milieus.

---

[63] Thomas F. Farr, "Diplomacy in an Age of Faith: Religious Freedom and National Security," *Foreign Affairs* 87, no. 2 (2008); Thomas F. Farr, "Undefender of the Faith," http://www.foreignpolicy.com/articles/2010/04/05/undefender_of_the_faith.

[64] See: berkleycenter.georgetown.edu/rfp

[65] GAO, "International Religious Freedom Act: State Department and Commission Are Implementing Responsibilities but Need to Improve Interaction," (Washington DC: United States Government Accountability Office (GAO), 2013).

[66] http://politics-of-religious-freedom.berkeley.edu/

3 Conclusion

With the end of the Cold War, a noticeable but sporadic interest emerged among American scholarly and policy elites towards exploring the ways that religion appeared to "matter" in international affairs and, *by fiat*, also to American foreign policy. Critiques of the secularization theory – its role in the production of social scientific knowledge about international affairs, as well as its influence over how the foreign policy establishment approached the world – were being put forward at this time.

The events of 9/11 and what followed provided a second turning point in this process. From then on, both a qualitative and quantitative explosion of post-secular expertise occurred as new centers, initiatives, programs, and courses were being launched within the secular and religious academic and policy research worlds. This American post-secular epistemic community sought to explore or critique the complex and multiple facets at the nexus of religion and international affairs. Those within this community would claim, from extremely diverse theoretical positions, that social scientists on the one hand, and American foreign policy makers on the other, should do a much better job in understanding and engaging with religion globally. As a result, over the past twenty years, the Washington foreign policy establishment's institutional and intellectual milieu has undergone what can be conceptualized as a process of *desecularization*.[67] Talking about religion is no longer taboo among intellectual and policy elites.

Some tentative links between the rise of this heterogeneous post-secular epistemic community on international affairs and specific changes in American foreign policy were provided in this article. In particular, it appears that certain sections of the American post-secular epistemic community was closely tied to the operationalization of religion in American foreign policy. Especially on issues of international religious freedom and religious engagement. Much closer scrutiny of the causal relationship between the emergence of the post-secular epistemic community, with its contestation of secular knowledge and practices, and changes in American foreign policy, is warranted. The opposite should also be investigated. To what extent has the desire to influence American foreign policy driven much scholarly research on religion in international affairs?

---

67 Vyacheslav Karpov, "Desecularization: A Conceptual Framework," *Journal of Church and State* 52.2 (2010).

Works Cited

Adler, Emanuel, and Peter M. Haas. "Conclusion: Epistemic Communities, World Order, and the Creation of a Reflective Research Program." *International Organization* 46.1 (1992): 367–90.

Albright, Madeleine K. *The Mighty and the Almighty: Reflections on America, God, and World Affairs.* Large print ed. New York, NY: Harper Large Print, 2006.

Appleby, Scott R. *The Ambivalence of the Sacred: Religion, Violence, and Reconciliation.* Lanham, MD: Rowman & Littlefield Publishers, 2000.

Bacevich, Andrew, and Elizabeth Prodromou. "God Is Not Neutral: Religion and US Foreign Policy after 9/11." *Orbis* 48.1 (2004): 43–54.

Berger, Peter L., ed. *The Desecularization of the World: Resurgent Religion and World Politics.* Grand Rapids, MI: Ethics and Public Policy Center; Eermans Publishing, 1999.

Berger, Peter L., ed. *The Sacred Canopy: Elements of a Sociological Theory of Religion.* New York, NY: Anchor Books, 1969.

Bettiza, Gregorio, "Constructing civilisations: Embedding and reproducing the 'Muslim world' in American foreign policy practices and institutions since 9/11," *Review of International Studies* 41.03 (2015).

Burnett, Stanton. "Implications for the Foreign Policy Community." In *Religion, the Missing Dimension of Statecraft*, edited by Douglas M. Johnston and Cynthia Sampson. New York, NY: Oxford University Press, 1994.

Casanova, José. *Public Religions in the Modern World.* Chicago, IL: University of Chicago Press, 1994.

Checkel, Jeffrey T. "Ideas, Institutions, and the Gorbachev Foreign Policy Revolution." *World Politics* 45.2 (1993): 271–300.

Chicago Council. "Engaging Religious Communities Abroad: A New Imperative for U.S Foreign Policy." In *Report of the Task Force on Religion and the Making of US Foreign Policy.* Chicago: Chicago Council on Global Affairs, 2010.

CSIS. "Mixed Blessings: US Government Engagement with Religion in Conflict-Prone Settings." Washington D.C.: Center for International and Strategic Studies, 2007.

Eyal, Gil and Larissa Buchholz." From the Sociology of Intellectuals to the Sociology of Interventions." *Annual Review of Sociology* 36 (2010): 117–37.

Farr, Thomas F. "Diplomacy in an Age of Faith: Religious Freedom and National Security." *Foreign Affairs* 87. 2 (2008): 110–24.

Farr, Thomas F. "Undefender of the Faith." http://www.foreignpolicy.com/articles/2010/04/05/undefender_of_the_faith.

Fukuyama, Francis. *The End of History and the Last Man.* New York, NY: Free Press, Maxwell Macmillan, 1992.

GAO. "International Religious Freedom Act: State Department and Commission Are Implementing Responsibilities but Need to Improve Interaction." Washington D.C.: United States Government Accountability Office, 2013.

Grim, Brian J. and Roger Finke. *The Price of Freedom Denied: Religious Persecution and Conflict in the Twenty-First Century.* Cambridge: Cambridge University Press, 2010.

Gunn, Jeremy T. "The United States and the Promotion of Freedom of Religion and Belief." In *Facilitating Freedom of Religious Belief: A Deskbook*, edited by Tore Lindholm, W. Cole

Durham Jr. , Elizabeth A. Sewell and Bahia G. Tahzib-Lie. 617–42. The Hague: Martinus Nijhoff, 2004.

Guth, James L. "Religion and American Public Opinion: Foreign Policy Issues." In *The Oxford Handbook of Religion and American Politics*, edited by James L. Guth, Lyman A. Kellstedt and Corwin E. Smidt. 243–65. New York/Oxford: Oxford University Press, 2009.

Haas, Peter M. "Introduction: Epistemic Communities and International Policy Coordination." *International Organization* 46.1 (1992): 1–35.

Hertzke, Allen D. *Freeing God's Children: The Unlikely Alliance for Global Human Rights.* Oxford: Rowman & Littlefield Publishers, 2004.

Hoffmann, Stanley. "An American Social Science: International Relations." *Daedalus* 106.3 (1977): 41–60.

Hoover, Dennis, and Douglas Johnston, eds. *Religion and Foreign Affairs: Essential Readings.* Waco, TX: Baylor University Press, 2012.

Hoover, Dennis R., ed. *Religion and American Exceptionalism.* New York, NY: Routledge, 2014.

Howorth, Jolyon. "Discourse, Ideas, and Epistemic Communities in European Security and Defence Policy." *West European Politics* 27.2 (2004): 211–34.

Huntington, Samuel P. "The Clash of Civilizations?" *Foreign Affairs* 72.3 (1993): 22–49.

IGE. "Inaugural Meeting of State Department Working Group on Religion and Foreign Policy." Institute for Global Engagement (IGE), http://www.globalengage.org/pressroom/releases/ 1236-video-now-available-from-the-working-group-on-religion-and-foreign-policy.html.

Johnston, Douglas M., ed. *Faith-Based Diplomacy: Trumping Realpolitik.* Oxford: Oxford University Press, 2003.

Johnston, Douglas M., ed. 10 June, 2011 Interview.

Johnston, Douglas M., ed. *Religion, Terror, and Error: US Foreign Policy and the Challenge of Spiritual Engagement.* Santa Barbara, California: Praeger Publishers, 2011.

Johnston, Douglas M. and Cynthia Sampson, eds. *Religion: The Missing Dimension of Statecraft.* New York, NY: Oxford University Press, 1995.

Karpov, Vyacheslav. "Desecularization: A Conceptual Framework." *Journal of Church and State* 52, no. 2 (2010): 232–70.

Lugo, Louis. 24 June, 2010. Interview.

Luttwak, Edward. "The Missing Dimension." In *Religion, the Missing Dimension of Statecraft*, edited by Douglas M. Johnston and Cynthia Sampson. New York, NY: Oxford University Press, 1994.

Marty, Martin E., and R. Scott Appleby. *The Fundamentalism Project.* 5 vols. Chicago: University of Chicago Press, 1991.

Mead, Walter Russell. "God's Country." *Foreign Affairs* 85.5 (2006): 24–43.

Overview of Courses on Religion in International Polities in the US: See http://globalengage. org/global-education/syllabi. Accessed October 14, 2014.

Rock, Stephen R. *Faith and Foreign Policy: The Views and Influence of U.S. Christians and Christian Organizations.* New York, NY: Continuum International, 2011.

Sandal, Nukhet A. "Religious Actors as Epistemic Communities in Conflict Transformation: The Cases of South Africa and Northern Ireland." *Review of International Studies* 37.3 (2011): 929–49.

Schmalzbauer, John, and Kathleen Mahoney. "Religion and Knowledge in the Post-Secular Academy." New York: SSRC Working Papers, 2012.

Schmalzbauer, John, and Kathleen Mahoney. "American Scholars Return to Studying Religion." *Contexts* 7.1 (2008): 16–21.

Smith, Christian. *The Secular Revolution: Power, Interests, and Conflict in the Secularization of American Public Life*. London: University of California Press, 2003.

Waever, Ole. "The Sociology of a Not So International Discipline: American and European Developments in International Relations." *International Organization* 52.4 (1998): 687–727.

Part II: **Case Studies: Global Secularisms**
B **The Public Sphere**

Roberta J. Newman

When the Secular is Sacred: The Memorial Hall to the Victims of the Nanjing Massacre and the Gettysburg National Military Park as Pilgrimage Sites

1 Introduction

In many ways, it's hard to imagine two nations with religious practices that differ more than those of the United States and China. Ideologically, America was built upon a foundation of Calvinist-flavored English and Dutch Protestantism; Protestant discourse exercises its influence on a wide range of American cultural practices. Chinese culture, in contrast, is strongly imbued with elements of Taoism, Buddhism, and, though more a philosophy than a religion in the strict sense, Confucianism. Nevertheless, by design, neither nation has an official state religion. Indeed, the establishment of an official church is expressly forbidden by the First Amendment to the United States Constitution, the cornerstone of the Bill of Rights. So, too, is it forbidden by the constitution of the Chinese Communist Party (CCP). Specifically, the CCP constitution grants citizens of the People's Republic of China (PRC) freedom to engage in "normal religious activities," and sanctions five specific "patriotic religious associations": Buddhist, Taoist, Muslim, Roman Catholic, and Protestant, but it does not endorse any.[1] Nor does the expressly Atheist CCP tolerate religious practices that lie outside its definition of "patriotic." Despite the absence of official state religions, in both the PRC and the United States, certain institutions have been established that provide each nation's faithful with what may be defined as collective, state-sponsored, cultural, and even vaguely spiritual – but expressly non-religious – sites at which contact the numinous is possible. These may be defined as secular pilgrimage sites.

This chapter will examine two such sites: the Memorial Hall to the Victims of the Nanjing Massacre in Nanjing, China, and the Gettysburg National Military Park and Cemetery in Gettysburg, Pennsylvania. Both sites are, by definition, secular; the former operates under the auspices of the CCP, while the latter is,

---

[1] "China: Executive Summary," United States Department of State, http://www.state.gov/documents/organization/192831.pdf. Accessed July 2014.

as its name implies, a United States National Military Park, operated by the National Parks Service, a federal agency legally bound by the First Amendment. On the surface, both are patriotic monuments to war dead. But on a deeper level, both exude a sense of the numinous that characterizes conventionally religious pilgrimage destinations, drawing the faithful by some unquantifiable force. The essay will seek to explain how, despite the fundamental contradictions inherent in the notion, each of these sites is able to function simultaneously as a secular monument and sacred space, doing so within a culturally specific context.

2 Defining Pilgrimage Sites

Before looking at the specific sites, it is useful to look at the practice of pilgrimage as a form of sacred tourism. The word 'pilgrimage' is rooted in the Latin *per agar*, meaning "through the fields,"[2] according to anthropologist Alan Morinis. In a very real sense, every pilgrimage takes the faithful on a protracted journey through the fields, be those fields physical, metaphoric, and as is most often the case, both, on a quest for contact with the numinous. Though their motives may differ, all pilgrims share in the desire to encounter the divine at a designated sacred space. Whether voluntary, like the Christian pilgrimage to Santiago de Compostela, or obligatory, like the Hajj, all pilgrimages are motivated by the individual pilgrim's need to approach the central node of a given spiritual world. Morinis defines these sacred *loci*, the central spiritual nodes, as places where there "is a rupture in the ordinary domain through which heaven peeks."[3] In simple terms, that which peeks through the rupture is what pilgrims identify as a representation of the spiritual ideal. What separates pilgrimage from other travel is the commitment on the part of sacred voyager to physically approach the rupture in the ordinary domain in order to worship in the projected presence of the spiritual ideal.[4] In a sense, the power of the ideal draws pilgrims to a given site in the same way iron filings are drawn to a magnet. As such, this power may be defined as "spiritual magnetism."[5] Without spiritual magnetism, a given site is little more than a travel destination. Although by definition and design, both the Gettysburg and Nanjing monuments are fundamentally secular, both are also spiritually magnetic. What peeks through the rupture in the domain

---

2 Alan Morinis, *Sacred Journeys: The Anthropology of Pilgrimage* (Westport, CT: Greenwood, 1992), 23.

3 Morinis, *Sacred Journeys: The Anthropology of Pilgrimage*, 19.

4 Morinis, *Sacred Journeys: The Anthropology of Pilgrimage*, 25.

5 Morinis, *Sacred Journeys: The Anthropology of Pilgrimage*, 25.

in the ordinary may not be defined as heaven in the conventionally religious sense, but it is definitely numinous.[6]

But what imbues these particular secular pilgrimage sites with their magnetic pull, if it is not the presence of a divinity? What is there specifically about the Nanjing Memorial and Gettysburg site that provides pilgrims with that all-important rupture through which they may encounter the ideal? In these two instances, the answer lies, much as it does in any number of European and East Asian expressly religious pilgrimage sites, in the cult of relics. In Medieval Europe, for instance, the Roman Christian Church promoted the notion of "the corporeal nature of the supernatural world and of its close contact with and influence upon the natural world of living men."[7] How better, then, to experience the corporeal nature of the supernatural than by worshipping in the presence of some physical remnant of a saint, the ideal's human epitome? Whether it was the physical remains of a saint or an object closely associated with a particular representative of the divine, the spiritual power of the ideal was made manifest through relics. Pilgrims devoted to the Apostle, Saint James, the remains of whom are said to lie in the Cathedral in Compostela, Spain, would travel on foot along the *Camino de Santiago* (Way of St. James), a specifically delineated pilgrimage route through France, often crawling the final mile on their knees to approach the ideal, God, by getting close to the physical manifestation of its epitome. So, too, did Buddhist pilgrims take arduous trips to reach the Famen temple, outside China's ancient capital of Chang'an (now Xi'an), attracted by the spiritual magnetism of the Sakyamuni Buddha's finger bone.

As memorials to war dead, both Memorial Hall to the Victims of the Nanjing Massacre and the Gettysburg National Military Park and Cemetery have no shortage of human remains to serve the function of relics. But so does every cemetery. However, both the Nanjing Memorial and Gettysburg are located atop earth that has literally been soaked in the blood of those defined by their respective national ideologies as heroes. Those entombed therein represent what might be thought of as a secular version of the spiritual ideal. The remains as well as the objects used by the individual martyrs housed at Nanjing and Gettysburg may not each have the same magnetic power as the body of Mao Tsedong, displayed in a crystal coffin in Beijing's Tiananmen Square, or the remains of John F. Kennedy, which lie beneath an "eternal flame" in the larger shrine of Arlington

---

6 Also see Roberta Newman, "The American Church of Baseball and the National Baseball Hall of Fame," *NINE: A Journal of Baseball History and Culture* 10.1 (2001): 46–63.

7 Michael Costen, "The Pilgrimage to Santiago de Compostela in Medieval Europe," in *Pilgrimage and Popular Culture*, eds. Ian Reader and Tony Walter (London: Macmillan, 1993), 138.

National Cemetery, but by sheer mass, both memorials have spiritual magnetism to spare.

3 The Gettysburg National Military Park

As the Gettysburg monument's website notes, the battle of Gettysburg, in which Confederate General Robert E. Lee's Army of Virginia invaded the North, clashing with the Union Army of the Potomac between July 1 and 3, 1863, is generally considered to have been the turning point of America's Civil War. It was also one of the war's bloodiest battles, with 7,863 killed, more than half of those Confederate. The shrine, the battlefield itself, was purchased by the State of Pennsylvania almost immediately after the battle in order to establish the Soldier's National Cemetery, to which the graves of the Union's fallen, previously scattered rather haphazardly across the battlefield, were moved. Not to be confused with Cemetery Hill, the site of some of the fiercest fighting, the National Cemetery, with its rows of small white tombstones, was dedicated later that year. It and the battlefield were transferred to the Federal government in 1895 and became a national park in 1933.[8] Although the shrine includes a modern museum and visitor's center, as well as the Gettysburg Cyclorama, in which pilgrims may watch *A New Birth of Freedom* – narrated, perhaps inevitably, by Morgan Freeman – and thereby experience the story of "the epic" battle in the round, the main attractions are the battlefield itself, with its period monuments to each company that fought there as well as its lovingly maintained peach orchard, and of course, the cemetery.

So magnetic is the site that it began to attract pilgrims four months after the battle was fought. Notes Jim Weeks:

> A correspondent on the battlefield in 1865 reflected, 'Not a few American writers and tourists have plaintively deplored the utter absence of all historic recollections connected with the scenery of our varied beautiful country.' But at Gettysburg, Americans could view a panoramic landscape fit for antiquity and equaling Sir Walter Scott's romanticizing, Thoreau wistfully mused that the American republic could revive the heroic ages, and many viewed Gettysburg as the occasion. Allusions to providential, heroic, and mythical events in press accounts prompted pilgrimages and encouraged travelers to anticipate an American Armageddon or Thermopylae.[9]

---

8 "History and Culture," National Park Service: Gettysburg National Military Park, http://www. nps.gov/gett/historyculture/index.htm. Accessed July 2014.

9 Jim Weeks, *Gettysburg: Memory, Market, and an American Shrine* (Princeton, NJ: Princeton University Press, 2003), 37.

The pilgrimage to Gettysburg, Weeks observes, was, at the time, one element of a new American civil religion. He writes:

> To some, veneration for past accomplishments promised to straighten the backbone of Americans. History infused a civil religion that offered both anodyne to change and compensation for religious doubt raised by science. Holidays and rituals of the new civic faith embraced by the public such as Memorial Day, flag worship, or pilgrimages accompanied the new commercial culture. Pilgrimages in particular were thought to be a particularly valuable approach to quickening the patriotic spirit.[10]

Given the fact that the Gettysburg shrine commemorates those who fell supporting the Union, thereby supporting the American national ideology of unity, it stands to reason that the site would attract a significant number of Northern pilgrims as well as the descendants of African slaves. But white Southerners, the descendants of the Vanquished, also seem to feel a personal connection to that which peeks through Gettysburg's rupture with the ordinary domain, despite the fact that it is the place where the tide turned against their ancestors – or perhaps specifically because of that fact. To a great extent, participation in the patriotic civil religion as described by Weeks may help explain why Gettysburg draws a significant number of pilgrims from below the Mason-Dixon line, and did so from the outset. After all, Southerners share in the romantic mythology of Civil War as Northerners do, perhaps even more so. Traveling to the site of the great defeat allows Southern pilgrims to partake in the heroism of their martyrs, too, without sacrificing their faith in the greater patriotic civil religion. The blood that soaked the ground at Gettysburg, the relics of those epitomes of the Southern ideal, representatives of the "Lost Cause," constitute, after all, as potent a spiritual magnet to the ancestors of the vanquished as to the victors. Indeed, of those who might be considered the fundamentalists of the cult of the Civil War, the most devout pilgrims to Gettysburg and other sites associated with the war, the re-enactors, individuals who recreate the battles in all their historic detail, the greater portion, save but a few, hail from Southern states. (Notably absent from re-enactments are live ammunition and actual starvation.) Writing of a re-enactment of the Battle of the Wilderness, Tony Horwitz observes, "[t] hough blue outnumbered gray almost two to one at the real battle of the Wilderness, the opposite was true here. In fact, a shortage of Yankees was endemic to reenactments [SIC], particularly those staged below the Mason and Dixon

---

10 Weeks, *Gettysburg: Memory, Market, and an American Shrine*, 5.

Line."[11] Certainly, Gettysburg is above the dividing-line between North and South, but still, Southerners are well-represented at Gettysburg re-enactments.

Yet, even though, arguably, Southern worshippers are drawn to Gettysburg by representatives of a different ideal than their Northern pilgrims, all of Gettysburg's pilgrims seem to be united by a specifically American ideology. In many ways, this ideology, the theology of the American secular civil religion, was best articulated during the shrine's dedication November 19, 1863. Lincoln's Gettysburg Address – uttered by one of America's central representatives of the ideal, at least to Northern pilgrims, who is associated far more closely with the shrine than with his actual burial place – may be seen as the very credo of the American civil religion: the idea that America was "conceived in Liberty, and dedicated to the proposition that all men are created equal," and that "this nation, under God, shall have a new birth of freedom – and that government of the people, by the people, for the people, shall not perish from the earth."[12] Of course, those faithful to the Lost Cause may interpret these words differently than those faithful to the victors. As such, a certain proportion of Southern pilgrims may be defined as belonging to a different sect of the same American civil religion than the majority of their co-religionists. But it is still the same civil religion.

4 The Memorial Hall to the Victims of the Nanjing Massacre

On the surface, the modern, minimalist Memorial Hall to the Victims of the Nanjing Massacre appears to be an entirely different type of war memorial and a different type of pilgrimage site than the Gettysburg monument. Most of the heroic martyrs, whose relics imbue the Nanjing site with its spiritual magnetism, were innocent victims of what amounted to genocide, the wholesale slaughter of Chinese by Japanese invaders over a six to eight week period. This genocide followed the occupation of Nanjing (then Nanking), the capital of the fledgling Chinese Republic, by the Imperial Japanese Army on December 13, 1937, during what is known in China as the War of Japanese Aggression (World War II to those outside of China). According to most estimates, more than 300,000 Nanjing resi-

---

11 Tony Horwitz, *Confederates in the Attic: Dispatches from the Unfinished Civil War* (New York: Random House, 2010), 135.
12 Abraham Lincoln, "The Gettysburg Address," November 19, 1863. http://avalon.law.yale.edu/19th_century/gettyb.asp. Accessed August 12, 2014.

dents and Chinese soldiers stationed there were murdered, often in unspeakably brutal ways, by the occupying forces.[13] Unlike those who fell at Gettysburg, where only one civilian was counted among the martyred, a significant portion of those massacred were non-combatants.

Like Gettysburg, the Nanjing memorial includes a museum and outdoor spaces. The shrine, itself, is adjacent to both a sculpture garden and a "peace park" meant for contemplation. Also like Gettysburg, the site includes what amounts to a cemetery, but of a very different nature. Built in 1985 by the Nanjing Municipal Government and enlarged in 1995, the focus of the memorial is a coffin-shaped hall containing what is essentially an open grave, where the skeletal remains of victims were buried in what is known as *wan ren keng* (pits of ten thousand corpses).[14] Through the darkened hall throng hundreds of pilgrims daily, the vast majority of them Chinese. Although there are signs everywhere admonishing visitors to be respectfully quiet and to refrain from taking pictures, the hall is oddly noisy and lit by numerous camera flashes, representing the attempt by pilgrims to capture some of the magnetism of the shrine. As such, attempts to regulate the form of worship at the memorial are largely unsuccessful.

Certainly, the site functions as an effective memorial to the victims of the massacre; but is it a pilgrimage site? In a very real sense, it is. It may be seen as a fundamentally secular site for a fundamentally religious practice – ancestor worship, "the central link between the Chinese world of men and their world of the spirits," according to Francis L.K. Hsu. Hsu continues:

> ancestor worship not only specifically embodies all the general characteristics of the Chinese approach to the supernatural but, to the Chinese, is itself positive proof and reinforcement of all their other religious beliefs. Ancestor worship is an active ingredient in every aspect of Chinese society, from the family to the government, from local business to the national economy."[15]

It is clearly also an ingredient in memorializing anonymous war dead. In fact, there are regular ceremonies at the shrine meant for these purposes, such as one in 2010, in which one pair of shoes was laid in the sculpture garden for each martyr. In this regard, the pilgrims who are attracted to the Nanjing memorial are engaging in a type of communion with a national collective ancestor.

---

13 Iris Chang, *The Rape of Nanking: The Forgotten Holocaust of World War II* (New York: Basic Books, 2012), 103–4.
14 David B. MacDonald, *Identity Politics in the Age of Genocide: The Holocaust and Historical Representation* (New York: Routledge, 2007), 153.
15 Francis L. K. Hsu, *Americans and Chinese: Passages to Differences* (Honolulu: University of Hawaii Press, 1981), 248.

Nanjing's pilgrims, like those drawn to Gettysburg, are also participants in the worship of a national ideology or a civil religion. The Nanjing Memorial is but one secular pilgrimage site that serves as a shrine to the Chinese national ideology. Unlike the cult of personality that surrounded Mao, however, the iteration of the Chinese civil religion practiced at the Nanjing Memorial is of a more recent vintage. Until 1982, the Nanjing massacre did not figure significantly in Chinese Communist rhetoric or mythology. It was, after all, an attack on the pre-Communist Chinese Republic, overseen by Nationalist leader, Chiang Kai-shek. In fact, until 1983, the official state position was that, though past Japanese militarism was definitely negative, it was, after all, past.[16] But since the mid-1980s, when not-so-coincidentally, the massacre was excised from Japanese textbooks, leading to an outcry from the centrally controlled Chinese press, the memorial has been used to reinforce a sense of "Chinese-ness," of nationalism, and more particularly to revive anti-Japanese sentiment.[17] Write Erica Streker Downs and Philip C. Saunders:

> The CCP's initial claim to legitimacy rested largely on its role in organizing resistance to Japan. Japan continues to provide a useful target that allows Chinese leaders to define China's national identity in opposition to Japanese aggression and imperialism. Appeals to anti-Japanese sentiment still pay domestic political dividends; the regime has used propaganda campaigns, exhibits depicting Japanese wartime atrocities, and anniversaries of past Japanese acts of aggression to exploit these popular feelings.[18]

In these terms, the entire Nanjing Memorial and especially the *wan ren keng* serve as perhaps the most potent appeals to anti-Japanese sentiment, thereby reinforcing the CCP's legitimacy. They also serve to support China's position in its ongoing dispute with Japan over the Daioyu Islands in the South China Sea, one that stretches back to the Japanese invasion shortly after that of Nanjing.

---

16 Caroline Rose, *Interpreting History in Sino-Japanese Relations: A Case Study in Political Decision-Making* (New York: Routledge, 2005) Kindle edition, Chapter 1.

17 Rose, *Interpreting History in Sino-Japanese Relations: A Case Study in Political Decision-Making*, Chapter 2.

18 Erica Streker Downs and Philip C. Saunders, "Legitimacy and the Limits of Nationalism: China and the Daioyu Islands," in *The Rise of China*, ed., Michael E. Brown (Cambridge, MA: MIT Press, 2000), 64.

5 Conclusion

Thus, in many ways, both secular pilgrimage sites serve similar functions in that they support at least some part of their respective national ideologies. In fact, both are what might be defined as nationalist shrines. Nevertheless, the two remain fundamentally different. Gettysburg, on one hand, draws pilgrims from both sides of the Mason-Dixon line to bathe in the spiritual magnetism of "one nation under God," though the definition of "One Nation" depends upon the viewpoint of individual pilgrims. Still, it serves to unify those who sought to separate with those who fought not to. The Nanjing Massacre memorial, on the other, serves to define its pilgrims by what they are not, Japanese, thereby affirming both their humanity and their Chinese-ness. And while both are fundamentally secular sites, pilgrims treat them as sacred. Spiritually magnetic in the narrowly defined sense, both the Memorial Hall to the Victims of the Nanjing Massacre and the Gettysburg National Military Park provide the faithful to their respective civil religions with that "rupture in the ordinary domain through which heaven peeks." They are, in fact, secular pilgrimage sites.

Works Cited

Chang, Iris. *The Rape of Nanking: The Forgotten Holocaust of World War II.* New York: Basic Books, 2012.

"China: Executive Summary". United States Department of State. http://www.state.gov/docu ments/organization/192831.pdf. Accessed July 2014.

Costen, Michael. "The Pilgrimage to Santiago de Compostela in Medieval Europe". In *Pilgrimage and Popular Culture*, edited by Ian Reader and Tony Walter, 137–55. London: Macmillan, 1993.

Downs, Erica Steker and Philip C. Saunders. "Legitimacy and the Limits of Nationalism: China and the Daioyu Islands". *The Rise of China*, edited by Michael E. Brown, 41–73. Cambridge, MA: MIT Press, 2000.

"History and Culture." National Park Service: Gettysburg National Military Park. http://www. nps.gov/gett/historyculture/index.htm. Accessed October 16, 2014.

Horwitz, Tony. *Confederates in the Attic: Dispatches from the Unfinished Civil War.* New York: Random House, 2010.

Hsu, Francis L. K. *Americans and Chinese: Passages to Differences.* Honolulu: University of Hawaii Press, 1981.

Lincoln, Abraham. "The Gettysburg Address." November 19, 1863. http://avalon.law.yale.edu/ 19th_century/gettyb.asp. Accessed August 12, 2014.

MacDonald, David B. *Identity Politics in the Age of Genocide: The Holocaust and Historical Representation.* New York: Routledge, 2007.

Morinis, Alan. *Sacred Journeys: The Anthropology of Pilgrimage.* Westport, CT: Greenwood, 1992.

Newman, Roberta. "The American Church of Baseball and the National Baseball Hall of Fame." *NINE: A Journal of Baseball History and Culture* 10.1 (2001): 46–63.

Rose, Caroline. *Interpreting History in Sino-Japanese Relations: A Case Study in Political Decision-Making.* New York: Routledge, 2005.

Weeks, Jim. *Gettysburg: Memory, Market, and an American Shrine.* Princeton, NJ: Princeton University Press, 2003.

Chika Watanabe
Porous Persons: The Politics of a Nonreligious Japanese NGO

1 Boundary Work in Religion, Secularity, and Development

In recent years, a growing number of scholars have begun to examine the relationship between religion and development. In some ways, it is curious that this attention to religion in development aid is new, given that many of these enterprises have historical roots in religious activities such as missionary work and charities. Yet, it is also not surprising when one considers the ways that development theories and practices, as well as the scholarship on development, have largely followed the standard modernization and secularization narrative in which religion was confined to the private sphere.[1] Today, as religious actors have become increasingly visible in the public sphere around the world – from political and military action to social services –scholars have taken an interest in questions of religion and secularism, re-evaluating the validity of the secularization thesis.[2] In anthropology, research on religion and development appeared in the mid-2000s with ethnographies of faith-based organizations (FBOs), mainly of Christian affiliations.[3] These studies have explored how religious beliefs and worldviews inform FBOs' development theories and practices, showing that development processes do not necessarily entail a separation of religion from other social spheres. In fact, scholars as well as aid practitioners are noting that religion plays an important role in development efforts around the

1 Frederick Cooper and Randall Packard, eds., *International Development and the Social Sciences: Essays on the History and Politics of Knowledge* (Berkeley: University of California Press, 1997); Marc Edelman and Angelique Haugerud, eds. *The Anthropology of Development and Globalization: From Classical Political Economy to Contemporary Neoliberalism* (Malden, MA: Blackwell Publishing, 2005).
2 Peter Berger, ed., *The Desecularization of the World: The Resurgence of Religion in World Politics* (Grand Rapids: Wm. B. Eerdmans Publishing Co., 1999); José Casanova, *Public Religions in the Modern World* (Chicago: University of Chicago Press, 1994); Jürgen Habermas, "Secularism's Crisis of Faith: Notes on Post-Secular Society," *New Perspectives Quarterly* 25 (2008): 17–29.
3 Erica Bornstein, *The Spirit of Development: Protestant NGOs, Morality, and Economics in Zimbabwe* (Stanford: Stanford University Press, 2005); Laurie Occhipinti, *Acting on Faith: Religious Development Organizations in Northwestern Argentina* (Lanham, MD: Lexington, 2005).

world. Given that these analyses have largely tended to address Christian and a few Muslim aid actors, there is clearly still a great need for anthropological studies of religion and development in the context of other faiths and societies.

However, my interest is not strictly on this question of FBOs or the impact of religion on development, but rather, on how aid actors engage in processes of boundary making and blurring regarding the categories of religion and secularism, and what might be their social, moral, and political effects. Beginning with Talal Asad's seminal work on the secular, a number of thinkers have examined how religion and secularity are interrelated historical categories that organize the world in particular ways and remain fluid in everyday practices.[4] Looking at international aid through this lens, I am interested in how the social life of these concepts and their (in)distinctions enable the emergence of particular worlds, knowledge, and subjects in efforts to "better the world." Several scholars have remarked that, in the practices of aid, the religious and the secular often blend into each other, or alternatively, they are kept distinct for particular purposes (intentionally or not).[5] I suggest that this work of blurring and delineating boundaries is not only an academic concern, but also something with which aid actors themselves engage. As this chapter will show, the analytical task, then, is not so much to illustrate how categorical distinctions are "only a fiction of the historical processes we are examining,"[6] but to trace how aid actors can themselves argue for indistinctions, with particular political effects. In short, how boundaries are made and blurred by the people we study – in the case of this chapter between religion and secularity, and relatedly, nature and the human – carry significant import on the consequences of development aid.

---

4 Talal Asad, *Formations of the Secular: Christianity, Islam, Modernity* (Stanford: Stanford University Press, 2003); Markus Dressler and Arvind Mandair, eds., *Secularism and Religion-Making* (New York: Oxford University Press, 2011); Saba Mahmood, "Secularism, Hermeneutics, and Empire: The Politics of Islamic Reformation," *Public Culture* 18.2 (2006): 323–347; Michael Warner, Jonathan VanAntwerpen, and Craig Calhoun, eds., *Varieties of Secularism in a Secular Age* (Cambridge, MA: Harvard University Press, 2010).

5 Michael Barnett and Janice Gross Stein, eds., *Sacred Aid: Faith and Humanitarianism* (New York: Oxford University Press, 2012); Cecilia Lynch, "Religious Humanitarianism and the Global Politics of Secularism," in *Rethinking Secularism*, eds. Craig Calhoun, Mark Juergensmeyer, and Jonathan Van Antwerpen (New York: Oxford University Press, 2011), 204–24.

6 Fenella Cannell, "The Anthropology of Secularism," *Annual Review of Anthropology* 39 (2010): 97.

2 Silence and the Nonreligious

My research focuses on one of the oldest NGOs in Japan, the Organization for Industrial, Spiritual and Cultural Advancement (OISCA), which derives from a
Shinto-based new religious group called Ananaikyō. OISCA is known for its
year-long training programs in sustainable agriculture and environmental education conducted at training centers in eight countries across the Asia-Pacific
world. The founder of OISCA and Ananaikyō, Yonosuke Nakano, was a man
who envisioned world peace through agricultural assistance and sustainable development aid, based on a worldview in which everything in the world, including humans, is connected through a life force running through the universe. He
spoke of the Great Spirit of the Universe (*uchū daiseishin*) and Great Nature
(*daishizen*) as the source of all life and things. According to Nakano, the way
to save the world from nuclear destruction and environmental catastrophe was
to create a world that exists according to the laws of nature. OISCA's organizational charter states:

> We recognize that all lifeforms are closely interconnected and that their source is in the uni-
> verse. We envision a world in which people coexist beyond differences of nationality, eth-
> nicity, language, religion, and culture, and strive to protect and nurture the basis of life on
> this earth ... As a way to realize this vision, we have chosen the work of cultivating people
> who can put to action efforts towards the coexistence of all life on earth, with a heart grate-
> ful for the fact that we are allowed to live thanks to the benefits granted to us by the uni-
> verse. (http://www.oisca.org/about/).

Given this organizational mission, as well as the fact that senior OISCA staffers
are all Ananaikyō members, one can see that OISCA is a religiously-derived organization.

However, Yonosuke Nakano established OISCA as an alternative to religion.
Throughout the 1950s, he organized international conferences with religious
leaders around the world in order to create a religiously-led global peace movement. But soon he realized that religious leaders tended to fight with each other,
and thus he envisioned OISCA as a beacon of a sustainable future that would
transcend religion while still adhering to the spiritual vision of Great Nature.
He turned his attention to the concrete activities of development aid and trainings in organic agriculture – "cultivating people" as the mission statement states
– as ways to actualize a new world. The assertion of being nonreligious was also
pragmatic: as a development organization without official religious affiliations,

OISCA was able to receive government subsidies from the 1970s to the early 2000s.[7] Moreover, OISCA staffers explained to me that donors and government aid officials often expressed resistance to OISCA's religious legacy, calling it "fishy" and "cultish," and so staff members had increasingly identified the organization as nonreligious. Today, more than half of the Japanese staffers are non-Ananaikyō – most of them young people in their twenties and thirties – and the organization's activities do not involve proselytization. Furthermore, during my fieldwork, OISCA's senior Ananaikyō staffers were reluctant to talk about their religion, and when they did, they generally whispered it to me behind closed doors.

This type of silence regarding the question of religion is actually prevalent among many other NGOs in Japan. Although Japanese NGOs are not often explained in terms of religion, I suggest that it is helpful to look at the trajectory of NGOs in Japan through the lens of religion and its position in Japanese society. Like OISCA, many of the other early NGOs also derived from religious organizations, such as the Asia Rural Institute (ARI) (Christian) and Shanti Volunteer Association (SVA) (Buddhist). But these NGOs have struggled against Japanese public suspicion toward "religion," and especially new religions. Particularly since Aum Shinrikyō's terrorist attacks on the Tokyo subway in 1995, the general Japanese public has tended to see new religions with apprehension, almost fear.[8] OISCA is no exception: a quick search of the terms "OISCA" and "Ananaikyō" online (in Japanese) shows comments by people who are alarmed at the connection between the two. OISCA's senior Ananaikyō staffers cultivated a culture of silence regarding the NGO's religious roots in response to such public concerns.

Rather than interpret this silence as a dissimulation of the "real" religious nature of such organizations, however, I suggest that it is telling of a "nonreligious" position that produces particular ideological and political effects. Working from the assertion that *how* the religion-secularity boundary is made and blurred is significant, in the following sections, I examine the ways that OISCA's Japanese staff members articulated the organization's nonreligious character, specifically through ecological ideas.

An early conversation that I had with Kimura, one of the senior staffers at the Tokyo headquarters and a prominent Ananaikyō member, captures the main dynamics at play in this formulation of the nonreligious in the context

---

7 According to Article 83 of the Japanese Constitution, public funds cannot be given to religious organizations.
8 Helen Hardacre, "After Aum: Religion and Civil Society in Japan," in *The State of Civil Society in Japan*, eds. Frank J. Schwartz and Susan J. Pharr (Cambridge: Cambridge University Press, 2003), 135–53.

of sustainable development aid. When I asked him what the relationship was between the NGO and the religious organization, he replied:

> It is not so much about Ananaikyō but about Shinto, and about valuing Japanese tradi-
> tions. When one says "religion," you might think of something like Sōka Gakkai [one of
> the largest new religious organizations in Japan], but that's not the case with OISCA. Shinto
> envelops many religions. Before, Ananaikyō was the parent organization and we had many
> OISCA members who were Ananaikyō, but that's different now. It's not that Ananaikyō
> gives us instructions, but it is the backbone of OISCA's philosophy. But that doesn't deter-
> mine the content of our projects. OISCA was made because we needed something that tran-
> scends religion to change the world. In the international conferences, religious leaders
> fought with each other all the time, and so we proposed Shinto. We removed the barrier
> of religion and proposed agricultural work. That is, a form of development that is in har-
> mony with nature, a sustainable form of development.

On the one hand, Kimura acknowledged OISCA's roots in a religious organization. Moreover, while he tried to distance the organization from the category of
"religion," he did not reject it all together, stating that "Shinto envelops many
religions." But on the other hand, he defined Ananaikyō as ultimately Shinto
and appealed to the historical constructions of Shinto as a national-cultural
moral system. Then, he took a further step: he appealed to the concept of nature
to propose that the Ananaikyō- and Shinto-derived values in OISCA – "development in harmony with nature" – were about a kind of ecological harmony that
could change the world by transcending religion without rejecting it.

This expression of a nonreligious Shinto in terms of arguments about "living
in harmony with nature" is a key aspect of, not only OISCA's mode of aid, but
also of a more general tendency in Japanese views of the environment and sustainable development. In OISCA, Nakano had taught that nature was infused
with the Great Spirit of the Universe, and as such, Ananaikyō staff members
talked about plants, animals, rocks, and other animate and inanimate beings
in nature as imbued with a vital force, suggesting animist worldviews. If only humans could live according to this Great Spirit, the thinking went, a sustainable
future would be possible. Although popular Japanese discourses about nature do
not appeal to ideas such as the Great Spirit of the Universe, the emphasis among
OISCA staffers on living in harmony with nature and seeing humans as merely
part of a wider spiritual world resonates with general understandings about
the environment in Japan. Significantly, this is a perspective about nature that
buttresses a culturalist claim about "Japaneseness" – that the Japanese have a
natural tendency to live in harmony with nature and that the unique natural environment of the Japanese archipelago is what made the Japanese a unique peo-

ple.[9] This view was advanced for many years by cultural nationalist writings known as *nihonjinron* ("discourses about the Japanese"), which touted the positive uniqueness of "the Japanese" and became a particularly popular genre from the 1970s to the 1990s during Japan's economic boom.

Thus, as I elaborate below, as transformative as Shinto ways of being with nature could be in reformulating nature-culture paradigms and transcending dualistic worldviews,[10] my concern is that the historical specificity of Shinto nationalism continues to overwrite the imaginaries and experiences of Shinto and nature in Japan. Admittedly, this is not a predetermined fact. But undeniable historical and political developments, as well as the *trainings* that go into cultivating ecologically harmonious persons, demand that we not take arguments of alternative human-nature relations only at face value, but also develop a view that is critical.[11] As much as permeable relations across human-nature divides and socialities beyond the human might provide hints for an environmentally sensitive and potentially sustainable future, these modes of being do not exist in a vacuum. In short, advocating for porous human-nature relations is something that some of the people we study already do, and scholars must beware of the political projects that non-dualistic worldviews can also advance.

3 Porous Persons

OISCA's organizational charter emphasizes the work of "cultivating people." The organization's use of training programs as a method of development aid can be characterized as a form of Japanese aid called *hitozukuri* ("making persons"). Hitozukuri is a term that has been used in other areas of Japanese society, from Toyota's business philosophy to municipal governments' projects of community revitalization. In international aid policies, Japanese officials have defined hitozukuri as "a concept unique to Japan," largely aimed at human resource devel-

---

9 Harumi Befu, "Watsuji Tetsuro's Ecological Approach: Its Philosophical Foundation," in *Japanese Images of Nature: Cultural Perspectives*, eds. Pamela Asquith and Arne Kalland (Richmond, Surrey: Curzon Press, 1997), 106 – 20; Peter Dale, *The Myth of Japanese Uniqueness* (New York: St. Martin's Press, 1986).

10 Casper Bruun Jensen and Anders Blok, "Techno-animism in Japan: Shinto Cosmograms, Actor-network Theory, and the Enabling Powers of Non-human Agencies," *Theory, Culture & Society* 30.2 (2013): 84 – 115.

11 Naoki Kasuga and Casper Bruun Jensen, "An Interview with Naoki Kasuga," *HAU: Journal of Ethnographic Theory* 2.2 (2012): 389 – 97; see also Ghassan Hage, "Critical Anthropology as a Permanent State of First Contact," *Cultural Anthropology* (online), January 13, 2014, http://cu lanth.org/fieldsights/473-critical-anthropology-as-a-permanent-state-of-first-contact.

opment efforts to develop and transfer knowledge through "mutual understanding" with aid recipients "who work in a situation where culture, history, and values are different from those of Japan."[12] This definition of hitozukuri as the cultivation of persons through inter-cultural relations and face-to-face interactions was reflected in the oft-used slogan for the Japan International Cooperation Agency (JICA) (the Japanese version of USAID), "Making Persons, Making Nations, Heart-to-Heart Contact" (*Hitozukuri, Kunizukuri, Kokoro no Fureai*). OISCA can be said to be the nongovernmental representative of hitozukuri aid.

OISCA staff members often stressed that hitozukuri for them was more about the holistic cultivation of persons than a simple transfer of skills. To this end, trainings were conducted in a communal lifestyle in which staff and trainees from diverse cultural backgrounds lived and worked together for a year, learning not only about organic farming, but more importantly, about living in a group. As a way to nurture particular kinds of collectively oriented people who would enable a sustainable future, OISCA's hitozukuri activities promised something more than "development." Specifically, the claims of nonreligious aid that depended on ecological arguments of "living in harmony with nature" aimed to bring about what I call a porous kind of person, borrowing Charles Taylor's phrase,[13] who would be intimately embedded in sustainable relations with nature. This porous person would be committed to organic agriculture, living symbiotically with the natural environment. OISCA's aid workers emphasized, for example, the importance of "listening" to the earth to learn what the soil might need to cultivate rice, and the value of incorporating human and animal waste into the agricultural system instead of using chemical products. But if in the agricultural activities in OISCA this was an exchange relation between humans and the natural environment, Ananaikyō members suggested that this approach was rooted in a more radical perspective. One Ananaikyō member – not an OISCA staffer – told me that the universe and the human body are one. "For example," he elaborated, "scientists have discovered that the human body is porous (*suka suka*) and it is mostly empty space, just like the universe." Although this man was not an OISCA aid worker, his explanation of the human body and the universe superimposed on each other was echoed in OISCA's hitozukuri activities, wherein an intimate connection between humans and the natural world – ideally to the point of becoming one – undergirded the ethics of organic farming.

---

12 Michio Kanda and Kyoko Kuwajima, "The Overview and New Orientation of Technical Cooperation of JICA—In the Framework of Capacity Development and Human Security," *Technology and Development* 19 (2006): 36–51.

13 Charles Taylor, *A Secular Age* (Cambridge, MA: Belknap Press/Harvard University Press, 2007).

Let me illustrate this with the words of a Japanese OISCA staff member. Furuichi was a man in his sixties with a slight build, but had an energetic gait that always made him seem a bit jumpy. During a three-hour interview, he reminisced about his life as a young boy in northern rural Japan, where his home was a regional chapter of Ananaikyō. He joined OISCA in his early twenties and was stationed in the East Timor project for many years.

In the second hour of our conversation, he told me about his philosophy of agriculture. "Agriculture can't lie, and if you can teach people through agriculture, you can cultivate a decent human being." He continued: "Agriculture is a means for OISCA to nurture people with a big and clean heart." In his view, the purpose of hitozukuri aid was not to create technically skilled farmers, but to shape persons with a particular kind of heart – using the word *kokoro* in Japanese, which refers to something like heart, mind, and soul. Furuichi believed that the person (trainee) should open oneself toward nature, taking a step to become more like a vegetable in an ethical self-making. "Nurturing the kokoro of vegetables will nurture the kokoro of humans," he stated. Illustrating what he meant with an example, he said:

> Daikon radishes grow by turning around and around like a screw [...] This means that you can understand the entire universe with just one daikon. It means that the daikon is looking toward the sun as its parent, turning around and around so that every side faces the parent equally as it grows. In that way, the daikon is teaching us everything.

According to Furuichi, vegetables have a kokoro that is moral, such as its inclination to face "the parent" (i.e. the sun), and this is an orientation that people should adopt through mimetic emulation. In this formulation, as much as people worked upon nature through agriculture, nature was working upon humans. Becoming a porous person vis-à-vis nature was an ethical act that would not only bring about a sustainable world based on the Great Spirit of the Universe, but also instill in humans the "nature" of nature. This form of constructing an ethical self through a mimesis of the natural world can be found in other spiritual-ethical practices in Japan.[14] Similar to the ways that Japanese mountain worshippers cultivate their ethical selves by simulating the shapes of the natural environment, Furuichi envisioned an ethical making of persons based on imitations of nature, such as daikon radishes.

However, as much as this was a transformative vision, it was a potentiality that was marked by particular political effects. Thus, as I elaborate below, non-

---

14 See for example Ellen Schattschneider, *Immortal Wishes: Labor and Transcendence on a Japanese Sacred Mountain* (Durham, NC: Duke University Press, 2003).

religious claims in Japanese aid might enable a new narrative of human existence that steps outside of the confines of modernity as we know it, but this is not without its political consequences.

4 The Potentiality and Politics of Shinto Ontology

Anthropologist Anne Allison's earlier work on anime and computer games in Japan shows how, in contemporary Japan, people often respond to social and ecological crises by pursuing the idea of becoming closer to nature based on a fundamental connection perceived between human and nonhuman worlds, or nature and artifice. She explains how Satoshi Tajiri, creator of the computer game *Pokemon*, invented the game as a way to recapture something that he felt had been lost with industrial capitalism. He remembered his childhood experiences in a town where nature was still abundant, and modeled the game based on his favorite pastime collecting insects and crayfish, which involved intimate interactions with both nature and other children.[15] Tajiri, therefore, designed Pokemon as an interactive game that was driven by a desire to (re)create porous human-nature relations through technology. Anne Allison calls this aesthetic wherein human and nature, thing and life, technology and human intermesh, "techno-animism."

Casper Bruun Jensen and Anders Blok take up this concept of techno-animism and argue that a re-examination of Shinto worldviews can offer a new perspective on human-nonhuman relations.[16] Taking Bruno Latour's explication that modernity has entailed the work of purification – of making separations between humans and nonhumans, nature and society – *and* that this work has never been successful,[17] Jensen and Blok propose that Shinto can be a fruitful lens through which to examine hybrid worlds and the fact that, therefore, as Latour claimed, "we have never been modern." Although scholars have shown that Shinto as a unified entity only appeared as a political project in the 18th century, and subsequently taken to its extreme by the military state in the Second World

---

15 Anne Allison, *Millennial Monsters: Japanese Toys and the Global Imagination* (Berkeley: University of California Press, 2006), 201.

16 Jensen and Blok, "Techno-animism in Japan : Shinto Cosmograms, Actor-network Theory, and the Enabling Powers of Non-human Agencies," *Theory, Culture & Society* 30.2 (2013): 84–115.

17 Bruno Latour, *We Have Never Been Modern* (Cambridge: Harvard University Press, 1993).

War,[18] there is a way of being that is associated with popular Shinto that treats gods, humans, animals, plants, and inanimate objects as permeable and part of a unified field of existence.[19] Jensen and Blok propose to take this Shinto animism seriously, beyond the political over-determination that attaches Shinto to imperial-militarist Japan. They argue that there is a human-nonhuman permeability in popular Shinto that challenges modernity's purification and opens new ways to understand how "we have never been modern."

I suggest that this potentiality of Shinto that Jensen and Blok identify arises from yet another position: that of the nonreligious. Webb Keane illustrates how the purification that Latour describes is also a mode of "dematerialization – the stripping away of bodily disciplines, rituals, icons, even texts – by which religious purification converges with the moral narrative of modernity."[20] This process of dematerialization is also part and parcel of secularization, in which religion is made into a matter of concepts and internal belief, thereby converging with the disenchantment of the world and the privatization of religion. In fact, in the non-Western world like Japan, religion as such came to be known at this moment of dematerialization, and hence, it is impossible to think of religion without the secular, and vice versa.[21] Hence, both religion and secularity are part of the same narrative of modernity's purification. I suggest that, against this background, the claim to be nonreligious is an attempt to sidestep this trajectory of modernity, religion-making, and secularization as we know it. In OISCA's formulation, the nonreligious converges with Shinto animistic worlds, making a strong case for a "non-modern" alternative future (as Jensen and Blok suggest), one where humans and nature coexist in harmony, or better yet, permeate into each other.

---

18 Helen Hardacre, *Shinto and the State, 1868–1988* (Princeton: Princeton University Press, 1989); Toshio Kuroda, "Shinto in the History of Japanese Religion," in *Religion and Society in Modern Japan: Selected Readings*, eds. Mark R. Mullins, Susumu Shimazono, and Paul L. Swanson (Berkeley: Asian Humanities Press, 1993), 7–30.

19 Some scholars have distinguished popular Shinto from state Shinto, the latter presented as the state-led effort to standardize and unify Shinto as a national moral system in the early 20th century. See John Clammer, "The Politics of Animism," in *Figured Worlds: Ontological Obstacles in Intercultural Relations*, eds. John Clammer, Sylvie Poirier, and Eric Schwimmer (Toronto: University of Toronto Press, 2004), 83–112.

20 Webb Keane, *Christian Moderns: Freedom and Fetish in the Mission Encounter* (Berkeley: University of California Press, 2005), 87.

21 Markus Dressler and Arvind Mandair, "Introduction: Modernity, Religion-Making, and the ," in *Secularism and Religion-Making*, eds. Markus Dressler and Arvind Mandair (New York: Oxford University Press, 2011), 1–36; Jason Ānanda Josephson, *The Invention of Religion in Japan* (Chicago: University of Chicago Press, 2012).

However, is it really possible to recuperate the capacity of Shinto, as Jensen and Blok argue, "to generate immanent connectedness in a more-than-human world,"[22] without its historically prescribed political ideology? Japanese intellectuals and state actors mobilized ideas of nature in various ways throughout history, from ideas of human-nature unity to those of humanity's duty to develop nature.[23] Until the early 20th century, local Shinto practices were diverse and, accordingly, people understood nature as sacred but in multiple ways. Nevertheless, it is also a historical fact that with the advent of nationalist and imperialist Japan in the early 20th century, the state consolidated Shinto practices into a national moral core and constructed an ideology of nature that was coterminous with the imagination of a modern Japanese nation.[24] As sympathetic as I am to the proposition to consider the potential of Shinto to offer alternative "nonmodern" human-nature relations, I also contend that such efforts cannot be divorced from specific histories. Shinto, as it appears in practice and discourse in Japan today, such as in OISCA's aid activities, is always already circumscribed by the legacies of what has come to be known as state Shinto and ultranationalism. As such, I argue that popular Shinto and state Shinto cannot be separated in practice. As Julia Adeney Thomas indicated, the conception of porous human-nature relations in the context of the nationalization of Shinto in early 20th century Japan is itself a history of modernity, albeit one that is based on hybridities rather than purification.

Kimura, the senior staffer mentioned above, talked about Ananaikyō as Shinto, which was, according to him, fundamentally about "Japanese traditions."[25] OISCA's Japanese aid workers mobilized Shinto in terms of porous relations between humans and nature, but this was also a definition of Shinto as an essentially Japanese national-cultural set of values. Furuichi's description of people becoming like vegetables cannot be simply taken at face value as an ontological claim; it is also part of a historically and politically specific project.

---

22 Jensen and Blok, "Techno-animism in Japan: Shinto Cosmograms, Actor-network Theory, and the Enabling Powers of Non-human Agencies," *Theory, Culture & Society* 30.2 (2013): 108.
23 Tessa Morris-Suzuki, "Concepts of Nature and Technology in Pre-Industrial Japan," *East Asian History* 1 (1991): 81–97; Julia Adeney Thomas, *Reconfiguring Modernity: Concepts of Nature in Japanese Political Ideology* (Berkeley: University of California Press, 2001).
24 Thomas, *Reconfiguring Modernity*, 179–208.
25 It is beyond the scope of this chapter to examine further, but Ananaikyō and Yonosuke Nakano have also been associated with rightwing public figures and emperor worship.

5 Conclusion

In 1967, Lynn White made the influential argument that the global environmental crisis was due to Western Christianity's human-nature dualism and ultimate anthropocentrism. He proposed that Christianity's destruction of "pagan animism" made it possible to exploit nature based on an indifference to the feelings of things in the natural world.[26] Although a number of scholars have questioned this correlation between anthropocentrism and ecological destruction (and, conversely, ecocentrism and environmental sustainability),[27] the idea – or hope – that a less oppositional form of human-nature relations could lead to better environmental practices continues to persist.[28] In this chapter, I have suggested that how aid actors conceive of porous human-nature relations in claiming to do nonreligious work could enable an ecologically sustainable future, but that this possibility is also marked by the political history of Shinto in Japan. Entangled human-nature relations are not only alternatives to Western dualistic understandings, but also already part of particular political projects.

As such, adapting Jensen and Blok's incisive question about Japanese techno-animism,[29] the question to ask is this: what happens when analyses that have relied on the hegemony of western nature-culture and religion-secularity dualisms to make their revelations about hybridity encounter situations where hybridization is explicit? Bruno Latour's point that modernity's purification has never been complete, Lynn White's contention that Christianity's human-nature dualism should be discarded, and anthropologists' views that categorical distinctions such as religion and secularism are only fictions become insufficient as analytical interventions when the people we study already make hybridities explicit and implicate them in political projects. Porous persons are not simply

---

26 Lynn White, "The Historical Roots of Our Ecological Crisis," *Science* (New Series) 155 (1967): 1203–07.

27 Ramachandra Guha, "Radical Environmentalism and Wilderness Preservation: a Third World Critique," *Environmental Ethics* 11 (1989): 71–83; Arne Kalland, "Culture in Japanese Nature," in *Asian Perceptions of Nature: A Critical Approach*, eds. Ole Bruun and Arne Kalland (Surrey: Curzon Press, 1996), 243–57.

28 Christopher Key Chapple, "The Living Cosmos of Jainism: A Traditional Science Grounded in Environmental Ethics," *Daedalus* 130.4 (2001): 207–224; John Grim and Mary Evelyn Tucker, *Ecology and Religion* (Washington, DC: Island Press, 2014); Gísli Pálsson, "Human- environmental Relations: Orientalism, Paternalism and Communalism," in *Nature and Society: Anthropological Perspectives*, eds. Philippe Descola and Gísli Pálsson (London: Routledge, 1996), 63–81.

29 Jensen and Blok, "Techno-animism in Japan: Shinto Cosmograms, Actor-network Theory, and the Enabling Powers of Non-human Agencies," *Theory, Culture & Society* 30.2 (2013): 92.

given, but rather, cultivated in specific ways and in the context of particular histories of modernity.

To say that Ananaikyō was ultimately about Shinto and therefore "simply" about Japanese traditional values enabled Yonosuke Nakano's teachings to enter the public and global sphere. This was, in a way, a formulation of development work as a redemptive dream to resuscitate things from the past – the nostalgic idea of the Japanese people's essential harmony with nature – that could guide the world toward a new future.[30] Certainly, the cultivation of porous persons attuned to the natural environment, based on "Shinto values," could potentially lead to a sustainable world. But the allusion to Shinto today always comes with political implications. The nonreligious might be evidence that "we have never been modern" in the context of Western trajectories, but the history of Shinto in Japan shows that the blurring of boundaries can itself be a story of modernity as well as the politics of development. It is a story that is both hopeful and hazardous, promising a sustainable future as well as a renewal of Shinto politics reminiscent of imperialist and nationalistic aspirations of the early 20th century.

Works Cited

Allison, Anne. *Millennial Monsters: Japanese Toys and the Global Imagination.* Berkeley: University of California Press, 2006.

Asad, Talal. *Formations of the Secular: Christianity, Islam, Modernity.* Stanford: Stanford University Press, 2003.

Barnett, Michael, and Janice Gross Stein, eds. *Sacred Aid: Faith and Humanitarianism.* New York: Oxford University Press, 2012.

Befu, Harumi. "Watsuji Tetsuro's Ecological Approach: Its Philosophical Foundation." In *Japanese Images of Nature: Cultural Perspectives,* edited by Pamela Asquith and Arne Kalland, 106–120. Richmond, Surrey: Curzon Press, 1997.

Berger, Peter, ed. *The Desecularization of the World: The Resurgence of Religion in World Politics.* Grand Rapids: Wm. B. Eerdmans Publishing Co., 1999.

Bornstein, Erica. *The Spirit of Development: Protestant NGOs, Morality, and Economics in Zimbabwe.* Stanford: Stanford University Press, 2005.

Cannell, Fenella. "The Anthropology of Secularism." *Annual Review of Anthropology* 39 (2010): 85–100.

Casanova, José. *Public Religions in the Modern World.* Chicago: University of Chicago Press, 1994.

---

30 Chika Watanabe, "Past Loss as Future? The Politics of Temporality and the 'Nonreligious' by a Japanese NGO in Burma/Myanmar," *Political and Legal Anthropology Review* 36.1 (2013): 75–98.

Chapple, Christopher Key. "The Living Cosmos of Jainism: A Traditional Science Grounded in Environmental Ethics." *Daedalus* 130.4 (2001): 207–224.

Clammer, John. "The Politics of Animism." In *Figured Worlds: Ontological Obstacles in Intercultural Relations*, edited by John Clammer, Sylvie Poirier, and Eric Schwimmer, 83–112. Toronto: University of Toronto Press, 2004.

Cooper, Frederick, and Randall Packard, eds. *International Development and the Social Sciences: Essays on the History and Politics of Knowledge*. Berkeley: University of California Press, 1997.

Dale, Peter. *The Myth of Japanese Uniqueness*. New York: St. Martin's Press, 1986.

Dressler, Markus, and Arvind Mandair, eds. *Secularism and Religion-Making*. New York: Oxford University Press, 2011.

Edelman, Marc, and Angelique Haugerud, eds. *The Anthropology of Development and Globalization: From Classical Political Economy to Contemporary Neoliberalism*. Malden, MA: Blackwell Publishing, 2005.

Grim, John, and Mary Evelyn Tucker. *Ecology and Religion*. Washington, DC: Island Press, 2014.

Guha, Ramachandra. "Radical Environmentalism and Wilderness Preservation: a Third World Critique." *Environmental Ethics* 11 (1989): 71–83.

Habermas, Jürgen. "Secularism's Crisis of Faith: Notes on Post-Secular Society." *New Perspectives Quarterly* 25 (2008): 17–29.

Hage, Ghassan. "Critical Anthropology as a Permanent State of First Contact." *Cultural Antropology* (online), January 13, 2014, http://culanth.org/fieldsights/473-critical-anthropology-as-a-permanent-state-of-first-contact.

Hardacre, Helen. *Shinto and the State, 1868–1988*. Princeton: Princeton University Press, 1989.

Hardacre, Helen. "After Aum: Religion and Civil Society in Japan." In *The State of Civil Society in Japan*, edited by Frank J. Schwartz and Susan J. Pharr, 135–53. Cambridge: Cambridge University Press, 2003.

Jensen, Casper Bruun, and Anders Blok. "Techno-animism in Japan: Shinto Cosmograms, Actor-network Theory, and the Enabling Powers of Non-human Agencies." *Theory, Culture & Society* 30.2 (2013): 84–115.

Josephson, Jason Ānanda. *The Invention of Religion in Japan*. Chicago: University of Chicago Press, 2012.

Kalland, Arne. "Culture in Japanese Nature." In *Asian Perceptions of Nature: A Critical Approach*, edited by Ole Bruun and Arne Kalland, 243–57. Surrey: Curzon Press, 1996.

Kanda, Michio, and Kyoko Kuwajima. "The Overview and New Orientation of Technical Cooperation of JICA – In the Framework of Capacity Development and Human Security." *Technology and Development* 19 (2006): 36–51.

Kasuga, Naoki, and Casper Bruun Jensen. "An Interview with Naoki Kasuga." *HAU: Journal of Ethnographic Theory* 2.2 (2012): 389–97.

Keane, Webb. *Christian Moderns: Freedom and Fetish in the Mission Encounter*. Berkeley: University of California Press, 2005.

Kuroda, Toshio. "Shinto in the History of Japanese Religion." In *Religion and Society in Modern Japan: Selected Readings*, edited by Mark R. Mullins, Susumu Shimazono, and Paul L. Swanson, 7–30. Berkeley: Asian Humanities Press, 1993.

Latour, Bruno. *We Have Never Been Modern*. Cambridge: Harvard University Press, 1993.

Lynch, Cecilia. "Religious Humanitarianism and the Global Politics of Secularism." In *Rethinking Secularism*, edited by Craig Calhoun, Mark Juergensmeyer, and Jonathan Van Antwerpen, 204–24. New York: Oxford University Press, 2011.

Mahmood, Saba. "Secularism, Hermeneutics, and Empire: The Politics of Islamic Reformation," *Public Culture* 18.2 (2006): 323–47.

Morris-Suzuki, Tessa. "Concepts of Nature and Technology in Pre-Industrial Japan." *East Asian History* 1 (1991): 81–97.

Occhipinti, Laurie. *Acting on Faith: Religious Development Organizations in Northwestern Argentina.* Lanham, MD: Lexington, 2005.

Pálsson, Gísli. "Human-environmental Relations: Orientalism, Paternalism and Communalism." In *Nature and Society: Anthropological Perspectives*, edited by Philippe Descola and Gísli Pálsson, 63–81. London: Routledge, 1996.

Schattschneider, Ellen. *Immortal Wishes: Labor and Transcendence on a Japanese Sacred Mountain.* Durham, NC: Duke University Press, 2003.

Taylor, Charles. *A Secular Age.* Cambridge, MA: Belknap Press/Harvard University Press, 2007.

Thomas, Julia Adeney. *Reconfiguring Modernity: Concepts of Nature in Japanese Political Ideology.* Berkeley: University of California Press, 2001.

Warner, Michael, Jonathan VanAntwerpen, and Craig Calhoun, eds. *Varieties of Secularism in a Secular Age.* Cambridge, MA: Harvard University Press, 2010.

Watanabe, Chika. "Past Loss as Future? The Politics of Temporality and the 'Nonreligious' by a Japanese NGO in Burma/Myanmar." *Political and Legal Anthropology Review* (PoLAR) 36.1 (2013): 75–98.

White, Lynn. "The Historical Roots of Our Ecological Crisis." *Science* (New Series) 155 (1967): 1.

Elayne Oliphant

Circulations of the Sacred: Contemporary Art as "Cultural" Catholicism in 21st Century Paris

"An immense scandal," read a comment scrawled in the *livre d'or* (Comment Book, or, literally, "Book of Gold") displayed next to the inaugural exhibit at a new contemporary art space, the *Collège des Bernardins*, in central Paris in 2008. "First the Louvre and Versailles," the writer continued, "and today *les Bernardins*. The Devil does his work in the light of day. What sadness." The critic's words clearly expressed his or her shock and dismay at the contemporary art installation exhibited at the *Collège* in the winter of 2008–09. For the installation, the impressive nave of the *Collège* had been cut in half in order to house row upon row of eight-foot-tall and one-inch-thick glass panels that the artist, Claudio Parmiggiani, and his assistants had smashed with mallets and shattered into pieces *in situ*, leaving a mixture of jagged pieces of glass scattered on the floor, along with the still-standing cracked fragments of panels. Like a painting, the sea of broken glass could only be viewed from one perspective and at a slight remove on the other side of a knee-high security wire. Along one side of sea of glass, the artist also had constructed *in situ* a "library of shadows." After collecting more than 20,000 books intended for destruction, he lit and then extinguished a controlled fire. As the shelves filled with smoke, he draped them with a light tarp that captured the soot, leaving the image of a shadowy negative of the books in the hollow of a burned shelf. Finally, in the sacristy, the artist Claudio Parmiggiani had placed on the empty tiled floor a collection of bells that once hung in village churches throughout Italy.

The *Collège* is a unique kind of exhibition space in Paris, located in the fifth arrondissement, within walking distance of several of the city's important historical and tourist sites, including the *Notre Dame* Cathedral. It is owned and operated by the city's Catholic archdiocese. But the critic took little notice of this exceptional status of the *Collège* in ways that betray the complexity of the city's religious and secular commitments. For the viewer of the contemporary art exhibit at the *Collège*, the former palace turned treasure-trove of the Republican state that is the Louvre, the monument to now discredited monarchical glory that is the *Palais Versailles*, and the newly renovated space of cultural Catholicism that is the *Collège*, all belong to a shared *sacred* space that, in recent years, has come to be tainted by contemporary art.

Here, I want to leave aside the critique of contemporary art to focus instead on the connections taken for granted between these religious and cultural spaces in and around Paris. The writer quoted above is not alone in making this equation; employees at the *Collège*, as one of its publicity staff explained to me, have worked hard to "install the *Collège* in the Parisian cultural landscape." Thus, while the critic's words disparaged the exhibit, the "scandal" that he or she identified, I argue, demonstrates the *success*, rather than the failure of this new project of the French Catholic Church. In order to implement this project, the French Church that has taken on significant debt and invested public, private, and corporate funds into this space where no one will be required to make a declaration of faith. The "success" of the space, I argue, requires us to rethink many of our assumptions about the French secular public sphere.

Museums and churches, as has often been noted, share a number of common traits. They are both sites of reverence, of carefully regulated movement, and of the appreciation of objects. Indeed, many early proponents of museums did not shy away from such comparisons. Rather, they explicitly borrowed techniques and language of viewing, beholding, and revering from churches and applied them to the newly forming "secular temples."[1] In France, and elsewhere, this transfer of the sacred also occurred by more material means. Follwing the Revolution of 1789, the institutions of the new Republican state expropriated (and often destroyed) many of the riches that had been displayed in spaces of the First Estate. The complex voyages taken by many of the masterpieces and treasures found in the Louvre are often displayed on the labels affixed on the wall beside artworks.[2]

What are the implications of the French Catholic Church's adoption of museum techniques in ways that may be understood as an expression of the ongoing circulation of the sacred between ostensibly religious and secular spaces in Paris? This circulation renders increasingly problematic the identification and separation of the categories of the "secular" and "religious." The Church, I

---

1 For the history of the formation of museums in Europe see Tony Bennett, *The Birth of the Museum: History, Theory, Politics* (New York: Routledge, 1995); David Carrier, *Museum Skepticism: A History of the Display of Art in Public Galleries* (Durham: Duke University Press, 2006); Andrew McClellan, *Inventing the Louvre: Arts, Politics and the Origins of the Modern Museum in Eighteenth-Century Paris* (Cambridge: Cambridge University Press, 1994); and Donald Preziosi and Claire Farago, eds. *Grasping the World: The Idea of the Museum* (Aldershot: Ashgate Publishing, 2004). For an analysis of museums of secular temples and the activities that occur within as rituals, see Carol Duncan Civilizing Rituals: Inside Public Art Museums (New York, Routledge, 1995).

2 Many such objects, of course, were also looted through French imperial expansion throughout Europe and North Africa in the early nineteenth century.

argue, is now hoping to take up (or back) some of the sacredness that has been vested in museums for much of the nineteenth and twentieth centuries. In addition to displaying objects that one might expect to find at Paris's modern and contemporary art museums, such as the *Centre Pompidiou* or the *Palais Tokyo*, the *Collège* also borrows museum language and techniques, while hiring professional artists, curators, and public relations specialists. This specialized labor aims to attract museum-going publics and engage them in contemporary modes of art viewing in a 'cultural' space owned and operated by the archdiocese. That such circulations between museum and spaces of the Church are possible is a fact of secular social life that requires further examination. What is more, the circulation of practices and objects from church to museum and back again, may have unanticipated consequences both for the Catholic Church and the public sphere in France.

In 2001, the archdiocese of Paris purchased from the city the thirteenth-century Cistercian building that holds the *Collège des Bernardins* 'back' from the city. Declared public property in 1791, its return to the French Church for just under two million euros brought it once again into the (private) possession of the Church. The archdiocece explicitly defines the space as one of "culture" rather than "worship" (in French, *culture* instead of *culte*). When Pope Benedict XVI came to give a speech at the opening of the *Collège*, his words inaugurated rather than consecrated the space. The category of 'culture' allowed the archdiocese to receive more than twenty million euros in state funding, and for *Collège* employees to invite representatives of the rigidly and famously secular state and public to hear the Pope speak. The *Collège* hosts debates, conferences, and lectures on 'religious' and 'secular' subjects alike, but it is the exhibitions of contemporary art that receive particularly wide coverage in the press and that attract a larger (although typically elite) public. I spent two years in Paris, arriving just after the *Collège* had opened to the public. Following my daily observations of its inaugural exhibit, I was hired to work as a mediator for three later exhibitions, between the summer of 2009 and the fall of 2010.[3] According to the brochures and the website accompanying Parmiggiani's installations, through the work, "the visitor is invited to find the silence of the space, the respect for the spiritual force that emerges."[4] The exhibit's curator, Catherine Grenier, produced much of the accompanying text in brochures displayed near the exhibit and a glossy catalogue

---

3 I describe these observations and the types of art viewing practices enacted at the Collège in greater detail in Elayne Oliphant. 2014. "Beyond Blasphemy or Devotion: Art, the Secular and Catholicism in Paris." *Journal of the Royal Anthropological Institute* 21 (2): 352–373.

4 Catherine Grenier, Exhibition Curator, Collège des Bernardins, "Parmiggiani au Collège des Bernardins, 22 novembre 2008–31 janvier 2009." Exhibition Brochure.

sold in the *Collège* bookstore. The *Collège* commissioned Grenier, the Director of Modern and Contemporary Art at the *Pompidou Center*, as curator for the exhibit at the request of the artist.

Of the single-artist exhibitions I observed, Parmiggiani's was the only to have benefited from the work of an external curator. This fact piqued my curiosity. One afternoon at the building's café, after the Parmiggiani exhibit had closed, I asked one of the coordinators of cultural programming at the *Collège* to help me understand this distinction. "The artistic program was set long before we arrived," she said. In fact, all of the exhibits of the first two years of the building's operation, she explained, were decided upon two or three years before the opening. This was necessary in order to ensure the availability of artists of fame and high caliber. These years of planning also highlight the forethought, planning, and strategizing that went into the *Collège*'s first few years of visual arts display. The need for Catherine Grenier, however, the cultural coordinator explained, had not been foreseen. Instead, as the time of the exhibit approached, Parmiggiani had requested that Grenier be brought in to act as an intermediary between himself and the *Collège*. He wanted to be sure that, in her words, "we took his point of view – the point of view of the artist – seriously." She continued that she had been "a bit surprised, because it was almost an act of defiance *vis-à-vis* the *Bernardins*, as if it was obvious that we would misinterpret, or do poorly by his *oeuvre*."

The circulations of the sacred I am describing here, it would seem, have not been as self-evident as the advertising surrounding the *Collège* would suggest. The work of making the *Collège* a secular sacred space of contemporary art display has required what anthropologists call significant social and cultural work. The artist's skepticism that the *Collège* could be a credible space for contemporary art display was perceived by the employee as an act of "defiance" because it called into question the Church's capacity to produce anything other than a religious sacred space.

The movement of the sacred from the church to the museum in the eighteenth and nineteenth centuries in France offers an early example of how the modernist project of purification was one that was always paradoxical. The religious language surrounding France's 'secular' museums demonstrates the slipperiness of the transformation of sites and objects from 'religious' to 'secular'. As Bruno Latour has demonstrated, the work required to maintain the separation of purportedly distinct spaces of modern life, in fact, produce the very categories that they presume to inhabit.[5] The production of these distinctions, moreover, is always incomplete and often contradictory. Both artist and viewers resisted the Church's attempts to meld two presumably distinct – religious and secular – sorts of sites. And yet, while Parmiggiani demanded the services of a curator to bridge a perceived distance between himself and representatives of the Church, he also found acceptable and important linkages between his work and the medieval *space* of the *Collège*. In a video recorded at the *Collège* and played on a wall during the exhibit, he described the installation in the following terms:

> Certain places have an energy; they palpitate; others don't. If one were to make a hole in the wall of any medieval cathedral, blood would flow; if one were to make a hole in the wall of a museum, nothing would come out [...] Some places have a voice, a heart that beats in the thickness of the walls.[6]

Thus, despite his concerns with the *Collège*'s handling of his installation, Parmiggiani produced precisely the sort of work the *Collège* hoped he would. He offered the institution the authenticity of the contemporary (as an evocative space in which to exhibit his work), while also situating this legitimacy in the premodern medieval past. The *Collège* could be contemporary, he argued, precisely because it escaped the trappings of modernity, when the "bloodless" national museums were formed. In its brochures and on its website, the *Collège* is described as a site of *renaissance*. Those who have worked very hard to transform the *Collège* into a contemporary space insist that, in fact, they had merely resuscitated a medieval site that had lain dormant in the city since its closure by the state. The meaning and intentions of the *Collège*, they suggest, had lain buried beneath the city, quietly awaiting resurrection. As Grenier put it in *Paris Notre Dame*, a weekly publication of the archdiocese, "the historical, religious and then civil elements of the *Collège* nourished [Parmiggiani's] imagination [...] He began with the idea of the book and of the memory of the vocation of the *Collège:* the diffusion of knowledge, which was lost and then reborn today."[7] The artwork he produced cannot easily be described as "Christian." It may be read, however, as a

---

5 Bruno Latour, *We Have Never Been Modern*, trans. Catherine Porter (Cambridge: Harvard University Press, 1991).
6 Collège des Bernardins, "Claudio Parmiggiani au Collège des Bernardins," *Daily Motion* video, 16:59. January 23, 2009. http://www.dailymotion.com/video/x84fir_claudio-parmiggiani-au-college-des_creation
7 Grenier, Catherine. "Quand l'art contemporain rejoint le 'génie d'un lieu,'" *Paris-Notre-Dame*, 20/11/2008, 6–7.

celebration of the Church's medieval past, as wells as its present-day *"renaissance."*

This circulation of the sacred from church to museum and back has a number of important implications. Members of the art world, including artists, curators, and art critics assist the Church, perhaps unwittingly, in its cultural project by supporting accounts of the self-evident place of its medieval space within Paris's cultural landscape. The *College's* project is significant precisely because it bridges the secular and the religious, the medieval and the contemporary. Just as at the *Collège*, museum practices are injected into spaces of the Church, in art works such as Parmiggiani's, the medieval church becomes a significant player in contemporary cultural life. Likewise, since medieval spaces bleed, and nothing emanates from a museum wall, the museum also benefits from a dose of the sacred. This co-articulation of medieval Catholicism and contemporary art, churches and museums, ultimately contribute to the production of elite 'high' French culture.

The *Collège* represents a significant investment by the French Catholic Church in a "cultural" project devoted to rituals of art viewing, rather than those of religious devotion. Those who came to the *Collège* seeking signs of explicity 'religious' art, left disappointed, perhaps, when they realized that this new cultural project aimed instead to display signs of secular elite sensibilities. What makes this type of project problematic is not the circulation of the sacred *per se*, but the fact that the signs of Catholicism are allowed such freedom of movement within the secular public sphere in ways that signs associated with other religions are not. The cost and effort expended in reshaping the Catholic Church so that it might slip indiscriminately into the secular landscape demonstrates not only the significant social and cultural work required to make Catholicism something other than just another "religion"; it also reveals the stakes involved in these circulations.

These stakes are those of inclusion and exclusion, of belonging and standing apart. At the *Collège*, a variety of activities including theology classes are available to visitors. They occur, however, not within a framework of deepening faith or attaining salvation, but of appreciating Catholic writings and history, as well as contemporary art, as remarkable cultural projects that are always already intertwined. For a certain class of educated Parisians, knowledge of Catholic history can serve as an important marker of a "cultivated" individual. Building on these connotations, those at the *Collège* aim to create a site that, in the eyes of these and other privileged groups, will become one of numerous spaces of culture in Paris that appear, as in Craig Calhoun's account of the secular, "normal, natural, and tacit."[8] It is through such strategies aimed at the production of Catholicism as "high" culture in France that the Church is able to by-pass concerns about the particularities of dress, behavior, or ritual that beset other religions in France, especially Islam.[9] By equating Catholicism with "high" culture in France, representatives of the Church are able to mark out an indisputable space in the "cultural landscape." While visitors may express qualms about the nature of contemporary "high" culture, their access to it and to French culture more broadly is guaranteed through their connection to the Church. This access, however, is not only to a religious identity, but a national and cultural identity as well.

Following Charles Hirschkind's theorizations of what makes an action, object, or symbol "secular," by way of conclusion, I suggest that the *Collège* wields, in Hirschkind's words "a distinct mode of power, one that mobilizes the productive tension between religious and secular to generate new practices."[10] In Paris today, however paradoxical it may seem, the Catholic Church is capable of producing secular spaces precisely by making use of the tension between its religious history and the contemporary secular uses that may be made of that history. Like Charles Taylor's "immanent frames,"[11] this new religious/secular space is not constructed in the aid of salvation. As Taylor notes, the practices that occur within "immanent frames" do not require deference to a higher power to justify their enactment. They appear instead as self-contained. Instead, the *Collège* offers an example of how Catholic spaces can slip between registers of the "secular" and "religious" by appearing as the tacit, the cultured, or the unmarked mode of being in France. The project I have described may (intentionally or otherwise) produce Catholicism as (in part) secular by promoting activities such as art viewing under its auspices. Despite appearing to be more open (or universal), these practices may, in fact, be all the more exclusionary. Rather than engaging in the particular rituals of a distinct religious community, those who come to

---

8 Craig Calhoun, "Rethinking Secularism," *The Hedgehog Review* Fall (2010): 38.

9 The *Institut du monde arabe* (Institute of the Arab World), located within five minutes walking distance of the *Collège*, provides a telling contrast. As a site of culture, it is explicitly defined as "Arab" (an ethnic rather than a religious identity) and employees actively discourages interpretations of the space as one that is "Muslim" in any way. The Louvre did recently open a new wing devoted to "Islamic Art," but its separation from the broader museum shows how this particular form of "religious" culture is perceived differently from art produced for Christian devotion. The numerous paintings expropriated from churches and monasteries mix unmarked with other more profane art of Europe throughout the museum's many galleries.

10 Charles Hirschkind, "Is There A Secular Body?" *Cultural Anthropology* 26 (2011): 643.

11 Charles Taylor, *A Secular Age.* (Cambridge: The Belknap Press/Harvard University Press, 2007), 542.

view (and critique) contemporary art at the *Collège* engage in practices that are merely (and undeniably) French.

Works Cited

Bennett, Tony. *The Birth of the Museum: History, Theory, Politics.* New York: Routledge, 1995.
Calhoun, Craig. "Rethinking Secularism." *The Hedgehog Review* Fall (2010): 35 – 48.
Duncan, Carol. *Civilizing Rituals: Inside Public Art Museums.* New York: Routledge. 1995.
Grenier, Catherine (Exhibition Curator), Collège des Bernardins. "Parmiggiani au Collège des Bernardins, 22 novembre 2008 – 31 janvier 2009."
Grenier, Catherine. "Quand l'art contemporain rejoint le 'génie d'un lieu.'" *Paris-Notre-Dame*, 20/11/2008, 6 – 7.
Hirschkind, Charles. "Is There A Secular Body?" *Cultural Anthropology* 26 (2011): 633 – 647.
Latour, Bruno. *We Have Never Been Modern*, trans. Catherine Porter. Cambridge: Harvard University Press, 1991.
McClellan, Andrew. *Inventing the Louvre: Arts, Politics and the Origins of the Modern Museum in Eighteenth-Century Paris.* Cambridge: Cambridge University Press, 1994.
Preziosi, Donald and Claire Farago, eds. *Grasping the World: The Idea of the Museum.* Aldershot: Ashgate Publishing, 2004.
Taylor, Charles. *A Secular Age.* Cambridge, MA: Belknap Press/Harvard University Press, 2007.

Charles Louis Richter

"A Deeply Held Religious Faith, and I Don't Care What It Is:" American Anti-Atheism as Nativism

In January of 1898, Lewis Knapp died in Kenosha, Wisconsin, and took his place under the tombstone he had made more than two decades earlier. His epitaph read in part: "...thanking God for sense enough to die as he lived ... thoroughly infidel to all ancient and modern humbug myths.... The Fear of the Right Reverend Doctors of Divinity, theological scarecrows of Hellfire and Damnation to all who refuse to pay tithes to their support, had no force or effect on Lewis Knapp."[1] This exclamation was one of the gentler attacks on religion that adorned the many tombstones Knapp had erected for himself and for his relatives and friends who had gone before him. Thousands of words worth of anti-clerical and anti-religious screeds were spread across the various stones, and had been something of a tourist attraction in Kenosha for some time. Regardless of his opinions on religion, however, Knapp was a well-liked man in town during his life, eulogized as an "eccentric, but warm and generous-hearted" man, who "literally [left] behind him sermons in stone and good in almost everything he did."[2] While even the local clergy could agree at his funeral that Knapp was a worthy citizen of Kenosha, in just a few years after his death, the blasphemous inscriptions had lost whatever charm they had once possessed. In 1909, with the approval of Knapp's surviving brother, the town cemetery association tore the monuments down and crushed them into dust, which they then divided amongst themselves so that – in the dead of night – each man could bury his share in the woods or sink it in Lake Michigan, ensuring that Knapp's blasphemy could never again tarnish the reputation of Kenosha.[3]

The question, then: what changed between 1898 and 1909 to turn public opinion so harshly against the memory of a beloved, if eccentric, citizen? Two events occurred that had ramifications not only for Lewis Knapp's memory, but also for the idea of irreligion in America: the death of Robert Ingersoll, the "Great Agnostic" and immensely popular orator of the nineteenth century, and the assassination of President William McKinley by Leon Czolgosz, an anar-

---

1 "Epitaphs from Wisconsin," *The Weekly Kansas Chief*, February 10, 1876, 1.
2 "He Died as He Lived," *The Weekly Wisconsin*, February 5, 1898, 8.
3 "Old Broad Gauge Knapp," *The Washington Post*, December 12, 1909, M4.

chist and atheist. With the loss of the nation's most eloquent proponent of irreligion and the accompanying decline of the freethought movement, and with the president slain in public by a suspiciously foreign-seeming man who acknowledged no gods, atheists and agnostics no longer seemed perplexingly harmless, but rather came to represent dangers to the fabric of civilization itself. While irreligion has never been a particularly popular notion in the United States, in the twentieth century individual non-believers and atheist organizations – as well as the idea of irreligion itself – transformed into domestic proxies for foreign and un-American threats, both real and imagined. As the United States became more involved on the international stage, the nation reinforced the religious nature of its citizenry, with the corollary – at times implicit, at others explicit – that American democracy was divinely inspired.

Throughout the twentieth century, in the wake of the these two deaths, American cultural, political, and religious leaders, as well as ordinary citizens, created a rhetorical world that removed irreligion as a legitimate grounding from which to participate in public life. This rhetoric has been used consistently to draw connections between irreligion and ideologies deemed hostile to American ideals: in particular, anarchism, socialism and fascism, communism, and secular humanism. This chapter will briefly discuss four phases in the twentieth century that characterized – but did not define – how Americans have demonstrated a nativist tendency toward irreligion with respect to these so-called foreign ideologies. Historian John Higham's useful definition of nativism, "intense opposition to an internal minority on the ground of its foreign (i.e., 'un-American') connections," adeptly describes the central trend of response to irreligion.[4] Higham originally used the term to describe nativism based on anti-Catholic, anti-radical, and racial delineations, but the model works equally well when applied to anti-atheist sentiment throughout twentieth-century America.

1 Anarchism

At the turn of the century, following Ingersoll's death in July of 1899, the nineteenth century freethought movement seemed to lose steam. Indeed, the freethought magazine *The Truth Seeker* increasingly lamented dedicating so much space to obituaries of former freethinking luminaries, rather than reporting on their activities. Ingersoll had long managed to combine vocal criticism of religion

---

4 John Higham, *Strangers in the Land: Patterns of American Nativism, 1860–1925* (New Brunswick, NJ: Rutgers, 1955), 4.

with a congenial and vivacious personality, and as a former officer for the Union during the Civil War, he commanded respect as a patriot. While his opinions on religion frequently provoked consternation, his status as a legitimate American typically went unquestioned. Among those who attempted to follow in his footsteps was Charles Chilton Moore, editor of *The Bluegrass Blade*, a nationally circulated Kentucky newspaper that promoted both freethought and prohibition ‒ possibly the two least popular ideas in Kentucky. Moore, however, was a frequently abrasive character, prone to more aggressive rhetoric than Ingersoll employed, and had served time behind bars for convictions of blasphemy.

Just two years after Ingersoll died, the assassination of President McKinley by an anarchist led to widespread association of atheism with foreign anarchism. Leon Czolgosz, the assassin, was born in Chicago to Polish immigrant parents, but his name marked him as foreign for the readers of the popular press. Reverend Benedict Rosinski, the pastor of the Church of St. Stanislaus in Cleveland, recalled an incident four years prior to the assassination when Czolgosz had refused his request for a donation. "He told me he had no religion and that he did [not] wish to help churches. He said anarchy was his religion. I tried to argue with him and drive the anarchistic principles out of his head, but it was to no purpose. I believe that he was mentally unbalanced."[5] Rosinski's linking of anarchism, atheism, and mental illness was widely echoed. In an editorial typical of the day, *The Independent* described the "dangerous anarchistic cranks [...] mostly foreigners, or of foreign parentage," as "atheists, having no fear of God or a future life."[6] Similar sentiments filled newspapers in 1901, claiming that "anarchists are always atheists;" or they "scoff at religion" and, therefore, must be "exterminated;" and calling for "the extinction of these imported atheists and murderers."[7] Meanwhile, sheet music producers published numerous songs commemorating the president's martyrdom, including several new arrangements of his favorite hymn, "Nearer, My God, To Thee." Although McKinley had been as subject to criticism as any politician, in death he attained near-sainthood, in large part due to the contrast with the irreligious and suspiciously foreign-seeming Czolgosz. The assassination may have been the single most significant contributing factor to the overall sentiment toward irreligion in the early years of the century.

---

5 "Czolgosz Says He Had No Aid." *The Chicago Daily Tribune*, September 8, 1901, 1.
6 "The Assassin's Deed." *The Independent*, September 12, 1901, 2187.
7 "Anarchism and Atheism." *The Chicago Daily Tribune*, September 22, 1901, 12; "Cure for Anarchy." *The San Francisco Call*, September 23, 1901, 3; "Prayer Topic." *The Mexico Missouri Message*, November 7, 1901, 2.

As the war in Europe drew closer, increased radicalism of all types, including anarchism, emboldened specifically atheist activism, prompting an increase in sermons and editorials linking religion and Americanism. Protestants, Catholics, Jews, and Spiritualists all used similar rhetoric to deny the possibility of an irreligious morality, and, consequently, the ability to participate fully in American life. The combination of atheism and anarchism presented a particularly frightening threat because it challenged the central assumption of the origin of law. As one newspaper editor put it, "Laws are [...] while they emanate from men, in a certain sense the commands of God. That is, conscience is the voice of God, and law is the uttered conscience of legislators. Human law is therefore divine law, and human government is therefore divine government."[8] From this perspective, anarchism threatened to do away with the laws of both man and God. Although atheism was a common component of anarchist philosophy, by no means were all atheists anarchists, of course. Nonetheless, the constant conflation of the two solidified the notion of the dangerous atheist in the American imagination.

2 Socialism and Fascism

After the First World War, concerns relating to atheism shifted away from lawless anarchy and centered on statist ideologies. Anarchism had failed to materialize as the threat it had been imagined to be prior to the war, but irreligion itself was still a concern. The interwar period was characterized in part by what Edward Purcell has called the "crisis of democratic theory" – the concern that after liberal democracy had failed to avert the First World War, perhaps it was not the best form of government after all, and only dictatorship was up to the task of managing twentieth century industrialized society.[9] Regardless of the actual religiosity on display in the various European dictatorships, Americans tended to speak of them as though they were fundamentally irreligious, in contrast to the profoundly religious United States. While the Bolshevik Revolution produced the First Red Scare, rhetoric explicitly linking Russian Communism and atheism was relatively rare after about 1921. Rather, fascism became associated with irreligion as early as 1925, when the Vatican condemned fascist violence in Italy. The immensely popular preacher Billy Sunday denounced America's universities as

---

8 "Anarchy and Atheism." *The Deseret Evening News*, April 4, 1908, 2.
9 Edward A. Purcell, Jr., *The Crisis of Democratic Theory: Scientific Naturalism & the Problem of Value* (Lexington: The University Press of Kentucky, 1973), 117.

breeding grounds for atheists. Indeed, as Leigh Eric Schmidt has recently noted, while many colleges found themselves home to godless societies of students in the twenties, their members counted for only a small minority of college students, themselves a small minority of the population.[10] Meanwhile, the increased fear of atheism led to blasphemy trials against Anthony Bimba and Charles Lee Smith. Bimba was a Lithuanian communist arrested on charges of sedition and blasphemy, under a seventeenth-century Massachusetts law.[11] He was cleared of the blasphemy charge, but Smith, the president of the newly formed American Association for the Advancement of Atheism, was convicted of blasphemy in Arkansas in 1928 after he set up an "Atheist Headquarters" storefront in Little Rock with signs proclaiming "Evolution is true. The Bible's a Lie. God's a Ghost."[12] He would later go on to hold the first "Blamegiving" service in 1931, at Webster Hall in New York City, complete with atheist hymns ("Blame God for nature's brutal plan/For jungle law of Kill who can/Blame him for all the grief and pain/Which hellish war brings in its train") as well as a remonstrance period for an airing of the grievances that predates *Seinfeld* and its satirical holiday of Festivus.[13]

Although domestic atheist activism was largely of this gadfly nature in the twenties and thirties, it still loomed large in the American imagination as a foreign threat. To combat the irreligion associated with European fascism and communism, American religious organizations instituted ecumenical observances and enlisted governmental support. The National Conference of Christians and Jews (NCCJ) was founded in 1928 to "moderate and finally to eliminate a system of prejudice which we have in part inherited and which disfigures and distorts our business, social and political relations."[14] The primary motivation for the founding of the NCCJ was the lack of action on the part of the Federal Council of Churches to sufficiently combat elements such as the Ku Klux Klan's anti-Catholic campaign and Henry Ford's popularization of anti-Semitic literature.[15] At one of the earliest organizing meetings, a near-unanimous resolution passed to limit membership in the NCCJ to those who "accepted a 'spiritual interpreta-

---

10 Leigh Eric Schmidt, "A Society of Damned Souls: Atheism and Irreligion in the 1920s," *Perspectives in Religious Studies* (June 1, 2011), 38:2, 220.

11 William Wolkovich-Valkavicius, *Bay State "Blue" Laws and Bimba: A Documentary Study of the Anthony Bimba Trial for Blasphemy and Sedition in Brockton, Massachusetts, 1926* (Brockton, Massachusetts: Forum Press, 1973).

12 "Atheist Hopes to Explain Views to 5,000 Teachers" *The Chicago Daily Tribune*, November 12, 1928, 21.

13 "Program of the First Annual Blamegiving Service," (New York: American Association for the Advancement of Atheism, 1931).

14 Harvey W. Lawrence, "Religion," *Current History*, July 1 (1939): 55.

15 James E. Pitt, *Adventures in Brotherhood* (New York: Farrar, Strauss and Co., 1955), 15.

tion' of the universe," a standard that would later be cited as a safeguard against infiltration by Communists.[16] After a few years of panel discussions and other small-scale, mostly localized outreach efforts, the NCCJ observed its first annual Brotherhood Day on April 29, 1934. The Conference explicitly stated that the event was not intended to promote common worship or bring up differences in doctrine, but rather to "suggest that the energies of Americans should be turned away from prejudice and toward joint constructive efforts."[17] To observe Brotherhood day, Americans had only to attend church or synagogue, where they might encounter a sermon on the topic of brotherhood. President Franklin Delano Roosevelt gave his support to Brotherhood Day and associated its goals with those of American citizenship, and a remedy to the fascisms growing in Europe. Roosevelt's Brotherhood Day letters reflected both the urgency of combating the Depression, as well as the rising threat of European dictatorships. In 1935, FDR exhorted Americans to "mobilize the forces of good-will across the country and to promote common effort ... in all that makes for human welfare and good citizenship."[18] His letter of 1936 described the world as engulfed in a conflict "between belief and unbelief," which the *Chicago Daily Tribune* interpreted as asking for a "united attack on 'irreligion.'"[19] In 1939, the nation's capital hosted its first "Red Mass," a Catholic service dedicated to the legal profession and open to Protestants and Jews. The annual service quickly began to attract Cabinet members, congressmen, and Supreme Court justices to hear sermons warning of the dangers of straying too far from religious principles in lawmaking. Both events became annual traditions lasting decades; the Red Mass still occurs every year. The ecumenically religious America of Will Herberg's popular book *Protestant, Catholic, Jew* was, therefore, not dependent upon World War II, but rather a long process that relied more on forging a cohesive religious national identity than simply on Cold War opposition to the Soviet Union.

By the beginning of the Second World War, the Nazis were not only a military threat, but according to warnings from the British Consul General, posed a "greater menace to Christianity than Lenin."[20] President Roosevelt repeatedly cited the threat of irreligion as an integral component of the phenomena of both the Nazi authoritarian state and its military belligerence, further reiterating the connection between American democracy and religious belief and affiliation. In the context of World War II, Roosevelt framed irreligion as an existential

---

16 Pitt, 38.
17 Pitt, 15.
18 "Church Activities of Interest in City," *New York Times*, February 23, 1935, 8.
19 "President Asks United Attack on 'Irreligion,'" *Chicago Daily Tribune*, February 24, 1935, 9.
20 "British Here Join in Annual Service," *New York Times*, January 8, 1940, 7.

threat to the United States. Having enumerated freedom of worship as one of the foundational pillars of civilization in his "Four Freedoms" speech to Congress on January 6, 1941, Roosevelt told the nation that Nazi Germany had "a plan to abolish all existing religions, Catholic, Protestant, Mohammedan, Hindu, Buddhist and Jewish alike."[21] This was no metaphor that Roosevelt described, but rather a detailed and documented scheme to eradicate religion and replace it with an international Nazi church, with *Mein Kampf* as its scripture and the swastika and sword as the symbols upon its altar. Although Roosevelt told the press that the Nazi documents outlining the anti-religion plan came from a reliable source, the map turned out to be a British forgery, as revealed decades later.[22] At the time, however, the President's claims were plausible to an American audience; invoking the fear of Christianity being erased by a foreign enemy was a canny tactic. Meanwhile, American propaganda posters depicting a Nazi dagger plunged through the pages of a Bible reinforced this fear. Ironically, the Nazi regime had previously boasted on several occasions that they had wiped out Germany's atheist movement in the thirties. Nevertheless, in America, a nearly unanimous idea that godliness would have to triumph over godlessness emerged as a motivating force throughout the war.

3 Communism

The Cold War era is commonly associated with the assertion of a national religiosity. The extended ideological conflict with the officially atheist Soviet Union lent credence to the belief that there existed a coherent and militant atheist movement, and increased the apocalyptic quality of the fight against irreligion. With the example of the expansionist USSR, critics of irreligion could imagine a teleology of atheism that would necessarily end with the destruction of American democracy, freedom and religion. At the same time, however, the post-war emphasis on social conformity created the illusion of religious unity in the nation. Several symbolic gestures toward explicit articulation of America as Christendom further characterized irreligion as a foreign phenomenon. The title of this chapter is drawn from a famous and often misquoted statement of then-President-elect Dwight Eisenhower: "Our form of government has no sense unless it is founded in a deeply-felt religious faith, and I don't care

---

21 "President Roosevelt's Navy Day Address on World Affairs," *New York Times*, October 28, 1941, 4.
22 Mark Weber, "Roosevelt's 'Secret Map' Speech," *The Journal of Historical Review* 6:1 (Spring 1985): 125–27.

what it is."[23] That is to say, democracy must be predicated on a religious, transcendent underpinning from which the ideal of equality is derived. Adding the phrase "under God" to the Pledge of Allegiance and adopting "In God We Trust" as the national motto were two more of the instances in which Congress and the Eisenhower administration expressed the importance of religiosity to the American project, but these gestures did not go far enough for some. In 1954, the National Reform Association (NRA) renewed an old campaign dating to the Civil War to amend the United States Constitution with language acknowledging "the authority and law of Jesus Christ, Saviour and Ruler of nations, through whom are bestowed the blessings of Almighty God."[24] The four hours of testimony before a Senate Judiciary subcommittee illustrate the realities of post-war religious pluralism in America: although the idea of a "Judeo-Christian" heritage was coming into vogue, the normative state of Protestant Christianity allowed for exclusively Christian language to be presented as an inclusive Americanism without any irony. Thus, the NRA saw the Christian Amendment to be immediately necessary because they believed the hegemony of the de facto Christian government to be threatened by the secular world, personified by Soviet Communism and American Jews. The Cold War preoccupation with the atheistic character of Soviet Communism was pervasive in American culture, but the NRA saw the threat as more than merely temporal. The *de jure* secular government of the United States would not be sufficient to repel the advance of global Marxism; only by "bring[ing] to bear the whole weight of our Christian conceptions and traditions" could the United States prevail, said John Coleman.[25] Otherwise, said R. E. Robb on behalf of the NRA, the nation would face the "cataclysmic and final battle between good and evil, between Christ and Satan."[26] Amending the Constitution to recognize divine law would, therefore, shield the nation from the armies of both the Soviet Union and Satan. It would set a precedent not only in the realm of federal jurisprudence, but also in a transcendent sense. The ratification of the amendment could prevent the apocalypse itself.

---

23 "President-Elect Says Soviet Demoted Zhukov Because of Their Friendship," *New York Times*, December 23, 1952, 16.

24 *Christian Amendment: Committee on the Judiciary, United States Senate. Hearings before a Subcommittee, Eighty-third Congress, Second Session, on S.J. Res. 87, Proposing an Amendment to the Constitution of the United States Recognizing the Authority and Law of Jesus Christ. May 13, 17, 1954*. 83rd Cong., 1. (1954).

25 *Christian Amendment*, 16 (statement of John Coleman, Professor of Political Science, Geneva College, Beaver Falls, Pennsylvania).

26 *Christian Amendment*, 30 (statement of R. E. Robb, Newspaper Columnist, South Carolina).

The run of Supreme Court decisions in this era that altered the relationship of religion and the state did much to make government more authentically secular, but also elicited concern that such changes would come at the detriment of religion. *McCollum v. Board of Education* (1948), *Engel v. Vitale* (1952), *Abington School District v. Schemp* (1963), and *Epperson v. Arkansas* (1968) all seemed to eject God from public schools. *Torcaso v. Watkins* (1961) and *Lemon v. Kurtzman* (1971) also presented critics of irreligion with evidence that the state was moving further from a *de facto* Christian foundation.[27] They interpreted secularization as capitulation to atheism, and by extension, to communism.

The founding of the John Birch Society in 1958 further exemplified the conflation of Americanism with apocalyptic Christianity. The Blue Book of the society accused one third of the country's ministers of not being "true believers in the Divine Names or the Divine History and Divine Teachings to which they give lip service," while gradually converting Christianity into communism.[28] The John Birch Society extended its criticism to the loss of faith in all religions, not only Christianity, making an explicit link between this trend and the rise of global communism. The answer was to reinforce an American faith, clearly identifiable as Christian in foundation, but resonant to all. Robert Welch, founder of the society, considered it his responsibility to take up the mantle of the fundamentalists, whom he believed to be fading from the nation's stage, in a Judeo-Christian Americanism founded on "unshakable confidence in absolutes."[29] And as Lisa McGirr has shown, the John Birch Society had enormous influence on the development of the new religious right of the late 70s and early 80s.[30]

Hal Lindsay's 1970 bestseller, *The Late Great Planet Earth*, both kicked off modern "rapture culture" and further pushed the nonreligious to the margins.[31] Readers learned of a world in which belief (of the correct sort) or non-belief determined whether people would experience a horrifying death in the apocalypse or be safely raptured away in advance. Dispensationalist end-times prophecies of this type had been a staple of Christian fundamentalism for a century, but Lind-

---

27 *McCollum v. Board of Education*, 333 U.S. 203 (1948); *Engel v. Vitale*, 370 U.S. 421 (1962); *Abington School District v. Schempp*, 374 U.S. 203 (1963); *Epperson v. Arkansas*, 393 U.S. 97 (1968); *Torcaso v. Watkins*, 367 U.S. 488 (1961); *Lemon v. Kurtzman*, 403 U.S. 602 (1971)
28 The John Birch Society, *The Blue Book of the John Birch Society* (Belmont, Mass.: Robert Welch, 1961), 49.
29 *The Blue Book* 47.
30 Lisa McGirr, *Suburban Warriors: The Origins of the New American Right* (Princeton: Princeton University Press, 2001), 75–78.
31 Hal Lindsey, *The Late Great Planet Earth* (Grand Rapids, Michigan: Zondervan Publishing House, 1970).

say's book exposed the ideas to a much wider audience at a time when the political world seemed on the verge of apocalypse. With worldwide apostasy as one of the signs of the times, irreligion took on ultimate meaning; the rise of new religious and spiritual movements during this time signified not simply a shift in morals or cultural expectations, but the approaching end of the world.

4 Secular Humanism

Although "godless communism" continued to be a threat until the collapse of the Soviet Union and the end of the Cold War, the rise of the new religious right, especially with the founding of the Moral Majority in 1979, forced a shift in focus from communism to liberalism and secular humanism as the primary irreligious targets. In the first part of this period, until the fall of the Soviet Union, the Christian right linked the two, but after 1991, liberalism could stand on its own as an apparent threat to American religiosity. Although secular humanism as a movement (such as it has existed at all) originated in America, its critics characterized it as foreign, alien to the American experience.

The Heritage Foundation fired one of the foundational salvos in a 1976 pamphlet by Onalee McGraw: "Secular Humanism and the Schools: The Issue Whose Time Has Come." In this tract, which school reformers mailed out to school districts and parents by the thousands, McGraw argued that "humanistic education" had replaced traditional teaching in America's public school system. The fifth grade humanities program, "Man: A Course of Study" (MACOS), exemplified this trend in curriculum. McGraw used the words of Peter Dow, one of its developers, to condemn MACOS as challenging "the notion that there are 'eternal truths' [e.g., the Ten Commandments] that must be passed down from generation to generation."[32] This challenge to essential truth lies at the heart of the fears of secular humanism and irreligion in general – the concern that if transcendent sources of morality are removed, people will have no reason not to act on their every base impulse.

Furthermore, McGraw argued, humanistic education was unconstitutional because it constituted government establishment of "the religion of secular humanism." To support the characterization of secular humanism as a religion, McGraw cited a footnote to the Supreme Court's decision in *Torcaso v. Watkins* (the case that upheld the prohibition on religious tests for state offices), in

---

32 Onalee McGraw, "Secular Humanism and the Schools: The Issue Whose Time Has Come." (Washington: The Heritage Foundation, 1976,) 5.

which Hugo Black wrote in a footnote, "Among religions in this country which do not teach what would generally be considered a belief in the existence of God are Buddhism, Taoism, Ethical Culture, Secular Humanism and others."[33] This one line of text in a footnote with no legal weight laid the foundation for framing secular humanism as not simply an analogue to religion, but rather a religion itself, and thus subject to the establishment clause of the First Amendment. The same reasoning was brought to Congress, which approved an amendment to the General Education Provisions Act prohibiting "grants, contract, or support ... for any educational program ... involving any aspect of secular humanism unless there is also a fair and equal teaching of the world and life view of Judaic-Christian principles set forth in the Old and New Testaments."[34] Of course, the new religious right of the seventies and eighties was not the first to describe secular humanism as a religion: the writers of the first Humanist Manifesto of 1933 described their movement as religious. Martin Marty called secular humanism America's "fourth religion" in his 1958 series of articles for *The Christian Century.*[35] But it made little sense to attempt to categorize secular humanism as a religion *in relation to the state* until the age of landmark Supreme Court rulings on religion in the public sphere. So while anarchism, fascism, and communism possessed clearly foreign elements, secular humanism was not so easily dismissed as completely alien to the American experience. Historian James Hitchcock attempted to delineate between two stages of humanism, arguing that modern humanism, what he called "Promethean Humanism," had its roots in Feuerbach, Nietzsche and Marx, and had lost the gentleness of the earlier humanism of the Enlightenment, which had not only informed the founding of the United States but also maintained Christian morality at its core.[36] By situating modern humanism in the world of the most disruptive German philosophers of the nineteenth century, Hitchcock stressed its foreign elements while largely ignoring the development of humanist philosophy in the United States during the twentieth century. This argument was fundamental to Judge W. Brevard Hand's opinion in the Alabama textbook case of 1987, in which he ruled

---

33 Hugo Black, *Torcaso v. Watkins,* 367 US 488 (1961).
34 Representative Conlan, speaking on H.R. 12851, on May 11, 1976, 94th Cong., 2nd sess., *Congressional Record,* 122 pt. 11:13427.
35 Martin E. Marty, "The new establishment. 3, An attitude toward 'realized pluralism' has become the fundamental article of America's national religion in its institutional aspect." *The Christian Century* 75:42 (October 15, 1958), 1179.
36 James Hitchcock, *What is Secular Humanism? Why Christian Humanism Became Secular and How It Is Changing Our World* (Harrison, NY: RC Books, 1982), 46.

that the use in Alabama schools of several textbooks had in effect established the religion of secular humanism.[37]

The final decade of the twentieth century saw an increase in millennial tensions, as well as the battles of the culture wars. The collapse of the Soviet Union eliminated an explicitly atheist nation from competition with the United States, but Conservative Christian organizations like the American Family Association, Alliance Defense Fund, and Concerned Women for America responded by re-situating their positions to articulate a clear opposition to secularism as a unifying threat. They saw secularization as inextricably linked to global unrest. In Patrick Buchanan's famous "culture war" speech at the 1992 Republican National Convention, he very specifically began his description of Bill Clinton immediately after defining George H. W. Bush as "a champion of the Judeo-Christian values and beliefs upon which America was founded," adding, "Mr. Clinton, however, has a different agenda."[38] Buchanan articulated the battle between right and left as a religious war for the soul of the nation. Later that year, in an essay by the same name, he argued that secular American culture was influenced not only by Marx but also by Mao Tse-tung, whose writings were "prescribed reading for the Herbert Marcuse-generation of the 1960s, who now run our cultural institutions."[39] This synthesis of earlier ideological enemies into the broader notion of looming secularism characterized the culture war rhetoric of the nineties. At the same time, however, the booming economy of the nineties produced declines in what *The National Review* and *Christianity Today* termed "social pathologies:" divorce, births to single mothers, abortion, people on welfare, and crime in general, leading to declarations of victory over the "isms" of "communism, socialism, nazism, liberalism, humanism, scientism."[40] The simultaneous and contradictory assertions of both imminent defeat by godlessness and resurgence of "traditional values" was an effective political tactic for the Republican party and the Christian right, but did not reflect changes either way in American religiosity. According to poll data, however, American attitudes

---

37 W. Brevard Hand, *American Education on Trial: Is Secular Humanism a Religion?* (Cumberland, VA: Center for Judicial Studies, 1987), 26–27.

38 Patrick J. Buchanan, "The Cultural War for the American Soul: Address to the Republican National Convention." August 17, 1992. Houston, TX. Text obtained from Buchanan.org, http://buchanan.org/blog/1992-republican-national-convention-speech-148. Accessed May 2014.

39 Buchanan, "The Cultural War for the American Soul," September 14, 1992. Text obtained from Buchanan.org, http://buchanan.org/blog/the-cultural-war-for-the-soul-of-america-149. Accessed May 2014.

40 Charles Colson & Nancy Pearcey, "The Sky Isn't Falling," *Christianity Today*, January 11, 1993, 104.

toward religion and morality were not becoming dramatically more liberal or permissive in the nineties. Between the years 1990 and 2000, there was an overall increase in the percentage of respondents who agreed with the statements: "Prayer is an important part of my daily life," "We will all be called before God on Judgment Day to answer for our sins," and "I never doubt the existence of God."[41] Strong majorities agreed with each statement, indicating not only that Americans still held the beliefs and attitudes Buchanan desired of them, but also that religiosity was not confined to one side of the culture wars. Respondents claiming no religious affiliation grew by only one percentage point over the decade.

Throughout the twentieth century, Americans consistently associated irreligion with foreign, existential threats, real or perceived, to its founding ideals. The facility with which irreligion has always been connected with these ideological bogeymen speaks volumes to the centrality of religion and religious authority in American culture and society. The accusation of atheism was a powerful tool politically and socially, and still is, only to a slightly lesser extent. Only recently have Americans begun to be able to claim legitimacy for their irreligious worldviews.

Works Cited

American Association for the Advancement of Atheism. "Program of the First Annual Blamegiving Service." New York: American Association for the Advancement of Atheism, 1931.

Buchanan, Patrick J. "The Cultural War for the American Soul." September 14, 1992. Text obtained from Buchanan.org, http://buchanan.org/blog/the-cultural-war-for-the-soul-of-america-149. Accessed in May 2014.

Buchanan, Patrick J. "Address to the Republican National Convention." August 17, 1992. Houston, TX. Text obtained from Buchanan.org. http://buchanan.org/blog/1992-republican-national-convention-speech-148. Accessed in May 2014.

Colson, Charles and Nancy Pearcey. "The Sky Isn't Falling." *Christianity Today* (January 11, 1993) :104.

Hand, W. Brevard. *American Education on Trial: Is Secular Humanism a Religion?* Cumberland, VA: Center for Judicial Studies, 1987.

Higham, John. *Strangers in the Land: Patterns of American Nativism, 1860–1925.* New Brunswick, NJ: Rutgers, 1955.

Hitchcock, James. *What is Secular Humanism? Why Christian Humanism Became Secular and How It Is Changing Our World.* Harrison, NY: RC Books, 1982.

---

41 Pew Research Center for The People and the Press, *Evenly Divided and Increasingly Polarized: 2004 Political Landscape* (November 5, 2003), 65.

John Birch Society. The. *The Blue Book of the John Birch Society.* Belmont, Mass.: Robert Welch, 1961, 49.

Lawrence, Harvey W. "Religion." *Current History* (July 1, 1939): 55–56.

Lindsay, Hal. *The Late Great Planet Earth.* Grand Rapids, Michigan: Zondervan Publishing House, 1970.

McGirr, Lisa. *Suburban Warriors: The Origins of the New American Right.* Princeton: Princeton University Press, 2001.

Marty, Martin E. "The new establishment. 3, An attitude toward 'realized pluralism' has become the fundamental article of America's national religion in its institutional aspect." *The Christian Century* 75:42 (October 15, 1958), 1176–1179.

McGraw, Onalee. "Secular Humanism and the Schools: The Issue Whose Time Has Come." Washington: The Heritage Foundation, 1976.

Pew Research Center for The People and the Press. *Evenly Divided and Increasingly Polarized: 2004 Political Landscape* (November 5 2003), 65.

Pitt, James E. *Adventures in Brotherhood.* New York: Farrar, Strauss and Co., 1955.

Purcell, Jr., Edward A. *The Crisis of Democratic Theory: Scientific Naturalism & the Problem of Value.* Lexington: The University Press of Kentucky, 1973.

Schmidt, Leigh Eric. "A Society of Damned Souls: Atheism and Irreligion in the 1920s." *Perspectives in Religious Studies* 38:2 (June 1, 2011): 215–26.

Torcaso v. Watkins, 367 US 488 (1961).

U.S. Congress, *Congressional Record*, 94th Cong., 2nd sess., Vol. 122 pt. 11: 13427.

U.S. Congress, Senate, Committee on the Judiciary. *Christian Amendment: Hearings before a Subcommittee, Eighty-third Congress, Second Session, on S.J. Res. 87, Proposing an Amendment to the Constitution of the United States Recognizing the Authority and Law of Jesus Christ.* 83rd Cong., 1st Sess., May 13 and May 17, 1954.

Weber, Mark. "Roosevelt's 'Secret Map' Speech." *The Journal of Historical Review* 6:1 (Spring 1985): 125–127.

Wolkovich-Valkavicius, William. *Bay State "Blue" Laws and Bimba a Documentary Study of the Anthony Bimba Trial for Blasphemy and Sedition in Brockton, Massachusetts, 1926.* Brockton, Massachusetts: Forum Press, 1973.

Newspaper and Magazine Articles

"Anarchism and Atheism." *Chicago Daily Tribune*, September 22, 1901, 12.

"Anarchy and Atheism." *Deseret Evening News*, April 4, 1908, 2.

"The Assassin's Deed." *The Independent*, September 12, 1901, 2187.

"Atheist Hopes to Explain Views to 5,000 Teachers." *Chicago Daily Tribune*, November 12, 1928, 21.

"British Here Join in Annual Service." *New York Times*, January 8, 1940, 7.

"Church Activities of Interest in City." *New York Times*, February 23, 1935, 8.

"Cure for Anarchy." *San Francisco Call*, September 23, 1901, 3.

"Czolgosz Says He Had No Aid." *Chicago Daily Tribune*, September 8, 1901, 1.

"Epitaphs from Wisconsin." *Weekly Kansas Chief*, February 10, 1876, 1.

"He Died as He Lived." *Weekly Wisconsin*, February 5, 1898, 8.

"Old Broad Gauge Knapp." *Washington Post*, December 12, 1909, M4.

"Prayer Topic." *Mexico Missouri Message*, November 7, 1901, 2.

"President Asks United Attack on 'Irreligion.'" *Chicago Daily Tribune*, February 24, 1935, 9.

"President-Elect Says Soviet Demoted Zhukov Because of Their Friendship." *New York Times*, December 23, 1952, 16.

"President Roosevelt's Navy Day Address on World Affairs," *New York Times*, October 28, 1941, 4.

James McBride
The Myth of Secularism in America

In a phrase that ironically mimes the millennial expectations of fundamentalism, Christopher Hitchens asked in his book *God Is Not Great*, "Could there be a change in the Zeitgeist coming on? I think it's possible. A 2001 study found that those without religious affiliation are the fastest growing minority in the United States."[1] The short answer to Hitchens' question is no – there is no such change in the offing. Although this subset of secular intellectuals, whom one journalist has called the "new atheists,"[2] argues that the American populace is increasingly turning toward secularism, poll numbers suggest otherwise. In the latest 2013 Pew Research survey on the "Religious Landscape" in America (based on interviews with 35,000 adults), only 1.6% of Americans are atheists and just 6.3% are unaffiliated secularists.[3]

Of course, we have heard such arguments before. Two generations ago, the 1960s brought not only dynamic change to the claustrophobic and patriarchal culture of the 1950s, but also the assessment by leading sociologists that a religious America was slowly fading away.

> Put simply, [...] the modern West has produced an increasing number of individuals who look upon the world and their own lives without the benefit of religious interpretation [...], it would seem, it is industrial society in itself that is secularizing, with its divergent

1 Christopher Hitchens, *God Is Not Great: How Religion Poisons Everything* (New York: Grand Central, 2009), 286. Hitchens does not identify this 2001 study. However, the 2001 *Religion and Spirituality on the Path of Adolescence* research report by the National Study of Youth and Religion reported that "[t]he majority of adolescents reported remaining at the same level of religiosity, and when adolescents did report a change in their overall religiosity, a higher proportion of them reported becoming *more* religious than becoming *less* religious. Thus, the least common response of adolescents was that they had become less religious over the previous three years." Melinda Denton, Lisa Pearce, and Christian Smith, *Religion and Spirituality on the Path of Adolescence: A Research Report of the National Study of Youth and Religion* 8 (Chapel Hill, NC: University of North Carolina, 2008): 4, http://youthandreligion.nd.edu/assets/102568/reli gion_and_spirituality_on_the_path_through_adolescence.pdf. Accessed September 5, 2013,
2 Ronald Aronson, "The New Atheists," *The Nation*, June 7 2007, http://www.thenation.com/ article/new-atheists#. Accessed September 5, 2013.
3 "Welcome to the U.S. Religious Landscape Survey," *Pew Research Religion & Public Life Project*. n.d., http://religions.pewforum.org/reports. Accessed September 15, 2013.

ideological legitimations serving merely as modifications of the global secularization process.[4]

However, the late 1960s and 1970s proved these academic pundits wrong. Instead of retreating, religion surged in what came to be known as America's "Fourth Great Awakening."[5] From a sociological perspective, America's revivalist turn in the 1970s and 1980s was a product of what Jürgen Habermas famously called a legitimation crisis in late modern capitalism.[6]

1 America's Legitimation Crisis

Introduced by Max Weber, the concept of legitimacy is implicit in all social orders as the claim of authority, whether in traditional, legal or charismatic forms.[7] The legitimation process, therefore, seeks to justify the institutions of the dominant order and, by means of a social ethic, mediates between the principles of socially-sanctioned activities and human experiences. Whenever experience and principles are dysfunctional, that is, whenever everyday life does not live up to the promises of that social ethic, the legitimacy, and hence authority, of the whole social system is placed in question.[8]

With the advent of American corporate capitalism and the development of a "post-industrial" technological society, the old social ethic of legitimation, the Protestant work ethic,[9] had collapsed. As a legacy of the Reformation, the Protestant work ethic had fueled the expansion of entrepreneurial capitalism both in Europe and the New World. Excluded from the salvific security of sacraments, Reformed merchants, business- and common-folk realized the self-confidence, indicative of God's Elect, only by subduing the world. This inner-worldly asceticism embodied the premise that God materially blesses his own. As the *summum bonum* of this ethic, the accumulation of capital *per se,* and the concomitant vir-

---

4 Peter Berger, *The Sacred Canopy: Elements of a Sociological Theory of Religion* (New York: Anchor, 1967), 108–09.

5 William McLaughlin, *Revivals, Awakenings, and Reforms* (Chicago: University of Chicago, 1980), 179.

6 Jürgen Habermas, *Legitimation Crisis*, trans. Thomas McCarthy (New York: Beacon, 1975).

7 Max Weber, "The Concept of Legitimate Authority," in *Basic Concepts in Sociology*, trans. H. Secher (New York: Kensington, 2000), 71.

8 Habermas, *Legitimation Crisis*, 41.

9 Max Weber, *Protestant Work Ethic and the Spirit of Capitalism*, trans. Talcott Parsons (New York: Routledge, 2001).

tues of frugality, hard work, and wise investment aggressively spurred on free enterprise ventures in the open market. Yet the very virtues of this ethic spelled its demise since capital accumulation reached such levels of concentration that the lone entrepreneur could no longer compete. Corporate capitalism, which had come into its own in the decades after World War II, discarded the Protestant work ethic as a relic of a bygone age.[10]

In the extensive post-mortems that followed its demise, sociologists detected the development of a new individual, markedly different from the American entrepreneur who had been infused by religious fervor and purpose. In place of this "inner-directed" individual, sure of salvation and confident in his or her own God-given abilities, came the "organization man."[11] As a business executive or bureaucrat, this new individual sought to dominate colleagues rather than the world and to accumulate kudos rather than capital. Some critics contended that this individual was a wholly new type of person – a psychological rather than economic "man," who nonetheless inherited the nervous habits of his predecessor – his shrewdness, his penchant for the accumulation of satisfactions, and his rejection of unprofitable commitments.[12] In an "other-directed" society where behavior flowed from conformity rather than conviction,[13] this "organization man" embodied a new world vision that jettisoned the religious anchor or work ethic and shifted the success pattern away from entrepreneurial proprietorship. This success ethic promised upward mobility, status, and wealth to those who learned to read the cues of organizational hierarchy and master the art of manipulating co-workers for one's own advantage.[14]

Although the success ethic dominated the 1950s, the social upheaval of the 1960s and 1970s destroyed its mass cultural appeal. The narrowing avenues for success caused by runaway inflation, unemployment, and increasingly intense competition among college graduates added to the disillusionment of middle-class sons and daughters, who found the promise of the American dream gnawingly empty. This persistent underlying emptiness created a motivational trauma, magnifying the cultural dilemma that plays off meaning against material compensation. As Habermas argued, "[m]eaning is a scarce resource and is becom-

---

10 Robert Bellah, *The Broken Covenant: American Civil Religion in Time of Trial* (Chicago: University of Chicago, 1992), viii-ix.

11 William Whyte, *The Organization Man* (Philadelphia: University of Pennsylvania Press, 2002).

12 Philip Rieff, *Freud: the Mind of a Moralist* (Chicago: University of Chicago Press, 1979), 356.

13 David Riesman, *The Lonely Crowd* (New Haven, CT: Yale University Press, 1952), 23.

14 Charles Mills, *White Collar: The American Middle Classes* (New York: Oxford University Press, 1956), 263.

ing ever scarcer. Consequently expectations oriented to use values – that is, expectations monitored by success – are rising in the civil public [...] The fiscally siphoned-off resource 'value' must take the place of the scanty resource 'meaning.' Missing legitimation must be offset by rewards conforming to the system."[15] In other words, disenchantment with the American *ethos* could be offset by material compensation. However, in an era of "lowered expectations," material compensation was not forthcoming and hence experience conflicted with the promises of the success ethic.

As scholars noted,[16] the new religious movements of the 1960s and 1970s arose in response to this "delegitimation" process.[17] Embodying the legacy of the counterculture, they grew rapidly because neither failed institutions nor a worsening economy addressed the crisis. With their emphasis on meaning rather than money, the new religious movements stood in stark contrast to traditional American religious institutions too closely identified with mainstream culture. Frequently challenging rather than comforting their flocks, the mainstream churches did not act to relieve the stress created within the social structure.[18] This quest for meaning in Asian philosophies, humanistic psychotherapies, or conservative Christianity attempted to resolve the anomic behavior endemic to an "other-directed" society. In this respect, religious awakenings act as a force of revitalization, since conversion can transform anxiety into functionally constructive activity. Indeed, Peter Berger's 1977 prognosis for the 1980s and 1990s proved to be correct, that is, that evangelical and fundamentalist Christianity would attempt to terminate the culture's crisis of meaning "by force, by the imposition of traditional values by the state."[19]

As a graduate student at Berkeley, I was part of the academic response to this burst of religious enthusiasm, serving as a research associate at the Center for the Study of New Religious Movements. Not only did we witness the rise of more exotic sects, from Hare Krishna devotees chanting on urban street corners to the mass weddings of Sun Myung Moon's Unification Church, but Americans

---

15 Habermas, *Legitimation Crisis*, 73.

16 Bellah, *The Broken Covenant*, 154; McLaughlin, *Revivals, Awakenings, and Reforms*; Dick Anthony and Thomas Robbins, "The Sociology of Contemporary Religious Movements," *Annual Review of Sociology* 5 (1979): 76.

17 Peter Berger, *Facing Up to Modernity* (New York: Basic Books, 1977), 159.

18 Charles Glock, Benjamin Ringer, and Earl Babbie, *To Comfort or To Challenge: A Dilemma of the Contemporary Church* (Berkeley: University of California, 1967), 211; Dean Kelly, *Why Conservative Churches Are Growing: A Study in Sociology of Religion with a New Preface* (Macon, GA: Mercer, 1996), 139–40.

19 Berger, *Facing Up to Modernity*, 161.

also saw the expansion of evangelical and fundamentalist Christianity. As wings of the "born again" revival, where the individual's relationship to Jesus is mediated by personal experience rather than by ritual, evangelical and fundamentalist Christianity made its presence felt among youth, that is, "Jesus freaks," and in the halls of political power, for example, the "Moral Majority.". Consequently, led by, *inter alia*, Jerry Falwell, Pat Robertson, and James Robison, the "New Religious Right" attempted to organize fundamentalists (who, as "in" but not "of" the world, had hitherto rarely participated in the political order) and evangelicals into an insurgent political force, which would seek to control a major political party and influence legislation and court decisions on key issues of importance to conservative Christians, for example, abortion, homosexuality, etc. The emerging born-again subculture erupted into the mainstream, from TV broadcasting, like Robertson's Christian Broadcasting Network (CBN), to the best-selling *Left Behind* series by preacher-turned-novelist Tim LaHaye. In contrast to traditional mainline Christians and Jews who embraced "[p]rogressivist moral ideals" that understood truth as a process, born-again Christians and their Catholic allies embraced orthodox beliefs as a commitment to external, definable and transcendent authority.[20]

Reaching its peak of influence in the early 1990s, the New Religious Right began to lose power under the George W. Bush administration, despite the President's own alleged evangelical beliefs. The *fin-de-siècle* decline of the New Religious Right's power stemmed in part from the end of the Cold War and the demise of Soviet atheistic communism and in part from the rising economy of the Clinton years. As the Cold War victor, global capitalism promised economic prosperity and its political and economic institutions regained their legitimacy. Today, Jerry Falwell, who helped to elect Ronald Reagan and placed fear in the hearts of political liberals, is dead, and the now-elderly Pat Robertson, founder of CBN and a candidate for President in the 1988 Republican presidential primaries, does not wield the influence he once had among political conservatives inside and outside the beltway. If anything, the surprising shift in public opinion on gay marriage within the past six years marks the decline of the New Religious Right as a political force. Indeed, born-again social conservatives have retained influence only by allying themselves with a hodge-podge of right-wingers, from libertarians to survivalists, in the Tea Party movement. Consequently, some academic commentators have read the passing of the New Religious Right's high-water mark as synonymous with the impending demise of religion. Nothing could be farther from the truth.

---

20 James Hunter, *The Culture Wars: The Struggle to Define America* (New York: Basic, 1991), 44.

Religious belief in the United States remains remarkably high, in fact higher than any developed nation in the world. As Frank Newport, Gallup's editor-in-chief and past president of the American Association for Public Opinion Research, reported last year:

> Books are published with names like *God Is Not Great: How Religion Poisons Everything*, and, as noted earlier, *The God Delusion.* Certainly the percentage of Americans who believe in God now would be lower now, right? Not by much. More than nine in 10 Americans still said "yes" when asked the basic question, "Do you believe in God" in May 2011. This is down only slightly from the 1940s when Gallup first asked this question. Despite the many changes that have rippled through American society over the past several decades, belief in God, at least as measured in this direct way, has remained high and relatively stable.[21]

Sociologically, the continued strength of religious belief in America can be attributed to a series of economic crises that rocked capitalism in the first decade of the twenty-first century, including the dot.com bust, the Enron scandal, the Long-Term Capital Management failure, and, above all, the 2008 collapse of the financial derivatives market, which nearly brought global capitalism to its knees. Widespread disillusionment with both government and Wall Street spells a new legitimation crisis, compounded by the stark disparity in the distribution of wealth between the 1% and 99% denounced by the Occupy movement. Today, the net worth of the American middle class has fallen to just $57,900 (in constant 2007 dollars) –– compared to $63,600 in 1969.[22] The deep-seated distrust of these social institutions suggests that people will compensate by seeking meaning elsewhere, above all, in religious faith and practices. Accordingly, Hitchens's expectation of a turn towards atheistic rationalism is largely unwarranted.

I suspect, however, that many intellectuals do not believe, as do the new atheists, that there will be a Western rejection of religious belief *per se*, but rather that the public square in America will become increasingly secular. Religion has been exiled to the private realm where it may influence individual behavior, a long-held sociological theory,[23] but it will and should not compromise the public sector, where both economics and politics ought to be governed by reason alone. Although politicians, conservative and liberal alike, invoke the name of God, secularist academic pundits frequently see such gestures as a *pro forma* appeal to

---

21 Frank Newport, *God Is Alive and Well: The Future of Religion in America* (New York: Gallup, 2012), 9–10.

22 Edward Wolff, *The Asset Price Meltdown and the Wealth of the Middle Class* (Cambridge, MA: National Bureau of Economic Research, 2012) (Working Paper 18559), 71.

23 Thomas Luckmann, *The Invisible Religion* (New York: MacMillan, 1967), 136–37.

the undereducated. However, urban sophisticates allegedly have no need of false pieties, for their world is dominated by logic rather than faith, and reason rather than irrationality. Belief in public square secularism is allegedly growing and will increasingly marginalize religion to the private sphere. Consequently, some advocates of secularism conclude that religion exercises diminishing influence in America.

2 Secularization of the Public Sphere

Ironically, secularism itself is a theological category, originating in the German Reformation. As Peter Berger acknowledged:

> With the disintegration of [Christendom as a social] reality, however, the world could all the more rapidly be secularized in that it had already been defined as a realm outside the jurisdiction of the sacred properly speaking. The logical development of this may be seen in the Lutheran doctrine of the two kingdoms, in which the autonomy of the secular "world" is actually given a theological legitimation.[24]

Written in 1523 in the wake of his excommunication by the pope and condemnation at the Diet of Worms, Martin Luther's treatise *On Secular Authority* gave voice to his "Theology of the Two Kingdoms." Whereas the medieval church laid claim to both spiritual and political authority, the abuses of the Vatican, particularly in the Indulgence Campaign of 1517, led Luther to advocate the reform of Christianity, limiting the church to spiritual government, both out of sincere conviction and political expediency. "Here we must divide Adam's children, all mankind, into two parts: the first belong to the kingdom of God, the second to the kingdom of the world."[25] Luther claimed that true Christians should follow the Matthean imperative to "resist not evil [...] but be compliant with your opponent and the person who takes your coat, let him also take your cloak" (Matt. 5:25, 39 – 40).[26] Their duty is to suffer the injustices of this world and not to seek recompense through the law or the courts from their fellow Christians. Although "true Christians need neither secular Sword nor law"[27] (scarcely one in a thousand being a true Christian according to Luther[28]), non-Christians, including the

---

24 Berger, *Sacred Canopy*, 123.
25 Martin Luther, "On Secular Authority," in *Luther and Calvin: On Secular Authority*, ed. and trans. Harro Höpfl (Cambridge: Cambridge University Press, 2002), 8.
26 Luther, "On Secular Authority," 3.
27 Luther, "On Secular Authority," 9.
28 Luther, "On Secular Authority," 10.

vast majority of Christians who are but Christian in name only, have need of secular authority, for "the Sword is indispensable for the whole world, to preserve peace, punish sin, and restrain the wicked."[29] Luther cited Paul's *Letter to the Romans* as evidence that God sanctioned the power of the state. "Let every soul be subject to power and superiority. For there is no power but from God and the power that exists everywhere is ordained by God. And whoever resists the power, resists God's ordinance" (Rom. 13:1–2).[30] Hence, Luther's Reformation theology gave birth to a secular realm hitherto unknown in the West.

As Luther argued, the world would "not tolerate a Christian government"[31] ruling secular society. However, Luther's worldview posed a dilemma to true Christians, for how could one "resist not evil" yet embrace secular authority whose whole function was to resist evil? Luther suggested that the boundary between spiritual and secular authority did not run between the institutions of church and state but rather ran right through the individual. Insofar as the true Christian lived and acted within the private realm of family and acquaintances, that person applied the Christian principle of nonresistance. However, when the true Christian interacted with secular authority, which had a God-given duty to establish and enforce the law for the well-being of all, the divine *imprimatur* of secular authority trumped the personal Christian ethic of the private realm. Accordingly, the true Christian would be obligated to follow the law, even if in so doing, the true Christian violated the tenets of Christianity practiced in private life. "And therefore if you see a lack of hangmen, court officials, judges, lords or princes, and you have the necessary skills, then you should offer your services and seek office, so that authority which is so greatly needed, will never come to be held in contempt, become powerless, or perish."[32] The Protestant Reformation, therefore, produced a secular reality where the Christian personal ethic did not hold sway in public life. Today American society maintains that split between the private and public spheres, and secularists echo the sentiments of Luther himself that it is imperative ""to keep these two governments distinct."[33]

---

29 Luther, "On Secular Authority," 13.
30 Luther, "On Secular Authority," 6.
31 Luther, "On Secular Authority," 11.
32 Luther, "On Secular Authority," 15.
33 Luther, "On Secular Authority," 12.

3 Capitalism, the Public Sphere and Religious Consciousness

While the origins of the split between the private and public spheres may be theological, some adherents to the secularization thesis argue that religious consciousness in the modern age has less and less a role to play in the public walks of life. However, although they think that the latter is largely free of religious influence, the secular realm in late modern capitalism is actually suffused by religious consciousness. As Marx suggested in Volume I of his *Capital*, religious consciousness has not disappeared. In one of the most famous passages ever written on political economy, Marx claimed that capitalist commodities, products created specifically for exchange, "abounded in metaphysical subtleties and theological niceties."[34] Seen in isolation from the labor-power that produced them, commodities are free-floating objects that assume "the fantastic form of a relation between things."[35] The complex web of social relations that constitute the object are effaced. Struggling to find an appropriate "analogy, we must have recourse to the mist-enveloped regions of the religious world."[36] Marx described this apparent autonomy of commodities as fetishism.[37]

In his *Passagen-Werk* or Arcades Project during the 1930s, Walter Benjamin analyzed the fetishized character of commodities, as evidenced in nineteenth century arcades, such as those in Paris and Milan, where objects on exhibit were not made on request but were rather mass-produced.[38] With the workshops of shoemakers, dressmakers, tailors, etc. no longer on site, the displayed goods appeared *de novo* to passersby, as objects with their own independent existence. Indeed, for the first time, it became fashionable for the bourgeoisie to *faire les vitrines* or window-shop – an activity which loosed the imagination to dream, not of the underlying social relations, but of associations with the attributes of the commodity, for example, power, elegance, sexual attraction, etc. The buyer – or what we have dubbed the consumer – engages in riotous feasting on the phantasmagoria of imagery roused by the commodity's fetish character.

---

34 Karl Marx, "Capital, Volume One" in *The Marx-Engels Reader*, ed. Robert Tucker, trans. Martin Nicolaus (New York: W.W. Norton, 1978), 319.

35 Marx, "Capital, Volume One," 321.

36 Marx, "Capital, Volume One," 321.

37 Marx, "Capital, Volume One," 321.

38 Walter Benjamin, *The Arcades Project*, ed. Rolf Tiedemann, trans. Howard Eiland and Kevin McLaughlin (Cambridge: Belknap, 1999).

The study of fetishism came to prominence in the nineteenth century by anthropologists like Edward Burnett Tylor whose work, *Primitive Culture*, distinguished between animism, which referenced "spirits in general," and fetishism, which referenced "spirits in or attached to, or conveying influence through, certain material objects."[39] Likewise, Alfred Cort Haddon in his *Magic and Religion* concluded that "[a]ll cases of Fetishism show that the worship is paid to an intangible power or spirit incorporated in some visible form."[40] According to both Tylor and Haddon, any object whatsoever may be a fetish. In typical social Darwinist fashion, however, nineteenth and early twentieth century British anthropologists, like Tylor, limited the effects of fetishism to "the lower races."[41]

These anthropological prejudices were reinforced by early twentieth century sociology. Max Weber, for example, argued that modern industrialized society had left this world of magic far behind. "[P]rincipally there are no mysterious incalculable forces that come into play, but rather [...] one can, in principle, master all things by calculation. This means that the world is disenchanted. One need no longer have recourse to magical means in order to master or implore the spirits, as did the savage, for whom such mysterious powers existed."[42] In short, the public sphere was marked by disenchantment (*Entzauberung*). Yet, Weber's claim is not altogether true. Indeed if anything, as Marx suggested, modern capitalism brought the re-enchantment of the world in the form of the fetishism of commodities. Marx's idea suggests that the relationship of consumers to commodities is akin to that of aboriginal peoples to "enchanted" objects. Consequently, the relationship of consumers to commodities is likewise mediated by the magical thinking of religious epistemology.

In his classic text *The Golden Bough*, James Frazer first described two modalities of magical thinking at work in fetishism: homeopathic magic and contagious magic.

> Both branches of magic, the homoeopathic and the contagious, may conveniently be comprehended under the general name of Sympathetic Magic, since both assume that things act on each other at a distance through a secret sympathy, the impulse being transmitted from one to the other by means of what we may conceive as a kind of invisible ether, not unlike that which is postulated by modern science for a precisely similar purpose, namely,

39 Edward Tylor, *Primitive Culture. Researches into the Development of Mythology, Philosophy, Religion, Art, and Custom.* Vol. 2 (New York,: Cambridge, 2010), 132.
40 Alfred Haddon, *Magic and Fetishism* (London: Archibald Constable, 1906), 70.
41 Tylor, *Primitive Culture*, 101.
42 Max Weber, "Science as a Vocation," in *From Max Weber: Essays in Sociology*, trans. and ed. Hans Gerth and Charles Mills (New York: Oxford University, 1946), 139.

to explain how things can physically affect each other through a space which appears to be empty.[43]

Frazier's book, like those of Tylor and Haddon, argued that sympathetic magic was limited to so-called "primitive" cultures. However, prominent psychologists and philosophers in the late twentieth century suggest otherwise. "Subsequent work [...] established that the laws of sympathetic magic characterize some types of cognitions, even among educated, Western adults."[44] As consumers, educated, rational individuals in late modern capitalist society are also subject to magical thinking.[45] Indeed, as one commentator concluded, "the only difference between primitive and advanced societies is that while the former openly accepts magical thinking, the latter denies being influenced by it."[46]

4 The Creation of the Fetishized Commodity

Although Marx placed emphasis on the negative dimension of commodity fetishism, that is, that it hides its underlying social relations of labor-power, modern psychologists and sociologists recognize the role played by sympathetic magic in animating the positive aspect of the commodity, that is, its charismatic power or *mana*, which seemingly arises *sui generis*. Of course, there is little doubt that advertising has a dispositive effect on the production of *mana* in the commodity-consumer nexus. The presence of sympathetic magic and its two components, homeopathic and contagious magic, is widely recognized in the marketplace by contemporary "consumer behavior scholarship."[47] However, sympathetic magic in the marketplace, which acts on the imagination of consumers, is contingent on the production of the commodity's fetish character.

---

43 James Frazer, *The Golden Bough: A Study of Magic and Religion*, http://www.gutenberg.org/cache/epub/3623/pg3623.txt. Accessed September 15, 2013.
44 Paul Rozin and Carol Nemeroff, "Sympathetic Magical Thinking: The Contagion and Similarity 'Heuristics,'" in *Heuristics and Biases: The Psychology of Intuitive Judgment*, ed. Thomas Gilovich, Dale Griffin, and Daniel Kahneman (New York: Cambridge University Press, 2002), 202.
45 Jean Baudrillard, *The Consumer Society: Myths and Structures* (London: Sage, 1998), 31.
46 Katya Assaf, "Magical Thinking in Trademark Law," *Law & Social Inquiry* 37.3 (2012): 596–97.
47 Barbara Phillips and Edward Mcquarrie, "Narrative and Persuasion in Fashion Advertising," *Journal of Consumer Research* 37 (2010): 370; see, for example, Yannik St. James, Jay Handelman, and Shirley Taylor, "Magical Thinking and Consumer Coping," *Journal of Consumer Research* 38.4 (2011): 632–49.

As Roy Ellen has argued, the fetish emerges from a four-step process: concretization, animation, the conflation of signifier and signified, and an ambiguous relationship between control of object by people and of people by object.[48] Just as certain ideas, such as holiness and forgiveness, are correlated with religious objects, so too are certain powers, for example, sexual attractiveness and success, objectified in commodities themselves. Like ecclesial authorities that took theological ideas and concretized them in relics, advertisers locate these desirable traits in the end-product of capitalist enterprises. The first step alone, however, cannot produce a fetish. "[W]hat concretization in itself does not do [...] is to attribute physiological and behavioral characteristics – truly to 'animate' what has first been concretised."[49] Hence, the second step in the advertising process is to animate the commodity by making the idea, externally associated with the commodity, an intrinsic attribute. Ellen notes that this step echoes Marx's description of the fetishization of commodities as "the personification of things."[50] "Products dance and sing, engage in relations with humans as if they themselves were alive and sometimes direct human actions because of the consumer's confusion in the marketplace."[51] In other words, the commodity represents sexiness, power, wealth, etc. The next step lies in the consequent conflation of the signifier and signified. Here the object no longer simply represents the idea. The object is the idea. Chanel is sex. Nike is athletic prowess. The attribute is enfleshed in the very presence of the commodity. The collapse of signified into signifier constitutes brand identification, the highest form of fetishization. Here the likeness of the commodity is no longer even necessary. Instead, the depiction of the commodity is replaced by the representational image of its brand name or logo. While the consumer may identify with and even purchase the product, the final step raises the question of whether the consumer masters or is mastered by the fetishized commodity.

Although in his essay "The Work of Art in the Age of Mechanical Reproduction," Walter Benjamin argued that mass-produced items lose the aura of the original,[52] modern advertising has reinvented the aura – indeed, the *mana* – of the fetishized commodity in the form of the brand. While some advertising

---

48 Roy Ellen, "Fetishism," *Man* 23.2 (1988): 219.
49 Ellen, "Fetishism," 223.
50 Ellen, "Fetishism," 224.
51 William Leiss, Stephen Kline, and Sut Jhally, *Social Communication in Advertising: Persons, Products & Images of Well-being* (New York: Routledge, 1997), 26.
52 Walter Benjamin, "The Work of Art in the Age of Mechanical Reproduction" in *Illuminations: Essays and Reflections*, ed. Hannah Arendt, trans. Harry Zohn (New York: Schocken Books, 1968), 223–24.

conventions attempt to transport the consumer into a narrative involving the commodity, more radical approaches replace narratives of utility with images of desire. Indeed, it is just this move which Baudrillard argued marks the advent of postmodern late capitalism.[53] Unlike traditional advertising which employs "conventional theories of persuasion," brand-focused advertising forgoes consumer evaluation of product claims, advanced in advertising text, for "a more intense brand experience."[54] Indeed, high fashion advertising most often omits text altogether and includes only photography and brand signifier.[55]

One commentator argues that "[m]odern advertising substantially correlates with Durkheim's idea of the sacred."[56] Katya Assaf compares commercial brands with the notion of a totemic mark of the *churinga* (a sacred wooden object used by peoples in Central Australia), described by Durkheim in his *Elementary Forms of the Religious Life*.[57] "Just like the totemic mark distinguishes *churinga* from similar pieces of wood and stone, a strong brand marks out goods from similar counterparts. Just like *churinga*, branded goods are valued much higher than their unbranded counterparts."[58] Branded merchandise therefore is not reducible to their actual physical characteristics. Frequently, certain categories of products may be virtually identical, and consumer evaluation of one's advantage over the other is negligible. Instead, the difference lies in the brand itself, its "totemic mark," which makes it unique.

5 The Reception of the Fetishized Commodity

One commentator suggests that advertisers "decontextualize the object from the real world and recontextualize it in the world of our imaginations."[59] (Farrell, 1998, 157). "By locating us imaginatively in the not-here and not-now, the commodity becomes an 'objective correlative' of a whole way of life that would be better than ours."[60] The process of fetishization alone, however, does not bring about the identification of the consumer with the commodity nor does it

---

53 Baudrillard, *The Consumer Society*, 192.
54 Phillips and Mcquarrie, "Narrative and Persuasion in Fashion Advertising," 390.
55 Phillips and Mcquarrie, "Narrative and Persuasion in Fashion Advertising," 372.
56 Assaf, "Magical Thinking in Trademark Law," 604.
57 Emile Durkheim, *The Elementary Forms of the Religious Life*, trans. Joseph Swain (New York: Free Press, 1969), 140.
58 Assaf, "Magical Thinking in Trademark Law," 604.
59 James Farrell, "The Moral Ecology of Consumption," *American Studies* 39.3 (1998): 157.
60 Farrell, "The Moral Ecology of Consumption," 157.

actualize the exchange value of the commodity. Here advertisers enlist the aid of sympathetic magic, in both its homeopathic and contagious forms.

As explained by Rozin and Nermeroff, sympathetic magic is first deployed in the form of homeopathic magic or what they call the law of similarity. "The *law of similarity* holds either that like causes like (causes resemble their effects) or appearance equals reality."[61] By employing signifiers of desire, skillful ad campaigns invite consumers to identify with the product displayed. Of course, the consumer need not even see the product itself for if the ad or commercial has sufficiently animated the commodity by displaying an attribute as an innate quality, one need only display the image of the attribute or even a name to effectively use sympathetic magic. Based on the law of similarity, the consumer need only see him or herself in the images associated directly or indirectly with the commodity that stimulates the consumer's imagination. Intuitively deploying the law of similarity, the consumer imagines that the desirable attribute of the fetishized commodity causes the emotional feeling of power, wealth, and sex displayed in the image and that the appearance of excitation is its own reality. As another commentator has argued, "[t]he commodity, a creative vehicle, draws the human into itself."[62] The fetishized commodity, therefore, compensates individuals for the disappointments suffered in everyday life.

Although advertising is effective in producing a hyperreality of surface effects, late modern capitalism cannot thrive without the realization of the exchange value of fetishized commodities through the sale of the actual merchandise. Here advertisers rely upon the power of contagious magic. As Rozin and Nemeroff note in their discussion of its anthropological context, "the law of contagion holds that *physical contact* between *source* and *target* results in the transfer of some effect or quality, which we call *essence*, from source to target."[63] This essence has a "holographic or metonymic nature" that contains all of the properties of the object.[64] Rozin and Nemeroff conclude from a study of scientific data gathered by questionnaires, laboratory experiments, and ethnographies that this essence – physical attributes, abilities, dispositions, and moral qualities – is transferred by contact. Indeed, this conveyance may occur even when the target is in close proximity to the source.

In the context of late modern capitalism, consumers share the product's fetishized essence through contact with the commodity, which may be either a

---

61 Rozin and Nemeroff, "Sympathetic Magical Thinking," 201.

62 Mauria Wickstrom, *Performing Consumers: Global Capital and its Theatrical Seductions* (New York: Routledge, 2006), 80.

63 Rozin and Nemeroff, "Sympathetic Magical Thinking," 206.

64 Rozin and Nemeroff, "Sympathetic Magical Thinking," 207.

physical object or even a service. Ideally for capitalist enterprises, the consumer buys the product, and, in possessing the product, incorporates the animated essence as his or her own. In short, the consumer is not immediate to him- or herself, but rather the individual is self-aware only through the mediation of the fetishized essence. For example, the consumer knows that he is powerful insofar as he possesses the indices of power, for example, a BMW, a Rolex watch, Chanel perfume, etc. The consumer's self-knowledge is reinforced by fellow consumers who are well-versed in the signification of fetishism and read his acquired possessions accordingly. They confirm a deeply-held belief that "the purchase of a commodity will give us control over the natural and social worlds, including our bodies."[65] Of course, one need not buy the product in order to enjoy the thrill of the commodity's essence. The consumer can vicariously imagine him- or herself in the advertisement and fantasize about the pleasures that one may experience. In this respect, the fetishized commodity is essentially a democratic *Döppelganger*, which offers everyone, no matter what their station in society, a share of happiness, however fleeting.

6 Conclusion

I recall a visit to East Berlin some thirty years ago when I was a graduate student conducting research on Walter Benjamin in Germany. At that time Ronald Reagan was President, and relations were strained between the United States and the Soviet Union, the alleged "evil empire." Having spent the previous month in West Berlin absorbing the phantasmagoria of images on the gigantic billboards that lined the Ku'damm, I waited to cross over at Checkpoint Charlie with a group of Americans. Although I expected East Berlin to be different, I was stunned by the absence of commercial advertising – no billboards, no signs except the occasional hammer-and-sickle. I remember in wonderment that I could actually see the buildings and appreciate the aesthetic qualities of the architectural remnants of old Berlin. Other Americans who accompanied me across the border, however, did not share my enthusiasm. They became exceedingly distraught, and I wondered what precipitated their reaction. When I asked whether they found the presence of Stasi guards threatening, they replied

---

65 James Farrell, "The Moral Ecology of Consumption," *American Studies* 39.3 (1998): 158. See also St. James, Handelman, and Taylor, "Magical Thinking and Consumer Coping," 636, citing Giora Keinan, "Magical Thinking as a Way of Coping with Stress," in *Between Stress and Hope: From a Disease-Centered to a Health-Centered Perspective*, ed. Rebecca Jacoby and Giora Keinan (Westport, CT: Praeger, 2003), 123–38.

no, for it was something altogether different that upset them. Without the huge billboards plastering the images of fetishized commodities that fueled their imaginations, these Americans found East Berlin dull, lifeless, and depressing. One said, "I now understand why communism is so horrible. Who would want to live here?"

Of course, under actually existing communist regimes, governed by an ideology of "scientific atheism," the authorities attempted to suppress religious consciousness, whether in its ecclesial or capitalist incarnations. With the collapse of the Soviet Bloc, religious consciousness in both forms not only survived but flourished, and today the religious consciousness of fetishism and sympathetic magic play their part in the People's Republic of China, where Maoist communist ideology has given way to "red capitalism." Some psychologists conclude that fetishism and sympathetic magic persist because they are innate, rather than incidental, to the human psyche. Whether this religious consciousness would survive the demise of capitalism is a provocative theoretical question; however, given the vitality of global capitalism, it is not one that we will be able to answer for many generations to come.

Works Cited

Anthony, Dick and Thomas Robbins. "The Sociology of Contemporary Religious Movements." *Annual Review of Sociology* 5 (1979): 75–89.

Aronson, Ronald. "The New Atheists." *The Nation*, 7 June 2007, http://www.thenation.com/article/new-atheists/. Accessed September 5, 2013.

Assaf, Katya. "Magical Thinking in Trademark Law." *Law & Social Inquiry* 37.3 (2012): 593–626.

Baudrillard, Jean. *The Consumer Society: Myths and Structures.* Translated by Chris Turner. London: Sage, 1998.

Bellah, Robert. *The Broken Covenant: American Civil Religion in Time of Trial.* Chicago: University of Chicago Press, 1992 [1975].

Berger, Peter. *The Sacred Canopy: Elements of a Sociological Theory of Religion.* New York: Anchor, 1967.

Berger, Peter. *Facing Up to Modernity.* New York: Basic Books, 1977.

Benjamin, Walter. *The Arcades Project.* Edited by Rolf Tiedemann. Translated by Howard Eiland and Kevin McLaughlin. Cambridge: Belknap, 1999.

Benjamin, Walter. "The Work of Art in the Age of Mechanical Reproduction." In *Illuminations: Essays and Reflections*, edited by Hannah Arendt, translated 217–52. by Harry Zohn. New York: Schocken Books, 1968.

Denton, Melinda, Lisa Pearce, and Christian Smith. *Religion and Spirituality on the Path of Adolescence: A Research Report of the National Study of Youth and Religion.* No. 8. Chapel Hill, NC: University of North Carolina, 2008, http://youthandreligion.nd.edu/as

sets/102568/religion_and_spirituality_on_the_path_through_adolescence.pdf. Accessed September 5, 2013.

Durkheim, Emile. *The Elementary Forms of the Religious Life*, translated Life. Translated by Joseph Swain. New York: Free Press, 1969.

Ellen, Roy. "Fetishism." *Man* 23.2 (1988): 213–35.

Farrell, James. "The Moral Ecology of Consumption." *American Studies* 39.3 (1998): 153–73.

Frazer, James. *The Golden Bough: A study of Magic and Religion*, http://www.gutenberg.org/cache/epub/3623/pg3623.txt. Accessed September 15, 2013.

Glock, Charles, Benjamin Ringer, and Earl Babbie. *To Comfort or To Challenge: A Dilemma of the Contemporary Church*. Berkeley: University of California Press, 1967.

Habermas, Jürgen. *Legitimation Crisis*. Translated by Thomas McCarthy. New York: Beacon, 1975.

Haddon, Alfred. *Magic and Fetishism*. London: Archibald Constable, 1906.

Hitchens, Christopher. *God Is Not Great: How Religion Poisons Everything*. New York: Grand Central, 2009.

Hunter, James. *The Culture Wars: The Struggle to Define America*. New York: Basic, 1991.

Keinan, Giora. "Magical Thinking as a Way of Coping with Stress." In *Between Stress and Hope: From a Disease-Centered to a Health-Centered Perspective*, edited by Rebecca Jacoby and Giora Keinan. 123–38. Westport, CT: Praeger, 2003.

Kelly, Dean. *Why Conservative Churches Are Growing: A Study in Sociology of Religion with a New Preface*. Macon, GA: Mercer, 1996.

Leiss, William, Stephen Kline, and Sut Jhally. *Social Communication in Advertising: Persons, Products & Images of Well-being*. New York: Routledge, 1997.

Luckmann, Thomas. *The Invisible Religion*. New York: MacMillan, 1967.

Luther, Martin. "On Secular Authority." *Luther and Calvin: On Secular Authority*, edited and translated by Harro Höpfl. 1–46. Cambridge: Cambridge University Press, 2002.

Marx, Karl. "Capital, Volume One." *The Marx-Engels Reader*, edited by Robert Tucker, translated by Martin Nicolaus. 294–438. New York: W.W. Norton, 1978.

McLaughlin, William. *Revivals, Awakenings, and Reforms*. Chicago: University of Chicago Press, 1980.

Mills, Charles. *White Collar: The American Middle Classes*. New York: Oxford University Press, 1956.

Newport, Frank. *God Is Alive and Well: The Future of Religion in America*. New York: Gallup, 2012.

Phillips, Barbara and Edward Mcquarrie. "Narrative and Persuasion in Fashion Advertising." *Journal of Consumer Research* 37.3 (2010): 368–92.

Rieff, Philip. *Freud: The Mind of a Moralist*. Chicago: University of Chicago Press, 1979.

Riesman, David. *The Lonely Crowd*. New Haven, CT: Yale University Press, 1952.

Rozin, Paul and Carol Nemeroff. "Sympathetic Magical Thinking: The Contagion and Similarity 'Heuristics.'" In *Heuristics and Biases: The Psychology of Intuitive Judgment*, edited by Thomas Gilovich, Dale Griffin, and Daniel Kahneman. 201–16. New York: Cambridge University Press, 2002.

St. James, Yannik, Jay Handelman, and Shirley Taylor. "Magical Thinking and Consumer Coping." *Journal of Consumer Research* 38.4 (2011): 632–49.

Tylor, Edward B. *Primitive Culture. Researches into the Development of Mythology, Philosophy, Religion, Art, and Custom*. Vol. 2. New York: Cambridge University Press, 2010.

Weber, Max. "The Concept of Legitimate Authority." In *Basic Concepts in Sociology*. Translated by H. Secher (New York: Kensington, 2000): 71–4.

Weber, Max. *Protestant Work Ethic and the Spirit of Capitalism*. Translated by Talcott Parsons. New York: Routledge, 2001.

Weber, Max. "Science as a Vocation." In *From Max Weber: Essays in Sociology*, edited and translated by Hans Gerth and Charles Mills. 129–56. New York: Oxford University Press, 1946.

"Welcome to the U.S. Religious Landscape Survey." *Pew Research Religion & Public Life Project*. n.d., http://religions.pewforum.org/reports. Accessed September 15, 2013

Whyte, William. *The Organization Man*. Philadelphia: University of Pennsylvania Press, 2002.

Wickstrom, Mauria. *Performing Consumers: Global Capital and its Theatrical Seductions*. New York: Routledge, 2006.

Wolff, Edward N. *The Asset Price Meltdown and the Wealth of the Middle Class*. Cambridge, MA: National Bureau of Economic Research. Working paper 18559. 2012.

Contributors

Rochelle Almeida, a postcolonial literary specialist, is a professor of South Asian Studies in the Liberal Studies Program at New York University. She has taught at NYU in London and is a Senior Associate Member of St. Antony's College, University of Oxford, UK. She is the author of *Originality and Imitation: Indianness in the Novels of Kamala Markandaya* (Rawat Publishers, Jaipur, India, 2000) and *The Politics of Mourning: Grief-Management in Cross-Cultural Fiction* (Fairleigh-Dickinson University Press, New Jersey, 2004). Other than postcolonial writing, she has published extensively on the subject of Anglo-Indian immigration, and her third book, tentatively entitled *Britain's Anglo-Indians: From Exodus to Assimilation*, is to be published shortly. She is a recipient of research grants and fellowships from the British Council to Exeter College, Oxford, and from the National Endowment for the Humanities to Hawai'i and Paris. She earned a PhD in Postcolonial Literature from the University of Bombay and a Doctor of Arts degree in Multi-Ethnic Literature from St. John's University, New York.

Jonathan Beloff is a PhD student at the School of Oriental and African Studies at the University of London, undertaking research on the African Great Lakes. His dissertation is entitled, "The Evolution of Rwandan Foreign Policy from Genocide to Globalisation." He received his Masters of Science in Global Affairs at New York University with a concentration in International Development and Humanitarian Assistance. He received his Bachelors of Arts with the honors of *magna cum laude* and Dean's Honor in Political Science with a concentration in Economics from the Richard Stockton College of New Jersey. He has been traveling to Rwanda since 2008, conducting research on Rwandan political, economic and social development.

Gregorio Bettiza is Lecturer in International Relations at the University of Exeter. His research interests are on religion and secularism, civilizational analysis, and non-liberal norms and identities in international relations. He is currently working on a monograph on the operationalization of religion in American foreign policy. Gregorio completed his PhD in International Relations at the London School of Economics and Political Science in 2012 and was also a Max Weber Postdoctoral Fellow at the European University Institute (2012–14).

Rajeev Bhargava is a Professor and former Director of CSDS, Delhi (2007–2104). He was Professor, JNU, New Delhi (1980–2005), and was Head, Department of Political Science, University of Delhi (2001–2005). He is Honorary Fellow, Balliol

College, Oxford and Professorial Fellow, ACU, Sydney. He has been a Fellow at Harvard University, University of Bristol, Institute of Advanced Studies, Jerusalem, Wissenschaftskolleg, Berlin, and the Institute for Human Sciences, Vienna. He has also been Distinguished Resident Scholar, Institute for Religion, Culture and Public Life, Columbia University, and Asia Chair at Sciences Po, Paris. Bhargava's publications include *Individualism in Social Science* (1992), *What is Political Theory and Why Do We Need It?* (2010), and *The Promise of India's Secular Democracy* (2010). His edited works are *Secularism and Its Critics* (1998) and *Politics and Ethics of the Indian Constitution* (2008). His work on secularism and methodological individualism is internationally acclaimed.

Arolda Elbasani is Jean Monet Fellow at the Robert Schuman Center for Advanced Studies, Florence. She received her PhD in Social and Political Sciences from the European University Institute, Florence in 2007. Her research interests lay at the intersection of Islamic politics, European integration, and comparative democratization with a focus on Southeast Europe and Turkey. Her publications include among others articles at *Democratization, Politics and Religion, Journal of Balkan and Near Eastern Studies, Transitions, Sudosteuropa* and an edited anthology, *European Integration and Transformation in Western Balkans*, published by Routledge in 2013. Another book entitled, *Revival of Islam in the Balkans*, is in press and will be published by Palgrave in 2015. Currently, she is working on a book-length project regarding Muslim communities' commitment to democratic regimes in Southeast Europe, particularly Albania, Turkey and Kosovo.

Philip Kitcher is John Dewey Professor of Philosophy at Columbia University. Before Columbia, he taught at the University of California, San Diego, and before that at the University of Minnesota. His books include: *Deaths in Venice: The Cases of Gustav von Aschenbach*, Columbia University Press, 2013; *Philosophy of Science: A New Introduction* (with Gillian Barker), Oxford University Press, 2013; *Preludes to Pragmatism*, Oxford University Press, 2012; *Science in a Democratic Society*, Prometheus Books, 2011; and, *The Ethical Project*, Harvard University Press, 2011. Kitcher's Terry Lectures, delivered at Yale in the Spring of 2013, will be published during 2014. Earlier book publications include: *Finding an Ending: Reflections on Wagner's Ring*, co-authored with Richard Schacht, Oxford University Press, February 2004; *In Mendel's Mirror: Philosophical Reflections on Biology*, Oxford University Press, 2003; *Science, Truth, and Democracy*, Oxford University Press, 2001; paperback 2003; *The Lives to Come: The Genetic Revolution and Human Possibilities* (Simon and Schuster [U.S.], Penguin [U.K.], January 1996, paperback editions 1997); *The Advancement of Science*, Oxford University Press, April 1993 (paper January 1995); *Vaulting Ambition: Sociobiology and the*

Quest for Human Nature, MIT Press, 1985 (paperback 1987); *The Nature of Mathematical Knowledge,* Oxford University Press, 1983 (paperback 1984); and *Abusing Science: The Case Against Creationism,* MIT Press, 1982 (paperback 1983).

Özlem Uluç Kucukcan is an Assistant Professor of Sociology and Anthropology at The Institute for Middle East Studies, Marmara University, Istanbul. She graduated with a BA in Public Administration from the Istanbul University. Uluc Kucukcan received her MA and PhD in Sociology of Religion from the Marmara University. She participated in summer schools on *Role of Religions in Public Discourse: Recent Developments in the Thought of Jürgen Habermas,* Washington Catholic University; *Eurosphere: Diversity and the European Public Sphere, Towards a Citizens' Europe,* Sabanci University; Institute for Human Sciences International Summer School on *Religion in Public Life,* Cortona. Her publications include *New Religious Movements: A Sociological Analysis* (Istanbul: 2012) and *Religion in Public Sphere: Intersections of State, Religion and Democracy* (Istanbul: 2013), both in Turkish. She works on secularism, religion in public sphere, citizenship and political systems.

Stijn Latré (1978) earned his PhD at the University of Leuven in 2008, with a dissertation on the philosophy of Charles Taylor. He is currently working at the University of Antwerp (Belgium) as lecturer. He was also funded by the Flemish Fonds voor Wetenschappelijk Onderzoek (FWO) for a research project on Theory of Secularization. Stijn Latré is also associated with the Centre Pieter Gillis of the University of Antwerp, where he teaches the courses entitled "The end of Secularization?" and "Levensbeschouwing" ("World views," German: "Weltanschauungen").

George Levine is professor emeritus of English, Rutgers University. Among his books, largely on Victorian literature, are three on Darwin: *Darwin and the Novelists, Darwin Loves You,* and *Darwin The Writer.* He is author as well of *Realism, Ethics and Secularism.* He was the editor of the anthology, *The Joy of Secularism: 11 Essays for How We Live Now.*

Patrick Loobuyck (Bruges, 1974) studied Religious Studies at the Catholic University of Leuven and ethics at Ghent University. He is Associate Professor in Religion and Worldviews at the Centre Pieter Gillis of the University of Antwerp and Guest Professor in Political Philosophy at Ghent University. His research focuses on political liberalism, church state regimes, religion in the public sphere, religious education, multiculturalism, and liberal nationalism. He has published in several national and international journals such as *Religious Education, Journal* *of Muslim Minority Affairs, Political Quarterly, Journal of Church and State, British Journal or Religious Education, Journal for the Scientific Study of Religion,* and *Ethnicities.*

James McBride holds a PhD in religion and social ethics from the joint doctoral program at Graduate Theological Union/University of California at Berkeley, an MA in religion from the University of Chicago, and a BA in the humanities from Johns Hopkins University. He also earned a JD from the Benjamin N. Cardozo School of Law. Prior to his position at New York University, he served as an Associate Professor in Religious Studies at Fordham University and for nine years practiced securities law at a major law firm in New York City. He is the author of numerous books and articles on religion, ethics, and law, including *War, Battering and Other Sports: The Gulf Between American Men and Women,* which received the "Outstanding Book in Human Rights" Award from the Gustavus Myers Foundation in 1996.

Ayşe Seda Müftügil is a Post-doctoral Research Fellow at Koc University (KU), Koç University Social Impact Forum (KUSIF), Istanbul. She graduated from American Robert College in 2001. She pursed her BA degree in Social and Political Science, at Sabancı University (SU), Istanbul. Via the help of British Chevenning Scholarship she got her master's degree in Human Rights (MSc in Human Rights) from London School of Economics (LSE), London. Her master's thesis was on Romani Self-Organisation in the Turkish context. After finishing her masters she moved to Amsterdam and worked with Prof. Ruud Peters, at the University of Amsterdam, at its ASCA (Amsterdam School for Cultural Analysis) Institute. Her PhD was on Compulsory Religious Education and Religious Minorities in Turkey. Since September 2012, she has been working at Koç University Social Impact Forum (KUSIF). She is researching social impact measurement tools and approaches as well as offering courses on social impact.

Roberta J. Newman is a specialist in critical sports and media studies and the author of *Black Baseball, Black Business: Race Enterprise and the Fate of the Segregated Dollar,* published in 2014 by the University Press of Mississippi. She has also published numerous articles and contributed to several anthologies dealing with sport, the media, and pilgrimage, the most recent being the Foreword to *A Locker Room of Her Own: Celebrity, Sexuality, and Female Athletes,* also from UP of Mississippi. Having received her PhD in Comparative Literature from NYU, her MA in English Language and Literature from the University of Chicago, as well as her BFA in Illustration from Parsons School of Design, she is currently a member of New York University's Global Liberal Studies/Liberal Studies program.

Elayne Oliphant is an Assistant Professor of Anthropology and Religious Studies at New York University. She received her PhD in Anthropology at the University of Chicago and was a Postdoctoral Research Fellow in Religious Studies at Brown University from 2013 – 15. Elayne is a visual anthropologist of Christianity, secularity, contemporary art, and the public sphere in Europe. In recent publications she has explored how the categories of religious and secular are applied in unequal ways to signs of different religious traditions in decisions of the European Court of Human Rights and cultural projects of the state and church in France. She is currently working on a book project that rethinks the state of the secular in France through an examination of the transforming place of Catholic symbols and institutions in Paris.

Michael Rectenwald studies nineteenth-century science, science and literature, secularism, the philosophy of science, the futures of science and technology, and composition theory and pedagogy. His work on secularism has been published in the *British Journal for the History of Science, The International Philosophical Quarterly,* and *George Eliot In Context* (Cambridge UP, 2013). His current book project, *Nineteenth-Century British Secularism: Science, Religion and Literature* (forthcoming from Palgrave Macmillan), explores a long-neglected and/or misrepresented nineteenth-century movement called "Secularism," founded by George Holyoake in 1851 – 1852, in conjunction with other secular interventions in nineteenth-century Britain. His textbook, *Academic Writing, Real World Topics* (co-edited by Lisa Carl), was published by Broadview Press in May 2015. He received his PhD in Literary and Cultural Studies from Carnegie Mellon University and is a professor of cultural history, science studies, and critical theory in the Global Liberal Studies Program at New York University.

Charles Louis Richter is a doctoral candidate in American Religious History at the George Washington University, where he is currently writing his dissertation on twentieth-century American responses to irreligion as a form of nativism. He received his master's degree in Comparative Religion and bachelor's degrees in Comparative History of Ideas and Russian History & Language at the University of Washington. He has worked at the University of Washington as a lecturer in the Jackson School of International studies and as a research assistant under a grant from the Luce Foundation to study religion and human security. His work has been published in *Teaching Theology and Religion.*

Bruce Robbins is Old Dominion Foundation Professor of the Humanities in the department of English and Comparative Literature at Columbia University. His books include *Perpetual War: Cosmopolitanism from the Viewpoint of Violence*

(2012), *Upward Mobility and the Common Good* (2007), *Feeling Global: Internationalism in Distress* (1999), *The Servant's Hand: English Fiction from Below* (1986), and *Secular Vocations: Intellectuals, Professionalism, Culture* (1993). He has edited *Intellectuals: Aesthetics, Politics, Academics* (1990) and *The Phantom Public Sphere* (1993) and co-edited (with Pheng Cheah) *Cosmopolitics: Thinking and Feeling beyond the Nation* (1998) and (with David Palumbo-Liu and Nirvana Tanoukhi) *Immanuel Wallerstein and the Problem of the World* (Duke UP, 2011). His essays have appeared in the *London Review of Books*, *n+1*, *The Nation*, *Public Books*, and the *LA Review of Books*. He is also the director of a documentary entitled "Some of My Best Friends Are Zionists," available on Amazon.

Jonathan Scott teaches writing and literature at New York University and Bronx Community College. He is the author of *Socialist Joy in the Writing of Langston Hughes*, as well as numerous articles in literary criticism, cultural studies, and composition studies. He lives in Brooklyn, New York.

Murat Somer is an Associate Professor of Political Science and International Relations at Koç University in Istanbul, specializing in comparative politics, political economy and Turkish politics. Somer's research on democratization, political moderation, social polarization, religious and secular politics and secularism, ethnic conflicts, political Islam, Muslim polities, and the Kurdish question have been published in numerous book volumes and academic journals such as Comparative Political Studies, Democratization, Third World Quarterly, Journal of Church and State, and The Middle East Journal.

Chika Watanabe is a Lecturer in the Department of Social Anthropology at the University of Manchester (UK). She received her PhD from Cornell University and has worked as a postdoctoral associate in the Inter-Asia Program at Yale University. Her research interests include development and humanitarian aid, NGOs, institutional expertise, religion and secularity, ethics and morality, ecology, and disasters. She is currently working on her book manuscript, *Muddy Labor: Nonreligion and the Moral Imaginary of a Japanese NGO in Myanmar*.

Index